T0289160

Better Bankers,
Better Banks

Better Bankers, Better Banks

PROMOTING GOOD BUSINESS THROUGH CONTRACTUAL COMMITMENT

Claire A. Hill and Richard W. Painter

THE UNIVERSITY OF CHICAGO PRESS *Chicago and London*

Claire A. Hill is professor and the James L. Krusemark Chair in Law at the
University of Minnesota Law School, where she is also director of the Institute
for Law and Rationality and associate director of the Institute for Law and
Economics. **Richard W. Painter** is the S. Walter Richey Professor of Corporate
Law at the University of Minnesota Law School. He is the author of several books,
including, most recently, *Getting the Government America Deserves*, and has
served as Associate Counsel to the President in the White House Counsel's office.

The University of Chicago Press, Chicago 60637
The University of Chicago Press, Ltd., London
© 2015 by The University of Chicago
All rights reserved. Published 2015.
Printed in the United States of America

24 23 22 21 20 19 18 17 16 15   1 2 3 4 5

ISBN-13: 978-0-226-29305-9 (cloth)
ISBN-13: 978-0-226-29319-6 (e-book)
DOI: 10.7208/chicago/9780226293196.001.0001

Library of Congress Cataloging-in-Publication Data
Hill, Claire A., author.
    Restoring responsibility in banking / Claire A. Hill and Richard W. Painter.
       pages cm
    Includes bibliographical references and index.
       ISBN 978-0-226-29305-9 (cloth : alkaline paper) — ISBN 978-0-226-29319-6 (ebook)
1. Banks and banking—Corrupt practices. 2. Banks and banking—Social aspects.
3. Banks and banking—History—21st century. 4. Banks and banking—History—
20th century. I. Painter, Richard W., 1961– author. II. Title.
    HG1573.H55 2015
    332.1—dc23   2015002748

♾ This paper meets the requirements of ANSI/NISO Z39.48-1992
(Permanence of Paper).

To my colleagues and to Eric

—CAH

To Sidney Homer Jr. and William H. Painter

—RWP

At the time this book was in galley pages for author review, William "Billy" Salomon, one of America's most prominent investment bankers passed away on December 7, 2014. Richard Painter is grateful for Mr. Salomon having given his grandfather, Sidney Homer Jr., a bond market analyst, a major career break—a partnership at age fifty-nine in Salomon Brothers & Hutzler, the first and only large firm of which Mr. Homer would be a partner. Mr. Salomon's concept of investment banking is discussed in some detail in chapter 2 of this book, and his views have inspired some of the normative observations made herein.

The *Los Angeles Times* obituary for Mr. Salomon states in part:

> Under Salomon's direction, the firm became an aggressive new player in the competition for underwriting business and a specialist in the high-stakes field of block trading. . . . After retiring in 1978 at 64, Salomon watched as the partnership was sold, transformed into a public corporation and ultimately folded into Citigroup Inc. It was his hand-picked successor, John Gutfreund, who struck the deal that made Salomon Bros. part of Phibro Corp. in 1981. Salomon was informed only after the accord was reached. "I was very upset," Salomon said in an interview with the New York Times. "I felt betrayed." Gutfreund's reign ended with his departure in 1991, after the company admitted violating U.S. Treasury Department auction rules by placing orders for securities in the name of customers who hadn't authorized them. In a 1991 interview with the Associated Press, Salomon expressed his displeasure at the direction of his former firm. "In my time, the customer was God, and we would no more take advantage of him than we'd fly out the window," he said. "We always felt that if we did the right thing the profits would take care of themselves."

CONTENTS

INTRODUCTION

> Just as any revolution eats its children, unchecked market fundamentalism
> can devour the social capital essential for the long-term dynamism of capitalism
> itself. To counteract this tendency, individuals and their firms must have a sense
> of their responsibilities for the broader system.
> — Mark Carney, Governor of the Bank of England, May 27, 2014[1]

> There is evidence of deep-seated cultural and ethical failures at many large
> financial institutions. Whether this is due to size and complexity, bad incentives
> or some other issues is difficult to judge, but it is another critical problem that
> needs to be addressed.
> — William Dudley, President and Chief Executive Officer, Federal Reserve
> Bank of New York, November 7, 2013[2]

On November 12, 2014, six banks—JPMorgan, Citigroup, Bank of America, UBS (Union Bank of Switzerland), RBS (Royal Bank of Scotland), and HSBC (Hongkong and Shanghai Banking Corporation)—were fined $4.3 billion by regulators in the United States, the United Kingdom, and Switzerland to settle charges that they had attempted to manipulate—and had aided and abetted other banks' attempts to manipulate—foreign exchange rates.[3] Investigations of foreign exchange rate manipulation by these and other banks are continuing; some of the investigations may yield criminal charges.[4]

On June 30, 2014, the French bank BNP Paribas agreed to plead guilty to a felony, conspiring to violate U.S. sanctions against doing business with entities in Iran, Cuba, and Sudan, and agreed to pay a penalty of nearly $9 billion.[5] On May 19, 2014, another bank, Credit Suisse pleaded guilty to "helping US taxpayers hide offshore accounts from [the] IRS," a felony, and agreed to pay penalties of $2.6 billion.[6] In the last few years, several banks, including JPMorgan Chase, Citigroup, Barclays, UBS, RBS, Deutsche Bank, Rabobank, and Lloyd's have settled charges that they manipulated or conspired to manipulate the London Interbank Offered Rate (LIBOR), probably the most widely used benchmark for setting short-term interest rates. In 2012, JPMorgan experienced an enormous trading loss, presently estimated at more than six billion dollars, from a supposed hedge originating out of its London office; it agreed to pay over one billion dollars in fines.[7]

Every month—if not week—brings new reports of allegations, settlements, and, in some cases, admissions involving the banking industry. The banks involved include JPMorgan, Goldman Sachs, Citigroup, Morgan Stanley, Bank of America, Deutsche Bank, Barclays, Credit Suisse, UBS, RBS, Rabobank, BNP Paribas, and others; the amounts of fines, penalties, and judgments at issue, and associated legal fees, exceed a hundred billion dollars.[8] Other matters include manipulation of currency exchange rates and electricity and commodities markets, and the use of financial engineering techniques to help their clients or themselves conceal excessive borrowing or other problematic aspects of their financial condition. Cases concerning illegal practices in the sale of mortgage-backed securities continue to be brought, proceed, and be settled. Large settlements have been reached in cases involving allegations of abuses in mortgage servicing and foreclosure.[9] The list of alleged (and in some cases admitted or proven) wrongdoing goes on and on.

These events suggest the severity of the problem. They suggest, too, that not enough has changed in the banking industry since the financial crisis of 2008. There are new laws and regulations, including the Dodd-Frank Act of 2010, with its thousands of pages of regulations. Some banks have deemphasized or exited certain businesses, or reemphasized other businesses. Morgan Stanley, for example, has moved away from proprietary trading and has reemphasized a traditional strength, private wealth management, while Barclays is paring back its investment banking and commodities trading operations.[10] Some banks have publicly announced commitments to cultural change.[11] But much remains the same.

Why isn't there more change? One major reason is that while banks have paid extremely large fines, these fines are effectively paid by the banks' shareholders. Individual bankers rarely have to pay anything themselves and are almost never put in jail. Law has not sufficiently constrained bank behavior. It did not do so before Dodd-Frank, and does not do so now.

But what about bankers' concern for their banks' (and their own) reputations? Why doesn't that serve as more of a constraint? Some bankers apparently believe that their clients won't hold problematic behavior against them—or even, that some sorts of problematic behavior are a sign of intelligence and skill. In a September 26, 2007, e-mail to Lloyd Blankfein, Goldman's chief executive officer, a senior Goldman banker said that "the institutions don't and I wouldn't expect them to, make any comments like ur good at making money for urself but not us. The individuals do sometimes, but while it requires the utmost humility from us in response I feel very strongly it binds clients even closer to the firm, because the alternative of take ur money to a firm who is an under performer and not the best, just isn't reasonable. Clients ultimately believe that association with the best is good for them in the long run."[12] The weight of evidence bankers have gotten thus far—the clients keep coming regardless of these scandals—is not inconsistent with these beliefs.

Much of the problematic conduct involves risk—to banks, bank clients and customers, and to the greater society. Banks in too many instances have not been responsible in their behavior toward risk. For example, in late 2006, when some market participants were concluding that subprime mortgages were overpriced, Goldman Sachs apparently reduced its own risk by selling part of its mortgage exposure to its clients and customers. The head of Goldman's mortgage department "extolled Goldman's success in reducing its subprime inventory, writing that the team had 'structured like mad and traveled the world, and worked their tails off to make some lemonade from some big old lemons.'"[13]

Some of the conduct involves apparent willingness to flout the law, as evidenced by BNP Paribas's conspiring to violate U.S. sanctions against doing business with entities in various sanctioned countries, Credit Suisse's assistance in its clients' tax evasion, and various banks' market manipulations. Some of banks' problematic conduct is of another type: bankers helping clients with complex transactions that cause client balance sheets to look different from what they actually are. Banks have been helping clients "manage" their financial statements for a long time. This skill was on abundant display in alleged attempts by JPMorgan, Citigroup, and other banks to "beautify" Enron's balance sheet in the 1990s. In the early 2000s, as Greece was adopting the euro, Goldman allegedly helped Greece conceal its debt so that it could avoid penalties under the Maastricht Treaty. Some banks put these same skills to work on their own bal-

ance sheets, particularly in maneuvering their way around capital requirements by overvaluing assets, undervaluing liabilities, and using other
complex strategies. Lehman Brothers, for example, during parts of 2007
and 2008, temporarily shifted up to $50 billion in bad assets off its balance
sheet at the end of each quarter but put them back again at the beginning
of the next quarter in a transaction known as "Repo 105."

The 2008 crisis prominently displayed harmful banker behavior, some
illegal, some legal, and some in the gray area in between. However, blame
for the 2008 crisis does not rest solely on banks or on bankers. The crisis
had many causes, including loose monetary policy, the rating agencies, the
housing bubble, and weak regulation of many industries. Arguably, the
government itself misled the market by saying it was regulating the financial sector and then failing to do so, a failure that shocked the markets and
might have been worse than not regulating at all. (One of the authors of
this book, Richard Painter, is exploring in separate work the role of campaign contributions from the banking industry to both political parties
between 1992 and 2008.) Homeowners too eager to borrow against their
home equity or own houses they could not afford, and homeowners and
investors too readily convinced of the ease of "flipping" houses for profit,
also were part of the problem.

Certainly, many bankers do not engage in behavior that damages their
banks or society at large; many are admirable people, courageous and self-
less. On May 13, 2014, President Obama, who has at times been very critical of bankers, bestowed the Congressional Medal of Honor for combat
in Afghanistan on Sergeant Kyle White, who is now an investment analyst
at the Royal Bank of Canada's office in Charlotte, North Carolina. Obama
characterized White as "a proud veteran welcomed into his community,
contributing his talents and skills to the progress of our nation."[14]

Still, banker behavior has caused significant problems—problems that
law has attempted to address. Since the 2008 financial crisis, there has
been an enormous amount of lawmaking: in addition to the Dodd-Frank
Act enacted in the United States, the European Union and its member
states have also enacted complex rules for banks, and other countries have
responded as well. Regardless, problems continue, and scandal has continued to plague the banking industry. This book is about how the banking

industry has come to be as it is and about the profound changes that are necessary for it to play more of a constructive role in our society.

The present trajectory began in the late 1970s and early 1980s, when investment banks converted from general partnerships, whose partners had unlimited personal liability for the debts of their firms, to corporations, whose managers do not have personal liability. In this period and subsequently, there has been a tremendous increase in financial innovation and globalization. Furthermore, the business model of banking has changed appreciably. Investment banks' core business has traditionally been capital formation (underwriting), intermediary services for investors (brokerage), and advisory services for investments and for merger and acquisition transactions, and commercial banks' core business has traditionally been lending. Now, a significant part of both investment and commercial banks' business involves other areas, notably including proprietary trading (although some banks have been pulling back on such trading since the 2008 crisis). Indeed, banks incur a great deal of risk in their trading operations (and even sometimes in their "hedges" against "risk").

Another part of the modern banking business is designing and selling complex financial instruments such as security-based swap agreements, collateralized mortgage obligations, interest rate hedges, and similar products. Banks create these financial instruments, or buy them from other banks, for resale (or sometimes to keep for themselves). Sometimes they are sold to investors who, notwithstanding their nominal sophistication, a bank may suspect or know are relatively naive. Indeed, the complexities of these instruments may be difficult for even the bank's most sophisticated customers or clients, or the bank itself, to understand sufficiently well. Yet another not insignificant business has been financial engineering, which banks sometimes take a step further, designing solutions to "problems" such as the client's desire to improve its debt ratios, to borrow money that is not recorded as debt on its financial statements, or to maneuver around regulations and contractual covenants. As noted above, some banks apply similar strategies to their own balance sheets, and a few banks take these strategies to extremes. Some types of maneuvering may have diminished in recent years, but others seem not to have done so.

Some of these business practices are hard to reconcile with banking's core function in society, which is, in the words of E. Gerald Corrigan, a managing director of Goldman Sachs and former head of the Federal Reserve Bank of New York, to play a constructive role in the "mobilisation of savings and their allocation to the most efficient possible uses that is at the end of the day the engine of economic growth [and] rising standards of living."[15] The 2008 crisis demonstrated, and a future crisis may demonstrate yet again, that bankers can undermine this core mission.

Society has not sufficiently condemned problematic behavior in banking and its underlying ethos. Indeed, there seems to be popular fascination with this behavior, reflected in books and movies. From Michael Lewis's 1989 book *Liar's Poker* to the 2013 film *The Wolf of Wall Street*, abusive banking practices have been frequently linked with conspicuous consumption, masculinity, and fantastic sexual exploits. Lewis's book begins with an older Salomon Brothers partner in the 1970s reminiscing in a Wharton School speech about how "at cocktail parties lovely ladies would corner me and ask my opinion of the market," but "when they learned I was a bond man they would quietly drift away."[16] *Liar's Poker*, however, quickly introduces a new character for the 1980s: the "Big Swinging Dick" who dominates Salomon's fixed-income trading floor. *The Wolf of Wall Street* takes this theme to an extreme: a broker hangs up a phone call with a customer by using his middle finger, snorts cocaine off of the bare posterior of a prostitute, and fornicates with a sales assistant in a glass elevator while other brokers cheer him on. Some of these scenes are unbelievable (a movie is more exciting when everything is extreme as well as open and notorious). The message, however, is clear: our society as a whole, and the banking profession in particular, celebrate single-minded pursuit of an objective—money, power, sex, et cetera—with little regard for what that pursuit means for the individual or those around him.

Many solutions have been proposed to the problems this book discusses. The solutions mostly fall into three general categories: increased regulation of banks (for example, prohibitions, limits, or other mechanisms to discourage particularly risky activities or make banks better able to withstand risk); enhanced fault-based litigation against banks and individual bankers (for example, shareholder derivative suits and securities fraud suits as well as regulatory actions and criminal enforcement); and compensation schemes designed to align bankers' interests with the long-term interests of their banks (for example, deferred compensation, compensation based on performance of bank debt, compensation clawback provisions, and mandatory holding periods for stock compensation).

We do not reject these solutions—some of them may, and probably do, have considerable merit. However, as to the first two types of solutions, as chapter 4 more fully explains, what regulation and litigation can do to improve behavior in the banking industry is limited for many reasons. Specifying with any precision what bankers should *not* do is difficult and in some cases impossible. "Too much" risk taking is undesirable but how much is too much? When is structuring around rules and agreements actually intended to deceive or to subvert a regulatory scheme or private agreement? When should it be punished? Laws that specify in detail and prohibit problematic transactions and behavior could also be part of the problem, encouraging the ethos that whatever is not prohibited is permitted. Those in the best position to choose conduct that is appropriate may not be regulators but, rather, bankers with a stake in the bank—that is, in its downside exposure as well as its upside prospects. Law is part of a broader push to encourage banker responsibility, but bankers themselves are perhaps the most important part of the solution. Even where law is able to specify what banks should not be doing, enforcement is often exceedingly difficult: banks have many ways to obscure, if not conceal, what they are doing.

Also, as chapter 3 explains, changes in bankers' upside compensation may not be enough to change banker behavior, especially when it comes to risk that might render their banks insolvent. Bankers who already have substantial personal assets may be willing to risk losing a substantial part of their upside compensation in order to pursue a course of conduct that could yield a huge payoff if it succeeds. Indeed, some bankers may be willing to risk not just their upside compensation but also the value of the stock they already hold in their banks, provided they would in any event retain enough assets to maintain a high standard of living. Bankers whose personal assets (other than their holdings of bank stock) are not on the line may be willing to take that risk, even if the risk is bad for the bank and for society at large.

We therefore argue for a different approach: that bankers be personally liable from their own assets for some of their banks' debts and that they be personally liable from several years of their past, present, and future compensation for some portion of fines and fraud-based judgments (including settlements) against the bank. In chapter 5, we describe our personal liability proposal, which consists of an agreement between the banker and his bank—a covenant. Our proposal, thus, is for what we will call covenant banking.

A successful solution to problematic banker behavior would change rewards in the banking industry, both monetary and nonmonetary. Ideally, such a change would filter through to the broader society, influencing what banker behavior the society celebrates, accepts, and condemns. Covenant banking operates directly on bankers' monetary rewards: highly paid bankers would bear some personal liability if their banks become insolvent, are fined by regulators, or are found liable in civil cases involving fraud. The liability would not be unlimited, but it should potentially adversely affect the banker's standard of living. By contrast with reforms that simply lessen bankers' potential upside, limiting their compensation, under covenant banking, bankers would bear a significant downside risk in the event of the bank's insolvency. Fines and fraud-based civil judgments against the bank could result in compensation cuts and compensation clawbacks so dramatic that bankers who are used to seven- and eight-figure paydays would definitely feel the impact.

In this book, we discuss various mechanisms by which covenant banking could be implemented. Bankers who meet certain compensation thresholds would be liable for these amounts regardless of any fault on their part; if banker compensation needs to be further increased to compensate for this liability exposure, then so be it.

Each such banker would be motivated to avoid problematic behavior themselves, watch for such behavior among their peers and subordinates (and those senior to them), and generally help to instill a culture that discourages bad behavior and its underlying ethos, the competitive pursuit of narrow material gain. Bankers subject to such liability should behave differently than bankers whose only exposure is to reduced compensation. Also, different people should be attracted to the banking profession to begin with, people who would make banking less volatile.[17] Because banks have such an important role in the business community, the culture change within banks might be reflected in a cultural change in the broader society, toward a better balance between competitive material self-interest and the community good.

The ultimate aim of covenant banking is a focus on banking as a profession, with bankers having greater responsibility for their conduct. The responsibility at issue is not just financial responsibility; it also encompasses a more holistic conception of a profession and a professional's role in society. Banks are entitled to seek profits, but not at society's expense. The law can do only so much; bankers' internal compasses, and their colleagues' compasses, need to do more. Society can do more as well, expecting more from its bankers.

Over the past decade, people of all political persuasions and philosophical outlooks have become increasingly worried about standards of conduct in the banking profession. We are no exception, and despite our differing outlooks on many issues, we have reached similar conclusions about problems in the banking industry and ways to solve them. Our conclusions are informed by our experiences as academics and lawyers, and our own knowledge of bankers. One of us (Richard Painter) had two grandfathers and a great-grandfather who were bankers at broker-dealer firms. Both of us represented many bankers when practicing law in New York, and continue to maintain close contacts with the banking industry.

Painter is skeptical of the ability of government regulation to solve the problems we describe, even if he is more worried about chaos that would emerge from a mostly unregulated banking industry. Hill shares Painter's skepticism, believing that regulation is no panacea, but that deregulation has at times encouraged (or not sufficiently discouraged) behavior that has harmed society. Indeed, we are both concerned that a distorted vision of free-market ideology has caused those questioning the behavior of market actors to be on the defensive; we believe that markets can impose harm as well as create good for the greater society.

Painter thinks that the decline of organized religion and a self-indulgent youth culture of the 1960s and 1970s did no favors for our society when younger people acquired powerful positions in the business world in the 1980s.[18] The banking industry was too eager to break with tradition and departed too quickly from established forms of business organization and social norms, even if isolated aspects of those norms, such as racial and religious segregation and sexism, were offensive and needed to change (both of us concur that the last of these norms has changed too little and that a distorted vision of masculinity in banking may be part of the problem). Hill thinks that social norms are a key part of the problem, and a key part of the solution. She thinks that what people (including bankers) want and what they think is acceptable to do to get it are highly influenced by the society's norms at a particular point in time, and that those norms can be influenced by well-timed, well-crafted, and well-delivered exhortations.

Our different perspectives impose some limitations on the analysis. We don't attribute problems to a particular cause unless we concur. Although both of us agree that behavioral economics offers valuable insights on the banking industry's problems and how they can be fixed, insights discussed in chapter 3, neither of us is inclined to ground an analysis within any specific theory of human interaction, including behavioral economics. Religious and general philosophical concepts are off limits. For that reason, the normative observations in chapter 6 about what bankers should do are based on assumptions about appropriate behavior in the business community that are stated but not derived from first principles. We generally agree on what bankers should do and should not do but would express our reasons differently, so extensive discussion of those reasons is omitted.

We share the widespread public dismay from all parts of the political spectrum at pervasive and costly episodes of misconduct in the banking industry. And we share the view of many people in the business community and the broader society that bankers have an important role in the betterment of our society and should be respected. In this book, we discuss how bankers can do better at earning and keeping that respect.

There are some encouraging signs that banks are recognizing the need for a change in culture and, in particular, the need for responsibility to be a key part of that culture. Deutsche Bank has on its website a section on responsibility; the web address includes the words "concrete cultural change." The website's introductory text reads as follows: "The impact of the economic crisis has made a long-term change of corporate culture in the financial sector absolutely imperative and cultural change is needed. We understand the message: Responsibility has to be the focus of our actions. In 2013, we laid the foundation for long-term change with the release of our new values and beliefs."[19]

In May of 2010, Goldman Sachs created a business standards committee (BSC) charged with reviewing Goldman's business standards and practices. The committee was created and overseen by personnel at the highest levels of Goldman Sachs, including the CEO and the board, and obtained independent advice from two consulting firms. In January 2011, the committee's report was published. It contained thirty-nine recommendations. At that time, a group to oversee implementation of the recommendations was established. Implementation was completed by February 2013 and an impact report was produced in May 2013.[20] Goldman identified "three unifying themes across the 39 BSC recommendations which capture the areas of greatest change and impact on the firm: (1) *clients*, and the higher standard of care we apply in serving them; (2) *reputational sensitivity and awareness*, and its importance in everything we do; and (3) the individual and collective *accountability* of our people."[21]

The specific recommendations Goldman Sachs implemented included review of client transactions by the newly created Firmwide Suitability Committee and the Firmwide New Activity Committee, which would apply "more thorough and comprehensive standards for transaction approvals, particularly for those transactions that present reputational risk."[22] Goldman also "changed [their] annual employee performance review and rewards processes to include an assessment of reputational excellence, linking 'cultural' behavior to how [their] people are recognized and rewarded."[23] Goldman articulated fourteen core business principles of the firm. Its articulation of these principles includes the following:

> We are dedicated to complying fully with the letter and spirit of the laws, rules and ethical principles that govern us. Our continued success depends upon unswerving adherence to this standard. . . .
>
> We expect our people to maintain high ethical standards in everything they do, both in their work for the firm and in their personal lives.[24]

In 2012, Barclays commissioned the *Salz Review* (discussed in chapter 3) on its business practices. In 2013, it received and responded to the review's recommendations and criticisms. The response noted that "following on from the financial crisis of 2008 and in light of the events of summer 2012, it was clear that Barclays needed a fundamental change of culture." In the response's introduction, Barclays said: "The Board asked for a rigorous and, crucially, independent view of how Barclays could spearhead industry changes in culture. Informed by unprecedented access to the bank and its people, that is precisely what we have received." The report then discussed how Barclays would do what the *Salz Review* recommends. The word "culture" appears thirty-nine times in the response; the phrase "culture and values" appears thirteen times.[25]

Of course, words are not enough. Enron had an exemplary ethics code. Nor are studies and recommendations enough. What is needed are actions that support and reflect the words.

Encouragingly, regulators, too, are stressing these same themes. On October 20, 2014, William Dudley, the president and CEO of the New York Fed, gave a speech titled "Enhancing Financial Stability by Improving Culture in the Financial Services Industry." He said:

> Although cultural and ethical problems are not unique to the finance industry, financial firms are different from other firms in important ways. First, the financial sector plays a key public role in allocating scarce capital and exerting market discipline throughout a complex, global economy. For the economy to achieve its long-term growth potential, we need a sound and vibrant financial sector. Financial firms exist, in part, to benefit the public, not simply their shareholders, employees and corporate clients. Unless the financial industry can rebuild the public trust, it cannot effectively perform its essential functions. For this reason alone, the industry must do much better.[26]

We agree with President Dudley—the finance industry "must do much better." In this book, we describe a way to bring this about.

A Note on Terminology

This note explains how we use many of the terms in this book.

First, banks are often organized in holding companies that own and oversee many corporations; also, they are commonly referred to by names that are not typically their formal legal names. In this book, we generally use the names commonly associated with the banks rather than the banks' specific legal names, and, except in direct quotes and specific historical references, we refer to all related entities using the same name or names (for instance, "Citigroup" or "Citi" for all Citigroup-related entities,

"JPMorgan" for JPMorgan Chase and other related entities, or "Goldman" or "Goldman Sachs" for Goldman Sachs and other related entities).

Second, more generally, we use the term "bank" to refer to many types of entities, including broker-dealers (brokerages), traditional investment banks, investment funds, and other financial services entities, as well as depository and lending institutions. Sometimes, other terms are used if doing so is appropriate in the particular context. For example, banks involved in the securities business are often referred to as investment banks, particularly if they are not closely affiliated with banks that also take deposits. Investment banks up through the 1970s may be referred to simply as firms because they were operated as partnerships much the way law firms still are today; they also may be referred to as partnerships. If generally applicable corporate governance norms or securities disclosure obligations are being discussed as to corporations, the word "company," "corporation," "firm," or, if applicable, "publicly held company" may be used. Finally, there are many financial services companies that are not commonly called banks, such as insurance companies, investment advisers, and fund managers, but that engage in businesses directly related to securities markets; appropriate terminology will be used to describe those companies when they are specifically being discussed, although many of the observations we make about banks in this book apply to them as well, particularly when they engage in businesses closely related to what banks do. Indeed, while most of what we say applies to banks (and bankers) generally, the heterogeneity of the entities we refer to as banks means that some characterizations are far more applicable to some types of banks (and bankers) than others. For instance, our discussions of the history of banking in chapter 2 and of particularly high compensation packages and extremely long working hours in chapter 3 are probably far more applicable to the larger national and international banks than to many regional banks.

Similarly, while we often use the term "banking," we sometimes refer specifically to "investment banking," which includes any business pertaining to buying or selling securities—a broad category of investments that includes, among other things, stocks, stock options, bonds and other debt securities, collateralized mortgage or debt obligations, and other asset-backed securities, as well as the many derivative products that are based on securities, such as "swaps." The term "commercial banking," by contrast, describes the business of taking deposits, some of which are federally insured, and lending to individuals and businesses.

The people working at banks who are engaged in banking activities will usually be referred to as "bankers"; when discussing bankers whose work is primarily related to securities, we may sometimes refer to them as "investment bankers." Sometimes, however, more specific terms may be appropriate, such as "investment adviser," "fund manager," or "trader." In many parts of this book, however, the discussion concerns the more highly paid bankers whom we believe should have more responsibility for the fate of their banks. These people are often referred to as "highly paid (or compensated) bankers," or "senior bankers." This group may include people more specifically described as "officers," "executives," "managing directors," or simply "managers," and these terms are used where appropriate (other highly paid bankers, such as traders, may fit in none of these other categories). When we discuss imposing some measure of personal liability on highly paid bankers or other similarly situated individuals by means of an employment agreement between them and the bank or other institution they work for, we may refer to a banker as an "employee."

One last terminological point involves the difference between "clients" and "customers." Customer is the broader category, encompassing the people or entities who transact with the bank, often simply as buyers or sellers of an investment product. Clients are a subset of customers. They often transact with the bank as well as retain the bank for specific purposes (underwriting clients, for example, often sell their securities to the bank in a "firm commitment" underwriting transaction). We use the term "client relationship" to describe a type of customer relationship that involves a substantial amount of trust being placed in the banker by the customer who hires or retains the bank for a specific task. Sometimes legal fiduciary obligations follow, sometimes they do not, but the banker's principal function is to look after the best interests of the client. Client relationships arise, for example, when the bank is hired to manage assets, to underwrite a securities offering, to arrange a merger-and-acquisition deal, or to design a particular type of transaction for the client. In other situations, the bank's principal and often only function is to transact with the customer, usually to sell the customer an investment product but sometimes to buy an investment product from the customer. Even though legal fiduciary duties rarely arise in these situations, the customer is still entitled, as a matter of good business practice, to put a high degree of trust in the banker, just as a customer buying a car or jewelry from a high-end retailer should be able to trust what the salesperson is saying and that the salesperson is helping him make a suitable purchase.

A Note on Sources

The material in this book, especially chapter 1, is based heavily on governmental reports, exhibits to those reports, court filings, exhibits to such filings, and other material on websites of governmental agencies. The correspondence, such as e-mails, quoted in the text, particularly in the introduction and chapter 1, is included as set forth in the source from which the quote was found, typically a document made public in a governmental report or website. The e-mails have been quoted without correction for typographical or other errors made by the e-mails' authors. Especially in chapter 1, we have included lengthy quotes from many sorts of documents: governmental press releases, agreed statements of facts, judicial decisions, internal e-mails, and complaints filed by parties (especially governmental parties, but in some cases private parties) in particular cases. While we cannot avoid some characterizations of what the relevant actors did, we very much wanted the actors to speak for themselves.

Chapter 3 makes extensive use of scholarly literature from psychology. More detail on the research discussed in the chapter is available in the endnotes. This book is, of course, also extensively informed by other sources, including local and national newspaper coverage.

Links to many of the sources referenced in the endnotes are given on the book's website, hosted by the University of Chicago Press.

PART I

The Problem

1 IRRESPONSIBLE BANKING

I n the spring of 2015, over six years after the 2008 financial crisis, and after the flood of regulation enacted in response, bank scandals — some new, some ongoing, and some in the recent past — are still much in the news. In this chapter, we discuss several of these scandals.

The examples we discuss are, of course, in the past, albeit in some cases in the very recent past. How common problematic behavior is now or, for that matter, how common it has been in the past, cannot be known. Certainly, much bank behavior is not problematic. But the behavior we discuss here is sufficiently common that it cannot fairly be considered exceptional or rare.

Many examples we discuss in this chapter involve financial risk taking and financial engineering. These are both part of banks' business models; the difficulties arise because the business models may not distinguish sufficiently well between the appropriate and the inappropriate.

Some examples involve conflicted behavior. It has been suggested that conflicted behavior itself may also be part of some banks' business models, such as when banks design or deal in complex products whose value they can misrepresent to their more credulous customers and clients. Greg Smith, who made headlines in 2012 when he left Goldman Sachs and simultaneously published an op-ed explaining why he had done so, was interviewed by Anderson Cooper on CBS's *60 Minutes*. In the interview, he described sales pitches made by "Wall Street" for complex products to "philanthropies, or endowments, or teachers' retirement pensions funds, in Alabama, or Virginia, or Oregon." The aim was, he explained, to get big fees from unsophisticated clients. Cooper then asked: "So, did the people you work with want unsophisticated clients?" to which Smith replied that "getting an unsophisticated client was the golden prize. The quickest way to make money on Wall Street is to take the most sophisticated product and try to sell it to the least sophisticated client."[1] It should be noted, however, that Smith's reasons for leaving Goldman Sachs are disputed and may have included dissatisfaction with his compensation.

Reputation should generally serve as a constraint to conflicted behavior. Apparently, though, there are times when it does not. Such behavior may be particularly tempting when banks (or bankers) are performing badly. Bankers may react in problematic ways, perhaps by attempting to sell bad investments to credulous but technically "sophisticated" customers and clients or by engaging in other undesirable behavior, such as doubling down on, or not fully disclosing, risk.

Just as reputation is not a sufficient constraint against conflicted or otherwise problematic behavior, neither apparently is the effect of the significant amounts banks pay, and presumably expect to pay, in settlements with regulators, especially the U.S. Securities and Exchange Commission (SEC).[2] A *New York Times* article discussing Citigroup's settlement of a case concerning subprime mortgages, to be discussed later in this chapter, noted that

> nearly all of the biggest financial companies, Goldman Sachs, Morgan Stanley, JPMorgan Chase and Bank of America among them, have settled fraud cases by promising the S.E.C. that they would never again violate an antifraud law, only to do it again in another case [and without admitting or denying that they did what they were alleged to have done, but typically paying significant financial penalties] a few years later. . . .
>
> A New York Times analysis of enforcement actions during the last 15 years found at least 51 cases in which 19 Wall Street firms had broken antifraud laws they had agreed never to breach.[3]

Some banks would respond that entry into a subsequent settlement as to the same law does not mean that they violated the prior settlement. This debate is ultimately beside the point being made here, which is that settlements do not seem to be doing enough to prevent future conduct that generates more charges of misconduct—charges that, again, are often settled with significant monetary penalties.

One of the best-known settlements in the years preceding the subprime bubble is the 2003 $1.4 billion global settlement that Bear Stearns, Credit Suisse, Goldman Sachs, JPMorgan, Lehman Brothers, Merrill Lynch, Morgan Stanley, Salomon Smith Barney, UBS Warburg, and USB Piper Jaffray entered into with the SEC (and the National Association of Securities

Dealers, the North American Securities Administrators Association, the New York Stock Exchange (NYSE), the New York attorney general, and state securities regulators), settling allegations that the banks' analysts' reports had been deceptive. The allegations concerned "undue influence of investment banking interests on securities research at brokerage firms."[4] Banks had given "buy" ratings and other favorable coverage to companies whose investment banking business they sought even though they believed the companies were of very low quality.[5] Documents meant for internal consumption within some of the banks used very evocative language to describe just how low. The more polite descriptions include "dog" and "junk"; less polite ones include "piece of crap" and "piece of shit."[6]

Also in the fairly recent past is Enron.[7] Enron collapsed in 2001, having used many bank-crafted techniques to depict its financial condition as far better than it was.[8] One type of transaction Enron used was a "prepay transaction."[9] Prepay transactions can be legitimate, but the SEC alleged that Enron's were not—that they were actually borrowings. JPMorgan and Citi helped Enron structure these transactions and participated in them, effectively lending Enron money. Both paid significant amounts to the SEC to settle allegations that they aided and abetted Enron's securities fraud. In a related proceeding, Citi also settled SEC allegations that it used similar techniques with another company, Dynegy.[10] In these settlements, in accordance with standard practice, the settling companies were allowed to neither admit nor deny the allegations.[11] But they settled for significant amounts of money—JPMorgan agreed to pay $135 million and Citi agreed to pay $120 million.[12] The two banks also agreed to pay over $2 billion each to settle private suits.[13]

The complexity of the transaction structure was intended to fool markets. One banker from JPMorgan explained the prepay structure used by Enron to another banker:

"Why do they want to hedge with gas where it is now?"
"They're not hedging . . . they do the back-to-back swap."
"This is a circular deal that goes right back to them."
"It's basically a structured finance—"
"It's a financing?"
"Yeah, its totally a financing"[14]

None of what follows is intended as a wholesale indictment of bankers or banking. Rather, the descriptions below are intended to provide a critical yet nuanced perspective on what banks and bankers did, avoiding reflexive demonization or overgeneralization. There are many different sorts of bankers, with many different roles, aptitudes, temperaments, and levels of knowledge and responsibility. As stated in the introduction, many bankers have done good things for our economy and for society as a whole. But bankers, together, created and inhabited a culture that has permitted, and at times encouraged, behavior that has proven highly problematic. Some of the behavior is clearly illegal. Some of the behavior may be in a gray area. And some may be legal but impose significant costs on many different types of people—taxpayers, homeowners, pension fund beneficiaries, and so on. Some types of misbehavior are probably no longer occurring—and some lessons may have been learned. But the all-too-recent examples in this chapter, many involving significant amounts of money, demonstrate that the problem in banking continues.

Some Examples
The 2008 Crisis: Subprime Securities

Investment banks were the driving force behind the structured finance products that provided a steady stream of funding for lenders originating high risk, poor quality loans and that magnified risk throughout the U.S. financial system. The investment banks that engineered, sold, traded, and profited from mortgage related structured finance products were a major cause of the financial crisis.[15]

That was the conclusion of the 2011 *Levin-Coburn Report*, the report produced by the Senate subcommittee that investigated investment banks' role in the crisis. The following briefly explains some of the main drivers of the report's conclusion.

BANKERS' RESPONSIBILITY FOR BAD MORTGAGES

When borrowers take out mortgage loans, those making the loans typically do not keep them. Rather, they sell them and use the funds to make more mortgage loans. The buyers of these loans—banks and others—pool many mortgages and sell interests (residential mortgage-backed securities, or RMBS) in the pools to investors on the capital markets. The capital markets thus provide financing for mortgages. Not only did banks structure and sell RMBS, they also structured and sold collateralized debt obligations (CDOs) made up of RMBS and other debt obligations. They also directly financed and, in some cases, acquired mortgage originators.

Prime mortgages, which are mortgages to borrowers with good credit, have been successfully sold into these pools for many years.[16] Starting in the early to mid-1990s, banks began structuring and selling interests in pools of subprime mortgages. The subprime mortgages that were pooled, while not of prime quality, were nevertheless purportedly carefully underwritten to be of a specified, albeit lesser, quality. Interests in pools of subprime securities proved quite popular, creating considerable demand for more interests and, thus, more mortgages. Transaction volume rose dramatically in the first decade and virtually exploded in the years immediately preceding the 2008 crisis.

The more demand there was for these mortgages, the more that were made. Moreover, the people originating subprime mortgages were compensated on volume. The demand was there; they just had to provide the supply. That they would try to stretch underwriting standards to and sometimes past the breaking point was to be expected. The subprime mortgages originated and pooled became progressively worse: loans were extended to borrowers with lower credit scores, based on highly inflated house appraisals. In some cases, mortgage originators simply lied.[17] Some borrowers were duped, but some were not: they were willing to take out a mortgage that depicted their financial situation as being far more favorable than they knew it to be. Whether or not lying was involved, considerable ingenuity was devoted to figuring out how to qualify (and indeed, recruit) more borrowers.[18] The term "liar's loans" and a somewhat less evocative one, NINA loans, for "no income no assets," tells the tale. The official terms for some of these loans were "low-documentation" (or even "no doc") or "stated income" (the borrower "stated" his income, and nobody checked). These kinds of mortgages, as well as mortgages requiring very low payments initially but much larger payments later on, where the ability to make the low payments sufficed to qualify the borrower for the mortgages, seem like open invitations to game underwriting standards.

Banks' assembly lines, buying these mortgages and structuring them into RMBS and selling them to investors, continued at breakneck pace. As the market heated up, banks sometimes, and perhaps often, didn't do enough due diligence. However little they knew about the quality of particular mortgages they were securitizing, they were increasingly aware that overall, mortgage quality was declining and that underwriting standards were not being adhered to. Where they knew that particular mortgages were of low quality, there was considerable pressure not to act on that knowledge and refuse to buy the mortgages, lest the sellers of the mortgages decide to take future mortgages elsewhere.[19]

BANKERS' STRUCTURING AND SALE OF LOW-QUALITY SECURITIES

Bankers structured and sold subprime securities they believed were bad, sometimes not fully disclosing and sometimes even affirmatively misrepresenting their views, including to their customers and clients.

Banks selling mortgage-backed securities represented them as being of high quality, with the underlying mortgages comporting with specified underwriting standards. Many lawsuits, both public and private, have been brought, alleging that banks, at best, knew they had not done enough due diligence or, worse, that the banks knew many of the mortgages were questionable. Some of these lawsuits have ended with settlements. The aggregate amounts of the settlements are in the billions, as discussed below, with settlements with one agency, the Federal Housing Finance Agency (FHFA), exceeding $18 billion. Of course, not all cases result in banks' settling or being found liable. Furthermore, even where banks do settle, as noted above and discussed in chapters 4 and 5, they often make no admission of wrongdoing. The settlements may, however, contain agreed statements of facts that can help explain the specifics of the conduct at issue. Moreover, whatever the legal situation may be—whether bank conduct was illegal or not and what the banks may or may not have admitted as part of settlements—considerable evidence has been unearthed, both in the litigation process and in governmental inquiries, that describes conduct of considerable concern. One particularly vivid source is internal e-mails, some of which are quoted or discussed below.

In November of 2013, JPMorgan entered into a $13 billion settlement with, among others, the Justice Department, the FHFA, and various states.

The settlement was "to resolve federal and state civil claims arising out of the packaging, marketing, sale and issuance of residential mortgage-backed securities (RMBS) by JPMorgan, Bear Stearns and Washington Mutual [which JPMorgan acquired when they collapsed] prior to Jan. 1, 2009. As part of the settlement, JPMorgan acknowledged it made serious misrepresentations to the public—including the investing public—about numerous RMBS transactions."[20] JPMorgan acknowledged that it "regularly represented to RMBS investors that the mortgage loans in various securities complied with underwriting guidelines. Contrary to those representations, as the statement of facts explains, on a number of different occasions, JP Morgan employees knew that the loans in question did not comply with those guidelines and were not otherwise appropriate for securitization, but they allowed the loans to be securitized—and those securities to be sold—without disclosing this information to investors."[21]

The statement of facts provides useful detail as to the quality of mortgages JPMorgan was securitizing and JPMorgan's knowledge on this point:

JPMorgan contracted with industry leading third party due diligence vendors to re-underwrite the loans it was purchasing from loan originators. The vendors assigned one of three grades to each of the loans they reviewed. An Event 1 grade meant that the loan complied with underwriting guidelines. An Event 2 meant that the loans did not comply with underwriting guidelines, but had sufficient compensating factors to justify the extension of credit. *An Event 3 meant that the vendor concluded that the loan did not comply with underwriting guidelines and was without sufficient compensating factors to justify the loan* . . . . JPMorgan reviewed loans scored Event 3 by the vendors and made the final determination regarding each loan's score. Event 3 loans that could not be cured were at times referred to by due diligence personnel at JPMorgan as "rejects." JPMorgan personnel then made the final purchase decisions.

From January 2006 through September 2007[,] . . . *JPMorgan's due diligence vendors graded numerous loans in the samples as Event 3's.* . . . The exceptions identified by the third-party diligence vendors included, among other things, loans with high loan-to-value ratios (some over 100 percent); high debt-to-income ratios; inadequate or missing documentation of income, assets, and rental/mortgage history; stated incomes that the vendors concluded were unreasonable; and missing appraisals or appraisals that varied from the estimates obtained in the diligence process by an amount greater than JPMorgan's fifteen percent established tolerance. *The vendors communicated this information to certain JPMorgan employees.*

JPMorgan directed that a number of the uncured Event 3 loans be "waived" into the pools facilitating the purchase of loan pools, which then went into JPMorgan inventory for securitization. . . . Some JPMorgan due diligence managers also ordered "bulk" waivers by directing vendors to override certain exceptions the JPMorgan due diligence managers deemed acceptable . . . without analyzing these loans on a case-by-case basis. JPMorgan due diligence managers sometimes directed these bulk waivers shortly before closing the purchase of a pool. Further, even though the Event 3 rate in the random samples indicated that the un-sampled portion of a pool likely contained additional loans with exceptions, JPMorgan purchased and securitized the loan pools without reviewing and eliminating those loans from the un-sampled portions of the pools.[22]

Another recent settlement involves Citigroup. In July of 2014, Citigroup entered into a $7 billion settlement with, among others, the Justice Department, the FHFA, and various states. "Contrary to [its representations 'about the quality of mortgage loans it securitized and sold to investors'], Citigroup securitized and sold RMBS with underlying mortgage loans that it knew had material defects. As the statement of facts explains, on a number of occasions, Citigroup employees learned that significant percentages of the mortgage loans reviewed in due diligence had material defects."[23]

The settlement's statement of facts provides additional detail, including the following passage:

In two [RMBS transactions] issued and underwritten by Citigroup in 2007, *Citigroup's due diligence vendor identified a number of loans that were outside of Citigroup's valuation rules and tolerances.* These included loans where the difference between the reported original appraisal and the vendor's valuation determination exceeded 15 percent, or otherwise exceeded Citigroup's thresholds. *Citigroup also instructed the due dili-*

gence vendor to change the grades of loans that its vendor had recommended for rejection, following Citigroup's review of those loans and loan grades. Citigroup then securitized hundreds of the loans that its vendor had identified as outside of Citigroup's tolerances.

In addition, early in the due diligence process, a trader at Citigroup wrote an internal email that indicated that he had reviewed a due diligence report summarizing loans that the due diligence vendor had graded as EV3s [Event 3] and had noted that "a lot" of these rejected loans had unreasonable income and values below the original appraisal, which resulted in combined loan-to-value in excess of 100 percent. *The trader stated that he "went thru the Diligence Reports and [I] think that we should start praying. . . . I would not be surprised if half of these loans went down. There are a lot of loans that have unreasonable incomes, values below the original appraisals . . . , etc. It's amazing that some of these loans were closed at all."*[24]

Thus far, FHFA has obtained over $18 billion in settlements in eighteen cases (including $4 billion from the JPMorgan settlement described above, which included FHFA as one of the parties), and two cases are still outstanding.[25] The cases involve banks' illegal practices, such as the ones described above, in their sales of mortgage-backed securities to Fannie Mae (the Federal National Mortgage Association) and Freddie Mac (the Federal Home Loan Mortgage Corporation).

The FHFA 2014 settlements have been with Morgan Stanley ($1.25 billion, February 3); Société Générale ($122 million, February 26); Credit Suisse ($885 million, March 21); Bank of America ($5.83 billion, March 25); Barclays ($280 million, April 23); First Horizon National Corporation ($110 million, April 29); RBS ($99.5 million, June 19); Goldman Sachs ($1.2 billion, August 22); and HSBC ($550 million, September 12).[26] On August 20, 2014, the Justice Department and other federal and state regulators reached a settlement with Bank of America for $16.65 billion for similar sorts of conduct (including conduct by Merrill Lynch and Countrywide, which Bank of America had aquired) as that involved in the FHFA settlements.[27] "The settlement includes a statement of facts, in which the bank has acknowledged that it sold billions of dollars of RMBS without disclosing to investors key facts about the quality of the securitized loans. When the RMBS collapsed, investors, including federally insured financial institutions, suffered billions of dollars in losses. The bank has also conceded that it originated risky mortgage loans and made misrepresentations about the quality of those loans to Fannie Mae, Freddie Mac, and the Federal Housing Administration."[28]

The buyers of mortgage-backed securities found the securities attractive, in significant part because they were very highly rated while offering yields higher than those of other comparably rated corporate instruments. Many of the buyers may have suspected that the AAA mortgage-backed securities were of lower quality than, for instance, U.S. government bonds, also carrying an AAA rating but offering a lower yield. But they probably did not suspect how much lower.

Many of the lawsuits, including many of those discussed above, relate to banks' sales of RMBS. In the years leading up to the crisis, many far more complex instruments were structured and issued, including CDOs. One type of CDO generating an enormous amount of litigation has been a "synthetic CDO."[29]

For RMBS and for CDOs that aren't synthetic, an investor's ultimate source of repayment is actual mortgages or the other debt obligations contained in the security. To simplify, an investor is buying the rights to a portion of many promises to pay, on mortgages and/or on other debt. The payments fulfilling the promises are made to a pool, which distributes the funds among the pool's investors. All the investors are betting that the mortgages comprising the transactions will do well. By contrast, synthetic CDOs are side bets: the money available to distribute to investors comes from the other investors in the CDO transaction. Synthetic CDOs specify or "reference" particular mortgages or RMBS (or CDOs). Investors who want to bet that the reference mortgages or RMBS (or CDOs)—called the "reference securities"—will do well make a bet with others who think the reference securities will do badly. Those making the bet that the mortgages will do well are taking the "long" position; those making the bet that the mortgages will do badly are taking the "short" position.

RMBS and CDOs (including synthetic CDOs) are typically structured so that each transaction offers different levels of seniority. An investor can buy the right to get paid back first, second, third, all the way to last. Not surprisingly, investors who buy the right to get paid first get the lowest promised return and investors who buy the right to get paid last get the highest promised return.[30] The hierarchy of payments will prove relevant to several aspects of the story, discussed below.

The RMBS lawsuits discussed earlier generally concerned investors who had bought an interest in mortgages and were told the mortgages were of higher quality than they actually were (and that the sellers knew them to be). The same is true of non-synthetic CDOs. Banks were selling securities they said were good, backed by good mortgages. The buyers now allege that the securities were in fact bad, backed by defective mortgages, and that the bankers knew this. There are additional, far more intricate, issues raised by synthetic CDOs.

Synthetic CDOs involve two opposing sides of a bet. One side will win and the other will lose. A bank structuring and selling such a transaction might have no strong view as to which side of the bet would win. And an investor without a strong view as to which side would win might have good reasons to want to buy either side, as might a bank that structured a deal and took a portion for itself. If the investor or bank had considerable "long" exposure, it might want some "short" exposure as a hedge.

One important impetus for the ramping up of production—if not for the creation—of synthetic CDOs was a demand for short positions to hedge long positions. But as more market participants began to think housing prices might decline, demand for short positions increased. To satisfy the demand, banks needed someone who would take the opposite bet, the "long" position. As more market participants were concluding that the market was overheated, the long bet became a harder sell. Banks involved in structuring and selling CDOs sometimes did have strong (and, in retrospect, correct) views as to which bet was likely to win—the short bet. In some cases, banks apparently were working with someone who wanted to buy the short position but were concealing that fact from those to whom they sold the long position; in some cases, banks seem to have structured deals that foisted part of *their own* losing positions onto their customers and clients.

How could investors be persuaded to take the long bet? To some investors, these securities were still "hot." And banks' sales staffs were on the case. Transactions also sometimes included a role for an independent party with a good reputation for picking valuable securities. Investors would be told that the "reference securities" on which they were making their bet were to be picked by such a party, and the offering documents for the CDOs would tout these parties' reputation and experience at some length. But these independent parties were sometimes discussing their securities selections with investors who were actually taking the "short" position and therefore benefited if the securities selected were of low quality. The independent parties generally did not know that these investors were taking short positions. They believed them to be taking long positions, often the lowest-priority position, which would only pay off if the securities paid off fully. But these short investors' short positions were far larger than whatever long positions they may have had. It is difficult to know in how many transactions this occurred.

None of this is to say that all synthetic CDOs were flawed — that, in each instance, banks knew that one side was "good" and the other "bad," and sold the bad piece by concealing their view (or knowledge) of its quality. Even when banks themselves took one side of the bet, they sometimes had a legitimate reason for doing so, such as a need to hedge other positions. But synthetic CDOs raise issues that are serious enough to warrant concern.

What investors buying synthetic CDOs were told in the disclosure documents makes the issues particularly complicated. While long investors were *not* told if the short party had been involved in collateral selection, they *were* generally told that the bank and others "might" have a conflict of interest (and indeed, that the bank might be taking the other side of the bet) and that the investment was subject to considerable uncertainties. Standard disclosure to the investors could include that the party selecting the collateral was not acting as an adviser or agent for them and that they should make their investment decision without relying on either that party or the seller of the security. Investors would generally be asked to represent that they had reviewed the collateral themselves.[31]

In perhaps the most notorious synthetic CDO, ABACUS, for which Goldman Sachs agreed to pay a $550 million settlement, the short party, Paulson & Co., dealt with the independent party described as selecting the securities, apparently giving the impression that it would be taking a long position and giving input on the reference securities. The involvement of the short party in selecting assets for the CDO was not disclosed to the investors buying the long position.[32] In the settlement, "Goldman acknowledge[d] that . . . it was a mistake for the Goldman marketing materials to state that the reference portfolio was 'selected by' ACA Management LLC without disclosing the role of Paulson & Co. Inc. in the portfolio selection process and that Paulson's economic interests were adverse to CDO investors. Goldman regrets that the marketing materials did not contain that disclosure."[33] The long investors lost a billion dollars, and Paulson made huge gains. A mid-level Goldman banker involved in the deal, Fabrice Tourre, was found liable for securities fraud for not disclosing Paulson's role and was fined more than $825,000.[34]

Another related gambit was for the bank itself to influence the selection of reference securities and acknowledge this but tout to long investors its own long position, while having a far greater short position.

An analogy is to a horse race with two horses, in which a person bets a small amount on a particular horse to win, while betting a much larger amount on the other horse. Because of his bet on the first horse, he is allowed input on the first horse's training and feed—indeed, he might condition his willingness to bet on the first horse on being allowed this input. He uses his input to suggest training and feed that he knows will make that horse perform very badly.

Second in notoriety to ABACUS may be Citigroup's Class V Funding deal. The facts as alleged are as follows. Citigroup had mortgage exposure it wanted to get rid of. It structured a synthetic CDO. But how would it get investors to buy the long position? Again, tell them the assets on which they were betting were selected by someone who had a reputation for picking high-quality assets, Credit Suisse Alternative Capital, Inc. (CSAC), while having a significant portion of the assets actually be picked by Citigroup, to enable Citigroup to short certain assets it wanted to short. CSAC went along with this. The SEC's complaint against Citigroup included a quote from an e-mail written by a Citi employee to his supervisor: "This is [Trading Desk Head]'s prop [proprietary] trade (don't tell CSAC). CSAC agreed to terms even though they don't get to pick the assets."[35] The portfolio selected by Citigroup included deals Citigroup had done, where Citigroup still held long positions. Almost all the names selected by Citigroup defaulted, whereas those selected by CSAC did not. Citigroup earned $160 million, while the investors lost all their investment.[36] Investors were not told of Citigroup's role in selecting the assets or its short position.

As recounted by the SEC: "Class V III proved to be one of the worst-performing CDOs issued during the relevant period. As soon as it was issued, certain knowledgeable market participants noted the poor quality of the portfolio, and much of the underlying collateral declined precipitously in late 2007. By November 2007, collateral representing approximately 83% of the value of Class V III had been downgraded. As a result, an event of default was declared on November 19, 2007, making Class V III the second-fastest CDO-squared transaction to default."[37]

Citigroup settled with the SEC, agreeing to pay $285 million. In their settlements with the SEC, CSAC agreed to pay $2.5 million and an individual from CSAC responsible for the transaction agreed to pay $50,000.[38] (Interestingly, Citigroup's settlement initially did not receive judicial approval. As was until recently the norm for these sorts of SEC settlements, the settlement did not require Citigroup to admit guilt. Judge Jed Rakoff of the Southern District of New York refused to approve the settlement, stating that he simply did not have sufficient basis to determine whether it was fair.[39] The Second Circuit overturned Rakoff's decision, holding that he had abused his discretion; on remand, Rakoff approved the settlement.)[40]

There are many more examples. JPMorgan agreed to pay $154 million to settle a suit containing similar allegations with respect to yet another synthetic CDO, Squared CDO 2007-1. In this transaction, a hedge fund, Magnetar, allegedly played a similar role to the one played by Paulson in ABACUS. JP Morgan allegedly helped Magnetar, at the expense of its other customers and clients, and, as it happens, itself: it made a losing investment in the transaction.[41] Yet again, the short party was secretly allowed input into what mortgages the transaction would be betting on. In Squared CDO 2007-1, Magnetar had a $600 million short position—a $600 million bet that the mortgages were bad—and an $8.9 million long position. In an internal e-mail, a JPMorgan employee noted: "We all know [Magnetar] wants to print as many deals as possible before everything completely falls apart." JPMorgan wanted to sell the deal as quickly as possible given the deteriorating market. In a March 22, 2007, e-mail, "the J. P. Morgan employee in charge of Squared's global distribution said . . . 'we are soooo pregnant with this deal, we need a wheel-barrel to move around. . . . Let's schedule the cesarian (sic), please!' Within 10 months, the securities had lost most or all of their value."[42]

Merrill Lynch agreed to pay $131.8 million to settle SEC charges in connection with other Magnetar deals. The charges are familiar: "Merrill Lynch marketed complex CDO investments using misleading materials that portrayed an independent process of collateral selection that was in the best interests of long-term debt investors. . . . Investors did not have the benefit of knowing that a prominent hedge fund firm with its own interest was heavily involved behind the scenes in selecting the underlying port- folios."[43]

Another example is a synthetic CDO sold by UBS to Pursuit Partners. Pursuit sued UBS; the court found probable cause that UBS would be held liable and required UBS to set aside $36 million to pay damages.[44] The court cited evidence that UBS was selling the securities to help its own financial position: it knew the securities were about to be downgraded at the time it was in the process of selling them to Pursuit. In describ- ing UBS's motivation in pitching the securities to Pursuit, the court men- tioned "UBS's awareness that these high grade securities on its hands would soon turn into financial toxic waste."[45] "The court takes UBS em- ployees at their word when they referenced their Notes, these purported 'investment grade' securities which they sold, as 'crap' and 'vomit,' for UBS alone possessed the knowledge of what their product, their inventory, was truly worth. While UBS would argue that such descriptors lack a precise meaning, the true meaning of these words and the true value of UBS's wares became abundantly clear when the Plaintiffs' multi-million dollar investment was completely wiped out and liquidated by UBS shortly after the last of the Note purchases was consummated."[46] Interestingly, Citi- group purchased AAA rated securities in this transaction and lost its $15 million investment.[47]

Other comparable deals have been the subject of suits (and some settle- ments), including Goldman's Hudson, Anderson, and Timberwolf deals, and Morgan Stanley's "Dead Presidents" deals. An internal e-mail from Thomas Montag, a senior Goldman executive, to the Goldman mortgage department head, Daniel Sparks, said: "Boy that [Timberwolf] was one shitty deal."[48]

As banks were increasingly concluding that the market was about to fall, they were sometimes aggressive in trying to sell bad securities, notably bets that mortgages would be valuable. Indeed, the Financial Crisis Inquiry Commission, a commission established in response to the financial crisis, wrote about Goldman:

> Back in October [2006], Goldman Sachs traders had complained that they were being asked to "distribute junk that nobody was dumb enough to take first time around." . . . In a December 28 email discussing a list of customers to target for the year, Goldman's Fabrice Tourre, then a vice president on the structured product correlation trading desk [who is now best known for his role in the ABACUS transaction], said to "focus efforts" on "buy and hold rating-based buyers" rather than "sophisticated hedge funds" that "will be on the same side of the trade as we will." The "same side of the trade" as Goldman was the selling or shorting side—those who expected the mortgage market to continue to decline.[49]

The *Levin-Coburn Report* recounts that,

> despite doubts about its performance and asset quality, Goldman engaged in an aggressive campaign to sell the Timberwolf securities. . . . Mr. Sparks and Mr. Lehman sent out numerous sales directives or "axes" to the Goldman sales force, stressing that Timberwolf was a priority for the firm. In April, Mr. Sparks suggested issuing "ginormous" sales credits to any salesperson who sold Timberwolf securities, only to find out that large sales credits had already been offered. In May, while Goldman was internally lowering the value of Timberwolf, it continued to sell the securities at a much higher price than the company knew it was worth. At one point, a member of the SPG [Structured Product Group] Trading Desk issued an email to clients and investors advising them that the market was rebounding and the downturn was "already a distant memory." Goldman also began targeting Timberwolf sales to "non-traditional" buyers and those with little CDO familiarity, such as increasing its marketing efforts in Europe and Asia.[50]

According to the *Levin-Coburn Report*, Goldman took a short position on approximately 36 percent of the assets underlying Timberwolf.

Another problematic CDO was Gemstone, a "hybrid" deal (consisting of both actual mortgage-backed securities and bets on specified mortgage-backed securities). The *Levin-Coburn Report* had this to say about Gemstone:

Gemstone 7 was a hybrid CDO containing or referencing a variety of high risk, subprime RMBS securities initially valued at $1.1 billion when issued. Deutsche Bank's head global trader, Mr. Lippmann, recognized that these RMBS securities were high risk and likely to lose value, but did not object to their inclusion in Gemstone 7. Deutsche Bank, the sole placement agent, marketed the initial offering of Gemstone 7 in the first quarter of 2007. . . .

Nearly a third of Gemstone's assets consisted of high risk subprime loans originated by Fremont, Long Beach, and New Century, three lenders known at the time within the financial industry for issuing poor quality loans and RMBS securities. Although HBK [the hedge fund serving as collateral manager] directed the selection of assets for Gemstone 7, Mr. Lippmann's CDO Trading Desk was involved in the process and did not object to including certain RMBS securities in Gemstone 7, even though Mr. Lippmann was simultaneously referring to them as "crap" or "pigs." Mr. Lippmann was also at the same time advising some of his clients to short some of those same RMBS securities. In addition, Deutsche Bank sold five RMBS securities directly from its inventory to Gemstone 7, several of which were also contemporaneously disparaged by Mr. Lippmann.

The Deutsche Bank sales force aggressively sought purchasers for the CDO securities, while certain executives expressed concerns about the financial risk of retaining Gemstone 7 assets as the market was deteriorating in early 2007. In its struggle to sell Gemstone 7, Deutsche Bank motivated its sales force with special financial incentives, and sought out buyers in Europe and Asia because the US market had dried up. Deutsche Bank also talked of providing HBK's marks, instead of its own, to clients asking about the value of Gemstone 7's assets, since HBK's marks showed the CDO's assets performing better. Deutsche Bank was ultimately unable to sell $400 million, or 36%, of the Gemstone 7 securities, and agreed with HBK to split the unsold securities, each taking $200 million onto its own books. Deutsche Bank did not disclose to the eight investors whom it had solicited and convinced to buy Gemstone 7, that its global head trader of CDOs had an extremely negative view of a third of the assets in the CDO or that the bank's internal valuations showed that the assets had lost over $19 million in value since purchased.[51]

Investors lost almost their entire investment and sued Deutsche Bank; some settlements have been reached, for close to $100 million.[52]

In another case, Morgan Stanley has been sued by China Development Industrial Bank, a buyer of Stack 2006-1, a "hybrid" CDO that lost much of its value. The case has survived early stage motions to dismiss. The now-familiar arguments are being made. The opinion allowing the case to proceed included the following:

> Plaintiff purchaser (China) alleges that defendant seller Morgan falsely promoted collateral debt obligations as having specified credit ratings, which Morgan knew to be overstated and misleading. Specifically, the ratings were allegedly generated with grandfathered models and protocols and assumptions that were no longer applicable. Such ratings for Morgan's products were allegedly procured by way of Morgan's financial influence over the rating agencies. We recognize that a sophisticated business entity, like China, that alleges it was fraudulently induced to enter a contract because of false representations as to a product's quality, may nonetheless be precluded by contractual disclaimers from pursuing such a claim. Nevertheless, such rule is not determinative in this case. China has sufficiently alleged that Morgan possessed peculiar knowledge of the facts underlying the fraud, and the circumstances present would preclude any investigation by China conducted with due diligence. . . . The element of scienter can be reasonably inferred from the facts alleged, including e-mails, which support a motive by Morgan, at the time of the subject transaction, to quickly dispose of troubled collateral (i.e., predominantly residential mortgage-backed securities) which it owned at the time.[53]

Various documents elicited through plaintiff's discovery have been made public. Among these have been e-mails among Morgan Stanley bankers in which they joked about what they would name the deal. Among the names considered were Nuclear Holocaust 2007-1 and Subprime Meltdown 2007, Mike Tyson's Punchout, and worse.[54] In another e-mail chain, in October of 2005, bankers discuss concerns over the quality of mortgages being securitized. In one e-mail, a banker expressed his concern that many of the loans were "stated income" loans and that the amount of income was "not reasonable for the credit profile." In another e-mail, the same banker noted that "most of the loans have some type of exception/ issue or Morgan would not have looked at it as a credit reject/exception. . . . The real issue is that the loan requests do not make sense. $900k in combined loans to a renter with no prior mtg history stated making $16k a month as a manager of a knock off gold club distributor via the internet and mailings, a borrower that makes $12k a month as an operations manager of an unknown company-after research on my part I reveal it is a tarot reading house. Compound these issues with the fact that we are seeing what I would call a lot of this type of profile." The e-mails indicate that there was considerable back and forth as the bankers tried to get comfortable with the transaction, which they eventually succeeded in doing.[55]

The mortgages at issue in the transaction had been originated by New Century Financial Corp. On April 2, 2007, New Century filed for bankruptcy. In July of 2010, several of its senior officers settled charges by the SEC that New Century had made false and misleading disclosures. They agreed to pay monetary settlements and to be barred for five years from serving as officers or directors of a public company.[56]

In most of the deals discussed above, the rating agencies, Moody's, Standard & Poor's, and Fitch played an important role. In order to sell the securities, the banks needed to persuade the rating agencies to give the securities high ratings. Because just a few banks were commanding an enormous amount of business, and because those banks were able to play the rating agencies off against each other, they succeeded in their persuasion: loss of any bank's business would cost a rating agency an enormous amount of money.[57] Rating agencies were no innocents in these matters, although in some cases, the agencies may have just let themselves be browbeaten and manipulated rather than actually knowing, especially at the time they were rating, that they were misrating. For instance, banks sometimes misrepresented aspects of transactions to the rating agencies, depicting them as of far higher quality than they were. In one e-mail, an S&P employee tells another "Regarding Delphinius [a synthetic CDO], it appears that the . . . assets that they included in our closing date portfolio that were dummies were replaced in less than 24 hours with assets that would have . . . made the portfolio worse. . . . Given they would have provided us with this portfolio . . . they would not have been able to close as they would not have been passing."[58] Bankers would request that "uncooperative" raters not be assigned to their deals, and their "requests" were not infrequently honored.[59]

BANKS' HOLDINGS OF SUBPRIME SECURITIES

Banks bought or held onto subprime securities they thought were good and, when the securities turned out to be, or became, of lesser quality, sometimes did not tell the truth about how many they owned. Banks' holdings of super-senior securities provide a good example.

As mentioned above, subprime mortgage securities were generally structured to have "tranches"—that is, orders of priority, such that some investors bought the right to be paid first, others second, others third, and so on. The securities sold to investors who are to be paid first are the safest, lowest yielding, and highest rated. Those to be paid last are the riskiest, the highest yielding, and the lowest rated (if they are rated at all). The safest securities, those experiencing the last losses, are called super-senior.

In the years leading up to the financial crisis, the super-senior interests were often kept by the banks, either because the banks wanted to keep them or because they had difficulty selling them: because these interests were deemed so riskless, they paid very little interest and, hence, were not desirable investments. But the super-senior interests were not riskless. Home prices had gotten so inflated, and underwriting standards for loans had gotten so lax, that even the most senior portion of the pool, the portion to be paid off first, declined considerably in value, as mortgages in the pool defaulted or were expected to default.[60] Banks with especially large exposure included Citigroup, Bank of America, Merrill Lynch, Lehman, Bear Stearns, and UBS. The latter even bought extra super-senior debt.[61] Citigroup allegedly misrepresented its exposure to super-senior and other subprime securities in its public filings and, while not admitting or denying the allegations, agreed to pay close to $1.5 billion in settlements: $590 million to purchasers of Citigroup stock during the relevant time period, $730 million to purchasers of their bonds and preferred stock, and $75 million to the SEC.[62] Two Citigroup bankers, the then chief financial officer Gary Crittenden and then head of investor relations Arthur Tildesley Jr., also agreed to make payments to the SEC. Crittenden agreed to pay $100,000 and Tildesley agreed to pay $80,000.[63]

According to the Financial Crisis Inquiry Commission report:

> As at Merrill [Lynch], traders and risk managers at Citigroup believed that the super-senior tranches carried little risk. Citigroup's regulators later wrote, "An acknowledgement of the risk in its Super Senior AAA CDO exposure was perhaps Citigroup's 'biggest miss.' [...] As management felt comfortable with the credit risk of these tranches, it began to retain large positions on the balance sheet. . . . As the sub-prime market began to deteriorate, the risk perceived in these tranches increased, causing large writedowns." *Ultimately, losses at Citigroup from mortgages, Alt-A mortgage-backed securities* [securities backed by the exotic types of mortgages described above, but made to borrowers somewhat better than subprime borrowers], *and mortgage-related CDOs would total about $58 billion, nearly half of Citigroup's capital at the end of 2006.*[64]

BANKERS' ACTIVITIES MAGNIFIED RISK

Banks' activities magnified risk as the banks themselves became riskier. First, they were holding significant volumes of AAA rated and super-senior securities against which the amount of regulatory capital they needed to hold was too low, given that the securities were not truly of AAA or better-than-AAA quality. Bank riskiness is supposed to be addressed, in part, by banks having to hold a particular amount of capital. For a safer asset like a senior bond from a company with very little debt, capital requirements are lower than they would be for a subordinated bond from a company with considerable debt. Of course, the requirements only work if riskiness is assessed properly, which it was not.

Second, banks became riskier by making "guarantees" structured so that they did not have to be recorded as potential bank liabilities. Banks created off-balance-sheet entities that bought securities backed by mortgage securities and other assets with funds that were effectively guaranteed by them but only for periods less than a year. The banks were not contractually required to renew the "guarantees," but markets expected them to do so, and they did so as a matter of course. This modus operandi allowed a bank's riskiness to be assessed as though it was not liable on these guarantees.[65] An analogy can be made to a parent's guarantee of her child's car rental payment. If the car rental is only for a few days, it makes sense to say that the parent's financial situation is not affected. But if the rental is regularly renewable and renewed as a matter of course, the parent's financial situation is very much affected if the amount in question is large.

Moreover, the creation of synthetic CDOs and other like instruments created more risk. When a borrower takes out a mortgage and the lender sells that mortgage, the risk the lender had is being transferred, and, in theory, no more risk has been created. But when banks created synthetic CDOs, they did create more risk. Synthetic CDOs allow side bets. Many people can be betting on whether a pool of mortgages will go up or down; so long as there are people to take both sides of the bet, there is very little limit to how much can be bet. Synthetic CDO issuance volume was probably well over a trillion dollars—exact figures are difficult to obtain because many of the transactions were private.[66]

Risk was also magnified by reason of the housing bubble and the enormous debt many people were incurring.

The 2008 Crisis: Repo 105

Subprime securities are probably the most salient example of problematic banker behavior in the crisis. But there are many other examples. A notable one is Lehman Brothers' Repo 105. Lehman Brothers declared bankruptcy in September 2008. During the preceding year, it used a complex form of financial maneuvering, Repo 105, to conceal its enormous debt and generally deteriorating finances.[67] In the period leading up to its collapse, Lehman especially feared being downgraded by the rating agencies; it therefore had to seem to have a great deal less debt than it actually had.[68]

The introduction to the report prepared by the Lehman bankruptcy examiner describes Repo 105 as follows:

> [Repo 105 helped Lehman temporarily remove] approximately $50 billion of assets from the balance sheet at the end of the first and second quarters of 2008. In an ordinary repo . . . such transactions were accounted for as financings, and the assets remained on Lehman's balance sheet. In a Repo 105 transaction, Lehman did exactly the same

thing, but . . . accounting rules permitted the transactions to be treated as sales rather than financings, so that the assets could be removed from the balance sheet. With Repo 105 transactions, Lehman's reported net leverage was 12.1 at the end of the second quarter of 2008; but if Lehman had used ordinary repos, net leverage would have to have been reported at 13.9. . . .

Lehman used Repo 105 for no articulated business purpose except "to reduce balance sheet at the quarter-end." Rather than sell assets at a loss, "[a] Repo 105 increase would help avoid this without negatively impacting our leverage ratios." Lehman's Global Financial Controller confirmed that "the only purpose or motive for [Repo 105] transactions was reduction in the balance sheet" and that "there was *no substance* to the transactions."

Lehman did not disclose its use—or the significant magnitude of its use—of Repo 105 to the Government, to the rating agencies, to its investors, or to its own Board of Directors. Lehman's auditors, Ernst & Young, were aware of but did not question Lehman's use and nondisclosure of the Repo 105 accounting transactions.[69]

The examiner concluded that there were both material omissions and affirmative misrepresentations in Lehman's financial statements.[70] The report noted that,

unbeknownst to the investing public, rating agencies, Government regulators, and Lehman's Board of Directors, Lehman reverse engineered the firm's net leverage ratio for public consumption. Notably, during Lehman's 2008 earnings calls in which it touted its leverage reduction, analysts frequently inquired about *the means* by which Lehman was reducing its leverage. Although CFO [Erin] Callan told analysts that Lehman was "trying to give the group a great amount of transparency on the balance sheet," she reported that Lehman was reducing its leverage through the sale of less liquid asset categories but said nothing about the firm's use of Repo 105 transactions.[71]

E-mails between some Lehman bankers describe the technique a bit less formally:

- "So, what's up with Repo 105? Why are we doing less next quarter end?"
- "It's basically window-dressing. We are calling repos true sales based on legal technicalities. The exec committee wants the number cut in half."
- "I see . . . so it's legally do-able but doesn't look good when we actually do it? Does the rest of the street do it? Also is that why we have so much BS [balance sheet] to Rates Europe?"
- "Yes, No and yes. :)"[72]

Did the executive committee want the number cut in half because it wanted to do fewer of these deceptive transactions? The bankruptcy examiner didn't think so. He concluded that Lehman attempted to limit the use of the transactions to keep them "under the radar," by limiting their total and the amount of a quarter-end spike.[73] Indeed, Lehman's president and chief operating officer said: "I am very aware . . . it is another drug we r on."[74]

The London Whale

In 2012, JPMorgan lost at least $6 billion in a "hedge" called the London Whale, after the enormous position taken by one of the bank's traders in London. The hedge represents a straightforward example of ill-advised and excessive risk taking. It is also an example of bankers being less than fully honest about the risks being taken, how little regulators were being told, and much else.

As discussed more fully in chapter 2, some banks earn a considerable amount of their income from trading on their own accounts, "proprietary trading." Fee income from traditional investment banking services such as underwriting and brokerage services has diminished in relative importance. When a bank engages in proprietary trading, it buys (and sells) securities that can gain or lose value. The bank can make an enormous amount of money—it can also lose an enormous amount of money. The Dodd-Frank Act seeks to limit proprietary trading by investment banks, such as JPMorgan, that are affiliated with depository institution holding companies. The specifics of the limitation, the "Volcker Rule," named after the former Federal Reserve Chairman who championed limitations on proprietary trading, have been vigorously debated. Hedging is to be permitted—it is ostensibly intended to lower a bank's risks. There is some debate as to whether the London Whale "hedging" would be prohibited. Treasury Secretary Jacob Lew says it would be: "The rule prohibits risky trading bets like the 'London Whale' that are masked as risk-mitigating hedges."[75] But some other commentators have expressed skepticism, with one noting that "portfolio hedging [which is how JPMorgan had characterized the Whale trades] is alive and well under the now-final Volcker Rule."[76] And in late 2014, the effective date of the Volcker Rule was extended, giving banks more time to comply.[77]

A Senate subcommittee held hearings on the London Whale trades and issued a report, the *Levin-McCain Report*. According to the report:

> JPMorgan Chase & Company is the largest financial holding company in the United States, with $2.4 trillion in assets. It is also the largest derivatives dealer in the world and the largest single participant in world credit derivatives markets. Its principal bank subsidiary, JPMorgan Chase Bank, is the largest US bank. JPMorgan Chase has consistently portrayed itself as an expert in risk management with a "fortress balance sheet" that ensures taxpayers have nothing to fear from its banking activities, including its extensive dealing in derivatives. *But in early 2012, the Bank's Chief Investment Office (CIO)*, which is charged with managing $350 billion in excess deposits, *placed a massive bet on a complex set of synthetic credit derivatives that, in 2012, lost at least $6.2 billion.*[78]

The *Levin-McCain Report* is over three hundred pages long and the exhibits to the report are close to six hundred pages. The most important points for purposes of this book are these:

- JPMorgan lost a huge amount of money.
- The transactions by which it lost the money were supposed to be a hedge against risk, but became risky themselves.
- The largest losses occurred as the traders were "doubling down" to try to reverse earlier losses.
- The bank's risk assessments and risk limits were manipulated to conceal what was going on.

- (Some) senior people knew about what was going on.
- Bankers, including senior ones, were not fully truthful with many people, including the public and regulators.

Each of these points is discussed briefly below.

SIZE OF THE LOSS

JPMorgan lost a huge amount of money—at least $6.2 billion.

THE "HEDGES" BECAME RISKY

Merriam-Webster dictionary defines "hedge" as "a means of protection or defense (as against financial loss)."[79] If you pay $10 for a share of stock, you can hedge by, for instance, paying someone to agree to buy the stock for $9 at some future time—a "put option." Of course, you hope the stock will go up. But it may go down. Buying the "put option" assures that the most you can lose is $1 (plus the amount you pay for the option).

So, a hedge is supposed to limit your losses. Douglas Braunstein, the chief financial officer of JPMorgan, characterized the synthetic credit portfolio (SCP), which made the money-losing trades, as "intended to provide 'stress loss protection' to the bank in the event of a credit crisis."[80] Roughly speaking, if some of the bank's assets declined in value, the SCP positions would go up in value: the bank's exposure to some losses would be limited, or hedged. But the bank "was unable to provide documentation . . . detailing the SCP's hedging objectives and strategies; the assets, portfolio, risks, or tail events it was supposed to hedge; or how the size, nature, and effectiveness of its hedges were determined."[81] The report notes that "the compensation history for key employees with responsibility for SCP trading suggests that the bank rewarded them for financial gain and risk-taking more than for effective risk management," suggesting that the SCP's aim was actually to make money rather than hedge.[82]

The report details the SCP's positions, and how they increased over time: "By the end of March 2012, the SCP held over 100 different credit derivative instruments, with a high risk mix of short and long positions, referencing both investment grade and non-investment grade corporations, and including both shorter- and longer-term maturities. JPMorgan personnel described the resulting SCP as 'huge' and of 'a perilous size'

since a small drop in price could quickly translate into massive losses."[83]
Hedges are by definition not perilous.

TRADERS DOUBLE DOWN

The largest losses occurred as the traders were "doubling down" to try
to reverse earlier losses.

The report notes that

The SCP went from a pattern of steady losses from January through
most of March, to a volatile pattern of much larger losses starting on
March 27, 2012. Those larger losses began after the CIO traders had
"doubled down" on the SCP's credit derivatives trading strategy by
placing a series of enormous trades in March, in which the CIO acquired $40 billion of notional long positions in several credit indices
which rapidly lost value.[84]

MANIPULATION OF RISK METRICS

The risk assessments and risk limits were manipulated to conceal what
was going on.

The report describes the steps taken to this end. The table of contents
includes the following subsections:

- Mismarking Begins;
- Mismarking Peaks;
- Disregarding the VaR [Value at Risk] limit;
- Breaching the VaR Limit;
- Ignoring Comprehensive Risk Measure [CRM];
- Ignoring Repeated Breaches of Credit Spread Risk Limits;
- Gaming the CRM Model; and
- Disregarding Stop Loss Advisories.[85]

E-mails in mid-February of 2012 show senior JPMorgan bankers,
notably the chief investment officer, Ina Drew, and her chief risk officer,
Irvin Goldman, discussing changing risk limits to avoid breaching them:
"We have a global credit csbpv [credit spread basis point value] limit. It
was set up at the initiation of the credit book, Unfortunately we have been
breaching for most of the year. Lavine's team is going to send out a noti-

fication (just within CIO) probably tomorrow. the big portfolio changes they made in the tranche book in Dec./Jan. caused the increase. We will need a one off limit increase." The response was: "I have no memory of this limit. In any case it need to be recast with other limits. Its old and outdated." "yes to all."[86]

The report discusses some JPMorgan personnel's reactions to the breaching of risk levels:

> The VaR and CRM results were not the only risk metrics that warned the CIO of increasing risk in the Synthetic Credit Portfolio. So did two additional risk metrics that JPMorgan Chase used to track how its portfolios would perform based on changes in "credit spreads," meaning risks linked to changes in credit derivative premiums. *The credit spread risk limits were repeatedly breached in the first quarter of 2012, with the SCP exceeding one limit by 100% in January, by 270% in early February, and by more than 1,000% in mid-April. But instead of heeding those risk warnings, which came on top of the VaR and CRM warnings, the CIO traders, risk managers, and management criticized the credit spread risk metrics as faulty and pushed for them to be replaced.*[87]

The report's executive summary states that: "While the bank claimed that the whale trade losses were due, in part, to a failure to have the right risk limits in place, the Subcommittee investigation showed that the five risk limits already in effect were all breached for sustained periods of time during the first quarter of 2012. Bank managers knew about the breaches, but allowed them to continue, lifted the limits, or altered the risk measures after being told that the risk results were 'too conservative,' not 'sensible,' or 'garbage.'"[88]

SENIOR BANKER KNOWLEDGE

(Some) senior people knew about what was going on.

The report provides ample evidence that this is not a case of rogue behavior by one junior or mid-level banker or by a small group of them. Senior people were heavily involved, some by what they did and others by what they knew. One example is the e-mails quoted above. Indeed, approvals for risk-limit increases were given by many senior bankers, including CEO Jamie Dimon.[89]

This is not to suggest all senior people knew what was going on. And certainly, that Dimon approved of a risk-limit increase does not by itself indicate that he had broader awareness of the situation, especially at the time of the approval.[90] Still, risk limits are meant to be just that—limits— and would not serve their purpose if they were breached lightly or regularly. The limit increase Dimon approved was couched as one-off, but somehow the positions at issue for which the increase was needed eventually became the Whale position, with its enormous loss.

One person who apparently didn't know enough about the SCP position for quite a while, until the April news reports, was John Hogan, JPMorgan's chief risk officer.[91]

BANKERS WERE NOT FULLY TRUTHFUL

Bankers, including senior ones, were not fully truthful with many people, including the public and regulators.

The less-than-truthful statements were about, among other things, the purpose of the transactions, the size of the losses, why risk measures were changed, and what regulators had been told.[92] The report details what the regulators and the public knew (not as much as they should have) and when they knew it (too late).

In early April, when informed that major news agencies were planning to publish news articles about the Synthetic Credit Portfolio and the Chief Investment Office, JPMorgan's chief spokesperson, who also had the titles "managing director" and "head of worldwide corporate communications and media relations," sent an e-mail to Dimon and others with several talking points, including that the CIO was intended and used to hedge. The other was that JPMorgan "cooperate[s] closely with [its] regulators, who [are] aware of [its] hedging activities."[93]

As stories started appearing in the media about the huge positions held by the trader who, on account of those positions, came to be known as the London Whale, JPMorgan was busily dealing with press and analysts, assuring them that it was hedging, not seeking short-term profits. In conversations with investors, including on a call with investors on April 13, 2012, the CIO results and SCP position were characterized as being "fully transparent to the regulators." On the April 13, 2012, call, JPMorgan chief financial officer Douglas Braunstein said that the regulators got "information on those positions on a regular and recurring basis as part of our normalized reporting."[94]

Evidence presented in the *Levin-McCain Report* indicates that these statements are incorrect.

On the April 13 call, Dimon was asked about the SCP's positions; his response was the now-famous characterization that it was a "tempest in a teapot." The report concluded that "when he made that statement, Mr. Dimon was already in possession of information about the SCP's complex and sizable portfolio, its sustained losses for three straight months, the exponential increase in those losses during March, and the difficulty of exiting the SCP's positions."[95]

On May 10, 2012, JPMorgan filed its quarterly report, Form 10-Q, with the SEC and also held a conference call with investors. It announced a $2 billion loss. (At that time, it was internally calculating the loss at $2.8 billion.)[96] On that call, Dimon continued to characterize the SCP as a hedge, saying the bank was reducing it.[97] Responding to a question about why the VaR model was changed, Dimon said that "there are constant changes and updates to models, always trying to get them better than they were before. That is an ongoing procedure."[98] He thereby made it seem as though the model was just being tweaked for technical reasons, not because, had it not been changed, the SCP positions would have breached the applicable risk limits.

Correspondence between personnel in the bank's regulator, the U.S. Treasury Department's Office of the Comptroller of the Currency (OCC), discusses how JPMorgan dealt with the OCC: "We [OCC] had some concerns about overall governance and transparency of the activities. We received a lot of pushback from the bank, Ina Drew in particular, regarding our comments. In fact, Ina called [Fred] Crumlish [of the OCC] when he was in London and 'sternly' discussed our conclusions with him for 45 minutes. Basically she said that investment decisions are made with full understanding of executive management including Jamie Dimon. She said that everyone knows what is going on and there is little need for more limits, controls, or reports."[99]

The *Levin-McCain Report*'s executive summary states that, "over the course of the first quarter of 2012, JPMorgan Chase's Chief Investment Office used its Synthetic Credit Portfolio (SCP) to engage in high risk derivatives trading; mismarked the SCP book to hide hundreds of millions of dollars of losses; disregarded multiple internal indicators of increasing risk; manipulated models; dodged OCC oversight; and misinformed investors, regulators, and the public about the nature of its risky derivatives trading."[100]

The Financial Services Authority (FSA), then the United Kingdom's financial regulator, fined JPMorgan almost £138 million over the Whale trades. The SEC also fined JPMorgan $200 million; JPMorgan admitted wrongdoing and publicly acknowledged that it violated federal securities laws. The acknowledgment was, however, very carefully worded to exclude any reference to specific laws that the bank had violated. In addition to the FSA and SEC fines, JPMorgan also was fined $300 million by the Office of the Comptroller of Currency, $200 million by the Federal Reserve, and $100 million by the U.S. Commodities Futures Trading Commission (CFTC). The SEC charged traders Javier Martin-Artajo and Julien Grout with fraudulently overvaluing investments to hide the SCP trading losses; both traders were also criminally indicted. Both the civil and criminal cases in the United States are still pending.[101] In May of 2012, JPMorgan announced that Ina Drew would retire. She, and a few other executives involved in the Whale losses, agreed to forfeit some past compensation and severance benefits.[102] No charges have been brought against CEO Jamie Dimon. In 2012, he earned $11.5 million in compensation, down from $23 million in 2011, reflecting the Whale difficulties; in 2013, he earned $20 million.[103]

LIBOR (and Other) Manipulation

A recent prominent example of banks' market manipulation involves LIBOR, the London Interbank Offered Rate, probably the most widely used benchmark by which short-term interest rates (such as rates on many adjustable mortgages) are set.[104] LIBOR itself is set by aggregating the responses provided by some large banks designated as "reference banks" as to their own borrowing rates. Rather than reporting their actual rates, banks instead reported self-serving rates for both LIBOR and another important rate, the Euro Interbank Offered Rate (EURIBOR).[105] Reference banks include Barclays, JPMorgan, Citi, Deutsche Bank, UBS, and RBS. How long the rate had been manipulated is not clear. A reasonable estimate is that it started in the mid-2000s, but the manipulation may have begun much earlier.[106]

Quite a few banks have been investigated for manipulation of LIBOR and EURIBOR. Some have been fined. Under a June 2012 settlement with the FSA, the British regulator, Barclays agreed to pay £59.5 million. Barclays settled as well with the CFTC, for $200 million and the Department of Justice, for $160 million.[107] In July of 2012, the head of Barclays, Robert Diamond, resigned.[108] Also fined by U.S. and British authorities were UBS, in 2012, and RBS, in 2013; UBS was fined $1.5 billion and RBS was fined $612 million. In April of 2015, Deutsche Bank agreed to pay $800 million to settle CFTC charges of manipulation, attempted manipulation, and false reporting of LIBOR and Euribor, the largest fine in the CFTC's history; it also agreed to make payments to other regulators in the United States and the United Kingdom, in an aggregate amount, including the CFTC penalty, of $2.5 billion.[109] Among the regulators fining RBS was the European Union, which also fined Citi, JPMorgan, Deutsche Bank, and Société Générale. The EU's fines totaled in excess of €1.71 billion and were assessed not just for the banks' rate manipulation but also for their collusion in that manipulation.[110] In 2014, Lloyds Bank was fined £105 million by the Financial Conduct Authority (a successor agency to the FSA), $105 million by the CFTC, and $86 million by the Department of Justice, for, among other things, manipulation of LIBOR.[111] In 2013, Rabobank settled charges relating to its LIBOR and EURIBOR submissions with U.S. and European regulators, paying in the aggregate more than $1 billion.[112] The rate-fixing investigations and lawsuits are continuing. JPMorgan, Deutsche Bank, Citi, Credit Suisse, and Bank of America are among the banks being investigated.[113]

The report announcing Barclays' settlement with the FSA contains many examples in which bankers requested, discussed, or acknowledged reporting inaccurate rates, including this one:

> On 26 October 2006, an external trader made a request for a lower three month US dollar LIBOR submission. The external trader stated in an email to Trader G at Barclays "*If it comes in unchanged I'm a dead man.*" Trader G responded that he would "*have a chat.*" Barclays' submission on that day for three month US dollar LIBOR was half a basis

point lower than the day before, rather than being unchanged. The external trader thanked Trader G for Barclays' LIBOR submission later that day: *"Dude. I owe you big time! Come over one day after work and I'm opening a bottle of Bollinger."*[114]

In a discussion of aggravating and mitigating factors, the FSA report noted that "Barclays' misconduct encompassed a number of issues involving a significant number of employees and occurring over a number of years. . . . The FSA has had particular regard to the routine nature of the Derivatives Traders' requests and of instructions to Submitters to reduce Barclays' LIBOR submissions during the financial crisis."[115]

RBS's conduct in LIBOR and other rate manipulation was described in the order under which RBS paid its $325 million settlement to the CFTC as follows:

- As recently as 2010 and dating back to at least mid-2006, RBS made hundreds of attempts to manipulate Yen and Swiss Franc LIBOR, and made false LIBOR submissions to benefit its derivatives and money market trading positions; RBS succeeded at times in manipulating Yen and Swiss Franc LIBOR;
- At times, RBS aided and abetted other panel banks' attempts to manipulate those same rates;
- The misconduct involved more than a dozen RBS derivatives and money market traders, one manager, and multiple offices around the world, including London, Singapore, and Tokyo; and
- The unlawful conduct continued even after RBS traders learned that a LIBOR investigation had been commenced by the CFTC.[116]

The press release describing the CFTC settlement with RBS also included "examples of misconduct" from various communications among traders, such as the following:

AUGUST 20, 2007:
    Yen Trader 4: where's young [Yen Trader 1] thinking of setting
        it?
    Yen Trader 1: where would you like it[,] libor that is[,] same
        as yesterday is call

Yen Trader 4: haha, glad you clarified ! mixed feelings but
  mostly I'd like it all lower so the world starts to make a
  little more sense.
Senior Yen Trader: the whole HF [hedge fund] world will be
  kissing you instead of calling me if libor move lower
Yen Trader 1: ok, i will move the curve down[,] 1bp[,] maybe
  more[,] if I can
Senior Yen Trader: maybe after tomorrow fixing hehehe
Yen Trader 1: fine[,] will go with same as yesterday then
Senior Yen Trader: cool
Yen Trader 1: maybe a touch higher tomorrow

MAY 7, 2008:
UBS Yen Trader: Hi [Sterling Cash Trader] if this is you can
  you pls ask for a low 6m in jpy for the next few days[.]
  Hope you are ok, was good seeing you last week[.] Cheers
  [UBS Yen Trader]
Sterling Cash Trader: Hi mate, I mentioned it to our guy on
  Friday and he seemed to have no problem with it, so fingers
  crossed.[117]

In addition to banks, individual employees have recently come under scrutiny of financial regulators.[118] Early in 2014, British regulators charged three former Barclays bankers with criminal violations in connection with their role in LIBOR manipulation.[119] Three Rabobank bankers were charged in the United States with conspiracy to commit fraud in connection with a five-year scheme to rig the Yen LIBOR, one of whom pled guilty to one count in August, 2014; an additional Rabobank trader pleaded guilty to LIBOR-related charges in June of the same year.[120]

As noted in the introduction, investigations of foreign exchange rate manipulation by U.S., UK, and Swiss regulators are underway and have so far led to nearly $4.3 billion in fines against JPMorgan, Citigroup, Bank of America, UBS, RBS, and HSBC over attempts to manipulate their own and other banks' foreign exchange rates, and criminal charges may be brought.[121]

Banks also may have manipulated an interest rate measure, ISDAfix, which affects the pricing of the $379 trillion global interest rate swaps market. (ISDA is the International Swaps and Derivatives Association.) A civil suit has been brought against thirteen banks—including Bank of America, Barclays, BNP Paribas, Citigroup, Credit Suisse, Deutsche Bank, Goldman Sachs, HSBC, ICAP, JPMorgan Chase, Nomura Holdings, Royal Bank of Scotland, UBS, and Wells Fargo—and investigations by various regulators, including the CFTC, the FCA, and Germany's BaFin, are under way.[122] Energy markets allegedly have been manipulated, too. Deutsche Bank recently settled with the Federal Energy Regulatory Commission (FERC) for $1.5 million, plus a disgorgement of $173,000 of profits.[123] JPMorgan was investigated for energy market manipulation, as was Barclays.[124] JPMorgan agreed to pay $410 million in penalties and disgorgement to ratepayers, $285 million to the Treasury, and $125 million disgorgement of unjust profits. FERC ordered Barclays to pay $470 million in civil penalties and other amounts, an order Barclays is presently contesting.[125]

Banks are under scrutiny for price and other manipulation of the commodities market as well; a Congressional investigation has released a report on the subject, with findings that are quite critical of banks.[126] Finally, the European Commission has informed Bank of America, Merrill Lynch, Barclays, BNP Paribas, Citi, Credit Suisse, Deutsche Bank, Goldman Sachs, HSBC, JPMorgan, Morgan Stanley, Royal Bank of Scotland, and UBS of its "preliminary conclusion that they [and two other organizations] infringed EU antitrust rules that prohibit anti-competitive agreements by colluding to prevent exchanges from entering the credit derivatives business between 2006 and 2009."[127]

Problematic Swap Transactions

The next examples concern swap transactions that have been highly problematic. The problems are of two general types. The swap may have been arranged by the bank for its client to help disguise the client's financial appearance. Or the swap may have been foisted by the bank on an unsophisticated customer or client for whom it was unsuitable or inadvisable.

Swaps are common transactions, and conceptually, they are perfectly legitimate. Indeed, all transactions can be understood as swaps: X and Y swap something each have for something the other has. In the world of finance, the term "swap" typically is used to refer to a transaction in which one or both parties' obligations are in the future. For instance, in an interest-rate swap, a person may swap the right to receive interest payments at a fixed rate (e.g., 5 percent per year) with the right to receive interest payments at a floating rate (e.g., LIBOR plus 1 percent). A simple currency swap is a swap of payments in one currency for payments in another at some future time based on a predetermined exchange rate. Many swaps are quite complex, such as those described below.

GREECE'S CROSS-CURRENCY SWAP

At the beginning of this decade, in the midst of recent economic turmoil in Greece, a transaction between Greece and Goldman Sachs entered into in 2001 became the subject of considerable press coverage.

Greece had entered the European Union in 1981; in 1993, a treaty came into force for members of the EU, the Maastricht Treaty, which, among other things, limited the amount of debt an EU member adopting the euro could have. As Greece was preparing to adopt the euro, it needed to conceal the amount of its debt. Goldman Sachs was ready to help.

Greece and Goldman Sachs entered into a cross-currency swap. The swap resembled a standard swap, except that it was made at an invented exchange rate, one that was not warranted by the underlying commercial realities. An example illustrates the problem with such an arrangement. Assume a very stable rate environment in which the present exchange rate between euros and dollars is one euro for $1.08, but a historical exchange rate is one euro for $1.50. What if the "swap" provided for one euro for $1.50? Standard swap documentation could be used, but clearly, something else would be going on. A close reading of the documentation would presumably reveal some sort of fee or other payment to the provider of the $1.50. And in Greece's case, it was indeed required to make additional payments to Goldman.[128] The success of this gambit turned on Greece's ability not to record on its books the full amounts it owed under the swap—something that was possible because it had been designed to exploit technicalities (what might be deemed loopholes) in the applicable rules. The rules have since been changed to "plug" the loopholes.

The swap reportedly reduced Greece's recorded debt by €2.4 billion. Greece initially "borrowed" €2.8 billion, but the amount it had to repay was much higher, reportedly, rather more than Greece might have expected, because of the way the repayment formulas worked.[129] Goldman reportedly made a lot of money on the transaction, in the hundreds of millions of dollars, an amount that reflected the transaction's size and complexity. It reportedly hedged its exposure in the swap, estimated at $1 billion, so that it would not lose money if Greece could not repay it.[130] Goldman reportedly subsequently sold its position to the National Bank of Greece.[131]

Where were the regulators? Eurostat, the agency that reviews and compiles member states' national accounts in accordance with EU accounting standards promulgated by the International Accounting Standards Board and adopted by the EU, claimed ignorance. It said in 2010 that "the Greek authorities had not informed Eurostat on this issue and no opinion on the accounting treatment has been requested from Eurostat as it should be the case for transactions that are not explicitly covered by its rules. In addition, Eurostat had been previously wrongfully informed by the Greek authorities that there had been no occurrences of off-market swaps in the past."[132] But Eurostat's ignorance is disputed: The *Financial Times* quotes a "former senior Greek finance ministry official" as saying: "Eurostat knew all about these deals, which were perfectly legal at that time. We didn't keep them secret."[133] Goldman says they consulted Eurostat; Eurostat acknowledged the possibility that Goldman asked them "for general clarifications."

An article in *Risk Magazine* concluded: "There is no doubt that Goldman Sachs' deal with Greece was a completely legitimate transaction under Eurostat rules. Moreover, both Goldman Sachs and Greece's public debt division are following a path well-trodden by other European sovereigns and derivatives dealers. However, like many accounting-driven derivatives transactions, such deals are bound to create discomfort among those who like accounts to reflect economic reality."[134]

Greece's cross-currency swap thus may have been one of many such deals; other countries in which such swaps may have been done include Italy and even Germany.[135] That these transactions may have been fairly common is troublesome for several reasons. First, it speaks to a general corrosion of values among bankers, regulators, and politicians and a willingness to do an end run around regulations. Indeed, to the extent regulators and politicians allow this type of transaction to conceal a government's true financial condition, government disclosure mandates for the private sector appear to be hypocritical, inviting evasion there as well.

Second, and less obviously, once one country is using this type of transaction, others may feel pressure to do so as well or, at least, feel justified in doing so. Consider in this regard the responses of E. Gerald Corrigan, former president of the Federal Reserve Bank of New York and now a managing director of Goldman Sachs and the head of its holding company, to questions before the British Parliament's House of Commons Treasury Committee:

> Q 295 Mr. Fallon: Turning to Goldman's international role, have
> banks like Goldman's not accentuated sovereign risk in countries
> like Greece by arranging loans for securitization against future
> revenue streams that do not appear on the books or currency
> swaps that have not been calculated at normal exchange ranges.
> Have you not you contributed to the risk?
> Mr. Corrigan. . . . . Let me respond to that on two levels. . . . First
> of all, on the currency swap question, . . . this Committee knows
> very well that governments, on a fairly generalized basis, do go to
> some lengths to try to "manage" their budgetary deficit positions
> and "manage" their public debt positions. There's nothing terribly
> new about this, unfortunately, and certainly those practices have
> been around for decades, if not centuries. . . .
> In the specific context of the question about Greece and
> currency swaps, it is true that a family of currency swaps that
> were entered into jointly by Goldman Sachs and Greece in the
> late 1990s and early part of the 2000s . . . did produce a rather
> small but . . . not insignificant reduction in Greece's debt-to-GDP
> ratios at that time. However . . . those transactions were very much
> consistent with and comparable with the standards of behavior
> and measurement used by the European community. There was
> nothing inappropriate. They were in conformity with existing rules
> and procedures when they were entered into. That is not to deny
> that they did in fact produce a very small reduction in Greece's
> debt-to-GDP ratio in the timeframe of 2000, 2001. . . . personnel
> from Goldman Sachs consulted with the appropriate authorities at
> Eurostat, as did, as I understand it, the Government of Greece and,
> again, there was no indication whatsoever that those transactions

were not in line with existing practices, policies and guidelines. I should also say that those guidelines and standards were modified in 2007 which suggests that perhaps they were more liberal than they should have been back in 2001.[136]

Goldman Sachs has since said that it would not engage in a transaction like the Greek cross-currency swap now: "We absolutely wouldn't do a transaction like that today. . . . There have been transactions of that ilk that have been presented to us by other European sovereigns that we've turned down because we felt there wasn't the appropriate transparency surrounding them."[137]

SOME OTHER SWAPS

Many types of swap transactions are quite complex: while the broad terms are understood, the specifics might not be, in ways that might prove very problematic for the bank's customer or client, the swap purchaser. One issue is therefore the extent to which the swap purchasers, nominally sophisticated entities, probably in some cases not as sophisticated as the seller banks, are chargeable with knowing what they are getting into. In some recent suits on these types of swaps, often brought by banks seeking payments due to them under the terms of the swaps, the swap purchasers argue that they did not understand the swaps and that the banks exploited that lack of understanding, charged excessive fees and commissions, and, perhaps, otherwise took advantage of the situation, protecting any possible downside risk the banks had. Some of the suits are ongoing, some have been settled, some have yielded liability for the banks, and in some cases the banks have been cleared.[138] In one case involving Deutsche Bank, the plaintiff, Unitech, provided evidence of an e-mail written by a Deutsche Bank employee that said: "Since you know [Unitech] so well and also know that [Unitech's] team is outrightly 'uneducated,' pls go ahead with what you think is best."[139] That case is proceeding.[140] In another case, Deutsche Bank reached a settlement with an Italian bank, Monte Paschi, in connection with a derivative that Deutsche Bank designed allegedly to obscure Monte Paschi's loss on another derivative.[141] But in yet another case, the convictions of JPMorgan, Deutsche Bank, UBS, and Depfa Bank and nine of their employees in connection with the banks' sale of interest rate swaps to the city of Milan were overturned, on grounds that the bankers had not deceived the city.[142]

JEFFERSON COUNTY

Jefferson County, Alabama, declared bankruptcy in 2011. It was at the time the largest municipal bankruptcy in U.S. history, now of course having ceded that distinction to Detroit.[143] The bankruptcy was caused in significant part by the county's inability to pay interest on complex swap transactions sold to them by JPMorgan, which allegedly paid people connected with local officials to get the business. Allegedly, the transactions were inappropriate for the county; they also carried excessive fees.

Charles LeCroy and Douglas MacFaddin, two managing directors of JPMorgan Securities, knew Jefferson County, Alabama, would need to raise money. The county had entered into a settlement with the Environmental Protection Agency and the Department of Justice, agreeing to renovate its sewer system, and the county commission had approved the issuance of more than $3 billion in bonds. What follows is based largely on the complaints filed by the SEC in the matter, which include e-mails written by LeCroy, MacFaddin, and others. The conduct at issue allegedly occurred in 2002 and 2003. As noted below, JPMorgan settled the SEC's charges without admitting or denying them. The SEC's case against LeCroy and MacFaddin is proceeding.[144]

LeCroy had heard that a rival firm had succeeded in getting business from the county by paying "small local firms in unrelated transactions to enlist those firms' 'political support' for the County hiring the rival firm." LeCroy estimated that the payments needed for JPMorgan to get the business from Jefferson County would be between $5,000 and $25,000 per deal. Some $8.2 million in payments later—to small firms (who had connections with the county commissioners) and not so small firms (including Goldman Sachs, for not bidding on the deals)—JPMorgan had the business: more than $3 billion of sewer bonds, and $2 billion (notional amount) of swap agreements.[145] (The $3 billion is an amount that would actually change hands. By contrast, one might enter into a swap of fixed interest on a $2 billion notional amount for floating interest on that same amount; the interest would be paid but the notional amount would not.) The bonds refinanced the county's previous debt, something the county had sought to do in any event. LeCroy had suggested a refinancing, as well as the use of adjustable-rate debt rather than fixed-rate debt, so the county could lower its interest payments. He also suggested that the county hedge its exposure with swaps.[146]

LeCroy told another JPMorgan banker: "At some point, we'll have to figure out who we have to pay off. I think instead of Goldman . . . we'll probably have someone like Bill Blount [the head of a local broker-dealer firm who had close ties with the commissioner] . . . who gets a percentage of the swap."[147] LeCroy described to the JPMorgan banker what Blount was doing for the amount he was requesting, 15 percent of JPMorgan's fees on one of the swap transactions. Blount would get the 15 percent for "not messing with us and, I said [to Blount], look the only way I'm willing to even entertain this is if you're successful in keeping every other firm out of this deal. . . . We've got a lot more latitude dealing with him than Goldman Sachs. And I've got to pay him some on the bonds. But, it's a lot of money, but in the end it's worth it on a billion-dollar deal."[148] LeCroy later reported to this banker: "B of A made a run at it yesterday, and I was able to get the Commissioner [Langford] to cancel the meeting. . . . That's gonna cost us, from the swap side about . . . $3.5 million, but part of that's coming out of the bonds."[149] Indeed, LeCroy sent a letter to Langford noting that "JPMorgan was incorporating the $3.1 million in payments . . . 'into the price of the interest rate swap at the time of execution.'"[150] JPMorgan did not mention the bulk of the payments, either in the disclosure documents or in response to questions.[151]

JPMorgan provided eighteen swaps for Jefferson County in all, including those referenced in the SEC's charges, with a total "notional amount" of $5.6 billion,[152] an amount that "surpassed the value of the bonds they were supposed to hedge."[153] The swaps carried fees significantly higher than those of comparable swaps.[154] A JPMorgan banker, asked to prepare materials explaining why the county should buy more derivatives, reportedly sent an e-mail to a colleague asking: "Do these guys know the risks they are taking (in large doses)? . . . Shouldn't we be pitching diversification arguments?"[155] Nobody seems to have acted on this sentiment.

All of the bonds were downgraded, and the JPMorgan swaps were terminated, with liability to the county of almost $648 million in "termination fees." In November of 2009, JPMorgan Securities agreed to pay $75 million to settle charges relating to its involvement in Jefferson County's bond and swap deals, $25 million to the SEC, and $50 million to the county, and agreed to forgive the $648 million.[156]

Jefferson County went bankrupt in 2011; its bankruptcy dwarfed the bankruptcy of Orange County, California, also related to problematic investments promoted and sold by an investment bank, discussed below. Describing Jefferson County's condition due to the bankruptcy, the *New York Times* reported that

> one county jail here is so crowded that some inmates sleep on the floor, while the other county jail, a few miles down the road, sits empty.
>
> There is no money for the second one anymore.
>
> The county roads here need paving, and the tax collector needs help. There is no money for them, either.
>
> . . . There is no money for holiday D.U.I. checkpoints, litter patrols or overtime pay at the courthouse. None for crews to pull weeds or pick up road kill—not even when, as happened recently, an unlucky cow was hit near the town of Wylam.
>
> "We don't do that any more," E. Wayne Sullivan, director of the roads and transportation department, said of such roadside cleanup.[157]

The county emerged from bankruptcy in 2013. Creditors agreed to settle their claims against the county for far less than the face value.[158] Sewer rates were scheduled to go up as well, albeit by less than was proposed by the county's bankruptcy receiver; a recent ruling allowing ratepayers to proceed with an appeal may further reduce the scheduled increase.[159]

In 2004, JP Morgan had fired LeCroy after he was indicted for fraud in a different matter: for disguising a payment made to help JPMorgan get bond business as being for legal services rendered. In 2005, LeCroy pled guilty to the fraud charge and was sentenced to three months in jail.[160] He was also barred from the securities industry.[161] The SEC sued him for this conduct, but lost.[162] Langford, who became the mayor of Birmingham after being county commissioner of Jefferson County, got a sentence of fifteen years, and Blount got fifty-two months.[163] JPMorgan fired MacFaddin in 2008, after he told them he was a target of a grand jury investigation relating to another (municipal marketing) matter.[164] JPMorgan terminated its business marketing derivatives to municipalities.

JPMorgan had also had issues when it marketed derivatives to non-profit organizations. The OCC accused JPMorgan of "unsafe and unsound conduct and/or illegal practices." While not admitting or denying the allegations, JPMorgan entered into a settlement in which it agreed to pay $22 million. (This settlement was part of the $228 million settlement described on the next page.) The settlement described the conduct as having lasted at least six years, from 2001 to 2006. The conduct included "participat[ing] in schemes with individuals outside of the Bank to agree on bids and to artificially set prices in connection with the sale of certain derivative financial products to certain municipalities and non-profit organizations." "Bank employees and/or agents . . . participated in the schemes by . . . submitting false or sham courtesy bids, communicating with direct competitors and/ or coordinating with third party brokers to fix bid prices, and/or coordinating with direct competitors and/or third party brokers to determine which bidder would win a particular transaction. In addition, Bank employees and/or agents . . . manipulated certain negotiated transactions to inflate the prices paid by certain municipalities and non-profit organizations that were counter-parties to such transactions."[165]

As mentioned above, the Jefferson County bankruptcy has some echoes in the large bankruptcy of Orange County, California, in which complex securities also played an important role. In 1998, Merrill Lynch was alleged to have sold highly complex and very risky securities to Orange County. The Orange County treasurer was allegedly lacking in sophistication, reportedly relying on nonstandard techniques for making his investment decisions, including a "star chart" he purchased from an astrologer.[166] By some accounts, Merrill used high-pressure sales tactics to obtain the sale. The securities performed disastrously, leading to the county's bankruptcy. Merrill Lynch agreed to pay over $430 million to Orange County and $2 million to the SEC.[167]

Municipal bond financing has been a fertile source of other varieties of investment banker misconduct. In 2000, Goldman Sachs, Morgan Stanley, Lehman Brothers, Salomon Smith Barney, Merrill Lynch, and other firms settled charges related to "yield burning" with the SEC, agreeing to pay an

aggregate of $172 million and agreeing to certain restrictions of their con-
duct going forward.[168] Yield burning involves overcharging municipalities
for securities.[169] Financial institutions also allegedly engaged in other techniques to manipulate the municipal market during this time. From 1998
to 2006, JPMorgan, Wachovia, UBS, and Bank of America entered into
settlements with the SEC and other agencies in connection with bid rigging (including the settlement JPMorgan made with the OCC mentioned
above).[170] Banks would rig bids in various ways, including by paying to get
information about competing bids before submitting their own, collectively determining in advance which bank would submit the winning bid,
or being paid to submit a losing bid. JPMorgan agreed to pay a $228 million
fine (which included the $22 million to the OCC discussed on the previous
page and which reportedly involved conduct by MacFaddin); UBS agreed
to pay $160 million; Wachovia agreed to pay $148 million; and a predeces-
sor of Merrill Lynch, Banc of America (a subsidiary of Bank of America),
agreed to pay $137 million.[171] On December 13, 2007, JPMorgan agreed to
pay the Financial Industry Regulatory Association (FINRA) $500,000 in
sanctions to settle allegations that, in violation of FINRA rules, it did not
disclose its use of consultants to obtain municipal bond offerings.[172] On
December 27, 2012, JPMorgan was sanctioned by FINRA for "unfairly obtaining the reimbursement of fees they paid to [a lobbying group] from the
proceeds of municipal and state bond offerings," "neglecting to disclose
that these costs were unrelated to the bond deals."[173] Citi, Merrill Lynch,
Goldman Sachs, and Morgan Stanley were also sanctioned by FINRA: the
total amount the five institutions agreed to pay was $4.4 million.[174]

Illegal Conduct: Dealings with Treasury-Sanctioned Countries and Assistance with Tax Evasion

Some scandals have involved allegations (and in some cases admissions) of violations of laws imposing prohibitions on dealing with certain
countries or entities in such countries and violations of tax laws.

PROHIBITED DEALINGS

As noted in the introduction, on June 30, 2014, BNP Paribas pled guilty
to a felony, conspiring to do business in violation of U.S. sanctions against
doing business with Cuba, Iran, and Sudan, and entities located in those

countries, paying close to $9 billion.[175] The Department of Justice press release announcing the settlement provided this description of what BNP Paribas did:

> Over the course of eight years, BNPP knowingly and willfully moved more than $8.8 billion through the U.S. financial system on behalf of sanctioned entities, including more than $4.3 billion in transactions involving entities that were specifically designated by the U.S. Government as being cut off from the U.S. financial system. BNPP engaged in this criminal conduct through various sophisticated schemes designed to conceal from U.S. regulators the true nature of the illicit transactions. BNPP routed illegal payments through third party financial institutions to conceal not only the involvement of the sanctioned entities but also BNPP's role in facilitating the transactions. BNPP instructed other financial institutions not to mention the names of sanctioned entities in payments sent through the United States and removed references to sanctioned entities from payment messages to enable the funds to pass through the U.S. financial system undetected.[176]

The press announcement stated that, "remarkably, BNPP continued to engage in this criminal conduct even after being told by its own lawyers that what it was doing was illegal."[177]

In 2009, Credit Suisse forfeited $536 million, agreeing that it had moved "hundreds of millions of dollars illegally through the U.S. financial system on behalf of entities subject to U.S. economic sanctions."[178] The countries at issue included Iran, Libya, Sudan, Cuba, and Burma.[179] The Department of Justice press release contains this description of some of what Credit Suisse did:

> According to court documents, beginning as early as 1995 and continuing through 2006, Credit Suisse, in Switzerland and the United Kingdom, altered wire transfers involving U.S. sanctioned countries or persons. Specifically, . . . Credit Suisse deliberately removed material information, such as customer names, bank names and addresses, from payment messages so that the wire transfers would pass undetected through filters at U.S. financial institutions. Credit Suisse also trained its Iranian clients to falsify wire transfers so that such messages would

pass undetected through the U.S. financial system. This scheme allowed U.S. sanctioned countries and entities to move hundreds of millions of dollars through the U.S. financial system.[180]

Moreover, as set forth in the factual statement agreed to by Credit Suisse in connection with the settlement, "in addition to training its Iranian bank customers how to format their payment messages to evade the [Office of Foreign Assets Control] filters, Credit Suisse also gave them materials to use in training other banks on how to prepare payment messages to evade the filters."[181]

Other banks have been sanctioned for violations of these laws. In 2011, JPMorgan agreed to pay $88.3 million to the Department of Treasury for processing wire transfers to persons in foreign states with which U.S. law prohibited dealings.[182] Most recently, HSBC and Standard Chartered settled allegations that they facilitated financial transfers to countries under U.S. sanctions programs. HSBC agreed to pay $1.9 million. Standard Chartered agreed to pay a $227 million fine to the Department of Justice and a $340 million penalty to the New York Department of Financial Services; the Federal Reserve Board also assessed a $100 million fine.[183]

Other banks have been involved, including Barclays. The *Salz Review* described Barclays' settlement for close to $500 million of charges relating to its "handling of $500 million in money transfers from banks in US-sanctioned countries including Cuba, Iran, Sudan, Libya and Burma between 1995 and 2006. Barclays was alleged to have removed details from payments to hide the identity of these recipients." The review also notes that "sanctions violations, especially relating to US rules, are an industry-wide issue. Since 2010, LBG has incurred sanctions-related costs of $350 million, Credit Suisse $536 million, RBS (via ABN AMRO) $500 million, ING $619 million and Standard Chartered $327 million. In the UK, the FSA fined RBS £5.6 million in 2010 for failing to have adequate systems and controls to prevent breaches of UK financial sanctions."[184]

TAX EVASION

In May of 2014, Credit Suisse pled guilty to a felony—helping U.S. taxpayers evade taxes—and agreed to pay $2.6 billion in penalties.[185] Credit Suisse "assist[ed] clients in using sham entities to hide undeclared accounts; solicit[ed] IRS forms that falsely stated, under penalties of perjury, that the . . . sham . . . entities were the beneficial owners of the assets in the accounts; . . . destroy[ed] account records sent to the United States for client review[;] . . . facilitate[d] withdrawals of funds from the undeclared accounts by either providing hand-delivered cash in the United States or using Credit Suisse's correspondent bank accounts in the United States; structur[ed] transfers of funds to evade currency transaction reporting requirements; and provid[ed] offshore credit and debit cards to repatriate funds in the undeclared accounts."[186]

In 2009, UBS had agreed to pay $780 million in connection with allegations of similar conduct.[187]

Conclusion

In this chapter, we have described many specific examples of problematic banker behavior—behavior involving inappropriate financial risk, legal risk, or both.

The first two sections concerned the 2008 crisis. The first section discussed the structuring and sale of what have come to be called "toxic securities," subprime mortgage securities. The second section discussed the use by Lehman Brothers, just before it collapsed, of a transaction structure that made its financial situation seem far better than it was, Repo 105. A third section discussed the London Whale scandal, JPMorgan's disastrous "hedge," which generated losses exceeding $6 billion and fines exceeding $1 billion. A fourth section discussed the manipulation by many banks of LIBOR (and other rates and markets). The fifth section concerned complex swap transactions, some in Europe and some in the United States, which arguably had very bad effects, including a country's concealment of its (bad) financial condition, and a U.S. county's bankruptcy. A sixth section discussed several banks' alleged (and in some cases admitted) illegal conduct in doing business with U.S. Treasury–sanctioned countries and in assisting clients in evading taxes.

These examples show that sometimes, bankers are (i) causing their banks to take on excessive or otherwise ill-advised risk or encouraging their customers and clients to do so; (ii) selling to their customers and clients securities they think are of low quality or are otherwise inappropriate without making sufficient disclosures; (iii) not sufficiently disclosing

their banks' risk exposures or conflicts of interest; (iv) engaging in conflicted behavior or financial maneuvering; (v) rigging or otherwise manipulating markets; and (vi) assisting customers and clients in evading
taxes or doing business with or in certain countries subject to U.S. sanctions.

What is wrong with conflicts and untruthful or otherwise inadequate
disclosure is obvious, as is what is wrong with manipulating or rigging
markets or otherwise violating the law or helping customers or clients to
do so. What is wrong with risk taking and financial maneuvering is less
obvious. Risk taking is certainly not always problematic or harmful, nor is
all financial engineering.

What risks should bankers not take? The answer is, of course, not ame-
nable to precise specification. Ideally, responsible risk taking would have
a socially beneficial objective; the risk would not be excessive in proportion to the expected social benefit; the person or entity deciding to take
the risk would have a significant downside if the risk did not pay off; and
other parties exposed to the risk would agree to bear it after being given
complete information that they could understand and use to protect themselves. These factors form a continuum, with risk taking that is obviously
irresponsible at one end and risk taking that is obviously responsible at the
other. Risk taking in the years immediately preceding the 2008 crisis that
left three of the United States' five largest investment banks insolvent was
surely on the irresponsible end of the continuum, as was risk taking by a
small group of traders, principally the one trader known as the London
Whale, who lost JPMorgan over $6 billion in 2012.

Financial maneuvering is another area that can cause enormous difficulties. As with risk taking, there is a continuum. Where financial engineering becomes maneuvering — where it is intended to deceive or subvert
a regulatory scheme or contractual obligation — it will be problematic. In
Goldman's cross-currency swap with Greece, there was an EU regulation
intended to limit Greece's debt level, which Goldman apparently helped
Greece to effectively subvert. Repo 105 involved Lehman's use of maneu-
vers intended to deceive the market into thinking it was not on the brink
of collapse. Enron used many bank-crafted techniques to create a wholly
false financial appearance, intending to deceive the market into thinking
it was far healthier than it was. These uses of financial maneuvering are

highly problematic, as are banks' attempts to reduce their regulatory capital requirements through creative structuring that exploits what can be considered loopholes in the regulatory capital rules.[188]

We do not take the position that regulated parties should not seek ways to comply more cheaply with regulations. The difficulty arises when the compliance is with the letter of the regulation and either the regulation's spirit is being violated or the letter or spirit of other regulations, such as disclosure regulations, is being violated. For instance, especially in the period leading up to the 2008 crisis, banks seem to have used various techniques to reduce their regulatory capital requirements without commensurately reducing the risk to which they were exposed, even though regulatory capital reductions are supposed to reflect reductions of risk.

Another problematic category of business practices is banks benefiting themselves at the expense of customers and clients. Unlike risk taking and financial engineering, which banks would acknowledge are part of their business, conflicts are not supposed to be how banks behave, much less make their money. But some examples above provide evidence that they may indeed engage in conflicted behavior. Sometimes, they may be doing so to bail themselves out of a bad situation, as was apparently the case with Citi's Class V Funding synthetic CDO. But sometimes, they may have been exploiting lack of sophistication, as seems to have been the case with Jefferson County's sewer bond deals and may have been the case in some other deals, including several discussed in this chapter.

In this regard, the Financial Crisis Inquiry Commission report depicts Goldman Sachs as having done some of both, bailing themselves out by taking advantage of their customers' and clients' lack of sophistication:

> On February 11 [2007], Goldman CEO Lloyd Blankfein questioned [Thomas] Montag [a Goldman partner] about the $20 million in losses on residual positions from old deals, asking, "Could/should we have cleaned up these books before and are we doing enough right now to sell off cats and dogs in other books throughout the division?"
>
> The numbers suggest that the answer was yes, they had cleaned up pretty well, even given a $20 million write-off and billions of dollars of subprime exposure still retained. In the first quarter of 2007, its mortgage business earned a record $266 million, driven primarily by short

positions, including a $10 billion short position on the bellwether ABX BBB index, whose drop the previous November had been the red flag that got Goldman's attention.

In the following months, Goldman reduced its own mortgage risk while continuing to create and sell mortgage-related products to its clients. From December 2006 through August 2007, it created and sold approximately $25.4 billion of CDOs—including $17.6 billion of synthetic CDOs. The firm used the cash CDOs to unload much of its own remaining inventory of other CDO securities and mortgage-backed securities.[189]

Bankers perhaps should not be expected to be overly solicitous toward supposedly sophisticated parties such as institutional investors engaging in large complex transactions. Yet many of these investors are not just "parties" on the other side of a trade; rather they are understood to be customers who buy investment products from the bank or clients who retained the bank for a particular transaction or other purpose. We discuss customer and client relationships—and their decline in importance in modern investment banking—in later chapters of this book, including chapter 2. Even clients and customers who don't rely on a bank for advice should not have to worry that the bank will knowingly or recklessly sell them a bad investment. A bank's business model should not include generating fees for encouraging transactions that the bank does not affirmatively think are good ideas unless clients and customers, armed with that knowledge, insist on proceeding. And banks should be especially mindful when they are dealing with entities such as municipalities or pension funds; the Jefferson County example we discussed in this chapter provides a particularly vivid example of why this is so.

The 2008 crisis has clearly affected, and may have reduced, at least for the present, certain types of problematic banker behavior. For instance, banks presumably have less ability and incentive to attempt to buy low-quality mortgages and package them into securities they misrepresent as high quality than they did prior to 2008. But less ability and incentive does not mean no ability and incentive. Indeed, one bank, SunTrust, one of the highest-volume mortgage originators in the United States,[190] recently paid nearly $1 billion to settle allegations relating to "deficient mortgage loan origination and servicing activities" occurring through mid-2012.[191]

Moreover, even as banks may have been less involved in selling securities backed by subprime mortgages, they have been involved in foreclosing on mortgages that defaulted; a number of those foreclosures have been conducted in ways that have been severely criticized and, in some cases, resulted in the imposition of significant sanctions. In 2013, five banks, Bank of America, JPMorgan, Wells Fargo, Citigroup, and Ally Financial Inc. (formerly GMAC), agreed to a $25 billion settlement of charges of "mortgage loan servicing and foreclosure abuses."[192] Sun Trust's settlement also encompassed allegations of foreclosure abuse.[193]

And investors' flight to quality, which would make them far less interested in risky securities, tends to be short lived. Many investors who fled to quality as the crisis began have returned to chasing yield.[194] Over a decade of very low interest rates has encouraged investor demand for yield—and it has also encouraged bankers' efforts to meet that demand.

As mentioned earlier, Goldman Sachs has said that if presented now with the opportunity to be involved in a transaction like the Greek cross-currency swap, it would refuse.[195] But financial engineering continues, as does interest in limiting the costs of regulatory compliance, compliance with debt covenants, and other obligations. At a certain point, financial engineering may cross the line into financial maneuvering, intended to deceive or subvert a regulatory scheme or contractual obligation.

Conflicted behavior, too, apparently continued after the crisis. In a 2011 case involving the acquisition of Del Monte Foods, Vice Chancellor Laster of the Delaware Chancery Court described Barclays' behavior in highly critical terms. While ostensibly working for the "sell-side," the business being sold, Del Monte,

> Barclays secretly and selfishly manipulated the sale process to engineer a transaction that would permit Barclays to obtain lucrative buy-side financing fees. On multiple occasions, Barclays protected its own interests by withholding information from the Board that could have led Del Monte to retain a different bank, pursue a different alternative, or deny Barclays a buy-side role. Barclays did not disclose the behind-the-

scenes efforts of its Del Monte coverage officer to put Del Monte into play. Barclays did not disclose its explicit goal, harbored from the outset, of providing buy-side financing to the acquirer. Barclays did not disclose that in September 2010, without Del Monte's authorization or approval, Barclays steered Vestar into a club bid with KKR, the potential bidder with whom Barclays had the strongest relationship, in violation of confidentiality agreements that prohibited Vestar and KKR from discussing a joint bid without written permission from Del Monte. Late in the process, at a time when Barclays was ostensibly negotiating the deal price with KKR, Barclays asked KKR for a third of the buy-side financing. Once KKR agreed, Barclays sought and obtained Del Monte's permission. Having Barclays as a co-lead bank was not necessary to secure sufficient financing for the Merger, nor did it generate a higher price for the Company. It simply gave Barclays the additional fees it wanted from the outset. In fact, Barclays can expect to earn slightly more from providing buy-side financing to KKR than it will from serving as Del Monte's sell-side advisor. Barclays' gain cost Del Monte an additional $3 million because Barclays told Del Monte that it now had to obtain a last-minute fairness opinion from a second bank.[196]

In another postcrisis case involving conflicted behavior, FINRA fined Barclays, Citigroup, Credit Suisse, Goldman Sachs, and JP Morgan $5 million each and Deutsche Bank, Merrill Lynch, Morgan Stanley, and Wells Fargo $4 million each for "allowing their equity research analysts to solicit investment banking business" and in exchange therefore, "offering favorable research coverage in connection with the 2010 planned initial public offering of Toys'R'Us."[197]

With the financial crisis of 2008, and the continuing scandals, it is apparent that, for investors, banks, and the financial system and society as a whole, too much of what has been going on in this industry doesn't work. In the remaining chapters of this book, we will discuss the historical and other reasons why the banking industry came to be what it is today and ways in which it could be changed for the better.

2 HOW BANKING BECAME WHAT IT IS TODAY

Perhaps the most symbolically important event of twenty-first-century finance has been the sale in 2013 of Wall Street's premier institution, the 220-year-old New York Stock Exchange, to Intercontinental Exchange, an upstart Atlanta-based derivatives exchange. For many member firms and their brokers, this represented an end of an era. The established players and established venues no longer controlled the business; new entrants and new venues have gained increasing prominence.

The exchange had a dramatic and at times tortuous history over a quarter of a millennium, beginning with its founding in a 1792 agreement among brokers under a buttonwood tree on Wall Street. The exchange was always a self-governing entity. Even after federal regulation of securities trading in 1934, the exchange was allowed to be a private self-regulatory organization. The SEC had the power to force changes to the exchange's rules and practices, but direct government interference in exchange governance was rare (SEC officials sometimes joking referred to prospective regulation as their "shotgun behind the front door" that would rarely have to be used). For most of the past two centuries, the largest corporations in the United States listed their securities on the exchange and most trading in these issuers' shares took place on the exchange. The buildings and letterhead of the most prestigious broker-dealers proudly advertised "Member NYSE."

In the past few decades, however, securities trading became far more competitive and the exchange lost market share to other exchanges at home and abroad. Although the exchange had been a "not-for-profit entity" since its founding, in 2006 it became a "for-profit" entity and had a public offering of its own stock. In the years after the financial crisis of 2008, NYSE Group, itself the result of a merger between the NYSE and the Archipelago Exchange (an upstart that had acquired an exchange formed in the late 1800s), struggled to compete in global markets and in the now enormous market in financial derivatives. A proposed merger with the

German Börse fell through in 2012. Finally, in December 2012, negotiations for sale of the NYSE Group to the Intercontinental Exchange were successfully concluded. In 2013 the acquisition was a done deal.

The NYSE/Intercontinental Exchange merger is a culmination of many trajectories—a definitive recognition that markets are now profoundly different. The industry's business models have changed; the "old ways" no longer work. Changes were forced by the increasing need for competition, increasing sophistication and globalization of markets, and increasing development of technology in trading and in the creation of complex new financial instruments.

These changes in securities markets were accompanied by significant changes in the organizational form of most NYSE member firms, technically referred to as broker-dealers and often also called investment banks. Many of these firms had been general partnerships since their early days, whose partners were potentially liable if their partnerships could not pay their creditors. In the 1970s and 1980s, most of these firms became publicly held companies with limited liability for their former partners, now executives, as well as their public shareholders. The executives could now be far less concerned about downside risk. These executives are supposed to be supervised by the company's directors, who are elected by the shareholders. Many of the directors are "outside directors," who are presumed to exercise independent judgment because they are not employed full time by the company, by contrast with the "inside directors," who are senior officers at the company. Often, however, the outside directors have deferred to the inside directors and other executives of the company. These changes at broker-dealer firms also reflected a move toward a "shareholder value" focused idea of business, in which business's goal is principally, if not exclusively, to increase stock price, a subject further discussed at the end of this chapter.

In this chapter we discuss these developments and how they affected the business of banking. One notable effect was a dramatic change in bankers' perceptions of their own personal and professional responsibilities. The problematic business practices that are the subject of this book stem in significant part from those changed perceptions.

As discussed in our introduction, for purposes of this book, the term "bank" does not refer only to entities that are called investment banks.

It also includes many other types of entities that might principally be thought of as commercial banks, insurance companies, or some other type of entity. In discussing banking during the period up through the 1990s, when investment banking (the securities business) and commercial banking (taking deposits and lending) started to converge, we will use the terms "investment bank" and "commercial bank" as appropriate.

The Changing Business Model of Investment Banking

Economic, political, sociological, and technological developments over the past forty years have converged to transform the business model of investment banking.

There has been enormous growth in the size and geographic reach of securities markets. Banks need huge amounts of capital to do business; they depend more on technology to execute and process trades, and on quantitative analysis to understand volatile and complex markets. At the same time, the regulatory posture toward Wall Street until 2008 prioritized competition over safety and soundness, from the federal antitrust suits initiated in the late 1940s and 1950s against the largest underwriters, to efforts in the 1960s and 1970s by Congress and the SEC to break up the old economic and social order and increase competition among broker-dealers, and efforts in the 1990s to promote competition by bringing commercial banks—Wall Street investment bankers' most feared competitors—into the investment banking business. Some bankers resisted these changes, but many seized on the new market opportunities and competitive ideology with enthusiasm.

Competition and regulatory changes, including negotiated brokers' commissions and shelf registration of new offerings, topics discussed in more detail later in this chapter, put price pressure on two traditional profit centers in broker-dealer firms: brokerage services and securities underwriting. Relaxation of New York Stock Exchange rules in the 1970s allowed broker-dealer firms to go public with sales of debt and equity securities to raise the capital needed to compete. By the 1980s, much of this capital was deployed for proprietary trading, which became a crucial profit center to counterbalance the decline of brokerage and underwriting profits. Because most investment banks had shifted to public ownership from private partnership, the investment bankers—now called managing directors instead of partners—took most of their trading and other risks with other people's money rather than their own. By the 1990s, investment banks were also designing and selling complex new financial instruments such as securitized mortgages, security-based swap agreements, and credit-default swaps. Compared with traditional brokerage and underwriting services, these new lines of business were lightly regulated until the passage of the Dodd-Frank Act in 2010. But, as we explain more fully in chapter 4, even recent regulatory changes may not be able to keep up with changes in the industry, and the assumption that regulation alone can solve problems may do more harm than good.

The Scale of Securities Markets

Trading volume on the New York Stock Exchange grew exponentially in the latter half of the twentieth century. In the past two decades, off-exchange or over-the-counter trading in derivatives and similar products has exploded as well.

In 1960, average daily share volume on the NYSE was three million shares; by 1967 this number reached ten million shares and by 1968 it was thirteen million shares.[1] Broker-dealers needed to make a large investment to automate trade processing. Substantial working capital was needed for quick execution of large block trades for institutional customers (broker-dealers often have to advance funds to execute customer trades quickly). This increased volume meant that broker-dealer firms needed to be larger and probably needed more capital than their partners could provide. Raising capital from outside investors became a tempting alternative for broker-dealer firms, even if doing so would change firm capital structure and governance.

By the early 1970s, securities markets were dominated by large institutional investors, as more individuals put their money into retirement funds and mutual funds rather than investments in individual stocks. Quick execution of trades, pricing of trades, and low brokers' commissions were important to institutional investors, and other aspects of brokers' services, such as stock recommendations, were less important to institutions that could do their own analysis and make their own investment decisions. Preexisting relationships between these investors and their brokers were also secondary. For all practical purposes, the broker could be a computer rather than a person, putting Wall Street on its way toward the computerized high-speed trading that by the 2000s would comprise at least half of total market volume.

The trend toward larger trading volume and a larger institutional presence has continued to accelerate. In the 2008–14 time frame, average daily trading volume on the NYSE has been between three and four billion shares, and at times higher. Hedge funds, private equity funds, sovereign wealth funds controlled by foreign governments, and trading operations of investment banks, dominate the market. A lot of trading activity is conducted outside of the organized exchanges, including some trading in stocks, bonds and other fixed income securities, collateralized mortgage, loan, or debt obligations (CMOs, CLOs, or CDOs, discussed in chapter 1), security-based swaps (contractual exchanges of payments based on the price of a "reference" security), credit-default swaps (CDS, or contractual exchanges of payments based on whether a particular borrower defaults on its debt obligations), and other financial products. Up to a third of trades in NYSE-listed stocks are conducted outside of public view in "dark pools," private trading platforms organized by broker-dealers off of organized exchanges.

Moreover, a lot of trading activity is no longer under the control of large New York–based broker-dealers but, instead, is conducted by computerized high-frequency trading firms. The "Flash Crash" of May 6, 2010, illustrated the enormous impact computers can have: the Dow fell almost a thousand points and recovered within minutes, all due to an apparent computer malfunction at an institutional investor in Overland Park, Kansas. Something similar happened in late July 2012, when a trading platform designed by a single company, Knight Capital, went haywire. Michael Lewis's 2014 book *Flash Boys* describes this high-frequency trading business in detail and alleges that the market is rigged by high-frequency traders who "front run," placing their own trades ahead of trades they or others will be placing for an investor. The SEC has for years sought to curtail such practices and is now seeking to address allegations similar to those raised in Lewis's book. In 2014, the SEC imposed a $4.5 million penalty on the NYSE for oversight violations on a range of matters, including connections between brokers' computers and the NYSE's timing of dissemination of trading information.

In sum, market fragmentation—much of it driven by loosely regulated or unregulated trading by people and computers—is undermining the national market system that Congress and the SEC built in the 1970s, as trading is increasingly conducted in venues that are themselves less regulated or unregulated. Regulators have worried since the 1970s that market fragmentation creates opportunities for broker-dealers and market professionals to use arbitrage and other strategies to profit at the expense of ordinary investors, yet the problem continues. The source of fragmentation today is not so much regional stock exchanges but, rather, trading of derivatives and other exotic financial instruments, private trading platforms, and computerized trading programs. Many investors do not understand these markets and trading mechanisms, giving professionals who do understand them an advantage, and arguably, one that is unfair. Indeed, multiple markets for fungible financial products create—for investment banks and some other professional investors—unique advantages that include opportunities for arbitrage between price differentials in different markets. In the words of former SEC chairman Arthur Levitt, these new market mechanisms have "scared the heck out of investors." Regulators are worried too: the SEC itself has contracted with a high-speed trading firm to give it up-to-date market information, and an official from the Berkeley National Laboratory has suggested that the SEC enlist the help of a supercomputer to keep track of markets.[2]

Finally, securities trading markets have expanded on a global scale. Germany and Japan emerged as economic powers in the 1970s, and securities trading markets in London rival those in New York. Other trading markets have emerged in Hong Kong, Shanghai, and other parts of Asia. Technological advances made it easier for investment capital to move quickly across international boundaries. By the 1990s, markets were driven by enormous amounts of capital originating from outside the United States, and U.S. markets were interdependent with markets elsewhere.

In this world of rapid change, institutional priorities move away from emphasis on stable business practices and personal relationships and toward ingenuity and innovation combined with aggressive new strategies for enhancing profitability. Regulators who try to rein in these strategies are told that stricter regulation will drive securities trading and investment banking services—and jobs—elsewhere. For example, many bankers and some academic commentators suggested that the Sarbanes-Oxley Act of 2002 would cause issuers to delist from trading in New York, and some commentators on the Dodd-Frank Act of 2010 complain that strict separation of commercial banking from investment banking and trading will drive both types of banking elsewhere. Global competition continues to cast a shadow on the debate over how much regulation a single country or even a group of countries such as the EU can impose without losing business to foreign trading markets, a topic we discuss later, in chapter 4. Meanwhile, money moves where it wants, and some trading markets for practical purposes may not exist in any one particular jurisdiction at all.

Increased Competition

Government's strong concern with making securities markets more competitive goes back to *U.S. v. Morgan*, the Department of Justice's unsuccessful antitrust suit against the leading underwriter firms in the late 1940s and the 1950s for allegedly restricting new companies' access to public markets and keeping underwriting fees high.[3] In the 1960s, broker-dealer firms that were not members of the New York Stock Exchange sued it under the antitrust laws; the Supreme Court held that the exchange's self-regulatory status under the federal securities laws did not exempt it from liability under the antitrust laws.[4] Going forward, Congress and the SEC remained concerned that established broker-dealers had too much power and were hurting competitor broker-dealer firms, issuers of securities, and investors.

New York Stock Exchange rules in particular were criticized as being overly protective of established firms at the expense of their competitors and customers. The sociological overlay to New York Stock Exchange and broker-dealer governance added emotional fuel to the controversy because many broker-dealers were identified with particular ethnic and religious groups (Protestant Christians were the dominant group through the 1970s, while non-whites were hardly represented at all in the senior ranks of broker-dealer firms or the exchange). Perceptions of fairness and equal opportunity — as well as money — were at stake when proposals were made to dismantle the existing order.

New York Stock Exchange rules were believed to impede competition in at least two areas: the ownership and governance of broker-dealer firms and the commissions that brokers could charge their customers for trades. Because regulators, Congress, and academic commentators believed that these rules reinforced privilege and restricted competition, broker-dealers challenging these rules knew that the NYSE and its most powerful firms were on the defensive.

Investment Banks Go Public

Up until 1970, an important NYSE rule required that voting interests in member firms be owned by individuals who were also members of the exchange and whose principal employment was as broker-dealers. The NYSE was not unusual; similar rules are still central to other professions where professionals work in a business owned by members of the same profession and not by outside investors. Many doctors used to own their own practices and some still do (the fact that many doctors today work for insurance companies, corporate-owned hospitals, and other providers has been a big criticism of modern medicine). Lawyers still own their own law firms and the American Bar Association Model Rules of Professional Conduct continue to bar law firms from being owned by non-lawyers or even accepting non-lawyers as law firm partners (the states continue to adhere to the American Bar Association rules, and U.S. law firms are not publicly owned). Before 1970, the NYSE and its member firms saw their own professional independence in a similar light.

This NYSE rule also had economic consequences. The rule protected member firms' brokerage commissions by keeping large institutional investors from having their own seats on the exchange. The rule also prevented large commercial banks from obtaining a seat on the exchange. One disadvantage, however, was that the rule made it difficult for broker-dealer firms—particularly newer firms—to accumulate the capital needed to quickly execute large block trades for institutional clients. Large block trades could only be done by established firms whose partners had already amassed substantial capital. Institutional investors did not like this situation and neither did brokers-dealers who wanted to break into the industry without large amounts of personal capital.

In 1969, the newly established Donaldson Lufkin & Jenrette firm informed the NYSE that it intended to go public regardless of the rule. William Donaldson, who became the chairman of the SEC more than thirty years later, in 2003, told the NYSE that the rule was not justified and that his firm needed outside capital in order to quickly execute large trades for institutional clients. The NYSE caved in and amended its rule in 1970 to allow brokerage firms to have a public float of securities. Merrill Lynch, the largest retail broker, went public the following year.

Up until this point, many of the most powerful investment banks on Wall Street had been partnerships—their owners had avoided the corporate form altogether. They preferred the "hands-on" governance norms of partnerships, the requirement that most if not all partners agree on major business decisions, and the ease of dissolving partnerships so individual partners could withdraw capital at the end of the year. These partners were willing to accept the personal liability that comes with general partnerships, and personal liability probably gave their firms added credibility with customers, clients, and other broker-dealers.

After the 1970 rule change, brokerage firms had the option of using the corporate form to raise outside capital, with the added side benefit of limited personal liability. During the 1970s and 1980s, many firms ceased being partnerships; by the mid-1980s, most of the major Wall Street firms had switched to corporate form and could at least argue that their reason for doing so was to raise outside capital. Before, when the NYSE rule prohibited outside capital, a large investment bank's switch from partnership to corporate form would have been difficult to justify. With most of the larger and better-known banks being partnerships, a competitor organized as an entity without personal liability for its owners would face a disadvantage, given the negative signal the lack of personal liability would send to customers. But when banks generally were switching, the corporate form became the new norm, not conveying any negative signal. The last holdout, Goldman Sachs, actually did a lot of its business through separate limited liability entities in the 1980s and 1990s until it also abandoned partnership form in 1999.[5]

Most of the capital in investment banks now belonged to someone else—the shareholders—rather than to the bankers themselves. The bankers had capital in the banks, in the form of shares of bank stock, but most of their return from being bankers was tied to their compensation, which in turn was tied to current reported earnings. When bankers took big risks in order to increase earnings, they would be richly rewarded if the risks paid off. They also knew that losses would be absorbed by the shareholders. If the losses were so severe that the firm failed, the bankers knew that they would not be personally liable. Creditors might not be repaid, and shareholders could be wiped out, but the bankers would keep what they had earned from the bank and whatever else they had previously accumulated.

Competitive Commissions

Another important change was the end of fixed-brokerage commissions. New York Stock Exchange rules before 1975 required member firms to charge the same percentage commission on trades, regardless of the size of the transaction. Large institutional investors thus subsidized individual customers. Broker-dealers for the most part competed against each other with respect to reputation and presumed quality of services, but not their commissions.

In the 1960s, the NYSE made some exceptions to fixed commissions for very large trades, but Congress pushed for more. In 1975, Congress finally mandated that the SEC abolish fixed-brokerage commissions and replace them with negotiated rates. On May 1, 1975 — "May Day" — negotiated rates went into effect. Institutional investors negotiated lower commissions on large trades and individual investors increasingly flocked to discount brokers and, with the advent of the Internet in the 1990s, online services such as E-Trade.

Negotiated commissions meant a better deal for frequent traders not in need of brokerage advice (with trading being cheaper, there would also be more of it, driving market volume up yet further, and beginning the shift toward high-speed trading that dominates today's markets). Negotiated commissions, however, also meant that most investment banks would make less money from giving advice to brokerage customers and other traditional brokerage services. The broker part of the broker-dealer combination became less important, and the dealer part (e.g., proprietary trading) would become more important as a profit center. Brokers would more likely play a supporting role for other lines of business. For example, brokers might be used for selling securities that the broker-dealer firm was also underwriting. In such an environment, personal relationships with brokerage customers who don't pay big commissions might be less important to the firm than opportunities to make money by selling customers securities in which the broker-dealer has another financial interest.

Shelf Registration and the Decline of Traditional Underwriting

In the early 1980s, a different regulatory change increased competition and price pressure in another highly profitable area of traditional investment banking: securities underwriting for corporate issuers. Concentration of power among the largest Wall Street investment banks (the major bracket underwriters such as Morgan Stanley and First Boston) had worried the government since its loss in the *U.S. v. Morgan* antitrust lawsuit in 1953. These few firms had an enormous share of the underwriting business. As discussed above, as late as the 1970s, predominantly "Protestant" firms (some of which were reluctant to hire and promote Jews and even Catholics) still dominated the market for blue chip corporate issues, including underwriting.

Then, in 1982, the SEC adopted a controversial rule, Rule 415, which allowed "shelf registration" of issuers' securities.[6] Some Wall Street bankers opposed Rule 415 because they believed it would cut into their profits and diminish the prestige of the corporate underwriting business. Under Rule 415, instead of being required to sell securities as soon as possible after a registration statement was filed with the SEC, larger corporate issuers could register securities "for the shelf" and then later do a "shelf takedown" when market conditions were most beneficial. In the volatile interest rate environment of the early 1980s, "shelf registration" was particularly helpful for issuers of debt securities who could register bonds with the SEC and then wait until interest rates dipped to quickly sell the bonds into the market. However, the procedure was soon used for stock issuances as well.

Rule 415 fundamentally changed the relationship between issuers and their underwriters. Prior to Rule 415, issuers had depended on a relationship with one or two underwriting firms that could put together a registration statement for a new issue of securities when it was needed. The underwriter's familiarity with the issuer, and ability to assist in a timely manner with preparation of a registration statement, was at least as important as the price charged by the underwriter for the transaction. Rule 415 now allowed an issuer to do most of the preparatory work for a registration statement ahead of time. Then, at the time of a shelf takedown, the issuer could price the deal with several underwriting firms and engage the firm that offered the lowest underwriting "spread" or commission. The fact that a corporation had always used Morgan Stanley, or that its CEO had gone to Saint Paul's School or Yale with a partner of First Boston, became irrelevant. When the registration statement was ready, the securities were "on the shelf"; when markets later were ready for a "takedown," presumably the only thing that mattered in selecting an underwriter was how quickly the securities could be sold and how much it was going to cost.

Rule 415 did for issuers what May Day and negotiated commissions had done for investors in 1975: the new rule brought price competition that appeared to benefit investment banking clients. Some opponents of the rule, such as Morgan Stanley, argued that issuers and investors get what they pay for because in traditional underwritings investment bankers know their issuer clients and more time is devoted to due diligence. The predominant view among policy makers and investment bankers who supported Rule 415, however, was that the old rules had favored a subset of investment bankers who had perpetuated their privileged position by charging issuers too much money for underwriting services. Rule 415 was celebrated as a success, and the procedures were liberalized yet further in 2005 with automatic shelf registration for the largest corporate issuers.

The Search for New Business

By the 1980s, the message was clear to investment bankers who had previously enjoyed generous brokerage commissions and underwriting spreads: they needed to find a new way to make money. Many investment bankers turned to proprietary trading as a profit center in the 1980s, a topic discussed under a separate subheading below. By the 1990s, securitization of mortgages, auto loans, credit card receivables, and other cash flow streams allowed an investment bank, or one of its subsidiaries, to be the issuer as well as the underwriter of securities and to internalize for itself the benefits from the speedy and more competitive shelf registration process. The investment bank could create as many new issues of securities as its bankers could invent and sell to investors. The bank could also make more money trading these new securities. The relationship between these types of activities and the funding of operating businesses, which had been the traditional purpose of underwriting, was increasingly attenuated. Bank-issued securities sometimes created *new* risks, notably in the case of synthetic securities, which consist of side bets on the performance of other securities. As discussed in chapter 1, banks probably knew more about what they were selling than many investors knew about what they were buying.

Banks also were involved in the development and sale of securities and other financial instruments that had purposes other than offering financial returns. For instance, some financial instruments helped buyers with regulatory requirements or tax minimization. Indeed, some banks became quite involved in the tax shelter industry that flourished through the 1990s, working with accounting firms and law firms to develop products that could be marketed and sold to individuals and corporations to significantly reduce tax liabilities.[7]

Some investment banks shunned these new lines of business and continued to focus on traditional brokerage services for individual and institutional investors and on underwriting and transaction advisory services for corporations. These investment banks, however, made less money than their competitors. In the social and professional world of Wall Street that emphasized rapid accumulation of money more than ever before—and relationships with clients and customers probably less—traditional investment banking as a stand-alone business was an anomaly as anachronistic as the portraits of long-since-departed partners that some banks still kept hanging on their walls.

For much of this same time (the 1980s, 1990s, and early 2000s), the political climate in Washington not only prioritized competition among investment banks but was also hostile to any effort to regulate securitizations and other new financial products that were increasingly important profit centers. (As noted in the introduction, one of us, Richard Painter, is working on a separate project exploring the role that the banking industry's campaign contributions may have had in this failure of the regulatory system.) For example, as discussed in chapter 4, the SEC tried to regulate security-based swap agreements in the 1990s but was told not to by Congress. The Gramm-Leach-Bliley Act of 2000 expressly provided that security-based swap agreements were not securities and that the SEC was prohibited from requiring their registration or taking any other steps to regulate them, even to prevent fraud. (After security-based swaps were a significant factor in the 2008 financial collapse, the Dodd-Frank Act largely reversed this position and introduced some new rules, including the requirement that swaps be traded on organized exchanges.) In the years since Dodd-Frank was passed, banks and their lobbyists have made significant efforts to minimize its effects. Some of these efforts have been focused on the language of regulations; more recently, in an omnibus spending bill passed in late 2014, a more significant roll-back was achieved. As we discuss in chapter 4, there are many limitations on the ability of regulators to police investment banking, and our political system, itself very responsive to moneyed interests, is one of them.

In sum, traditional brokerage and underwriting services for many investment banks are less important than they once were. By the late 1980s and into the 1990s, many investment banks had turned to new areas of business that either did not exist or were nowhere near as important when the securities laws had been enacted. Up through the enactment of the Dodd-Frank Act in 2010, and continuing to this day, investment bankers in these new areas of business have had a lot of influence over the rules that govern those businesses.

New Competitors

Yet another important manifestation of Wall Street's competitive drive over the past several decades has been the entrance of new categories of competitors into investment banking, two of the most important being depository institutions such as JPMorgan, Bank of America, and Citi and insurance companies such as American International Group (AIG). Hedge funds, the finance arms of major corporations such as GE, and other competitors have also jumped into investment banking.

Prohibitions on investment banking activity by commercial banks gradually loosened until the 1999 Gramm-Leach-Bliley Act finally repealed the 1933 Glass-Steagall Act that had required investment banking and commercial banking to be separated. Commercial bank holding companies, if not the banks themselves, can now carry a considerable amount of risk on their balance sheets. Citi bought Salomon Brothers, and other large depository institutions also went into the investment banking business. The two parts of the former J.P. Morgan & Co. that were separated due to Glass-Steagall—the commercial bank JPMorgan and the invest-ment bank Morgan Stanley—still remain separate. Their respective busi-ness models, however, are not as distinct as they were twenty years ago. J. P. Morgan (now JPMorgan Chase) is no longer just a traditional lending institution and is, perhaps, even more focused than Morgan Stanley on making profits from securities and derivative markets. Finally, banks in Europe and other places where investment banking had traditionally been combined with commercial banking, supposedly under strict government regulation of both, could now use their combined business model in the United States as well.

From 1994 through at least 2010, and probably continuing today, the largest bank holding companies became increasingly dependent on sources other than "traditional" income (income from interest on loans and fees for services) and more dependent on income from "nontraditional" func-tions such as trading, investment banking, and insurance commissions and fees.[8] In this environment, the commercial bank subsidiary of the largest bank holding companies is of diminished importance relative to the investment bank subsidiary, a development that is very likely to have an impact on which bankers will hold the most power within the firm.

Describing the investment bank's culture at Barclays, the 2013 *Salz Re-view*, commissioned by Barclays in the wake of publicity surrounding Bar-clays's bankers' manipulations of LIBOR and discussed elsewhere in this book, said:

The interpretation and implementation of "winning" went beyond the simply competitive. It was sometimes underpinned by what appeared to have been an "at all costs" attitude. This was insufficiently tempered by permission to decide that it was better sometimes to compromise and move on. This may have led to a tendency to argue at times for the letter rather than the spirit of the law. Winning at all costs comes at a price: collateral issues of rivalry, arrogance, selfishness and a lack of humility and generosity. . . .

If winning was a stated value, then "cleverness" was an unstated—but equally strong—one. They were somewhat related. Barclays undoubt-edly hired clever people. For the investment bank, this was the key to its success. Cleverness manifested itself in the way the team clearly built a very successful business on the back of a well thought-through strategy. But the cleverness showed through in other ways described elsewhere in this report: the tendency to take robust positions with regulators, to determine its position by the letter rather than the spirit of the rules, and in the "edgy" way it pushed its own business agenda.[9]

Barclays, to its credit, made changes to its management team and to its business model. In the wake of the LIBOR bid rigging scandal, Robert Diamond resigned as CEO of Barclays in July of 2012 and was replaced in August of 2012 by Anthony Jenkins. In November 2013, Robert Hoyt, who had been general counsel to the U.S. Treasury during the 2008 financial crisis, was appointed as group general counsel of Barclays. Jenkins then led Barclays on a "bold simplification" plan that included cutting back substantially on its investment banking operations and the sale of retail banking operations in France, Italy, and Spain. Barclays is also exiting the metals, energy, and agricultural commodities-trading business—a business that not only was volatile but also exposed the bank to regulatory problems. "It's just no longer doable for us to be a global, universal bank," Michael Rake, deputy chairman of Barclays, said in a press interview.[10]

Not all banks have gone Barclays's route toward simplification, and debate continues over what types of businesses should be conducted under one roof. Sandy Weill, the architect of Citigroup, which was a combination of many different financial services companies, Mervyn King, the former governor of the Bank of England, and Paul Volcker, former chairman of the Federal Reserve, have all expressed concern about the combination of proprietary trading and other types of banking. While restrictions are being imposed on proprietary trading by broker-dealers affiliated with commercial banks—the Volcker Rule—the government otherwise shows no intention of reintroducing the separation between the two lines of business, and banks show no signs of breaking up. The very large commercial banks, through their holding companies, were the competitors that traditional investment banks always feared, and now with the government's blessing they are important—arguably the most important—players in the game.

Insurance companies also are increasingly engaging in banking-like activities. One especially important such activity is the sale of "insurance" on financial instruments, "credit-default swaps." Currency and interest rate swaps were discussed in chapter 1. In a credit-default swap, a swap provider gets a premium to provide insurance against a particular borrower's default on a loan. If the borrower defaults, the swap provider—or, the "protection seller"—has to pay the "protection buyer," who may or may not be the lender, the amount of the loan. Swaps can thus be used for speculation as well as for hedging a preexisting position. Many of the buyers are banks or other financial institutions, and as shown by the failure of AIG and by the troubles at MBIA, some traditional insurance companies have put their survival on the line by going into this area of business. Insurance companies are regulated by state regulators in the states in which they sell insurance. State regulators cannot be expected to do better at regulating swaps than federal regulators have done. Although federal regulators have increased their scrutiny of insurance companies' investment banking activities since the Dodd-Frank Act, it remains to be seen how this federal investor-protection mandate will square with the traditional view that insurance regulation is the business of the states and not the federal government.

Many other developments in the 1990s and 2000s made it easier for investment banking to be conducted in many different types of entities. Thus, investment banks compete with each other as well as with commercial banks, insurance companies, and other entrants in the investment banking industry. In the interest of brevity these developments will not all be discussed here.

The highly fluid and competitive environment that has emerged in the past forty years shapes how investment bankers make money, the incentives they have when doing so, and whether investment bankers are more or less likely to make money at someone else's expense. The tight-knit Wall Street club that the government attacked in the late 1940s and the 1950s in the *U.S. v. Morgan* antitrust suit is gone but the uneven playing field between banks and their customers remains, and the financial institutions that dominate the industry are even bigger than they once were.

Trading and Technology

Since the 1980s, trading has been very important as a profit and power center in Wall Street firms. Lehman Brothers, until its demise one of the most prestigious of the large underwriting firms, appointed a trader, Lewis Glucksman, as its CEO in 1983. Glucksman soon introduced management changes that drove many traditional bankers to leave. Michael Lewis's 1989 book *Liar's Poker* described the rise of the trading culture that came to dominate Salomon Brothers in the 1980s, complete with vulgar trading floor language and an enormous appetite for gambling on anything, including the serial numbers of dollar bills.

Since the 2000s, trading operations in many banks have become so large that traders in a few banks have the power to move markets. Traders can now influence prices for large numbers of securities simultaneously, and, as discussed in chapter 1, traders in several banks apparently successfully manipulated the London Interbank Offered Rate (LIBOR). Interest rates had been assumed to be an economic benchmark, beyond the control of any one financial institution except the Federal Reserve, the Bank of England, or some other central bank. But trading operations at Barclays and other banks became so powerful and their treasuries had gotten so much "firepower" that they could manipulate even a widely followed benchmark of short-term interest rates. As we discuss in chapter 4, regulators are attempting to address banks' ability and incentive to manipulate rates and markets, but their success in doing so is scarcely assured.

Trading's rise in importance has occurred at the same time as the rise of technology. Wall Street realized the importance of technology in the back-office crisis of 1969, when old-fashioned methods of processing trades—including using paper stock certificates to settle trades—made it impossible for many firms to keep up with market volume. A firm that was run by people who did not understand technology could not survive. The 1970s and 1980s also saw a need for rapid dissemination of information, particularly in increasingly volatile bond markets. Michael Bloomberg was promoted to partner at Salomon Brothers at a relatively young age because he designed the computer systems that bond traders used to keep track of trades and value bonds. After he left the firm in 1981 following the Phibro merger (discussed later in this chapter), Bloomberg designed computerized information systems that he sold to almost every broker-dealer on Wall Street. Computers have now taken over almost all of the trading operations of investment banks, hedge funds, and other market participants.

In today's markets, trading success depends in significant part on predicting what computers will do. Computers are, of course, programmed by people. But they can "act" randomly. The information they are programmed with can be manipulated. And they are sometimes reacting to what other computers are doing. In this environment, the notion of personal responsibility of human beings for market fluctuations—and occasional market chaos—is conceptually remote. As discussed further in chapter 3, bankers may not feel a sense of personal responsibility with regard to what computers do. Moreover, even if they are attempting to rein in the computers, they may not be able to do so, and the computers may be able to cause massive damage.

Meritocracy and Mathematics

Another mid-twentieth-century development was the growing importance of objective measures of merit in hiring and promoting investment bankers, as well as the growing emphasis on quantitative analysis of investments. These developments were linked with sociological changes on Wall Street and the country as a whole, and marked a profound shift in the investment banking business away from human relationships toward more quantitative measures of value.

Part of this trend—like some other trends in finance—originated in academia, where quantitative assessment in standardized tests transformed and democratized higher education. Scholastic Aptitude Tests were introduced into college admissions in the 1930s, when President Conant of Harvard used the Scholastic Aptitude Tests' measure of academic ability to increase the fairness of an admissions process that had previously drawn students principally from well-known private schools. The Scholastic Aptitude Test soon spread to other colleges after the beginning of World War II, and admissions for many top colleges became increasingly selective. Overall, the result was for many colleges—particularly the Ivy League colleges that had traditionally been pipelines for large investment banks—a student body that was more diverse and more academically focused than ever before. (The fact that the objective measure embodied in the tests could be manipulated by coaching and might contain sociocultural biases that worked against certain minority groups was not given much thought until the 1970s.) These college graduates presumably believed they achieved what they did in significant part because they had excelled along a quantitative metric—first, Scholastic Aptitude Tests and then, perhaps grade point averages. For those joining investment banks, their faith in an institution's ability to quantifiably measure merit may not have receded when other metrics, such as earnings and stock price, took over.

The concept of measurable merit also has come to influence hiring and promotion on Wall Street. There has been decreased emphasis on personal connections, particularly those within a tight-knit social group, and increased emphasis on what a prospective banker knows and what he can do with his knowledge to make money. Guesses about a candidate's personality traits, to the extent they are important, have come to be closely linked with the bank's principal mission of making money in the new business model. Appetite for risk would, for example, probably be more important in a bank that emphasized trading profits and operated under the shield of limited liability than in a bank that emphasized underwriting or brokerage profits within a partnership with joint and several liability.

Meanwhile, bankers and investors have turned to more sophisticated quantitative tools for measuring the performance of investments themselves. This was, at first, a welcome—and inevitable—development, but it has ended up having a dark side. Quantitative tools have an aura of legitimacy that they do not always warrant: as sophisticated as these tools become, the subject matter is simply too complex for them to be used mechanically. The computations require assumptions provided by fallible and sometimes self-interested humans. The system can be gamed so trades will mistakenly be computed to be profitable; the banker engaging in the trade can collect a bonus based on his "profits," when there in fact are none, and there may even be losses.

The recent history of quantitative analysis on Wall Street begins in the late 1960s, when Salomon Brothers' bond market research department urged market participants to have a greater understanding of mathematical concepts and enlisted a young mathematician, Martin Leibowitz, to provide mathematical calculations for the *Inside the Yield Book*, which he coauthored with an older Salomon partner, Sidney Homer.[11] Leibowitz, now a senior officer at Morgan Stanley, was one of the earliest, if not the earliest, pioneers to bring sophisticated mathematical reasoning to Wall Street, and *Inside the Yield Book* is still widely used today.

Leibowitz and his colleagues attracted customers to Salomon Brothers with their bond market publications, but their work was essentially academic and not intended to sell a particular product. These analysts worked for investment banks, but those early days of quantitative analysis were nonetheless relatively free of conflicts of interest. Bond market researchers' work was not used by their firms to create their own investment products, sell those products, and then write about them in favorable terms. Instead, researchers observed and wrote about fixed-income securities that were trading in existing markets. These early quantitative analysts also had a very public role of explaining markets to investors as a whole. They did this in part to bring prestige to their firms but also to contribute to the general level of human knowledge in their field. (Leibowitz alone has published dozens of scholarly papers.)

The genuine successes of these early quantitative analysts encouraged the all-too-human hope, especially on the part of investors, that risk could be conquered—that financial instruments with high expected return and low risk could be created—although the quantitative analysts themselves presumably understood the difficulty if not impossibility of this and other strategies for creating money out of thin air. Bankers fed into this hope, crafting and selling financial instruments they promoted as offering low risk but high return. Bankers' own views presumably ran the gamut, with some genuinely believing they had conquered risk, some being perhaps willfully ignorant, and others being quite skeptical.

Brilliant quantitative minds have flocked to Wall Street in increasing numbers. Many economists and mathematicians from this later generation of "quants" would be enlisted in the design of complex derivative securities. The securities were sufficiently complex that many people who bought them, and even some people who sold them, didn't fully understand them. Bankers sometimes seem to have taken advantage of securities' complexity: certainly, in the period leading up to the 2008 crisis, they at times looked for buyers who they thought would more or less blindly rely on high ratings from the major rating agencies, and buy securities the bankers knew or strongly suspected were very bad indeed.

The Uneasy Relationship between Banking and Limited Liability

As discussed above, a change in New York Stock Exchange rules in 1970 eventually led almost all investment banks to do business as limited liability entities. Bankers in banks organized as corporations are generally not legally responsible for the debts of their firms. It is easy to assume that limited liability is the natural state of affairs in banking. But limited liability has historically engendered substantial skepticism, in banking and in other industries as well. Investment banking and law, both fields requiring education, offering prestige and styling themselves as professions, traditionally were conducted largely in general partnerships. Both fields now are generally conducted in entities offering significantly limited liability to those running the firms. But law firms today are still owned by lawyers who practice in them; those lawyers thus experience real downside risk when their firms do poorly. Such is far less true for executives at banks.

The South Sea Trading Company and the Bubble Act of 1720

One of England's best-known early experiments with limited liability in banking was a disaster. England's South Sea Company was chartered in 1711 by Tory politicians and their friends.[12] Parliament gave the company a monopoly on trade in the South Seas, while a competitor company with Whig roots received considerably less favorable treatment. Ostensibly a trading enterprise, the company was quickly converted into an investment bank for refinancing large quantities of government debt that England had from its wars with Spain. This government-sponsored enterprise was a win-win situation for everybody—at least for a while. Members of Parliament were given free stock in the company and began trading in the stock. Even the king's mistress—but apparently not the queen—had a stake in the company. The most important trading was not in goods from the South Seas but in the company's own stock.

When the South Sea Company stock crashed in 1720, many people were left in financial ruin. A few of the promoters were sent to the Tower of London, and many others lost all of their property. The financial crisis of 1720 was blamed, rightly or wrongly, on the combination of limited liability and freely tradable shares. The South Sea Company—in reality an investment bank more than a trading company—had abused this combination with disastrous results. Parliament quickly covered its own tracks by passing the Bubble Act of 1720, which forbade publicly traded limited liability company interests without a specific grant of authority from Parliament.

London solicitors made a significant business devising ways to circumvent the Bubble Act. Then, as now, regulation of banking and other business activities invited efforts to circumvent the regulation, and regulatory constraints on limited liability were no exception. The Bubble Act was finally repealed in the mid-nineteenth century, but doubts about the advisability of limited liability would remain.

Assessable Stock

Concerns with limited liability have historically been addressed in different ways. One way is to require the owners of limited liability businesses to deposit, and retain, a certain amount of capital in the business as an equity cushion for the benefit of creditors. A related method is to require the owners of the business to invest more capital if it is needed to pay creditors. Banking institutions in particular were frequently subject to these rules and norms until the mid-twentieth century.

Commercial banks historically used arrangements that tried to tie financial interests of senior bankers, who were bank employees and bank owners, to the fate of depositors and other creditors. Commercial banks arguably needed such arrangements in the era before extensive federal regulation. Most of them were corporations, with limited liability of stockholders, unlike, as discussed above, the investment banks, which were typically partnerships with unlimited personal liability of partners. One notable arrangement, used particularly before the 1930s, was assessable stock—stock that requires the holder to agree to pay amounts in addition to amounts initially paid for the stock. Some commercial banks, as well as some other corporations, issued assessable stock to their directors and officers. When banks failed after the 1929 crash, state bank regulators and other receivers raised funds by making assessments on the assessable stock. Stockholders challenged the assessments, raising constitutional and statutory interpretation issues, but courts often upheld the assessments. For example, in *Broderick v. Rosner*, in an opinion written by Justice Brandeis, the Supreme Court held that, under the Full Faith and Credit Clause of the U.S. Constitution, the New York superintendent of banks could bring suit for assessments against New Jersey residents holding stock in a New York bank.[13] The court held that the defendants could not avail themselves of a New Jersey statute prohibiting bringing suit in New Jersey under the laws of another state to enforce stockholders' personal liability. The court, Justice Brandeis observed, would not allow the New Jersey defendants to escape their voluntarily assumed statutory obligation consistent with their moral obligation to the bank's depositors:

> In respect to the determination of liability for an assessment, the New Jersey stockholders submitted themselves to the jurisdiction of New York. For "the act of becoming a member (of a corporation) is something more than a contract, it is entering into a complex and abiding relation, and as marriage looks to domicil [sic], membership looks to and must be governed by the law of the State granting the incorporation." . . . Obviously recognition could not be accorded to a local policy of New Jersey, if there really were one, of enabling all residents of the State to escape from the performance of a voluntarily assumed statutory obligation, consistent with morality, to contribute to the payment of the depositors of a bank of another State of which they were stockholders.[14]

Stock ownership as described here is a lot more than a simple contract; it is a relationship that includes legal and moral obligations to the corporation's creditors. As the New York statute demonstrates, these obligations are particularly strong when the corporation is a bank. In this era, before extensive federal regulation of banks, the state where a bank was chartered had the primary responsibility for defining the terms of the relationship between stockholders and creditors. New York and many other states rejected the notion that unqualified limited liability should control that relationship, particularly when many of the stockholders were also the people who ran the bank. (If a bank was publicly traded, however, the publicly traded shares usually were not assessable.)

In the 1930s, without adequate federal government oversight of banks, state-mandated stockholder assessments proved inadequate to control banks' excessive risk taking and insolvency. The litigation over assessable stock in the 1930s shows that at least some capital calls were not being honored. After the mid-1930s, the federal government guaranteed commercial bank deposits, forced commercial banks out of investment banking in the Glass-Steagall Act, and regulated commercial banks for safety and soundness. In this world, assessable stock was presumably no longer necessary because the government would tell the commercial banks how to manage their affairs. As discussed earlier in this chapter, however, with the repeal of Glass-Steagall in 1999 and other regulatory changes, these assumptions about government oversight of commercial banks may no longer hold. Assumptions about the proper role of limited liability in banking should be revisited as well.

Investment Bank Partnerships

Through the 1970s, most investment banks, particularly the largest and most prestigious investment banks, were general partnerships run by partners who were therefore personally liable for their partnerships' debts.[15] This arrangement was not required by law—New York Stock Exchange rules only prohibited member firms from raising outside capital through the sale of stock, and some broker-dealer firms were corporations with limited liability. Many investment banks, however, chose to be partnerships, thereby assuming a legal obligation to put personal assets on the line. This choice was not particularly costly in their world, because putting one's assets on the line was also the societal norm for investment bankers. Indeed, as noted above, the choice not to put one's assets on the line could have been the costly one, since customers might shun such firms in favor of firms whose owners did put their assets on the line.

Lehman Brothers traced its roots back to the 1870s. Until it incorporated, in 1983, its partners were personally liable for the debts of their partnership; they could lose their savings, their houses, and just about everything else. In investment banking partnerships, it often took many years for someone to become a partner because the other partners had to be willing to risk everything on decisions made by that partner. Because they bore the collective responsibility of paying creditors, they were collectively involved in whatever risk taking the other partners did. Not infrequently, partners huddled together on the trading floor to discuss big trades before they were made.

Salomon Brothers provides a good example of risk taking informed and constrained by the potential for unlimited liability. Salomon Brothers specialized in bonds and developed its business with the expansion in government and corporate bond offerings in the years after the Great Depression. In an era before credit-default swaps and other recent innovations in debt markets, Salomon's bond business was perhaps mundane but was generally profitable. The firm's partners probably appreciated the lack of excitement. As young men, during the Depression, many of them had seen too much "excitement" on Wall Street as stock brokers jumped out of windows and families were ruined. Others had immigrated to the United States from Europe, particularly Germany, where they had seen that financial chaos can cause political instability, which in turn can have a devastating impact on human civilization. Their life experiences were inconsistent with the notion that personal profit was all that banking was about and that inflation, unemployment, and other societal problems are somebody else's worry. These bankers were rich, but they also had good reason to worry about things other than their own money, including the political system and the economy as a whole.

In an investment bank operating as a partnership, the bank's capital belonged to the partners; there were no shareholders. Partners invested their own money, and they had to leave as much of it as possible in the firm so the firm could grow. Large cash distributions to the firm's partners were not an option; raising capital from public investors simply was not feasible and, as noted above, was not allowed under pre-1970 NYSE rules. Partnership tax rules made the cash flow situation even more challenging: partners paid taxes on the firm's profits whether or not the profits were distributed to them (the top federal tax bracket on earned income was significantly higher than it is now). Between taxes and the capital requirements of the firm, investment banking partners had to lead relatively modest lives. Investment bankers in those days could live in nice homes and put food on the table; they even rode in limousines to work and probably spent too much of their money on cigars. But few of them had the equivalent to the large cash paydays of more recent years.[16]

When partners retired, they would become limited partners and get access to their capital, but that capital was paid out in slow installments over time during retirement. The partners' and retired partners' capital was often the only capital the firm had. Many limited partners left their money in the firm as long as they could, trusting the younger generation to use it wisely. Some limited partners also kept an office at the firm, where they could observe what was happening even if they did not participate in day-to-day management. These limited partners had an opportunity to weigh in with their perspective, even a contrarian perspective, on the conduct of the general partners, something that younger partners had to adjust to when they took over management of the firm.[17] These limited-partner contrarians perhaps had less influence when intergenerational tension intensified in the 1960s, but they were the men who had hired and promoted the general partners, their hard work had been largely responsible for the wealth they all enjoyed, and their views on how to protect that wealth were most likely respected.

As mentioned above, and explained more fully below, this system was soon to change, and the change was to make a big difference in the way bankers behaved. Henry Kaufman, formerly chief economist for Salomon Brothers, recently observed: "I know from my own experience as a senior partner of Salomon Brothers that the shift from partnership to corporation had profound impacts over time on the level of our risk-taking and in our relationship with clients."[18] Kaufman recalls that "Sidney Homer, one of my mentors, told me that I would become a partner [of Salomon Brothers]. He said, 'I'm sure that you will rush to tell your wife.' Then he added, 'But be sure to tell her that once you sign the partnership papers next week you will be personally liable for $2 billion.'"[19]

From Partnership to Liar's Poker

As discussed earlier in this chapter, once the New York Stock Exchange in 1970 changed its prohibition on member firms having a public float, investment banks could access huge amounts of capital from stockholders and other investors. For the investment bankers who ran these firms, the switch also brought important new developments: liquidity for the money they had locked up in their firms; a compensation system based on bonuses, stock, and stock options instead of accrual of partnership capital within the firm; and no personal liability for the debts of the firm. Each firm had its own trajectory, but the impact on investment bankers' behavior seemed uniform. Wall Street changed in the 1980s, from a fairly staid place to one where considerable risk taking became the norm. Limited liability, and the moral hazard that comes with it, is an important reason for the change.

Again, Salomon Brothers is a good example of a trend throughout the industry. Salomon switched from partnership to corporate form in 1981 when it merged with Phibro Commodities, Inc. After the merger, partners became "managing directors," and traders began making their bets with shareholders' and creditors' money rather than their own money. Managing directors' personal assets outside of the firm were not at risk. Former partners who it was thought could not contribute sufficiently to the short-term bottom line were asked to leave. (As mentioned above, one of these partners, Michael Bloomberg, took his $10 million interest in Salomon Brothers, along with technological know-how that enabled him to develop what became a multibillion dollar financial information network.) The retired limited partners who had built Salomon Brothers were paid back their capital, but only the general partners shared in the premium paid by Phibro in the merger. A few of the limited partners retained their offices, including William Salomon, who at age ninety-nine still had an office at Citigroup, which bought Salomon in the 1990s.[20] In the new corporate structure, however, the retirees' "contrarian" role in questioning management would be much reduced. (Former chief executive officers are viewed with suspicion in many corporations if they say anything about the way the firm is being managed by their successors; directors are presumed to have the oversight role, a role which they carry out with varying degrees of vigor.) It is highly unlikely, for example, that senior managers at Citi consulted with William Salomon about how to run the investment banking operations that Citi had acquired from Salomon Brothers. And the way those investment banking operations were run in the two decades before 2008 appears to be very different from the way Salomon had run his firm.

The age of *Liar's Poker* had begun at Salomon almost immediately after the merger and extended all the way through the firm's integration into Citigroup in the 1990s and beyond.

That landmark book on Wall Street culture had its roots in a decision by Michael Lewis, a recent Princeton graduate, to accept a job offer at Salomon in 1984. Salomon had been a corporation for three years, and Lewis's description in the book has little resemblance to the firm that William Salomon had run only a decade before. Lewis joined a training class where other recent recruits acted more like students in a junior high school—they shot spitballs during class, told crude jokes, and took care to ignore much of what they were told. *Liar's Poker* discusses the common term for a star trader—"big swinging dick"—which reflected not only the rise of obscenity on trading floors but also an ethos in which investment bankers' risk taking was a sign of their masculinity.

Then disaster struck. In 1991, one of Salomon Brothers' "star" bond traders was caught illegally cornering the market in Treasury securities. Senior officers, including CEO John Gutfreund, were told about it. The firm's general counsel told them that they had to report it to the Treasury Department. Instead they kept it secret, continuing to break the law. The general counsel did not go to the board of directors. The Treasury Department found out anyway and almost shut down the firm. The SEC began an enforcement action and suspended Salomon's three most senior bankers from the industry.[21] When the dust settled, top management was fired, board member Warren Buffett installed new management, and the firm was merged into Smith Barney.[22] Salomon Brothers, which for decades had been a gold-plated brand name in fixed income markets, was irreparably tarnished. The culture of the "big swinging dick" had swung back to knock one of Wall Street's premier investment banks off its pedestal. By the late 1990s, what remained of Salomon's investment banking business was, along with Phibro, merged into Sandy Weill's financial empire at Citigroup.[23]

And there the story continued. Citigroup's investment banking business has experienced significant financial and legal risk taking, including the conduct that led to the settlements discussed in chapter 1 of this book. Phibro's business also turned out to be as risky as its executive compensation was generous. By 2009, Phibro's compensation arrangement with its top executive, Andrew Hall, required the firm to pay him over $100 million in the year after Citigroup had gotten billions of federal bailout dollars. The embarrassment led Citigroup briefly to rethink limited liability. Citigroup for a time considered spinning off Phibro as a general partnership with Mr. Hall as managing partner. Citigroup, however, finally sold Phibro, along with Mr. Hall's bonus problem, to Occidental Petroleum.[24]

The history of Salomon Brothers and many other firms—including Lehman Brothers, which also switched from being a partnership to being a public company in the 1980s—suggests that when investment banks became public companies, they changed dramatically from what they had been as partnerships. Because so many other aspects of the business model changed, as discussed earlier in this chapter, one cannot definitively say that bankers were more "responsible" before this change than they are now. What it means to be an "investment banker" has changed over time, so such comparisons are of limited utility. Moral hazard and other perils, however, should be anticipated when unlimited liability is combined with bonuses based on current profits. Risky conduct in this environment was likely to come to pass, and it did.

This new moral hazard first affected the investment banks—such as Lehman Brothers—that had switched from partnership to corporate form. Later, however, it also became a problem for the large commercial banks that acquired investment banks after the demise of regulatory barriers between the industries (e.g., Citigroup's acquisition of Salomon Smith Barney in the 1990s) and then the commercial banks that acquired more investment banks in the wake of the 2008 financial crisis (e.g., Bank of America's acquisition of Merrill Lynch and JPMorgan's acquisition of Bear Stearns).

Bankers' Changing Relationship with Customers and Clients

Another fundamental change in investment banking has been the relationship between bankers and their customers. Customers are sold investment products by the bank and rely on the bank for good advice. Some of these customers are also clients who have hired the bank for a particular purpose such as asset management, underwriting securities, mergers and acquisitions, or structuring other transactions. (We discuss the difference between customers and clients in the terminology section of the introduction to this book.) Some of the reasons for the changes in banks' relationships with clients and other customers have already been discussed earlier in this chapter, including the decline of brokerage profits with the advent of negotiated commissions in 1975 and the decline of underwriting relationships and profits with the advent of shelf registration of new issuances of securities in 1981.

Some of this change was also cultural. Many of the "old line" relationships in investment banking, and between banks and their clients and other customers, were among persons from narrowly defined social and religious backgrounds who preferred to do business with each other. In the modern age, particularly after the 1960s, this mindset was viewed as morally objectionable, regardless of whatever value might be derived from bankers repeatedly interacting with their clients and customers in a wide range of settings (business, clubs, alumni organizations, and churches or temples). Expanding opportunities for a diverse group of people in investment banking and in business generally presumably required dismantling many of these old relationships.

In traditional investment banking, the business model assumed that revenue would come from repeat interaction with customers. In order for a bank to be successful, reputational capital was as important as financial capital. The people who ran investment banks understood that temptation to take advantage of customers for short-term gain was always present, but they made a concerted effort to control it. Henry Kaufman recalls the way this problem was handled at his firm:

> During one of our executive committee meetings back in the 1970s, a young trader interrupted the meeting that was then being held by Bill Salomon, the managing partner, and he gave him a slip informing him of a very large bond trade we had just completed with one of our institutional clients.
>
> Bill asked, "How much did we take out of the trade?"
>
> The young trader replied, "A point," meaning one percentage point.
>
> Bill then called in the partner in charge of transactions, who reaffirmed that the firm had made one point.
>
> Bill Salomon's admonition was brief and to the point. He said, "Salomon Brothers does not take such a profit." The bonds purchased were highly marketable, of high quality, and they were sold by an institution that was a valued client.
>
> He ordered the trading partner to return part of the profit to the institution. In addition, he told the trading partner that the participation in the profits of the firm for him was going to be reduced.
>
> The question then is: What prompted Bill Salomon to take this action in the 1970s? It was, among other things, to protect the relationship with an important institutional client. But it was also to ensure that this wouldn't happen in other transactions of this kind by the firm.[25]

The dispute William Salomon had with this trading partner was about an issue on which the law was neutral—the size of the profit Salomon took on a trade. Imagine his reaction if he had been told that the trader did something to cheat a customer that was in fact illegal. How often traders did something illegal, if they did so at all, when Salomon was head of the firm, is not known; the firm did, however, violate the law after he retired from the firm. Probably the most valuable business relationship Salomon Brothers had was with the U.S. Treasury, a relationship that was shattered by the Treasury bid scandal of 1991 discussed earlier in this chapter. Senior management, when told about the problem, didn't fix it and didn't disclose it. They didn't even tell the board of directors. They did not address the violation until they were caught and the Treasury Department almost shut the entire firm down.

Nearly twenty years later, in 2012, former Goldman Sachs vice president Greg Smith, whose departure from Goldman we discussed in chapter 1, described Goldman's proud history of serving clients for over one hundred years and what he claims to be the recent deterioration of its client relationships:

To put the problem in the simplest terms, the interests of the client continue to be sidelined in the way the firm operates and thinks about making money.

What are three quick ways to become a leader [at Goldman Sachs][?] a) Execute on the firm's "axes," which is Goldman-speak for persuading your clients to invest in the stocks or other products that we are trying to get rid of because they are not seen as having a lot of potential profit. b) "Hunt Elephants." In English: get your clients—some of whom are sophisticated, and some of whom aren't—to trade whatever will bring the biggest profit to Goldman. Call me old-fashioned, but I don't like selling my clients a product that is wrong for them. c) Find yourself sitting in a seat where your job is to trade any illiquid, opaque product with a three-letter acronym.

Today, many of these leaders display a Goldman Sachs culture quotient of exactly zero percent. I attend derivatives sales meetings where not one single minute is spent asking questions about how we can help clients. It's purely about how we can make the most possible money off of them. If you were an alien from Mars and sat in on one of these meetings, you would believe that a client's success or progress was not part of the thought process at all.

It makes me ill how callously people talk about ripping their clients off. Over the last 12 months I have seen five different managing directors refer to their own clients as "muppets," sometimes over internal e-mail . . .

It astounds me how little senior management gets a basic truth: If clients don't trust you they will eventually stop doing business with you. It doesn't matter how smart you are.[26]

Smith may or may not be right on this last point about the importance of trust to clients (he also may or may not be right in what he alleges about Goldman Sachs, although what he says echoes what some other observers have said about Goldman and other banks as well). As we discussed in the introduction, some accounts suggest that clients have been willing to accept untrustworthy behavior to get the smartest bankers. It's not clear whether the niche of "smart and trustworthy" is being sufficiently exploited. What is clear is that individual banker time horizons are far shorter than those of their banks. As banks have done progressively larger transactions, and as some bankers have become more mobile—moving from bank to bank rather than staying with the same bank for their whole careers—much has changed about bankers' relationships to their banks, and consequently, banks' relationships to their customers and clients. This is especially so for those bankers who in a good year may make enough to live on for the rest of their lives. A banker may be motivated to behave in a manner that might harm the bank's long-term reputation for integrity if doing so will yield the banker a sufficiently large short-term payout. If bonuses, and even continued employment, are based on the current year's bottom line, and the bottom line does not require a reputation for integrity, bankers may not do as much as they could to preserve that reputation.

Indeed, given present-day norms, a banker may not just benefit financially, he also may not suffer in terms of reputation from less than honest conduct. And the same may be true of the bank. Partners in the old investment banking partnerships might have thought about the firm's reputation for integrity because that is where their retirement income came from, but managing directors of incorporated banks have no such incentive. (Goldman calls its most senior managing directors "partners," but this is in name only; these partners have larger equity holdings in the firm than other managers, but they have no personal liability and the firm is governed as a corporation.) It may also be that what a bank's shareholders and management want is a reputation for "street smarts" rather than one for integrity. They might even consider a bank too concerned with integrity as somehow lacking in street smarts—as though having street smarts meant using them to make profits regardless of the cost to others.

Lloyd Blankfein, the CEO of Goldman Sachs, and his deputy at Goldman, Gary Cohn, had both previously worked for J. Aron and Company, a precious metals trading firm that had been acquired by Goldman Sachs. Blankfein once joked: "We didn't have the word 'client' or 'customer' at the old J. Aron. We had counterparties—and that's because we didn't know how to spell the word 'adversary.'"[27]

As discussed earlier in this chapter, unlike underwriting and brokerage, the proprietary trading business is not a customer-oriented business. Traders are more powerful at investment banks than they once were. When they move into leadership positions, these traders could change their personal priorities to suit the more customer-oriented areas of the investment banking business, but it appears that many of them have helped change their banks instead.

There are many other reasons investment banks' attitudes toward clients and other customers changed between the era of the old investment banking partnerships and the era that began with *Liar's Poker* in the 1980s and extended to the 2008 financial crisis and beyond. Part of the problem, discussed at the beginning of this chapter, was that investment banks made less money from traditional client and customer relationships, such as securities underwriting and brokerage services, and made more money in trading operations and then, later, in designing and selling exotic securities such as mortgage-backed securities. (*Liar's Poker* tells the story of how Louis Ranieri, who had worked in Salomon's mailroom, moved up the ranks of senior management in the 1980s when he designed and marketed some of the earliest mortgage-backed bonds.) Another part of the problem was the demise of the close-knit business and social organization that characterized the business for decades prior to the 1980s.

Many of the social and economic forces that used to temper investment banker behavior have disappeared. In his 2011 Carnegie Council speech, Henry Kaufman used the word "civility" to describe the relationships that bankers had with clients and with each other in an earlier era. This word "civility" connotes something more than the extended quid pro quo that is now often assumed to be at the heart of business deal making.

The Changing Aims of Business

Historical changes in the banking business also reflect a broader change in the objectives of businesses in general in the late twentieth century, in particular in public companies. As explained earlier in this chapter, by the 1980s most investment banks had become public companies; by the early 2000s, and particularly after 2008, many of these investment banks had merged into commercial bank holding companies such as Citigroup, Bank of America, and JPMorgan.

The reassessment of publicly held companies' business objectives goes back at least to the mid-1970s, when a lackluster stock market, disappointing business results, and increasing competition from Germany, Japan, and other countries led to soul searching by investors, business leaders, and academics concerned about the future competitiveness of U.S. business. Corporate executives' fixed pay and apparent pursuit of their own interests rather than those of their companies—by, for instance, supposedly pursuing acquisitions simply to form and lead larger conglomerates—led to a search for ways to better align executive incentives with the interests of company shareholders. Institutional investors increasingly sought to focus managers' attention as much as possible on earnings and stock price. To that end, compensation schemes shifted toward bonuses, stock, and stock options.

In principle, the approach seems sensible. Company executives are supposed to advance their companies' interests. Those interests include the interests of the companies' owners, the shareholders. Managers are not supposed to advance their own interests except insofar as doing so advances their companies' interests. But the emphasis on shareholder value has not been wholly good and, in some respects, it has been harmful.[28]

First, the emphasis on shareholder value has deemphasized the importance of other constituencies, particularly customers and clients (a topic discussed above), creditors (another topic discussed above in the context of limited liability), and society as a whole. Managers who believe themselves strictly accountable only to shareholders often feel that they do not need to consider, and perhaps even should not consider, these other interests as well. For example, excessive leverage (high debt load) can be used to dramatically increase profits and stock price if things go well and may be favored by diversified shareholders who believe that they are insulated against risk because they invest in so many companies. Creditors, however, do not share much of the upside of this risk and are more likely to suffer the downside than if the company were more conservatively managed; employees also do not fare well if their company becomes insolvent. Creditors may try to protect themselves by withholding credit or raising the cost of borrowing for overleveraged borrowers, but this creates an incentive for borrowers' managers to find ways to hide the amount of debt they are incurring.

Second, the way in which shareholder value is measured—both reported earnings and stock price—has led to other difficulties. The measures are objective ones that allow for easy comparability, but few measures, including "objective" ones, are invulnerable to manipulation. This is as true for test results reported by school districts subject to objectives measures of success, such as the No Child Left Behind Act, as it is for financial results reported by public companies. The obvious ways to measure shareholder value are accounting results and stock prices. Financial maneuvering of the sort we describe in this book is directed at both of these measures. Indeed, some observers claim that the move toward emphasizing shareholder value was promoted by self-interested actors, notably institutional fund managers, who are compensated based on their funds' performance (e.g., stock prices in the portfolio) and who wanted to motivate company executives to engage in maneuvering of precisely this type to increase their companies' stock prices.[29] Increases not based on fundamentals presumably can't be sustained in the long or even moderate term, but they can be sustained long enough to benefit people with shorter time horizons.

Third, another important factor was the increasing role and professionalization of companies' chief financial officers (CFOs), whose work became important when corporate officers and directors focused more on earnings, cash flow, debt to equity ratios, and other reported metrics.[30]

In earlier times, many companies did not have a CFO and, instead, relegated accounting to back office personnel. By the 1960s, however, having a CFO became increasingly popular.[31] Chief financial officers focused on minimizing the cost of capital and on preparing financial statements, but sometimes they worked on developing methods for making financial statements meet investor expectations, management projections, or both.

Given the increased pressure to maximize shareholder value, companies became more focused on improving their financial appearance. Bankers could help, sometimes with techniques that stretched accounting rules to (and in some cases beyond) their limits. Meanwhile, a stylized dance developed between companies and securities analysts, in which companies gave analysts information by which the analysts could make predictions.[32] Given all the techniques available and accepted by which earnings could be manipulated, analysts came to expect that companies would somehow manage to "earn" what the analysts had predicted. If a company missed the analyst's prediction, even by a few pennies a share, its stock could plummet on the theory that, given the techniques available to manage earnings, its results must be truly catastrophic. Once this kind of interaction becomes the norm, it is difficult for the cycle of expectations and reactions to change.[33]

In this environment there was more demand for financial maneuvering from highly skilled professionals—their jobs apparently included creating good numbers for companies, even if doing so meant "creativity" in the euphemistic sense. Some banks responded by meeting the demand. And, the skills and ethos at issue also permeated some of these banks' own operations: the professionalization of financial maneuvering led to some banks using the techniques for their own purposes, perhaps regulatory or contractual, or simply to show markets how well they were doing. As these banks were gaming their results and those of their clients, individual bankers were doing the same, gaming their results to obtain the highest possible bonuses from their employers.

3 EXPLAINING BANKER BEHAVIOR

Addressing the problem of banker behavior requires an account of why bankers did what they did and what might cause them to behave differently. We reject a simple story, in which people seek the most money they can regardless of the costs to others, in favor of a more complex one in which the history and present-day culture of banking determine what behavior is rewarded, accepted, or punished. Much of this chapter applies to bankers generally; some of it, however, is particularly focused on an important subset of bankers, those who make the most money and work the longest hours in the largest national and international banks.

The concept of culture in this context is well captured in the 2013 *Salz Review*, the independent review of Barclays's business practices discussed earlier in this book. The review characterizes culture in "an organisational context" as encompassing practices, "the acts or the way things are done," as well as values, "the judgments about the way things should be done."[1] It discusses at length the culture that yielded the LIBOR manipulations and other problematic banker behavior; it also discusses the culture that Barclays should seek to develop and instill to avoid such behavior in the future and to encourage more desirable behavior.

In this chapter, we discuss the culture in some banks that led up to the 2008 crisis, and that persists in some banks today. We consider a more constructive bank culture in chapter 6. (As pointed out in the introduction and in chapter 2, to their credit, some banks, such as Barclays, seem to be moving in this direction.)

An effective solution to problematic behavior in the banking industry will directly affect monetary incentives. But it will also need to affect culture: how banking is viewed as a career and who it attracts, what bankers are proud of doing and what they are ashamed of doing, how bankers influence each other within their institutions, and what values are considered important, both within the industry and in the broader society.

Bankers act as they do because they are rewarded for doing so. Those rewards include money, but they also include status, improved professional prospects, and presumably, a sense of pride and achievement.

What is rewarded is often what should be rewarded: genuinely good results of some sort, such as a truly profitable transaction or trade. But sometimes, what is rewarded reflects problematic behavior. The results yielding a bonus might be fleeting, timed precisely to coincide with the measurement period. The results are sometimes at a customer's expense, such as where a bank makes a big profit by selling a customer an unsuitable investment—sometimes an investment that the bank itself made and wishes to dispose of. Results that yield bonuses also might reflect creation of a transaction structure or other mechanism designed to help clients do end runs around regulation, accounting rules, or contractual covenants. A culture, or ethos, has developed in which these and other problematic "results" are aggressively pursued, and societal and other constraints that might have hindered that pursuit are muted. Some bankers become involved in a competition not just for money, which they might in theory get enough of, but also, or instead, for accomplishment or status vis-à-vis their peers—"points." In the broader society, too, problematic banker behavior is not sufficiently discouraged and, indeed, is in many instances lauded.

We describe in this chapter the arena in which some bankers have competed and the mechanisms that have permitted and encouraged the competition. This chapter describes as well how some bankers have reacted when difficulties arose. The difficulties sometimes related to an individual banker, such as when his trades lost money, and sometimes they related to more than one banker or even the bank itself, such as when the bank's financial condition was deteriorating. The ethos described here has not discouraged, and in some instances has encouraged, bad reactions, like doubling down on risk, foisting bad investments on customers, and lying about the risk one has taken. The result can be to exacerbate the problem, sometimes calamitously so.

The "banker behavior" described here is of course not the behavior of all bankers; while some banker behavior is problematic, clearly not all (or even most) of it is. But there is enough problematic behavior that it cannot simply be regarded as anomalous, with the bankers engaged in the behavior characterized as outliers. When a former senior banker at Credit Suisse, Kareem Serageldin, was sentenced for fraudulently marking up bond prices, "Judge Hellerstein showed mercy [sentencing him to thirty months in jail, far less time than the five years suggested by advisory sentencing guidelines], in part because of what he said was a toxic culture at Credit Suisse and its rivals. 'He was in a place where there was a climate for him to do what he did,' the judge said. 'It was a small piece of an overall evil climate inside that bank and many other banks.'"[2] In a recent speech, Dan Tarullo, a governor of the Federal Reserve Board of Governors said: "The hypothesis that this [bad behavior that led to the 2008 crisis] is all the result of 'a few bad apples,' an explanation I heard with exasperating frequency a year or two ago, has I think given way to a realization within many large financial firms that they have not taken steps sufficient to ensure that the activities of their employees remain within the law and, more broadly, accord with the values of probity, customer service, and ethical conduct that most of them espouse on their websites and in their television commercials."[3]

A simple account of human motivation underlies many accounts of banker behavior: it's all about the money and, ultimately, what the money can buy. But motivation is complex, and goes well beyond money, even a more complicated view of money. Indeed, the pursuit of money for its own sake is not likely to be a sufficient explanation, especially for the many bankers whose income or assets are already quite high. Something else—status, which is largely conferred by others—is at issue.

Many bankers (and many other people) want status. Status is associated with money. But it is also associated with doing better than one's peers, at whatever the benchmarks for achievement are deemed to be. Having good professional prospects, not just within the bank but within other firms in the industry, also bestows status. Besides the external rewards, there are internal analogues, including being pleased at one's accomplishments and taking pride in one's skills.

Banking culture has provided all of these rewards for behavior that is in some cases harmful to particular banks, the banking industry, or even the society as a whole. Because this behavior is rewarded, the result is more of it—and promotion of the underlying ethos, one that encourages and to some extent glorifies narrow material self-interest, including craft at its advancement. A solution needs to reduce simple money rewards to the harmful behavior. But it should also work to change this ethos in banking and hence change the way factors other than money affect what bankers think and do.

The rewards offered by money are not merely what the money can buy. Money can buy more possessions, more leisure time, and less financial worry about the future. But for many high earners, including many senior bankers at the highest paying financial institutions, there's not much that they can't already buy. They can't trade off some of their money for leisure given what their jobs require—they already have the possibility of complete leisure (never working again) and they don't take it. And finally, they also have few if any financial worries about the future. They might seem to have reached a point where the utility of more money would be declining—more money wouldn't be worth much, if anything, to them. But we still observe many such people pursuing more money. Others who pursue more money may not be in a position to retire for life, but do not seem to value the money for its ability to provide them with increased material comforts. The pursuit of more money under these circumstances must be serving some other purpose, such as conferring status points.

People want status for both external and internal reasons. What determines the availability and amount of status points is not internal—status is conferred by others.[4] And what confers status is contingent, and may change over time. Indeed, while pursuit of supposed improvements in standard of living is based on love for things anointed (and priced) as the finer things in life, much of what people enjoy, particularly people who already have a lot of material possessions, is determined through a social process.[5] Even something as purportedly unmediated as a person's musical taste is highly influenced by what the person thinks others like.[6]

Money can also act like a drug, offering internal rewards. Extending the analogy, people may be or become addicted to getting money, increasingly needing more of it to get the same psychological effect.[7]

A banker will do what he believes will yield the highest rewards for him, both monetary and nonmonetary. While some components of a banker's potential monetary rewards can be computed mechanically—the banker's salary is set at some amount, and some of his bonus may be payable based on a mechanical formula—other components may turn on the banker's judgment of how what he does will turn out and, more generally, how others will appraise him. A banker may know that his bonus will be based in part on the success of a particular transaction; he may, or may not, correctly estimate the prospects for success. The same can be said about rewards such as promotions. The banker may know, or think it likely, that doing x volume of deals will make a promotion more likely. The banker will want to do what he thinks his bank will reward.

A banker will also assess the nonmonetary social rewards or status points available to him. The banker may have an assessment, correct or not, as to social rewards associated with particular behavior—"If I figure out a great way for company X to get money that doesn't count as debt, my colleagues will be impressed. If I can sell the 'dog' deal and help us reduce our exposure to subprime mortgages, my colleagues will think I can sell anything." (Or, more uncontroversially, "If I land the IPO business for the next hot issue, I will be considered a big hero.")

But the availability of social rewards is highly contingent on history— on a particular state of affairs in a particular context at a particular point in time. More money may command status, though in some contexts and fields it does not. The ability to "sell anything" may command status, or it may not. Aggressive business practices may be reviled by the greater society or some important constituency of it, they may be admired, or somewhere in between. In banking, participation in activities in which the bank might be acting in conflict with its clients and other customers, or looking out for itself far more than it looked out for them, has apparently been accepted and at times rewarded. In chapter 1, we discussed allegations about Goldman's efforts to foist CDOs onto less sophisticated clients and customers; we included a passage from the *Levin-Coburn Report* on Goldman Sachs's role in the financial crisis in which a senior Goldman banker suggests trying to motivate salespeople to sell a low-quality deal by giving them "ginormous" sales credits, only to find out that such an offer had already been made to the salespeople.[8] A single-minded focus on profits, even gained at the expense of customers, could and apparently did become accepted, and perhaps even became the norm. The *Salz Review* says of Barclays that "the culture that emerged tended to favour transactions over relationships, the short term over sustainability, and financial over other business purposes."[9]

The discussion above has mainly concerned external rewards, in the form of money, improved prospects, or esteem. It touched as well on internal rewards, which are also very important. The availability of internal rewards turns on a banker's worldview, identity, and values. A banker might laud his own cleverness for designing a transaction structure that helps him maximize his compensation by allowing him to record expected future gains in the present. He might think: "If I come up with techniques that 'minimize' debt, or design and execute a transaction by which my bank can sell bad assets to its clients at premium prices, I am clever and am doing a good job." The banker may think of himself as someone who can sell anything to anyone, no matter how bad it is—he may have a "salesman" identity. Insofar as he might otherwise feel internally conflicted about selling "dog" securities, he could, perversely, take comfort in the fact that the conflicts were revealed in the disclosure documents.[10]

The banker's internal rewards may, or may not, track the external rewards. A banker may experience with pride his craft at maneuvering around rules, or he may find the fact that his job expects him to do this a cost. He may not focus on third parties adversely affected by his actions, or he may focus on it but consider it irrelevant. He may even take pride in it, an example being the infamous "Grandma Millie" incident involving traders at Enron: the traders gloated that the energy bill of a hypothetical grandmother, Grandma Millie, had gone up because of their manipulation of California energy prices.

Many aspects of a banker's worldview, values, and temperament affect his overall assessment of the benefits and costs of his job. A banker might think business ought to be conducted in accordance with a strong Golden Rule, with bankers looking out for all of their customers, especially if they think their customers may not be doing a good enough job of looking after themselves. Alternatively, a banker might be a strong believer in the principle of caveat emptor: he may think, perhaps genuinely or perhaps self-servingly, that those with whom he has business dealings should be looking out for themselves and if they don't, they deserve what they get. A banker may also focus on serving a client, doing what might benefit the client even if there are significant costs to others, including his own employer. Stated differently, the banker may have some of the "zealous advocate" ethos that sometimes leads lawyers to do fairly extreme things on their clients' behalf. This may be part of the explanation for why banks structured synthetic CDOs that offered their favored clients an opportunity to short subprime mortgage securities, even though the transactions also required sales to apparently less-favored clients or customers who would lose a great deal of money.

Indeed, becoming caught up in the pursuit of success in banking may have made the effects on third parties, such as the citizens of Jefferson County or people investing with the investment managers who bought synthetic CDOs, seem remote indeed. In a well-known *Star Trek* episode, a war has been going on for hundreds of years, killing many people, because the leaders of the respective countries are conducting warfare by pushing buttons. Real people are being killed as a result of the button pushes, but the leaders are not seeing casualties in any visceral way. Captain Kirk is able to stop the war quickly by getting the leaders to face the specter of actual combat.[11] A banker may deal largely with his colleagues, customers who are sophisticated investors and may be investing for other people, and with computer screens: more remote third parties may never enter into his consciousness at all.

The intensity of the work schedule and work environment is another aspect of bankers' lives that could skew their perspective.[12] Being so thoroughly in the bank environment may make bankers more apt to dehumanize "more distant others," such as third parties affected by what they do as bankers.[13] Bankers' assessment of costs and benefits may also be affected by the pace of their professional lives and the short time frame they have to make many decisions. The fast-paced work environment can lead to "automatic egocentrism," in which a person automatically—almost reflexively—takes a narrow self-centered perspective into account to the exclusion of other considerations.[14]

Going further, that banking involves constant reminders of money may make bankers be less inclined to focus on the effect of their actions even on people in closer proximity. Recent research demonstrates a connection between money and self-sufficiency: people reminded of money were more likely to focus on their own individual efforts and interests, be less sensitive to the needs of others, and be less inclined to see things from others' perspectives.[15] Stated more broadly, a set of values and goals, a mindset supporting those values and goals, and various other aspects of present-day banking, may have made bankers more inclined to appreciate the rewards present-day banking offers and blunted their assessments of what they might otherwise have experienced as costs.

That banking involves constant reminders of money also may weaken "the pull of morality," perhaps making some bankers more inclined to be unethical.[16] Some recent research suggests that banker identity itself encourages dishonesty. In an experiment involving employees of a large international bank, the experimenters found evidence that when "their professional identities as bank employees [was] rendered salient to them" (they were asked questions about their professional background in the banking industry), more of them became dishonest, cheating in reporting the results of coin tosses so as to increase their monetary payoffs than was the case with people from various other professions—making those other professional identities salient did not increase dishonesty. The experimenters also found that bankers whose banker identity had been made salient to them—and bankers most likely to have cheated—were more apt to agree that social status was "primarily determined by financial success."[17]

Also affecting a banker's internal rewards is the banker's view as to whether he is in a meritocracy.[18] Many bankers have very good quantitative and technical skills—there is a certain mystique about such skills, a mystique that the banker may internalize. The banker may think the bank's meritocracy saves the industry from dependence on the class- and ethnic-based social connections that, as discussed in the previous chapter, used to be so important for advancement: industry norms that receded decades ago can still be a convenient straw man. In this regard, Goldman Sachs CEO Lloyd Blankfein stated: "When you're wrestling with the market, the market doesn't care whether you're black or white, tall or short, gay or straight. . . . I always thought that the best forum for democracy and meritocracy was a trading room floor."[19] The narrative is of an ideological struggle between two diametrically opposed views of the world, one based on entrenched privilege and the other on merit, where merit has prevailed.

Bankers may also have bought into a broader worldview in which success consists of jumping through hoops of alignable metrics, scales on which people are easily compared and ranked—the best grades, entry into the best schools, obtaining a job at the most prestigious firm, getting the quickest promotion and the biggest bonus.[20] Bankers may have come of age jumping through these hoops, initially created and held out by others; this may have logistically crowded out consideration of their own values, taking all the conceptual "room" available for such consideration. The crowding out is logistical in two distinct senses. The competition with other highly motivated and talented people takes considerable time: there may be little time to do anything else. Indeed, there is some evidence that people can get into a mode in which they mindlessly accumulate, working until they are tired (probably exhausted), beyond the point when they have earned "enough."[21] As important, the worldview itself crowds out alternatives. When a person is involved in hoop jumping, he presumably believes in it as an endeavor or, at least, does not actively question it. The ethos is on vivid display at those youth sporting events at which parents and coaches stress the importance of winning above all else, and in various other examples of overaggressive parenting.[22] Similarly, bankers' competition over progressively larger pay packages can crowd out morality.[23]

Consider the activities of Kareem Serageldin, mentioned at the beginning of this chapter, who has gone to jail in connection with his conduct in mismarking subprime securities, and some of his subordinates. The SEC and the U.S. Attorney alleged that in late 2007, as the prices of mortgage-backed securities were plummeting, Serageldin, the global head of structured credit trading at Credit Suisse, together with his subordinate, David Higgs, the global head of hedge trading, and two traders reporting to Higgs, Salmaan Siddiqui and Faisal Siddiqui, marked unprofitable trades as though they were profitable. They did this to avoid recording losses — to preserve their bonuses. Serageldin was also trying to preserve his prospects for a promotion.[24]

For some bankers, crowding out may play another important role. They may narrowly focus on maneuvering around regulations, formulas or agreements, operating as though everything that is not prohibited is permitted. This mindset can displace any deeper assessment they might make as to what they are doing. It can allow them simply to focus on the craft of maneuvering to a particular end and assessing their success based on how well they achieve that end, without regard to whether the maneuvering may have violated the spirit of the regulation, formula, or agreement at issue. Indeed, where the maneuvering is to get around legal rules, the rules might work perversely, perhaps allowing a banker to assume that others — here, rule makers — have permitted and found legitimate whatever was not exactly and precisely prohibited. New rules to limit a particular result might be viewed as a challenge to be surmounted — to achieve the desired result notwithstanding the rule.[25]

Going further, this mindset, and indeed, many other features of banking, serve to encourage what has been called a "promotion focus" over a "prevention focus."[26] "A promotion focus emphasizes hopes, accomplishments, and advancement needs." By contrast, "a prevention focus emphasizes safety, responsibility, and security needs."[27] The many stories of how banks marginalize their risk management departments support the idea that the promotion focus is encouraged and the prevention focus is discouraged. There is some malleability in the respective focuses, although people often have tendencies in one direction or the other. It seems likely that, in banks, those with a promotion focus have dominated and that many aspects of banking culture have encouraged that focus even in people with tendencies more toward a prevention focus.

The preceding discussion speaks principally of a banker's own assessments, but of course, a banker's assessments are not made in isolation. As noted above, a group of bankers working together on designing or selling a transaction may work such long hours that they rarely see their families. To each banker, the other bankers may therefore be his most important reference group. The bankers may be able to convince each other, and hence themselves, that the behavior they are engaging in is appropriate.[28] The effect is to encourage a dynamic in which the benefits seem larger and the costs seem smaller. The bankers in a particular unit of a bank may collectively focus on keeping their heads above water on a day-to-day basis, having very little time to reflect. These group dynamics, together with related individual dynamics, may keep far from bankers' consciousness the effects of what they are doing on third parties, such as those whose money was being invested by the money managers to whom they sold toxic investment products. The increasing specialization in banking (a subject discussed in chapter 2 of this book) as well as job insecurity (another subject discussed in chapter 2) also may hinder a banker or a group of bankers from seeing "the big picture" — the aggregate effect of the activity in which they are playing a small part.[29]

There are thus many possible rewards from the problematic behavior of some bankers described in chapter 1 of this book. Bankers may get money (that they may value for what they can do with it, for the status it brings them, or because it makes them feel successful, or some combination of these things); they may get better professional prospects; they may get status among their peers or the greater society (perhaps not for the behavior, but for their seniority or power or title); they may get status from crafting an ingenious instrument, fulfilling client needs, or outsmarting the system; and they may get status from successful risk taking. They may even get status from being indifferent to or causing suffering among clients or other customers (including by selling them unsuitable investments) or third parties. They may get pleasure from some or all of these things as well. Different bankers will assess the value of these rewards differently, and many of them will also be affected by the way in which their peers assess that value. Indeed, for some bankers, valuing these types of rewards may come easily and might reflect previously held values, whereas for other bankers, valuing such rewards may require some combination of self-serving rationalizations and peer influence. A former Lehman banker writes:

> The part of Wall Street that I worked in was simply transferring wealth from the less sophisticated investors, often teachers' pension funds and factory workers' retirement accounts, to the more sophisticated investors that call themselves proprietary trading desks and hedge funds. Of course, the traders had all sorts of excuses and jargon to deal with this truth. 'Oh no,' they would say, 'We are important providers of liquidity that create stable financial markets. We're a crucial part of a system. And besides, if we don't do it, someone else will.' These are the lies that people tell themselves so that they can buy larger homes.[30]

A banker will also assess the costs from the same behavior, costs the banker expects to incur or thinks it possible if not likely that he will incur. Some of these costs were discussed above. They might include potential financial losses for the bank (or himself) from taking too much financial risk or legal risk, potential loss of a client or other customer or even a friend for selling him an unsuitable investment, or a feeling that he has compromised his values or violated central tenets of his religious faith. What influences a banker's assessment of costs? As with the rewards from behavior, culture is one factor, mediated by the banker's own attributes.

People assess rewards and costs of behavior differently. That being said, people who work together influence each other and play an important role in determining who thrives in their profession. Many, and probably most, of those who stay in banking presumably assess the rewards as high, exceeding the costs.

One particularly important difference influencing assessments relates to risk. People vary enormously in their attitudes toward risk. Some people get pleasure from risk, some see risk as a psychologically painful experience, and some are in the middle.[31] Thus, different people are likely to respond differently if offered a job in which they could make or lose significant amounts of money every day, such as being a trader controlling a large fund at an investment bank (or a hedge fund). Some people would be sanguine about the prospect. Others might take the job but then seek out ways to minimize their risk. Some people might be horrified and refuse the job. Yet other people might be delighted at the chance to risk so much money.

Risk taking can be a means to an end (money, status points, or both). It can also be an end in itself. The first perspective has been called instrumental risk taking, and the latter perspective has been called stimulative risk taking.[32] Those who see risk only instrumentally may be better at risk assessment than those who either are pure stimulative risk takers or are both instrumental and stimulative risk takers. Stimulative risk takers may assess risk less clearly initially and update their assessments less clearly as well—they may get carried away, for instance, panicking at losses and "doubling down." Stimulative risk takers may be particularly inclined to underestimate risk at the outset, so as to better justify taking it.[33] Some, perhaps even many, modern bankers seem to be stimulative risk takers, whether or not they are also instrumental risk takers. This may help explain why they took (usually on behalf of their banks) the types of ill-advised risks discussed in chapter 1. Indeed, this may also help explain why they encouraged their customers and clients to do so as well. Discussions in academic literature and the popular press of risk takers of different sorts, as well as people's "risk preferences," generally refer to a person's view of his own risk taking, where the risks are being taken on his own behalf. The behavior with which this book is concerned encompasses as well a person's involvement in others' risk taking—in particular, a banker's involvement in having his bank take risky positions and in selling risky financial instruments to clients and other customers. Being in proximity to big risks being taken is something some people are drawn to—and others run away from.[34] Stimulative risk takers should be inclined to run toward it.[35]

Besides the person's general attitude toward risk, his attitude toward risk in a particular instance may be influenced by the worst-case scenario to him: might the risk, if it failed, appreciably impair his quality of life? In this regard, people's attitudes toward risk may be affected not just by how much they might lose but also by what they might keep after a possible loss.[36] For instance, if they will keep enough to retain their standard of living or their social standing, they may be relatively sanguine about even extremely large losses. Also, people's attitudes about risk may be different depending on how what they are risking was acquired: was the money at stake inherited, was it earned by hard work over a long period of time, or was it recently acquired by taking similar risks? A person winning a certain amount in a casino may be more inclined to make a bet with that money—"house money"—than with money in his savings account accumulated over several years.[37] Indeed, the loss of "house money" may be experienced as far less costly than the loss of one's "own" money. Insofar as bankers, especially very senior bankers, have a great deal of money that they experience as house money, such as large shareholdings in their banks awarded to them as part of their compensation, they may be quite sanguine about having their banks take big risks that could adversely affect others, notably the banks' own shareholders and creditors.

Moreover, bankers' attitudes toward risk also may reflect whether they are in a "loss frame," choosing among negative outcomes. Research indicates that people who find themselves in losing situations are inclined to take greater risks, doubling down and risking much greater losses in the hope of avoiding what seems like a sure loss.[38] Where a banker has already incurred losses and fears detection, he is in a "loss frame." A recent example of this type of behavior, in which the trader keeps placing larger and larger bets in hopes of digging himself out of his loss "hole," eventually being discovered after enormous losses, is JP Morgan's London Whale trades; a less recent example, from 1995, is that of star trader Nick Leeson, who bankrupted Barings Bank, a bank founded in 1762, having lost one billion dollars.[39] Lehman Brothers' Repo 105 can be seen in this light too: bankers, aware that their bank's financial condition was deteriorating, making a desperate and ultimately futile attempt to prevent the truth from becoming known. Whether the loss frame manifests itself in the psychology of desperate traders or the psychology underlying a complex cover up, decision makers sometimes incur extraordinary financial, legal, and ethical risks because they are not willing to accept modest losses, embarrassment, or other consequences of earlier poor decisions.[40]

Physiology may contribute to the problematic outcomes of bankers in loss frames. People in the midst of huge losses may have physiological reactions that lead them to behave in less than ideal ways.[41] The trader-turned-neuroscientist John Coates, of Cambridge University, argues in his recent book, *The Hour between Dog and Wolf*, that

recent advances in neuroscience and physiology have shown that when we take risks, including financial risk, we do a lot more than just think about it. We prepare for it physically. Our bodies, expecting action, switch on an emergency network of physiological circuitry, and the resulting surge in electrical and chemical activity feeds back on the brain, affecting the way it thinks. In this way body and brain twine as a single entity, united in the face of challenge. Normally this fusion of body and brain provides us with the fast reactions and gut feelings we need for successful risk-taking. But under some circumstances the chemical surges can overwhelm us; and when this happens to traders and investors they come to suffer an irrational exuberance or pessimism that can destabilize the financial markets and wreak havoc on the wider economy.[42]

A press account about Kweku Adoboli, the UBS rogue trader who in 2011 lost $2.3 billion and was given a seven-year jail sentence after his conviction for fraud, provides a data point supporting Coates's argument.[43] After extreme pressure from his colleagues, Adoboli changed from holding short positions to long positions. Immediately after this change, the market started declining. He described losing control, noting that it led to "an increasing number of breaks (accounting problems), a more frantic trading activity, a less controlled decision-making process."

Later that month, as losses mounted in a volatile market, Adoboli re-called that exhaustion and stress levels reached such a peak that it caused him to briefly break up with his long-term girlfriend.

He said that on the evening of July 23 [2011] the couple had been sup-posed to go out for dinner but he found himself unable to talk to her.

"I went a bit catatonic. I was curled up on my bed. She was asking me what was wrong. I just couldn't explain," he said.[44]

This suggests that the "circumstances" Coates is talking about are to be avoided if at all possible, certainly with respect to people whose actions can have broad effects: what triggers the cycle is trading, with its enor-mous and immediate gains and losses. Steps to limit the magnitude and importance of trading (including perhaps some of the measures suggested in chapters 5 and 6 of this book) might dampen the cycles.

Finally, assessments of risk among a group of people, such as bankers, can change over time, depending on who is in that group, how they influ-ence each other, and the incentives offered to members of the group indi-vidually and collectively to assess risk in a certain way. A financial jour-nalist, Nick Dunbar, observed that, "for most of its history, our financial system was built on the stolid, cautious decisions of bankers, the men who hate to lose." But more recently, "men who love to win," "came to funda-mentally change not just the practices of a financial system that had been in place for centuries, but its very DNA."[45]

A more common but related observation made by several recent com-mentators is that "banking used to be boring."[46] Dunbar's account de-scribes how bankers' attitudes toward risk have changed. Many in the pre-vious generation of bankers, those who hated to lose, didn't like risk. The present generation, those who love to win (or those heavily influenced by them), like risk quite a bit. To return to terminology used above, bankers generally used to have a prevention focus; they now frequently have a pro-motion focus. These observations suggest that bankers overall assess the rewards and the costs of risk taking differently than they used to. Banks are probably attracting different sorts of people. And many people within banking, whatever they were like before they became bankers, have or are adopting the now-prevailing ethos. How much that ethos has changed again since the 2008 financial crisis—some might argue toward more prevention—has yet to be seen. The many post-2008 examples in chapter 1, however, show that a promotion focus is still widespread.

In summary, a banker's assessment of costs and benefits of conduct is importantly contingent. It is contingent on the individual banker, his co-workers, the bank in which he works, and the ethos of the industry and of the society as a whole. Many people, including many bankers, would not sell unsuitable financial products or craft end runs around rules and regulation for the amounts paid to bankers who do these things—or even for considerably more money. Some people are more inclined to do such things than others, but social forces also make a big difference.

These different assessments of rewards and costs of behavior are well illustrated by two of the examples discussed in chapter 1. One is the Greek cross-currency swaps. Greece needed to conceal its debt so that it would not incur penalties under the Maastricht Treaty, a treaty that restricted debt levels of countries adopting the Euro. Imagine the mindset of a banker tasked with this assignment. Perhaps he is proud that he can help the client. But what about the effect on others? And what about the fact that the client is trying to do end runs around regulation and is paying a great deal of money to do so when its financial condition is already bad? The worldview in which bankers "rationally" regard this situation purely and narrowly instrumentally, the banker thinking he will get a nice bonus, and Greece will avoid the penalties that could be assessed for violating the treaty, has no privileged claim to legitimacy or truth: "rationality" does not consist in advancing narrow material self-interest without regard to the broader consequences. Maybe the result of the Greek swap is that people are fooled into thinking Greece has less debt—maybe (and apparently, for many people) not. The latter is the better case scenario, but it still depicts the banker as subverting rules designed for legitimate purposes. The trajectory by which a junior banker becomes the kind of banker who helps his client subvert regulations and takes pride in his cleverness at doing so is disturbing, and certainly not inexorable or inevitable.

Another example is the alleged attempts to market low-quality CDO tranches to dupes, as discussed in chapter 1, and even, in some cases, taking delight in dupes being dupes. Consider in this regard former Goldman banker Greg Smith's claim that Goldman bankers in England secretly called their clients muppets, which, in English slang, means dupes. Frank

Partnoy, a banker-turned-academic, sounded almost incredulous when interviewed about this. His incredulity was not about how callous the bankers sounded; rather, it was about how much more callous he was used to them sounding. He recalled that bankers used to talk about "ripping clients' faces off," meaning making high fees selling clients something the clients did not understand.[47] This also is not a "natural" or "inevitable" ethos, but it was apparently rather more common than it should have been—and than was good for society.

PART II Solutions

4 LAW AND ITS LIMITS

Bankers' conduct in the U.S. has been regulated at the federal and state levels for a long time. In response to the stock market crash and banking collapse of 1929 and the early 1930s, Congress passed the federal securities laws in 1933 and 1934. In response to Enron, Worldcom, and other scandals, Congress passed the Sarbanes-Oxley Act of 2002, presumably to better assure corporate compliance with the securities laws. In response to the financial crisis of 2008, the Dodd-Frank Act of 2010, with its many hundreds of pages of law and thousands of pages of regulation, was enacted. Still, the problems continue. Other countries, particularly in the European Union, have adopted their own laws and regulations to address the causes and consequences of misconduct within the banking industry. In a global economy, sometimes several countries' laws apply to a bank or its financial transactions. Sometimes it is clear which laws apply, but sometimes it is not clear, and sometimes, particularly when transactions are moved off shore, it may appear that few if any laws apply.

Governments will no doubt continue to modify existing laws and regulations and promulgate new laws and regulations to address these problems. Many of these laws can accomplish a useful purpose. But regulatory solutions alone will not be sufficient to change bankers' behavior. Regulatory solutions mostly directed at banking institutions, rather than at individual bankers, are particularly unlikely to achieve the desired result.[1]

In this chapter, we explain some of the reasons why the law is limited in what it can accomplish. An analogy with the tax system illustrates one reason why this is so. Some—perhaps many—sophisticated taxpayers and their advisers expend significant resources to pay the least tax possible, using strategies that adhere to the letter of particular regulations while violating the spirit. "Well"-advised taxpayers reduce their tax liability considerably, below what the law intends them to pay. Tax advisers get internal and external rewards from coming up with the best strategies to avoid tax. The history of tax regulation is a history of approaches to this problem.

There are tangible rewards in paying less tax, and prevailing norms do not penalize, and may even celebrate, clever ways of achieving this result—of staying one step ahead of the regulators and using other "minimal compliance" strategies to make colorable arguments that justly earn the epithet "legalistic." Indeed, for some taxpayers, and particularly for tax advisers, both lawyers and accountants, the pursuit of tax loopholes may become an end in itself, even apart from the saved tax. They may view tax as a complex game, like chess, affording them the personal and perhaps professional satisfaction of having "checkmated" the Internal Revenue Service. A similar dynamic was described in the previous chapter with respect to some aspects of banking, especially financial maneuvering and, more broadly, bankers' attempts to minimize legal constraints that might limit banks' ability to make profits. Indeed, bankers and banks have both the ability and the incentive to minimize such constraints, as this chapter discusses. And there are many other reasons to suppose law's ability to deal with the problem of banker behavior is limited. Law can do considerable good— but more than law is needed.

Many of the specific examples discussed in this chapter involve regulations in the United States. The challenges discussed below, however, are also likely to arise, and in some instances have already arisen, with respect to regulation in Europe, Asia, and elsewhere.

Banks versus Regulators

It is difficult for regulators to control bank and banker behavior. Below we discuss reasons why this is so.

Resources

Bankers usually have far more resources to figure out both how to comply minimally or only facially with regulations and how to complicate regulatory efforts to get them to comply more maximally. Regulators often lack the resources to match the efforts of regulated industry.

Resources for detection of violations and enforcement are usually scarce relative to the enormous size of the playing field that most regulators are expected to cover. Regulators have to choose when to investigate alleged misconduct further and when to drop an investigation and move on to something else. Regulators have to choose when to litigate enforcement cases and when to settle those cases. It is easy for observers to criticize regulators for doing too little, as members of Congress did in a May 2012 hearing in which they criticized the SEC's willingness to make settlements with Citigroup and other financial institutions that did not require the institutions to admit fault. But regulators often make the best judgment calls they can with the resources available to them. (In this regard, several witnesses at the hearing, including one of the authors of this book, Richard Painter, testified that increasing the SEC's enforcement budget would be advisable.)

Most regulators have a lot more to do than policing the conduct of large banks. Bank regulators also have small and midsized banks to supervise, a process that is extremely time-consuming. Securities regulators are searching for securities violations perpetrated all over the country by promoters other than banks. Many of these promoters are relatively unsophisticated and their violations easy to detect and prosecute, yet following through with these cases requires a substantial time commitment from the SEC. The SEC could not justify politically falling behind in pursuing regional fraud cases while focusing on large banks. Indeed, it is tempting for the SEC to devote resources to smaller-scale fraud and other "low-hanging fruit" and the immediate results and publicity the successful enforcement provides. Resources devoted to convoluted arguments with large banks about novel investment vehicles are less likely to yield immediate and tangible results for the SEC than enforcement action against unsophisticated promoters who have obviously committed fraud. Sometimes even low-hanging fruit—including warnings the SEC received about Bernie Madoff's massive Ponzi scheme—is ignored. Perhaps this is because of negligence, but perhaps it is because SEC officials have to make thousands of judgment calls about whether to investigate suspected violations, and sometimes they guess wrong.

Meanwhile the largest financial institutions have enormous sums to spend on studying regulations, lobbying agencies for exceptions to regulations, devising transactions that avoid regulations, avoiding detection of violations of regulations, and so forth. They can afford to pay their advisers substantially more than these advisers would earn at the SEC, the Treasury, or another agency (indeed many of these advisers are alumni of these agencies and have moved on to "greener" pastures). The institutions can afford to put their advisers to work for many hours on whatever problems the institutions have with a regulator, and, most important, the advisers can afford to focus just on that problem. If a regulator chooses to launch an investigation or an enforcement action, financial institutions will devote even more resources to the matter, making it correspondingly much more expensive for the regulator.

One recent example illustrating a typical "dance" between regulators and regulated banks involves the EU's recent adoption of bonus caps for bankers. The rationale for the caps was that bankers had engaged in risky behavior (of the sort this book discusses) in order to get higher bonuses. Soon after the bonus caps were adopted, some banks restructured their compensation packages to include what they called "allowances," established at the beginning of the year and paid during the year, which they characterized as being a component of fixed pay and hence not subject to the cap.[2] After studying the issue, regulators rejected this characterization, announcing that "allowances" that were discretionary, as some of them essentially were, would not be considered part of fixed pay.[3] This particular dance between banks and regulators is probably not at an end.

Agency staff members are in the position of chess masters who have to play ten or fifteen games simultaneously against different opponents, each of whom is focused exclusively on his or her own game. In times of economic expansion, when banking activity increases but agency enforcement budgets may stay the same, there may be a substantial increase in the number of simultaneous games agency staff members must play. Sometimes government officials achieve sufficient mastery of their work that they can win some—or perhaps even most—of these games. (Although the agency official who is too good at this is likely to be hired away by private industry for a lot more money.) Sometimes, however, the effort that agency staff can expend on any one game is overwhelmed by the effort that the single-minded opponent can exert in the other direction.

The SEC's lack of resources very much constrains what it can do. For example, the SEC was not equipped to regulate the largest U.S. investment banks for safety and soundness despite its promise to do so in the Consolidated Supervised Entity Program that it introduced in 2004. The program was never funded with additional resources and ended only four years later, less than two weeks after the Lehman Brothers bankruptcy, in September 2008.[4] The SEC's Division of Enforcement failed to detect massive frauds such as the $50 billion Ponzi scheme orchestrated by Bernie Madoff that collapsed in 2008. The SEC has pursued only a few cases against large financial institutions and their officers and directors stemming from the financial crisis of 2008. It is also taking several years to promulgate the massive new regulations required under the Dodd-Frank Act of 2010; the process is still continuing. The SEC's 2014 budget allocation from Congress of $1.35 billion was sizable, but modest in comparison to other agencies (the FBI's budget was about $8 billion).[5] The SEC's 2015 budget of approximately $1.5 billion is only somewhat better. This budget is also very modest compared with the amount of money the Treasury has received in multibillion-dollar fines in U.S. government cases in the past few years against major banks, some of which we described in the introduction and chapter 1: these fines are payable to the Treasury, or sometimes are used to compensate victims, but are not plowed back into enforcement of banking and securities laws.

Regulators in many other countries have sometimes fared even worse. Although London is a world financial center on par with New York City, the United Kingdom's Serious Fraud Office (SFO) has won few, if any, major cases against large banks. The *New York Times* said in 2014 of the SFO's budget: "At £38 million [$64 million], it is 7 percent lower than the £41 million it had in 2008–9. Credit Suisse spent 169 times that on compensation in 2013."[6] It should be clear from these numbers that when the SFO gets into a legal scuffle with a major bank, including Credit Suisse, the odds are probably stacked in favor of the bank in all but the most straightforward cases of misconduct.[7]

Staying Current

Both regulators and banks have to keep up with new financial instruments, new technologies, and other developments. For several reasons regulators have more trouble keeping up than the banks do.

First, the banks usually set the pace of change. Many innovations come from within industry itself, so industry participants have an inherent advantage in understanding how they work. If regulatory approval of an innovation is needed, bankers can present the innovation to the regulatory agency, and pressure the agency for prompt approval before the agency has had time to fully understand all the implications.

Second, staying current is more difficult for regulators in times of substantial and rapid change. As pointed out in chapter 2, beginning in the 1980s, banking underwent substantial change. Notably, many investment banks were shifting from partnership to corporate form, becoming public companies. Moreover, their business models were shifting from traditional underwriting and brokerage services to trading, derivatives, securitization, and other new areas. The pace of change—particularly in computerized trading programs and new financial instruments—accelerated starting in the 2000s. Regulators may have encouraged some of these changes, and may have believed these changes promoted competition in the industry, but they also were probably slow to realize the other implications of change. In an age of rapid technological advancement, the SEC now depends on the industries it regulates for essential information about how securities markets work—for example, in 2012 Tradeworx, a high-speed trading firm based in New Jersey, sent its experts to tutor SEC regulators on a computer program called Midas, designed by Tradeworx, that would give the SEC a "real-time" window into the stock market similar to that which Tradeworx and other such firms have had for years. One former SEC employee told Congress that the SEC using the Tradeworx program was "reminiscent of the fox guarding the hen house," but the SEC, with its own rudimentary technology, has little alternative to relying on the private sector for the expert advice it needs.[8]

Third, regulators are not subject to the competitive pressures that require private businesses to respond to change. Some old-fashioned investment banks did not keep up with the changes discussed in chapter 2 and receded into relative obscurity compared with the giant banks that now dominate the industry. Regulators that failed to keep up with these changes in most instances, by way of contrast, were not replaced by other regulators. They just failed to do their jobs and nobody stepped forward to do their jobs for them (occasionally state regulators have addressed problems left alone by federal regulators, but these situations are the exception rather than the rule). The one area where regulators face competition is in retention of their staff—their opponents in private industry routinely hire away the best agency staff to come over to the other side and work for them.

Reaction Time

Bankers not infrequently design a product or transaction to help their clients get around regulations the clients find costly. The regulators respond with a new regulation, the bankers respond by making changes to the product or transaction, and so it continues. As was the case with reaction to innovative products, regulators' reaction to attempts to get around old or new regulations is also likely to be sufficiently slow as to give banks the advantage.

First, the bank will probably be allowed to proceed with an innovation that is not already specifically prohibited before the agency acts to stop it. The alternative is a regulatory regime that requires the bank to get prior approval for each innovation, a politically unpopular and probably unfeasible arrangement that bankers may derisively refer to as a "mother may I" regime.[9] Most, although not all, regulation of investment banking falls in the first category: banks are usually allowed to move forward with an innovation before getting regulatory clearance. (By contrast, federally insured depository institutions are more used to getting prior approval for innovations). Where the bank introduces its innovation before any sort of regulatory clearance, regulators are left to react. They may not do so in a timely manner or with the precision required to effectively address a problem. Even if the regulators spot a problem and try to stop or change the innovation, banks may be able to continue using it or merely vary it slightly for a significant amount of time.

Second, administrative procedure and agency politics delay reaction time. Regulators have to decide which agency is to regulate a financial instrument or practice. Notorious turf battles between the SEC and the Commodities Futures Trading Commission (CFTC) heat up whenever financial futures or derivatives are involved. (The CFTC traditionally regulated futures and derivative contracts; these contracts began in the agricultural commodities markets but then spread to the financial services sector traditionally regulated by the SEC). Regulators at the appropriate agency, or at multiple agencies, then deliberate over how to regulate a new transaction or financial product and then draft a regulation. The notice and comment period required by the Administrative Procedure Act may add to the delay before a rule is in place. By the time a regulation is in place, bankers may have moved on to a new and different financial instrument or business practice that is not subject to the regulation.

The Role of Advisers

Bankers hire lawyers, accountants, and other advisers to help them get around regulations. As pointed out in chapter 2, this phenomenon is at least as old as the 1720 Bubble Act in England, which created a robust business of London solicitors advising promoters of joint-stock companies on how to get around it. Today, regulatory law practice, accounting, and consulting services directed at regulatory compliance, are an enormous business.[10] The more regulations there are, the larger and more lucrative this business becomes.

First, advisers can help bankers technically comply with a rule—or at least arguably comply so they can defend themselves in litigation—even though they are not complying with the intent of the rule. For example, an insolvent or near insolvent institution may meet net capital requirements with assets that are overvalued because net capital rules fail to distinguish between appropriate and inappropriate methods of valuing complex assets such as derivative securities. Advisers can facilitate valuation methods that are dubious or even fundamentally unsound. Advisers who are former employees of the regulator sometimes have a decided advantage at this "technical compliance" aspect of the regulatory game.

Second, advisers can help bankers engage in business practices that lie outside a particular metric defined in a rule. These practices may undermine the general intent of the regulatory regime but are not prohibited by the rule. For example, many factors define the safety and soundness of a financial institution, but safety and soundness rules look at some factors and not others. (The Dodd-Frank Act mandates a broader range of factors than regulators used previously, but it is probably impossible for regulations to consider all factors important for safety and soundness.) Advisers, including those inside a bank and outside it (such as lawyers, accountants, and other bankers) can help bankers identify permissible risks that lie outside the defined metrics set forth in the current rules. For example, before 2008, banks were advised by legal and financial experts on how to place risky bets using derivatives that were originally designed to reduce risk. After a major financial failure, regulators may update the rules to consider safety and soundness metrics that were previously ignored, but advisers can then help their clients find yet other risks that remain outside the rules. Advisers for financial institutions can help even their clients who have serious problems look good to regulators.

Regulators probably know that the system is skewed in favor of banks that can afford advisers who tell them how to game the system, although many regulators may not admit this. The "objective" metrics of quality that are increasingly stressed in our society, including for banks, give gaming a convenient focus and allow for the development of specialized techniques. The many advisers who are former regulators add "value" in part by their knowledge of the metrics and the techniques that are most likely to satisfy the regulators.

Third, advisers can help some bankers (or their clients) avoid detection when they violate the rules or avoid the most severe consequences of a violation when they are caught.

Bankers also advise other bankers, and bankers sometimes advise their clients, on how to avoid the intent if not the letter of the law, or sometimes even the letter of the law. Depending on how the advice is framed, it may be legally permissible, even if unethical, for the bankers to give it regardless of whether the client uses it to break the law. Advisers also may inform clients about agency detection practices. (This "fuzz buster" method is the equivalent of telling a speeding motorist the location of police radar.) Advisers may inform clients about agency enforcement criteria, for example, which types of violations are usually ignored. (This method is the equivalent of the well-known rule of thumb that up to five miles per hour over the limit—ten in some places—does not result in a speeding ticket.) Advisers furthermore stand by ready to advise a client on dealing with the agency, and in serious cases with prosecutors, if the regulator decides to escalate the game to these next steps. Banks know that they will have excellent advisers on their side in the heat of battle with the government. This knowledge in some cases probably influences the risks banks are willing to take that draw them into those battles.

Fourth, banks' advisers sometimes also advise the regulator. The fact that many lawyer and accountant advisers are former agency staff members makes this practice much easier. Accepting advice from professionals paid by banks is also tempting for agency staff overwhelmed with work and in need of someone to explain to them the complexity of a bank's products or transactions. Agency staff knows that the advice is biased, but it may be better than nothing, and at least provides a logical argument for reaching a certain regulatory result, which just happens also to be the result that the bank that paid the adviser wants.

As pointed out in chapter 3, gaming the system is ingrained in the psychology of many people in our society, including some of the lawyers, accountants, and other professionals who are paid to advise bankers on how to play the regulatory game. Whether manipulating financial statements in Lehman Brothers' Repo 105 or engaging in some other strategy, bankers do not do it alone. Expert advisers are almost always close by. (Repo 105 involved, among others, Lehman's coterie of advisers and the Linklater's law firm in London that issued a narrowly crafted opinion that the transaction technically complied with UK law.) These advisers are well paid for enabling banks to do what they do, and when things go wrong, these advisers often claim that moral and legal responsibility for what went wrong is attributable to someone else.[11]

Capture

Much has been written for decades on how regulated industries "capture" their regulators and persuade regulators to do what the industry wants. Finance is no exception.

Agency capture results in part because of the revolving door of employees between the financial services industry and government, particularly at the most senior levels. Government is supposed to regulate banks, but many decisions are made by a group of people who work for government and banks consecutively, a group the media, singling out one bank in particular, derisively referred to after the 2008 crisis as "Government Sachs." The United States has chosen not to staff the highest levels of government agencies with career civil servants, as France and some other countries do. The revolving door has its advantages in that regulators understand the industry they regulate because they have worked in it, but this system also gives regulated industry more influence over the content of regulation.

Banks also have other means of influencing regulators. Powerful lobbying groups, such as the Securities Industry Association and the International Swaps and Derivatives Association, devote resources to studying regulations and informing agencies and lawmakers about the downsides of regulations they believe are too onerous. These groups sponsor parties, dinners, symposia, and even weekend retreats at luxury resorts that federal ethics rules permit regulators to attend free of charge. These groups provide a steady supply of information and prepared arguments for agency commissioners and other staff who want to argue to their colleagues that less regulation or certain types of regulation are desirable. These lobbying groups contribute substantial sums to political campaigns, making them a voice very likely to be heard in Washington. Some of them get additional help: they hire outside lobbyists who are often former congressional or White House staff members.

Congress

Regulators have another player—Congress—looking over their shoulder. Congress has the power to interfere if the regulator is not playing the way powerful members of Congress like. Sometimes Congress wants regulators to be more aggressive against banks, but often it (or at least some of its powerful members) wants the opposite.

Regulators are overseen by both House and Senate committees and have to deal with Congress on a regular basis. Congress makes laws that set up federal regulatory agencies and that define their authority. Congress also makes the laws that regulators enforce. Many laws give agencies the power to promulgate regulations, but banks will sometimes argue that regulations do not comport with the laws passed by Congress. The views of individual members of Congress will have a substantial influence on the way regulators interpret the laws. Finally, Congress decides what budget to give each agency, and this decision alone can put substantial pressure on regulators if powerful members of Congress do not like the way they are doing their jobs.

Congress's power was on prominent display in 1999, when it amended the federal securities laws to specifically prohibit the SEC from adopting regulations to prevent fraud in security-based swaps. The SEC had been trying to regulate security-based swaps; it was concerned that disruptions in these unregulated markets could affect not only parties to swaps but also investors in the underlying securities. Congress, however, believed that regulation was not appropriate: swap parties were sophisticated players who should be allowed freedom to design and trade their own contracts free of government interference. The effort to pass the amendment was led by Senate Banking Committee chairman Phil Gramm; his wife, Wendy Gramm, sat on the Enron board. Booming markets and the political atmosphere of the 1990s made passing the amendment possible. Congress did not reverse this position and regulate these swaps until 2010.

Congress also puts pressure on regulators on behalf of particular regulated companies that are politically well connected. For example, former SEC chairman Arthur Levitt in 2001 wrote a book about his tenure at the commission and the pressure from Senator Gramm and others to back off on regulating the accounting industry. The appendix to Levitt's book includes letters he received from Congress and very similarly worded letters he received from Enron CEO Ken Lay complaining that the SEC was interfering in Enron's relationship with its auditor Arthur Anderson.[12] Levitt was expected to listen to Congress and someone in Congress was apparently listening to Lay.

Our system of campaign finance is a big part of the problem. Corporate political action committees and other vehicles for giving make it easy for banks and other regulated entities to communicate their views to Congress (campaign finance laws, like banking laws, are notoriously easy to manipulate, with the added complication that some campaign finance laws are ruled unconstitutional). Even if Congress, in the heat of wrath at banks, enacts a seemingly strict new law such as the Dodd-Frank Act, subsequent Congresses oversee regulators' implementation of that law. After heads have cooled, the composition of Congress may change, and campaign contributions from financial institutions will have time to buy sufficient access to Congress for financial institutions' views to sink in. In December of 2014, President Obama signed into law a budget bill that substantially narrowed the scope of some of Dodd-Frank's regulation of derivatives trading as part of a deal that would avoid a government shutdown.[13] According to some news accounts, much of the narrowing language had been drafted by Citigroup, and calls had been made to lawmakers by the CEO of JPMorgan, Jamie Dimon, urging them to back the narrowing.[14]

The Global Playing Field

It is a lot easier for banks to move around the global playing field than it is for the entities that regulate banks to do so.

Regulation is generally confined to national boundaries. Theoretically, countries with major financial centers can coordinate their regulation, but often they don't. Regulation across national boundaries, even within a group of countries such as the EU, is difficult. Worldwide regulation is nearly impossible; indeed, some jurisdictions will seek to lure banking business by assuring bankers that few if any rules apply.

Global banking is rapidly expanding, creating yet more opportunities for regulatory arbitrage. One of many examples was the Lehman Brothers Repo 105 transactions discussed earlier, which concealed Lehman's true leverage ratio. When New York lawyers refused to bless a dubious short-term sale of Lehman's bad assets to get them off its balance sheet for a few days at the end of the quarter, the deal was done in London and blessed by English solicitors who reported it as a legitimate transaction to Lehman's accountants in New York.

Efforts to apply national law extraterritorially to reach transactions in other countries also run into strong resistance from other countries and sometimes within. In 2010 the U.S. Supreme Court, for example, held in *Morrison v. National Australia Bank* that the Exchange Act's antifraud provisions do not apply to securities transactions that take place outside of the United States.[15] Although Congress quickly inserted a provision in the Dodd-Frank Act that purported to give the SEC some extraterritorial enforcement authority, it is unclear how much authority the SEC has under this provision and how it will be used in conjunction with enforcement efforts by other countries.[16] The United States is not, and cannot effectively be, the world's policeman against securities fraud. Neither can the European Union or other countries or groups of countries with robust bank regulatory regimes aspire to effectively regulate transactions beyond their borders. While there is hope for more global cooperation than at present, worldwide government regulation of securities transactions will be very difficult.

The Limited Role of State Regulation and Corporate Law

The foregoing discussion is mostly focused on regulation at the global and national level. State and local regulation might in theory constrain banker behavior—a state or locality could simply say that a bank could not do business within its borders if the bank did not adhere to certain rules. Some states impose additional rules in important areas of concern, such as consumer protection. Some state attorneys general have been active in bringing lawsuits that pursue bank misconduct when the federal authorities do not.

There are, however, limitations on what states can do. First, federal law sometimes specifically provides that states cannot impose additional regulatory burdens. (More than once, Congress, at the behest of regulated companies, has preempted state law, as it did in 1998 when it enacted the Securities Litigation Uniform Standards Act, which provides that most class action securities fraud lawsuits must be brought under defendant-friendly federal law rather than state law.)[17] Second, if regulated entities do not like a particular state's laws, or the way a state enforces its laws, they can move many of their transactions to another state. The threat to move transactions, and jobs with them, is often enough to change the minds of state regulators who are getting too far ahead of the federal regulatory regime.

One body of state law, state corporate law, is particularly unlikely to help control banker behavior. Corporate directors—with the shareholder consent that is almost always forthcoming—can choose the state where they incorporate (or reincorporate) and perhaps for this reason, the law is very deferential to corporate officers and directors. Corporate law also focuses on process rather than substance, making it easy for corporate managers with good lawyers to comply. Absent evidence of self-dealing of the sort the law prohibits—an officer selling the company headquarters to himself, for instance—or of conscious and intentional disregard of duty, courts rarely find directors to have breached their duty. For example, when shareholders sued Citigroup's directors for failing to exercise their oversight duties in permitting Citi to invest in subprime securities, the Delaware Chancery Court dismissed the suit, noting that "oversight duties under Delaware law are not designed to subject directors, even expert directors, to personal liability for failure to predict the future and to properly evaluate business risk."[18] Excessive risk is an issue that state courts deciding corporate law cases do not want to address—and the highly deferential "business judgment rule" under which director conduct is typically reviewed allows courts to avoid doing so.[19] Congress addressed this problem in the Dodd-Frank Act by requiring many financial services firms to have a risk committee and avoid executive compensation arrangements that encourage inappropriate risk taking. It has yet to be seen how effective these new federal rules will be at addressing the problem. Indeed, one potential downside of risk committees is that they may paradoxically give some bankers an apparent excuse not to seriously consider risks. People on the risk committee are charged with considering risks, but those not on the risk committee may then believe that they do not need to do so. Compounding the problem, the risk committee could have a ritualized way of proceeding that is better suited to explaining and defending what the committee is doing than to doing the best possible job of ferreting out issues concerning risk. These concerns don't argue against risk committees—rather, they underscore the limits of state corporate law at addressing banker and bank risk taking.

Limitations on the Effectiveness of Financial Penalties

Regulators and prosecutors, particularly in the United States, rely heavily on imposing enormous financial penalties to deter corporate misconduct. The fines imposed on banks run into the hundreds of millions of dollars and in the past few years have run into the billions of dollars. For example, as we discussed in the introduction and chapter 1 of this book, the year 2014 saw several multibillion-dollar settlements. The cost of these fines is absorbed by bank shareholders, there only being an indirect effect on bank managers whose careers, future compensation, or stock holdings may or may not be affected, but who do not typically have to personally pay even a portion of the fines. The banks are willing to agree to these enormous fines in order to settle the claims, and regulators apparently believe that fines of this magnitude are needed to deter future misconduct.

This approach of only indirectly penalizing bankers who cause misconduct or allow it to occur by imposing huge fines on banks and bank shareholders has obvious costs for investors, even if the government profits from the fines. In a global economy, the U.S. government's reliance on fines as a deterrence mechanism is also causing serious problems in international relations. French public opinion and perhaps even the French government (behind the scenes), for example, objected strongly to the size of the 2014 fine imposed against BNP Paribas for violating U.S. sanctions laws.[20] Fines of such enormous magnitude could even create an international trade dispute if foreign banks are perceived to be disproportionately affected. Foreign governments might retaliate by imposing larger fines on U.S. banks and other U.S. companies for actual or perceived violations of foreign law (the European Union is now using large fines to enforce not only its banking laws but also privacy and antitrust laws). There is a limit to how high fines imposed on companies and their shareholders can go, and we may reach that limit before the fine is large enough to deter the executives who cause misconduct or allow it to occur. Regulators and prosecutors may be forced by international political considerations, as well as considerations of fairness to shareholders, to consider whether smaller fines imposed in part on individuals in a position to prevent misconduct—even if those individuals cannot be shown to have been legally at fault—may be a better alternative than massive fines imposed only on institutions.

Why Some Bankers May Not Fear the Law
Obstacles to Legal Actions for Fraud

Antifraud statutes and other similar laws and regulations are the "heavy hammer" that regulators purportedly have to hang over the head of regulated financial institutions. Criminal prosecutors and plaintiffs' lawyers are also supposed to back up agency enforcement actions where appropriate: there are criminal sanctions and potential civil liability for violations of antifraud statutes. In an ideal world, bankers would be deterred from conduct anywhere near to the line with respect to fraud.

However, this heavy hammer of antifraud law is very narrow in its focus and hits only a few nails in the broad framework of risky banking behavior.

For decades the U.S. Supreme Court has narrowed the definition of fraud under the federal securities laws, requiring proof of the defendant's knowledge of the fraud or recklessness, and in civil suits, requiring clear proof that the defendant's fraud actually caused the plaintiffs' loss and that the defendant was the primary violator. Private suits against aiders and abettors and even co-conspirators are not allowed, meaning that a bank that intentionally helps a client defraud investors can almost never be liable in such suits; they can only be liable in a suit brought by the SEC, which for reasons of politics and resource conservation will generally only bring suits that they think they are very likely to win. To make matters more difficult for plaintiffs, Congress in 1995 intervened with very strict pleading requirements and other procedural limitations on plaintiffs' suits. Then, as mentioned above, in 1998 Congress preempted similar suits under state law so plaintiffs could not take advantage of more lenient substantive and procedural requirements there. Finally, as also pointed out above, in civil litigation, U.S. antifraud laws only apply to transactions inside the United States, and it is often easy for bankers to move transactions off shore. Other countries, or groups of countries such as the EU, may experience a similar problem in that their efforts to regulate banks may lead bankers to move transactions elsewhere.

In short, the enforcement mechanisms behind some of the laws against financial fraud are relatively weak. For reasons discussed elsewhere in this book, little social stigma attaches to bankers whose conduct comes close to fraud especially if it does not result in legal liability. (Indeed, as we have noted, in some banks, sharp dealing with others may be celebrated rather than looked down upon.)

Bankers Don't Have to Pay

Some banks, knowing all of the above advantages they have in the regulatory game, play their hand too aggressively and lose. They are sued by the SEC or some other regulator. Rather than go to trial and risk a big loss, many agree to settle with the regulator. Most such settlements do not involve an acknowledgment of wrongdoing (such an admission would invite civil lawsuits, so defendants usually refuse to admit anything). Many settlements do, however, involve payment of a substantial fine. Often the fine is substantial enough to make the regulator look good—average citizens are likely to be impressed with any number with many zeros after it. The bank pays the fine out of its earnings—that is, the shareholders effectively pay—and then goes on about its business, which may involve violating the same provision or a similar provision in the near future.

Sometimes regulatory violations, particularly in the safety and soundness area, are so severe that a bank fails. Here also, however, the people who likely were responsible do not pay. Partners in investment banks that were organized as partnerships had to pay their firms' creditors when the firms failed (for them, refusing to listen to regulators' warnings about safety and soundness would have been like refusing to listen to one's own doctor's orders). The managing directors and other officers of modern investment banks (and commercial banks) can take their compensation and walk away. If they have stock in the bank, they will lose its value along with the other shareholders, but assets they have invested elsewhere are theirs to keep, well beyond the reach of bank creditors.

When Law Crowds Out Morality

Another source of law's limits is law itself. Law seeks to attach consequences to behavior. To do so, it needs to define the behavior. There are perils to both a narrow formulation using detailed rules and a broad one using standards. The narrow rule may miss behavior that should have been included; the broad rule's coverage is uncertain and may give people latitude to claim something is permitted (or give regulators the ability to overreach in claiming something is not permitted) and, thus, may cost a lot along the way. Not surprisingly, law uses a mix of rules and standards.

When regulation is being changed after some bad outcome, regulators make use of not only rules that prohibit what regulators now know is bad but also standards, broad language meant to capture things similar to the thing that has been prohibited, in an attempt to address efforts to get around the spirit of the rule. But the push toward rules is a strong one. Moreover, standards become more rule-like over time, as they are interpreted by courts and regulators. The ability to plan is societally valued, especially so in business. A great many doctrines in business and financial law elevate form over substance.

Law's reaction to problematic banking behavior necessarily includes both standards and rules, but most of the emphasis is on rules. In the Dodd-Frank Act and similar legislation in the EU and elsewhere, the law yet again has sought to describe with some specificity—and prohibit—the problematic conduct. As was the case before the crisis, however, the more specific the prohibition, the more likely it is that the rule's scope is too narrow and that it serves as a roadmap for how to avoid its applicability. The time and energy spent in following the roadmap establishes and reinforces the ethos discussed in chapter 3, that what is not prohibited is permitted. Following the roadmap logistically crowds out other things, such as a broader contemplation of whether one's activities comply with law in fact and in spirit. People get caught up in being just at the right side of the line, or so little over the line that they expect they won't be discovered or, if they are, it won't be worth the regulator's while to proceed against them. They may regard regulations (as well as other rules, private agreements, and other private appraisal mechanisms, such as accounting rules, debt covenants, or financial ratios determined by analysts or rating agencies) as obstacles to be worked around; they may even welcome the challenge, competing with one another on their creativity and skill and perhaps even daring. In sum, spending considerable time working on financial maneuvering affects a banker's values and mindset in profound ways, making the banker regard the practice of such maneuvering as normal and acceptable.

The solution we propose in the next chapter is what we call covenant banking—a personal liability regime under which highly compensated bankers would be personally liable if their banks became insolvent or if their banks had to pay a fine, fraud-based judgment, or a settlement in lieu thereof. The liability would be subject to certain limits, but it would not be fault based. Covenant banking would usher in a new era of personal and professional responsibility, as bankers became more invested in their banks' effects on the greater society.

5 COVENANT BANKING

In this chapter, we discuss contractual promises, or covenants, that banks could use to make some bankers—highly compensated bankers—assume more responsibility for the costs to society imposed by their banks. As we discussed in chapter 2, the investment banking partnership model largely accomplished this objective because bankers owned their banks, were liable to their banks' creditors, and absorbed the cost of regulatory fines and civil judgments the banks had to pay, and the settlements the banks entered into. Some commercial banks up through the 1930s effectively imposed liability on some of their shareholders, including officers who were shareholders, by having them hold stock that could be assessed if a capital call was required.

Banks today, almost all organized as corporations, are not likely to become general partnerships. But they could contractually impose some measure of personal liability on highly paid bankers in connection with insolvency, bailouts that result in a substantial net loss to the government, regulatory fines, and civil judgments involving fraud, which for this purpose include settlements in lieu of fines or possible judgments. Just as personal liability in general partnerships was not predicated on fault, neither should the liability proposed here. Unlike in general partnerships, the liability would not be unlimited. In this chapter, we discuss what some such contractual arrangements, or covenants, might look like.

Giving bankers some personal liability for their banks' insolvency, fines, and judgments should change their incentives to take risks. Bankers now have incentives to take inappropriate financial risks with their banks' money and with customers' and clients' money, and to take legal risks in areas such as institutional safety and soundness, proprietary trading, compliance with tax laws and anti–money laundering laws, transactions with customers and clients, transactions with third parties, and disclosure to investors. Personal liability should encourage bankers to reduce these risks and, since the liability is not fault based, to monitor each other's behavior to the same end.

Moreover, personal liability ultimately should discourage people who are inclined to take inappropriate financial risks and legal risks from being bankers—and discourage banks from recruiting, retaining, or promoting such people. People who are disinclined to consider the interests of other people, and of society as a whole, are also less likely to become bankers if they have to internalize more of the associated costs.[1] Changed incentives and infusion of bankers with different attitudes and values should also change the influences that bankers have on each other. Under covenant banking, highly compensated bankers would be responsible for other bankers' conduct. Monitoring other bankers' activities would therefore be a wise liability-avoidance strategy. A measured, if not conservative, attitude toward financial risk and a conservative attitude toward legal risk, including legal risks taken in relationships with customers, clients, investors, and other third parties, would become embedded in the institutional culture. The cultural shift from the world of William Salomon's partnership in the 1960s to the world of *Liar's Poker* that engulfed Salomon Brothers and many other firms in the 1980s, after limited liability became the norm, can be reversed. Bankers might demand higher compensation than they now get in return for this personal liability exposure, an issue that would have to be worked out with their boards of directors, but even if they do, the incentives and the culture created by a covenant banking regime are very likely to be worth the cost.

Why would banks adopt covenant banking? One possibility is that they could be required to do so under law. Another is that they would do so voluntarily. Voluntary adoption is preferable and is probably more likely. It also could be encouraged with regulatory preferences. Even if adoption of covenant banking were required, the requirement would be specified by means of a minimum standard—one size would not be expected to fit all. We discuss implementation of covenant banking later in this chapter.

One desirable change to the law, whether covenant banking is voluntary or required, is that banks that are publicly held companies subject to U.S. securities law filing requirements should be required to disclose to shareholders in their annual filing with the SEC—a filing that contains detailed disclosures about the filer's financial condition and results of operations (called Form 10-K)—the specifics of personal liability agreements with its highly compensated bankers and, if there are no such agreements, the reasons why there are no such agreements. Such required disclosure might help motivate more banks to adopt such agreements. It would also help ensure that covenant banking arrangements entered into genuinely provide for personal liability for bankers and do not include loopholes rendering the liability illusory. Banks in other countries could be subject to comparable requirements under their countries' securities laws.

Described below are examples of arrangements — contractual provisions, or covenants — under which a bank's highly compensated bankers, sometimes referred to below simply as "bankers" (or "employees"), would potentially be liable to the bank's creditors — or for a portion of the cost of government bailouts — if the bank was insolvent. If a solvent bank was assessed fines or found liable for a fraud-based civil judgment (securities fraud, bank fraud, mail fraud, etc.), its highly compensated bankers would be responsible for payment of a portion of those fines or judgments out of their compensation from the previous two years as well as the next two years. Arrangements for the insolvency context are described first, followed by a description of arrangements to have a portion of the cost of fines and judgments against the bank (and settlements in lieu thereof) paid for out of the compensation of individual bankers. In this book, we refer to both of these types of arrangements, together, as a "personal liability regime," or a "covenant banking regime." The liability under such a regime is limited. A specified amount of personal assets — perhaps $2 million — is exempt from the personal guarantee arrangement described first below. The assessable stock arrangement that follows imposes liability only in proportion to the amount of assessable stock owned by the banker. Finally, the arrangement for fines and fraud-based civil judgments against the bank imposes liability only out of the previous two years', and the next two years', compensation without recourse to the bankers' other personal assets. But in all of these situations the personal liability is far less limited than is presently the case.

A general outline of these arrangements is set forth below; different banks would craft specific contractual provisions that fit their particular needs.

Personal Liability for Bank Insolvency: In General

In many respects the relationship between highly compensated bankers and their banks is a joint venture, insofar as a substantial portion of a bank's profits are paid out in compensation. Joint liability for a venture's debts, also part of a typical joint venture relationship, was present when investment banks were partnerships. Personal liability for bank insolvency should still be part of the venture terms for the most highly paid bankers, even if their banks do business as corporations or other limited liability entities.[2]

One way to accomplish this, discussed more fully below, is a personal guarantee of bank obligations signed by the banker or a partnership/joint venture agreement between the bank and the banker. Bankers earning over a certain amount, perhaps $3 million in the previous year, could be asked to enter into such arrangements, with the amount of personal liability perhaps being proportional to compensation but limited insofar as the banker would be allowed to retain an absolute amount (such as $2 million) of his assets in any event. The covenant would impose personal liability on these bankers, similar to, albeit less onerous than, that of investment bankers who were partners not so long ago. In traditional partnerships, the guarantee was for all of the firm's debts, and all of the partners' assets were potentially available to pay those debts.

A second approach, discussed in another section below, is for the bank to pay any employee whose annual compensation exceeds a certain amount, perhaps $1 million, the excess over that amount in assessable stock. In the event of firm insolvency, the stock would be assessable in an amount fixed by the board of directors at the time of its issuance. The assessment would be a personal debt of the record holder of the stock. As discussed in chapter 2, this method of imposing personal liability also has historical precedent, as in the 1930s when holders of assessable stock had to contribute additional capital to banks that failed.[3]

The personal liability resulting under either of these approaches would not depend on fault. The covenant would be for strict personal liability in the event of bank insolvency.

This approach differs from the many proposals made to enhance fault-based personal liability. Indeed, even before the 2008 crisis, commentators urged making it easier to impose personal liability on corporate officers and directors for securities fraud.[4] Similarly, commentators have also proposed that corporate officers sued for breach of fiduciary duty in shareholder suits should not be allowed to avail themselves of the protection of the highly deferential business judgment rule, a rule that vastly reduces the chance that they will be held liable.[5]

Fault-based approaches are not sufficient. Bankers will not behave differently if they do not believe they are likely to be held personally liable, and there are many reasons bankers might doubt they will be held liable in a fault-based regime. Their reasons could include perceived or actual ability to blame behavior on others, inadequate government enforcement, procedural and substantive barriers to private lawsuits, difficulties in assigning fault for institutional conduct to individuals, or ambiguities in legal standards of care. They might also think that even a finding of liability would not result in any out of pocket cost to them given the availability of indemnification from their corporation or insurance their corporation obtains for them against such liability. Fault-based liability also will likely motivate bankers to organize and assign work or create "paper trails" so as to minimize the chance that they will be found liable. Thus, some bankers might think that what they are doing could not result in a determination of fault, that they could escape liability given the legal resources available to them, or both. Bankers making such an assessment, whether or not it is correct, probably will not improve their behavior or their monitoring of others' behavior because of fault-based liability. Without better behavior, the main effects of a fault-based approach will be that bankers spend more time documenting the legitimacy of what they are doing in anticipation of any litigation. An enhanced fault-based legal regime would thus probably have a negative impact on the ethos of the industry. Fault-based liability discourages people from acknowledging and accepting responsibility for the consequences of their actions. Indeed, lawyers are paid to deny their clients' responsibility for alleged conduct and to deny a causal link between the conduct and alleged harms.

Some measure of no-fault, strict personal liability would have a more desirable impact on individual incentives and the ethos of the banking industry. Bankers profit enormously from their banks' success in good times and would share in their banks' troubles in bad times. This sharing would go beyond simply sharing in the decline in value of any bank stock that they may own and losing their job if the bank fails.

If a bank fails, some of its bankers could lose money because of their personal liability for bank debts. This liability would turn on the banker's level of compensation, not the banker's formal level of responsibility. Some highly compensated bankers have a greater formal role in bank decision making or monitoring other bankers, and are hence in a sense more responsible for their bank's overall results, but other highly compensated bankers, such as traders, who may not have managerial or broader decision-making responsibility at all, can have an enormous effect on a bank's results. The personal liability regime proposed here does not differentiate among these groups and confers liability on the basis of compensation, in order to motivate all highly compensated bankers, whatever their formal job descriptions, to have a considerable stake in their own and others' conduct at the bank.[6]

The principal reason to impose personal liability is not to obtain the bankers' payments for the benefit of creditors, although that would occur. If a bank of any appreciable size were insolvent, the liable bankers' combined assets probably would not make a significant dent in the amount by which the bank's debts exceeded its assets. Rather, the exposure to personal liability should make bankers more circumspect about risk, so that the damage to creditors would not arise in the first instance or, at least, would not be as extensive.

Bankers are aware that personal guarantees reduce risky behavior: they already use this strategy in dealing with their own borrowers. Before bankers extend credit to riskier incorporated enterprises, particularly start-up companies, they often insist on personal guarantees from the principals, even those with relatively modest personal assets. Bankers know that companies whose managers have guaranteed corporate indebtedness will be managed more conservatively than companies whose managers have not made personal guarantees. A personal guarantee or joint venture agreement between the bank and its own highly paid bankers should help accomplish a similar objective with respect to how the bank itself is managed and operated.

Specific Covenants

Joint Venture Agreement/Personal Guarantee

The most direct way of imposing liability for bank debts is with a personal guarantee. The most highly paid bankers (perhaps those making more than $3 million) would be asked to make a substantial portion of their personal assets (all except perhaps $2 million) available to pay the debts of the bank if it fails. This approach would in some respects be a return to the industry norm for investment bankers up until the 1980s, except that under this approach, the bank would be a corporation or other limited liability entity, and the personal liability at issue would not reach all of a banker's assets.

A related approach would be joint venture/partnership agreements (JVPA) between a bank and each of its highly paid bankers. A JVPA between the banker and the bank could be created regardless of the organizational form chosen by the bank and the liability rules that normally attach. The advantage of imposing personal liability through a contract such as the JVPA is that it could not only include the personal guarantee of the bank's indebtedness but also allow the bank to include other provisions, for example, giving the banker higher compensation or a share of the bank's profits in years in which the bank does well. (Most of these other provisions presently are found in executive employment agreements that provide for bonuses, stock, stock options, and phantom stock, but no personal liability for debts.) By addressing compensation as well as personal liability, the JVPA would set forth the entire relationship between the banker (employee) and the bank, and clearly set forth the consideration paid to the employee in exchange for the personal liability covenant.

Variations on the JVPA concept might allow the employee to reduce personal liability exposure to a limited extent in return for accepting lower compensation. For example, an employee who agreed to accept less than $3 million in compensation might be relieved of personal liability for the bank's debts altogether unless the bank failed within a certain period of time (perhaps twelve months) after the employee earned $3 million or more from the bank. An employee who agreed to accept no more than $5 million might be allowed to keep a larger share of his or her own personal assets (perhaps $3 million instead of $2 million) in the event of the bank's insolvency. Such choices by the bank's most highly paid employees would need to be disclosed in compensation descriptions in the bank's annual 10-K and other securities filings. These choices would be a valuable signaling device to shareholders, regulators, customers, clients, and creditors. These constituencies might be wary of a bank whose employees shifted toward protecting a larger share of personal assets in return for lower compensation. They might suspect that the bank has significant exposure to the risk of insolvency.

Which employees would be subject to these personal liability provisions? Again, an appropriate threshold amount would probably be somewhere around $3 million in annual compensation during the previous year, where compensation is broadly defined to include, among other things, stock options and phantom stock. Provisions would be needed to deal with "creative" ways of structuring compensation so as to fall below the threshold, although presumably directors who voluntarily adopted such a personal liability regime would want to make the regime effective rather than a sham, and in any event a bank that misrepresented such a personal liability regime to shareholders (e.g., "everyone who makes more than $3 million at our bank is subject to the personal liability covenant" when such is not the case) could be liable for, among other things, securities fraud.

What type of event would trigger personal liability under the personal guarantee or JVPA? Triggering events should, with one exception noted below, include only situations where the bank cannot pay amounts due to creditors; in this regard, a basic premise of the guarantee or JVPA is that the bank itself should be primarily liable for its debts and the banker should only stand in the position of a guarantor when the bank cannot pay. Thus, the triggering events would include bankruptcy, receivership, and similar events but not situations where the bank merely refuses to pay. The guarantee or JVPA could not be used by the bank's counterparties to pressure its bankers into settling contested claims. Proceedings against the bankers or their assets under the JVPA should not be permitted unless the bank is clearly *unable* to pay legally valid claims against it. The exception is government bailouts in which the government does not ultimately lose money; these are discussed later in this section. (In another section, below, we describe a separate provision under which some bankers could be made personally liable for a portion of fines or fraud-based judgments against a solvent bank, but this provision is outside the scope of the JVPA discussed here.)

How long would a guarantee or JVPA last? The beginning date is relatively easy to specify: the time the employee crossed the compensation threshold that required him to sign the guarantee or the JVPA. The ending date is harder to specify, as the arrangement should include some period after the employee ceased to receive the requisite level of compensation and indeed, after he ceased to be an employee at all. Otherwise the employee could terminate the guarantee or JVPA by accepting a reduction in compensation or resigning from employment (an employee who knew about solvency problems might have better access to the information that would allow him to take such action to avoid liability). A one-year time period is probably appropriate. The employee thus would be personally liable under the guarantee or JVPA if the triggering event, including the bank's insolvency, occurred within one year of the date on which the employee lost the status that required him to sign the guarantee or JVPA in the first place. Alternatively, the extent of the employee's personal liability for bank debts under the guarantee or JVPA could be phased out over this one-year time period. As pointed out above, the employee should perhaps be permitted to reduce exposure of personal assets to creditors of a still solvent bank by accepting a reduction in compensation, but the employee should not be able to escape liability altogether unless the triggering event is more than a year later.

Furthermore, as discussed above, the guarantee or JVPA probably should allow an employee to designate an amount—perhaps $2 million— in personal assets that would not be subject to attachment by creditors of the bank. Arguably, this exemption should be higher for older employees, who would not have sufficient opportunity to rebuild their assets after a bank failure (otherwise the JVPA might be counterproductive if it encouraged older, more experienced bankers to retire). The guarantee or JVPA should also probably exempt assets acquired in the future from reach by the bank's creditors, saving the employee from the humiliation and expense of filing bankruptcy in order to protect future income or assets. These asset preservation provisions would be more lenient than the joint and several liability of traditional investment banking partners, whose present and future assets are reachable by bank creditors with no such exceptions. These provisions in a personal guarantee or JVPA, how-ever, would temper the potentially harsh impact of the agreement while preserving enough personal liability to encourage a more responsible ap-proach to risk taking.

Like any other guarantee or similar agreement, this covenant will be vulnerable to some gaming, including personal asset protection strate-gies. (The possibility of gaming does not discourage bankers from obtain-ing personal guarantees from the principals of corporate borrowers, even when collection on guarantees can be complicated.) A well-drafted guar-antee or JVPA would address many such strategies and prevent or miti-gate most of them. Banking lawyers are good at drafting personal guaran-tees for officers and directors of corporations to which banks loan money; these skills can be used to work on guarantees to be obtained from the banks' highly paid bankers, and the directors and lawyers performing this function would be legally responsible for due care in the process. As dis-cussed above, requiring the bank to describe the JVPA or other liability arrangement in its securities filings, such as its Form 10-K and annual proxy statements (the statements sent to shareholders that solicit their vote on directors), would also encourage a bank's directors and its lawyers to assure that exceptions to personal liability, if they did exist, were publicly disclosed.

Another issue is whether employees who sign a guarantee or JVPA should be permitted to purchase liability insurance to cover their pay-ments. A guarantee or JVPA provision should allow bank creditors to proceed against all of the employee's assets including liability insurance proceeds that are subsequently paid to or on behalf of the employee, in effect negating the effect of the insurance policy. A guarantee or JVPA that instead allowed the employee to have an insurance company pay the amount he or she would have paid or later reimburse the employee for pay-ments would have a different effect of shifting risk of bank failure to the insurance company. An employee or his family members might also avoid losses from his contractual liability by making a "bet" that the bank would fail; such a bet could take the form of a credit-default swap. Such a hedge position would have to be prohibited on the part of the employee and probably his spouse. (Most officers of public companies are now prohib-ited from shorting the stock of their own company.) An employee could also be required to disclose to shareholders his knowledge that a family member—for example, a son or daughter—has entered into such a bet against the bank's solvency.

Another mechanism by which the guarantee or JVPA might be circumvented is that senior management of a troubled bank could arrange a government bailout as an alternative to bank failure. Without proper safeguards, the guarantee or JVPA could even result in political pressure for bailouts that otherwise would not occur. Thus, for this approach to be effective and not just become a catalyst for yet more government bailouts, bailouts would have to be conditioned on contribution by employees bound by a JVPA of the same amount they would have been required to contribute if the bank had failed. A well-drafted JVPA, however, would only require individual bankers to pay these amounts if and when the government ended up losing money in the bailout. Banks that identify solvency problems early enough and then ask central banks or other government agencies for help are likely to receive bailouts in the form of loans that eventually get paid off. (The government even made money or broke even on some of the 2008 bailouts, although the government lost a lot of money on others.) The objective of the JVPA thus should not be to discourage necessary bailouts or bailouts with a realistic chance of turning a struggling bank around, but to discourage bankers from arranging a bailout that is costly to a central bank or to taxpayers in order to avoid their own personal liability.

Assessable Stock

Another approach would be for bankers to receive part of their compensation in the form of assessable stock. Assessments on the stock would be made if their banks became insolvent and additional funds were needed to pay the banks' creditors. The assessable stock would be transferable, but the obligation to pay the assessment would remain with the original holder. The maximum amount of the assessment would be equal to—or some multiple of—the value of the stock at the time of issuance. One approach would be to follow the traditional, if archaic, approach of assigning a "par value" to the stock at the time of issuance that, instead of the "penny par" stock common today, had a reasonably close relationship to the purported book value of the company's stock. An alternative would be to set the assessment amount equal to the market value of the stock at the time of issuance. The recipient of the assessable stock would be required to pay to the company the full assessment amount on a capital call or an event of insolvency.[7]

Historically, assessable stock has been a significant exception to the limited liability that normally comes with the corporate form, but it is not common today. The norm today is stock that is fully paid and nonassessable: a stockholder of a company cannot be forced to contribute to the company's capital by reason of being a stockholder. His shares are deemed fully paid for (even if the payment is services and the shares are part of a compensation package) and cannot be assessed. As discussed in chapter 2, however, assessable stock was commonly used in an earlier era, particularly by banks and other corporations that had large numbers of creditors and sometimes urgently needed additional equity capital to survive. Generally, the assessment reflected that the stock had been sold at a discount: it was intended to assure that shareholders finished paying for their stock and did not simply walk away if the company's fortunes declined. If the company needed additional capital, amounts not paid for the stock, usually up to its par value, could be assessed by a vote of the board of directors.

Assessable stock could be used once again to help assure that bank employees who receive generous stock-based compensation do so with adequate attention to the capital on hand to conduct the bank's business. The premise for the arrangement would be that the employee's services are deemed to fully pay for the stock if the bank remains solvent, but if the bank becomes insolvent, regardless of who is at fault, the employee's services are deemed to be insufficient consideration for the stock, which can then be assessed as if it was not fully paid for. In sum, regardless of what the employee's services were actually worth, this portion of his compensation is conditional on the bank's future solvency for the time that the employee holds the stock (probably as long as he is employed by the bank), and if the solvency condition is not met, the compensation is clawed back by making the employee pay for the stock.

Assessable stock could be an appropriate medium of compensation for bankers in excess of a certain amount, perhaps $1 million annually. Compensation up to this amount, but no more, could be paid in cash, nonassessable stock, stock options, or other consideration; compensation over this amount could only be paid in assessable stock. Employees should perhaps receive steadily decreasing percentages of their compensation in assessable stock. For instance, after working at a company for five years, an employee might be permitted to get 25 percent of her annual compensation or $1 million, whichever is greater, in a medium other than assessable stock; after ten years, the percentage might increase to 50 percent. This would limit employees' incentive to change jobs to avoid the accumulation of too much assessable stock (and too much exposure to their firms' downside risks). Employees would be liable for assessments on their stock for some period (perhaps one year) after the employment ceased. After that period the assessable stock could become nonassessable.

How much could the assessment be? It could be the stock's book value on the date the stock was issued. Alternatively, it might be the stock's fair market value, or the fair market value of comparable publicly traded shares that are not assessable, on the date the stock was issued to the employee. This approach to assessable stock has the added benefit of discouraging the bank from inflating the reported value of net assets on its balance sheets. If the assessment is tied to the stock's book value at the time of issuance, the incentive would be to state net assets conservatively. A potential assessment tied to the stock's market value on the date of issue also would discourage bankers from using accounting techniques and other practices to inflate stock trading price.

For reasons similar to those discussed in the context of a personal guarantee or JVPA, it might be appropriate for the contract to exempt up to $2 million in personal assets from the assessment. Although assessable stock used in earlier years contained no such exemption for stockholders, such an exemption avoids the undue hardship that some families still remember from assessable shares held by relatives during the Great Depression. For the reasons explained above, making assets in excess of $2 million subject to the assessment probably imposes sufficient downside risk to encourage prudent decisions by bankers who hold the stock. Recall, in this regard, that the aim is not to create a pot of assets available to bank creditors or to "the public" but, rather, to discourage inappropriate risk taking. Moreover, unlike the personal guarantee or JVPA, under which a banker's liabilities could be extremely high, with assessable stock the banker's liability would be capped at the maximum amount of the assessment on his shares, thus potentially letting him keep more than $2 million.

Whereas the personal guarantee, JVPA, or the personal liability of a traditional partnership, are all a strong version of personal liability, assessable stock is a more limited version of personal liability, but it could be effective nonetheless. The incentives created by assessable stock are somewhat different from those created by a personal guarantee or JVPA. The guarantee or JVPA discussed above applies automatically and to its full extent when an employee earns over $3 million per year. The assessable stock instead gradually phases in personal liability depending on the amount of accumulated compensation over $1 million per year that is paid in assessable stock. The longer an employee has been with the company accumulating stock, the more personal liability exposure that employee has. Those who have been with the company longest are likely to pay the most, although some employees who have been with the company a shorter time but have nonetheless accumulated a lot of assessable stock would pay a lot as well. As discussed above, if the amount of assessable stock accumulated by long-term employees is deemed excessive by the directors, a reduction in the percentage of compensation paid in assessable stock could be phased in as such employees' tenure at the company lengthens.

Because of its lower compensation threshold, $1 million, assessable stock could be extended to more employees than could the JVPA, with its $3 million threshold. Perhaps most employees of a bank should hold some assessable stock (the stock might, for instance, be held in their pension plans), creating an incentive for these employees to monitor for conduct that puts the bank at risk of insolvency. As pointed out above, a complicating factor with assessable stock is that it could accumulate in an employee's account, creating an incentive for employee turnover. As also pointed out above, this problem could be mitigated by phasing out accumulation or capping the amount of assessable stock in an employee's account.

Responsibility for Fines, Judgments, and Settlement Payments
The conduct described in chapter 1 identifies several problems: taking inappropriate financial risks for the bank's own account and acting in a way that could subject the bank to liabilities to third parties or for fines and regulatory sanctions, as well as loss of reputation. The conduct that

causes these problems includes disclosure violations, financial maneuvering, conflicts of interest, market manipulation, rigging benchmarks such as interest rates, as well as violations of laws relating to sanctioned countries, and assisting with tax evasion. Some conduct in all these categories will be illegal; some will not be illegal but perhaps should be; other conduct is in a gray area where liability is possible. An effective personal liability arrangement will encourage bankers to be responsible with respect to legal risk as well as financial risk. This is particularly important to assure that bankers treat their clients, customers and other parties to transactions appropriately.

Highly paid bankers—here, with a lower earnings threshold than would be applicable for liability for bank insolvency, perhaps those making $1 million or more the previous year—also should be personally responsible for paying out of their compensation a substantial portion of any fine imposed by the SEC or other regulator when the bank is alleged to have violated the law. This personal liability could also extend to certain specific types of civil judgments against the bank, for example, for securities fraud or other actions involving fraud. As with personal liability for bank debts in insolvency, such personal liability for specific types of fines and judgments would be assessable against all bankers based on their compensation, and without regard for who is at fault. Unlike the personal liability for bank insolvency, discussed earlier in this chapter, the amounts would only be payable out of, and to the extent of, the past two years' and the next two years' compensation.

All bankers meeting the earnings threshold should be subject to a clawback from the previous two years' compensation and should also be required to take a reduction in their current year's and the next year's compensation sufficient to cover a portion (perhaps half) of the cost of fines imposed by regulators or prosecutors on the bank as well as civil judgments in cases against the bank involving fraud. Fines and judgments for this purpose include such amounts agreed to be paid in settlements in lieu of fines or possible judgments. A banker's liability would be prorated such that the most highly paid bankers would have to pay more than the bankers who barely made $1 million. To discourage bankers from leaving the bank to avoid contributing from future compensation to the fine or judgment, a banker who leaves the bank during this two-year window for employment in another comparable private-sector job would be required to contribute to the fine or judgment the amount he would have contributed had he remained at the bank and earned the same compensation as he earned at the time of the fine or judgment.

Because this compensation reduction would be imposed regardless of fault, there should be some limitations, including perhaps a provision that no banker whose compensation is reduced because of the fine or judgment would make less than $250,000 per year, or $1 million over the specified four-year period, because of the clawback and automatic reduction. (The banker could make less than that for other reasons, including poor performance or being found by the bank to be responsible for the conduct that resulted in the fine or judgment.)

One type of compensation should be made immune from reduction on account of a fine or judgment: additional compensation awarded by a bank to an individual in connection with detection and prevention or mitigation of conduct that resulted in, or could result in, a fine or judgment. A compliance officer or in-house counsel, for example, could be awarded additional compensation for detecting a violation, putting a stop to the conduct, and promptly notifying regulators. A trader who blew the whistle on violations by other traders could be rewarded pursuant to whatever internal whistleblower reward system the bank chooses to establish. (Under the Dodd-Frank Act, federal regulators pay "bounties" to people who blow the whistle to regulators if the regulators later collect a fine for the same conduct, and banks may wish to respond by providing a reward for internal whistleblowing that mitigates or prevents the conduct in the first place.) Banks would need to set their own policies for rewarding effective compliance efforts and internal whistleblowing, but these rewards should probably be paid on top of net compensation calculated after pro rata reductions for fines and judgments.

Indeed, regulators may want to encourage banks to have internal whistleblower reward programs. For instance, when fines are imposed, regulators could expressly state whether compliance, whistleblowing, or mitigation efforts of particular employees most likely reduced the amount of the fine (e.g., "the commission believes that but for the aforementioned efforts of Employee Z the fine the commission would have imposed [agreed to settle for] in this case would have been a higher amount of $X instead of the Y actually imposed"). These statements by regulators would be invitations, but not a requirement, for the bank to appropriately reward the employee or for another institution that wants to avoid or mitigate future violations to hire that employee.

A pro rata compensation reduction for fines and fraud-based judgments, along with any promise of a compensation increase for compliance efforts or internal whistleblowing, could be inserted in employment agreements. These provisions would need to be designed by each bank for its own employees, and at the outset probably should not be required by regulators. The SEC and other regulators, however, could consider the presence or absence of such a provision in determining the appropriate amount of a fine. Nowadays, it is scarcely news when a bank agrees to a settlement in the hundreds of millions of dollars. Smaller fines may achieve adequate deterrence if individuals are responsible for some or all of these fines. If regulators make it clear that who pays for banks' fines is a factor in determining the amount of fines, banks that do not make their highly paid bankers absorb a portion of these fines would have to explain to their shareholders why they agreed to an arrangement that could result in higher fines. If the SEC also requires detailed disclosure of these arrangements in Form 10-Ks and proxy statements, shareholders, creditors, customers, and clients will have ample information to push for changes if they want them.

As with the personal guarantee and assessable stock proposals discussed above, the focus of this covenant would not be on blame but, rather, on shared responsibility and accountability, and on ex ante incentives to collectively prevent business conduct likely to result in the loss, here a fine or fraud-based civil judgment.

Some mechanism would be needed to prevent a bank's officers from refusing to settle enforcement cases in order to avoid this personal responsibility for fines. If a case were litigated rather than settled, the contractual arrangement could specify that the same bankers who are subject to the personal liability arrangement also would have to pay, from amounts otherwise due to them as compensation, for a portion of the bank's legal bills incurred in the litigation as well as for a portion of any judgment in the case. Independent directors, those not otherwise employed by the bank, could, and probably should, supervise negotiations of settlements with regulators. Directors who in bad faith turned down a settlement offer in order to protect highly paid bankers from contributing to settlement payments might themselves be liable in shareholder suits for breach of fiduciary duty to the bank.

Finally, if such a personal liability provision is to be effective, banks could not reimburse individual bankers or increase their pay to offset compensation reductions in connection with fines or judgments (an exception would be the separate compliance and whistleblowing payments discussed above if a bank chose to provide for them). Once again, it would be up to directors, shareholders and sometimes regulators to make sure that offsetting payments that undermine the purpose of the compensation reduction provision are not made.

Covenant banking would address a problem that has concerned courts, members of Congress, and the public: government enforcement actions against major financial institutions are often settled with a fine but no acknowledgment of wrongdoing, and later, the same institution violates the same or a similar law again. This problem came to a head when, in 2011, Judge Jed S. Rakoff of the Federal District Court in Manhattan rejected a proposed settlement between Citigroup and the SEC. As discussed in chapter 1, the SEC alleged that Citi had misled investors by selling them collateralized debt obligations that included assets the bank handpicked and then bet against. In rejecting the settlement, the judge cited in particular that Citi had not admitted guilt even as it agreed to pay $285 million and promised not to violate securities laws in the future. The SEC and Citi appealed the rejection; in 2014 the Second Circuit sided with them, reversing Judge Rakoff's rejection of the settlement, after which Rakoff approved it. Mary Jo White, the chair of the SEC, has said that the SEC will seek more settlements in which financial institutions admit wrongdoing, and some recent settlements indeed have included admissions, albeit quite limited ones, of some wrongdoing.

The May 2012 hearing of the House Financial Services Committee mentioned in chapter 4 focused on such settlements and, particularly, whether the SEC and other regulators should insist on an admission of wrongdoing in settlements. Most witnesses testified that settlements should not require such admissions because defendants would refuse to settle on terms that included an admission of guilt that would in turn invite private suits. Testifying at the hearing, Richard Painter told the committee that the problem with many SEC settlements was not the lack of admission of guilt as much as the fact that a penalty assessed against an entity is effectively paid by its shareholders.[8] The shareholders neither caused the behavior that led to the fine nor were they responsible for preventing it. The officers, by contrast, are only affected by the penalty to the extent they are shareholders or indirectly, insofar as their bonuses are tied to earnings reduced by the penalty unless the directors take the rare step of removing them as a result of their behavior. They thus have less incentive to change their behavior or that of the bank than they would if they were personally liable for a portion of the fine.

Covenant banking would give them the appropriate incentive.

Implementation of Covenant Banking

How would covenant banking be implemented? A government mandate has obvious problems, particularly specifying to which institutions it should apply. Banks, and better bankers, might flock to the jurisdictions without such mandatory covenant banking. It seems best, therefore, for banks to adopt covenant banking on their own.

Why would banks voluntarily adopt such personal liability arrangements? With increasing attention paid to the continuing problems in banking, banks might conclude that such arrangements would be advisable and, indeed, good for business. They might also conclude that adopting such arrangements might forestall far less desirable regulatory action. Shareholders, creditors, or bank customers and clients might urge banks to adopt such arrangements, as could regulators, perhaps in return for various regulatory concessions and preferences described more specifically below. Voluntary arrangements could be tailored by banks to address their particular circumstances; the regulatory preference would be available so long as those arrangements met certain specified minimum standards. These points are discussed in more detail below.

The many private actors who have a stake in and interact with banks should benefit from a covenant banking regime. If a bank's cost of credit goes down because some of the most important bank employees are personally liable for its debts, shareholders will benefit enormously. Creditors also are likely to take personal guarantees or other personal liability provisions into account not only in determining interest rates but other terms of credit as well. Clients and customers may think they will get better treatment if senior bankers are personally liable out of their past, present, and future compensation for a portion of regulatory fines and fraud-based civil judgments assessed against the bank. Counterparties in arm's-length transactions such as security-based swap agreements may be reassured, and provide better terms, if they know that in the event of insolvency, a fine, or a fraud-based judgment, the bankers are liable. The objective, again, would not be creating an additional pool of assets for recovery of the loss as much as creating an incentive structure, and an ethos within the bank that makes the loss much less likely to begin with.

A bank's outside directors also may press for personal liability of its bankers. These outside directors are themselves subject to suit by shareholders and other investors when financially and legally risky business strategies go wrong. Even with directors' liability insurance, outside directors may be eager to rein in the type of conduct that gives rise to litigation and investigations. Making highly paid bankers personally liable out of their compensation for a portion of regulatory fines and for some types of civil judgments may help close the gap between the interests of outside directors, in not regularly being investigated and sued, and the interest of inside directors, who are also officers, sometimes have in running the bank in a way that makes as much money as possible in the current year in which their compensation is determined.

Government can also play a role, not just as a regulator but as a customer, client, and counterparty as well. State and local government bonds are almost all underwritten by broker-dealers, and these issuers could insist that their underwriters' highly compensated bankers be personally liable for their own bank's debts in insolvency as well as for certain fines imposed in connection with the offering. The U.S. government is one of the largest borrowers in the world and could give privileged status in Treasury bond auctions and other markets to banks willing to make their highly compensated bankers personally liable for some things. (One firm, Salomon Brothers, achieved its preeminence in Treasury auctions at a time when its partners were personally liable for its debts.)

Rating agencies would be likely to take personal guarantees and other liability provisions into account in assessing the credit quality of a bank's debt securities. Other private organizations—such as Institutional Shareholder Services—that advise investors on the quality of corporate governance and on proxy voting, including election of directors, might be expected to take personal liability provisions into account in assessing the quality of a bank's management.

Institutional shareholders themselves, particularly pension funds investing the assets of "ordinary citizens," could promote covenant banking. Institutional investors are increasingly involved in questions of executive compensation, and they might add personal liability provisions to their list of concerns. Shareholder ballot proposals, which the bank can be required to include in its proxy materials under SEC Rule 14a-8, could urge directors to implement covenant banking, and many shareholders may vote in favor of these provisions if they believe they are consistent with the long-term value of the bank. Proposals for reducing banker compensation on account of civil and criminal fines in particular might be attractive if shareholders believe that conduct yielding fines would be less likely and that, if it did occur, regulators and prosecutors might agree to impose smaller fines on banks that make individual bankers responsible for a substantial portion of those fines.

Finally, regulators—both self-regulatory organizations such as the New York Stock Exchange (and its regulatory arm, the Financial Industry Regulatory Association) and government regulators such as the SEC—could play a role. The New York Stock Exchange could rethink its 1970 decision to allow member firms to have a public float of their own securities, not by reverting to its old rule prohibiting a public float but by requiring that member firms with a public float assure firm creditors that their executives are personally liable for firm debts, at least in some circumstances. Other member-based organizations in the United States, in Europe, or elsewhere could consider similar rules. Banks that want to be members of those organizations would have to follow the rules to enjoy the reputational and other benefits that come along with them.

Regulators could promote covenant banking in other ways. Regulators could consider making concessions with respect to post-2008 rules designed to control risk, such as the Volcker Rule limiting proprietary trading and rules imposing stricter capital requirements. Regulators' views regarding what the minimum standards of covenant banking are for such regulatory concessions should influence the form and content of covenant banking regimes, whatever the trajectory may be to their adoption: constituencies such as shareholders, creditors, customers, clients, or the bank's directors, discussed below, will presumably encourage the adoption of regimes that make regulatory preferences available.

If regulatory relief were potentially available, bank directors would have a choice: either the bank could do business under the stricter regulations that came after the 2008 crisis or it could adopt covenant banking and then do business under less strict regulations and with the other available regulatory preferences. The bank directors would probably need to explain their choice when shareholders or analysts ask whether the directors are prioritizing the interests of the bank or the personal interests of its most highly paid bankers. Banks that choose to have covenant banking provisions could even increase compensation if necessary to attract talented bankers, probably a worthwhile tradeoff for the society and ultimately for shareholders as well. In this regard, one regulatory response to the problems posed by banker behavior has been to restrict banker compensation insofar as it is viewed as incentivizing risk taking. The Dodd-Frank Act has such a provision, and, as noted in chapter 4, the EU recently enacted a bonus cap on banker pay. If regulators were to consider relief from such provisions for bankers who were personally liable for a portion of their banks' debts, fines, and fraud-based judgments, the regulatory purpose might be served in a manner that was attractive to bankers and banks.

More regulatory relief might be offered to smaller and medium-sized banks. The less systematically important the bank, the more certain sorts of relief might be warranted and the more meaningful to the bank the cost savings of the relief might be. Large financial institutions can spread legal and other compliance costs over larger operations. They can also afford to invest in devising ways to get around regulations, and absorb the fines and other penalties if they are wrong. Competition among banks might be better promoted by a greater degree of regulatory relief for smaller and medium-sized banks and such banks might agree to covenant banking in order to get such relief.

Furthermore, regulators could determine that certain types of transactions or financial products inherently involve so much financial or legal risk that banks should be permitted to engage in these lines of business only if certain individual bankers are personally liable in some circumstances for bank insolvency, for fines, and for fraud-based civil judgments against the bank. The regulators' conditions could be tailored to the particular situation: regulators might insist only that certain people such as business unit heads or traders be personally liable, or regulators might insist on personal liability for all highly paid bankers at the bank. Even if only some countries' regulators imposed such conditions on banks doing certain types of business within their borders, these efforts would help covenant banking gain traction in the industry as a whole.

Prosecutors could weigh in as well. They already are entering into deferred and nonprosecution agreements with corporate defendants that involve key issues of corporate governance.[9] These agreements could include provisions that condition deferred prosecution on a bank's adoption of an arrangement that prospectively imposes personal liability for fines, fraud-based judgments, and insolvency, which might be more effective at controlling future misconduct than the complex corporate governance provisions that now characterize these agreements.

Settlements of pending regulatory enforcement proceedings that involve payment of a current fine could include a provision that a portion of the fine will come out of the compensation of highly paid bankers. Settlements could also include personal liability provisions with respect to fines for future violations and perhaps with respect to all bank debts in insolvency. In exceptional cases — for example, where there have been repeat violations or particularly egregious violations — the settlement could provide that the bank must obtain from its most highly paid bankers a contractual commitment to be personally liable for any future fines imposed on the bank for the same or similar conduct that takes place while they are employed by the bank, even if those fines exceed compensation. (These payments would have to be out of personal assets.) Judges who approve settlements of regulatory enforcement actions, to the extent they have discretion in reviewing settlements, could look for personal liability provisions, in effect saying: "I will approve this settlement provided X percent of this fine comes out of banker compensation and provided the bank has obtained a contractual commitment from its most highly paid Y bankers, stating that if there are any future fines for similar violations these bankers will be personally liable for Z percent of those fines."[10]

The alternative to voluntary arrangements is, of course, arrangements imposed by regulation. Regulatory imposition of covenant banking could present significant challenges. Who would be required to have such an arrangement? Defining comprehensively the types of banks to be covered would be nearly impossible. Entities might organize themselves so as not to be treated as banks. Indeed, the result might be the widespread development of techniques to subvert the spirit of the regulation, contributing to an ethos, discussed in chapter 3, that has already done considerable harm in the banking industry. Moreover, banks doing business in more than one jurisdiction could game choice of law rules, arranging where they did different components of their business to their advantage, and compete based on the regime whose rules they adopted, perhaps fueling a cycle in which regulators appeal to bankers with the weakest possible personal liability rules.

The foregoing may overstate the difficulties of regulatory imposition of a personal liability regime. Banks might be willing to choose to be regulated under a personal liability regime created and enforced by a governmental entity, a securities exchange, or some other entity for the same reasons they might choose to adopt such a regime voluntarily. Just as companies may choose to list their securities in the United States in part to signal their willingness to be subject to a more demanding regulatory regime for disclosure to investors, the branding effect might be a significant lure. Some jurisdictions might choose to increase the competitiveness of their banks on the global stage by imposing a personal liability regime on banks that are headquartered within their borders, if not all banks that do business within their borders. Some exchanges and other member organizations might also choose to opt into such a regime to distinguish their members from other institutions (recall that, as described in chapter 2, before 1970 the New York Stock Exchange did not allow its members to be public companies at all, which meant that many were general partnerships with unlimited personal liability.)

As stated above, whether the regime is imposed voluntarily or is required, the U.S. securities laws and perhaps the disclosure regimes of other countries should require disclosure by banks of their covenant banking regimes. Congress should amend the Securities Exchange Act to require that all public companies in the financial services industry disclose in their annual Form 10-K whether the company (in SEC parlance, registrant) has a covenant banking regime and, if so, what its terms are and, if not, the reasons why not. As discussed above, an important advantage of using the federal securities laws to require disclosure of personal liability arrangements—without requiring any specific arrangement to be used—is that whatever a bank does with respect to personal liability, the bank will be legally required to tell the truth about it. Untruthful disclosure of personal liability arrangements would trigger the civil and criminal penalties associated with securities fraud and false statements to the SEC. Once a bank does disclose its personal liability arrangements, its shareholders, creditors, customers, and other constituencies can use this information and information about personal liability arrangements at other firms to encourage whatever changes they believe to be appropriate.

Among the matters that should be disclosed are: the presence or absence of a personal guarantee or joint venture agreement between the registrant and any of its bankers meeting a specified compensation threshold, the specific terms of any such agreement, whether assessable stock is included in the compensation of such bankers, the specific terms of any such stock, and, if the registrant did not have such agreements and/or stock, the reasons why not. With respect to the impact of regulatory fines on compensation, Form 10-K should require disclosure of (1) the amount of any regulatory fines imposed on the registrant within the past three years, (2) the portion of these fines, if any, that was paid for through reduced compensation of the registrant's bankers, (3) the specifics of the arrangement the registrant used to cover the cost of the fine through reduced compensation of its bankers, including the bankers whose compensation was affected and the portion of the fine absorbed by each banker, (4) whether the registrant has formally or informally made any arrangements to increase compensation in future years to offset compensation reductions on account of fines, and (5) the presence or absence of compensation-based incentives for compliance and/or internal whistleblowing. Similar disclosure could be required in 10-Ks and in proposed settlement agreements themselves with respect to the proportion of judgments and settlements to be effectively paid by bankers. Congress could enact a law requiring all federal agencies and courts asked to approve settlement of a regulatory enforcement proceeding against a publicly held bank or its affiliate to publicly disclose: (1) the portion of a fine imposed on the institution that is to be absorbed by its own bankers through reduced future compensation and/ or clawbacks from prior compensation and the portion of the fine to be effectively absorbed by the institution's shareholders, and (2) an explanation of why the regulatory agency believes the proportion of the fine to be paid by the bankers is appropriate. Congress could also provide that courts should consider the proportion of the fine to be paid by the bankers, not just the amount of the fine, in deciding whether to approve a settlement. Exceptions should be made for cases where the court determines that the principal objective of the fine is recovering investors' losses and that this is more important than deterring future violations. In these cases, maximizing investor recovery with large fines imposed on banks would take priority over deterrence objectives that could be furthered with a smaller fine paid for in part by individual bankers.

Similar measures could be adopted by state legislatures with respect to state enforcement proceedings, such as those brought against financial institutions in New York and Massachusetts. Also, both federal and state law could provide for similar disclosure to shareholders of settlement terms for securities class actions as well as other civil litigation involving fraud against publicly held banks. The portion of the settlement absorbed by the company—that is, its shareholders—also should be disclosed to the court and considered as an important factor in the evaluation of any proposed settlement.

What types of firms would be expected to seriously consider covenant banking? These firms probably include federally insured banks or bank holding companies; firms that originate, buy, or sell mortgages; firms registered as broker-dealers or investment advisers under the Securities Exchange Act; and perhaps the larger investment funds, including hedge funds. All or almost all of the firms that have been discussed thus far in this book would fall into one of these categories.

Some Objections

Our covenant banking proposal will face objections. One objection is that the proposal is somehow illegitimate insofar as it treats banks differently from other types of entities. Another objection is that even if the proposal is legitimate, it is inadvisable. A third objection is that the proposal would be too difficult to implement. We respond to these objections below.

One aspect of the illegitimacy objection concerns the different treatment of the banking industry. Covenant banking provides for personal liability that highly paid employees of other corporations do not have. Why should the banking industry be treated so differently from other industries? This objection has the most apparent force insofar as covenant banking is sought to be imposed through regulatory encouragement or regulatory mandate. To the extent that covenant banking is adopted voluntarily by banks, the bank is treating itself differently rather than being treated differently by law. However, bankers may still argue that bank directors, shareholders, creditors, and other constituencies should not attempt to impose personal liability when highly paid corporate officers in other industries don't have it.

We take no position as to what ought to happen in other industries. It is clear, however, what ought to happen in banks—we have seen that what has happened, and what is apparently now still happening in at least some banks, has caused considerable damage.

There are many reasons why banks are in a position to cause so much damage. As is well known, banks are highly leveraged. High leverage is very risky and also encourages risk taking. Moreover, banks' assets may be extremely hard to value, and banks may at times have both the incentive and ability to assign valuations that may give creditors unwarranted comfort. For these and many other reasons, it is difficult for shareholders, creditors, customers, clients, and regulators to assess risks that bankers are taking. Those risks can have repercussions throughout the global economy, as has been seen so dramatically in recent times. But, as we have discussed earlier in this book, bankers now have many incentives not to take costs to others into account, given that they are not presently liable for the bank's losses and that neither they nor their banks necessarily suffer reputational costs from engaging in behavior that could, or indeed does, appreciably raise the chance that the bank might run into legal or financial difficulties. And many banks, especially large ones, have a good chance of being bailed out, foisting the cost onto third parties. The potential negative externalities from failures in the banking industry are extremely high, probably higher than in most other industries.

A related objection is that covenant banking would impose no-fault liability and that liability without fault is somehow illegitimate. As we discussed in chapter 2, no-fault liability in this context has ample historical precedent. Indeed, personal liability of senior bankers for firm debts in insolvency was not historically premised on collective guilt, individual guilt, or any other notion of fault. Personal liability in these circumstances had to do with collective responsibility for the consequences—both good and bad—of collective conduct. Perhaps most important, collective responsibility for outcomes—good and bad—encouraged bankers to concern themselves not only with their own actions but those of their colleagues. People are more likely to work to change the cultural norms in institutions when some norms (appetite for risk, skating close to the legal line, etc.) pose a risk of collective liability regardless of who is at fault.

Another related objection is that some highly paid bankers who could be liable are not senior managers (e.g., traders). Why should these people, simply because they are paid a lot, have liability exposure similar to that of senior managers chargeable with the consequences of whatever happens to the firm, even beyond their own departments?

One answer to this objection is "moral"; another is more practical. A "moral" answer is that with high compensation should come some responsibility with respect to what happens at the bank, including as a result of others' behavior. This means personal liability for the bank's insolvency as well as certain types of fines and fraud-based civil judgments against the bank. If bank directors genuinely believe that bankers need to be paid more money to take on this added responsibility, they can always increase compensation accordingly. A practical answer is that requiring a fault-based inquiry into "whodunit" even on a division-by-division basis within a bank is not likely to discern fault in any meaningful way and, instead, is more likely to yield attempts to avoid or shift blame. If group culpability were to be a controlling factor in assessing personal liability, divisions with more clout could make it seem as though the "mistake" happened somewhere else in the bank.

These objections concerned legitimacy of a personal liability regime for banks; other objections concern the advisability of such a regime.

One such objection is that a no-fault personal liability regime might curtail desirable risk—that more precisely targeting undesirable risk taking would be preferable. Particularly after the Dodd-Frank Act, much law and regulation has been aimed at curtailing undesirable risk taking: very detailed regulations have been proposed and in some cases adopted. But relying on this legalistic approach unrealistically assumes that legislatures and regulators are adept at identifying undesirable risks and preventing them. Furthermore, banks' experience with financial engineering suggests that some bankers will figure out how to get around the regulations. If bankers are not personally liable even for a portion of fines imposed against their banks, they are particularly likely to maneuver their way around regulations.

A related objection is that a personal liability regime might curtail "financial innovation." "Innovation" sounds as though it is always a good thing, but the 2008 crisis suggests that a more critical perspective is warranted. In an interview quoted in the Wall Street Journal, Paul Volcker said:

> I hear about these wonderful innovations in the financial markets, and they sure as hell need a lot of innovation. I can tell you of two—credit-default swaps and collateralized debt obligations—which took us right to the brink of disaster. Were they wonderful innovations that we want to create more of? You want boards of directors to be informed about all of these innovative new products and to understand them, but I do not know what boards of directors you are talking about. I have been on boards of directors, and the chance that they are going to understand these products that you are dishing out, or that you are going to want to explain it to them, quite frankly, is nil. I mean: Wake up, gentlemen. I can only say that your response is inadequate. I wish that somebody would give me some shred of neutral evidence about the relationship between financial innovation recently and the growth of the economy, just one shred of information [sic].[11]

If more personal liability means less innovation in banking, then so be it.

Yet another objection is that, in some scenarios, personal liability in the event of insolvency could, perversely, encourage excessive risk taking. If a bank approaches the zone of insolvency, personal liability might encourage particularly risky behavior by some bankers who believe extreme risk taking might succeed in reversing the bank's losses and returning it to profitability. The likelihood of this occurring cannot be established. Clearly, there is considerable risk taking now, without personal liability, when banks are approaching insolvency. Indeed, recent failures, including Lehman Brothers, demonstrate that bankers engaged in very risky, and perhaps illegal, behavior as their firms were nearing financial collapse. It is not clear what the incremental effect of more personal liability in such a situation would be. Also, bankers exposed to personal liability in the event of insolvency might not take more risks but instead, as discussed above, reach out to central banks and government regulators for help sooner in order to bring their bank's financial situation under control. Furthermore, personal liability for bank debts and for fines and some civil judgments would likely curtail the risky decisions that put these firms on the brink of insolvency to begin with.

A final objection is that the proposal is too difficult to implement; we considered this objection in the implementation section above, providing reasons why banks might voluntarily adopt a personal liability regime, especially with regulatory encouragement, and showing how even regulatory imposition of such a regime might succeed. But if implementation did prove too difficult—if bank directors and bank regulators were not prepared to require or even encourage implementation of a full-scale covenant banking regime, there are halfway measures that could be implemented instead. For example, highly paid bankers could be compensated mostly in preferred stock in the bank and also given the option to buy, and be encouraged to buy, preferred stock with their personal assets. The preferred stock would have a fixed liquidation value and a fixed dividend providing a high rate of return (perhaps 10 or 12 percent). This dividend would be required to be paid by the bank as a contractual obligation, although dividends would be paid in more preferred stock instead of cash if the banker were still employed by the bank. The crucial point is that the preferred stock—both the fixed liquidation value and any accrued dividends—would only be paid in cash one to two years after the banker left employment with the bank. And the preferred stock would of course be subordinate to the bank's obligations to creditors, so if the bank failed, the banker would lose his entire investment in the preferred stock. Although such a regime would lack some of the benefits of the full-fledged covenant banking regime described in this chapter, a preferred stock investment plan could increase the personal exposure of bankers to the financial health of their banks. One approach, urged by New York Federal Reserve Bank president William Dudley in a speech on October 20, 2014, "Enhancing Financial Stability by Improving Culture in the Financial Services Industry," would be to require a bank's top managers and "material risk takers" to post "performance bonds" from deferred executive compensation. These amounts would be sacrificed if the bank were required to pay substantial fines and, presumably, if the bank were to become insolvent. A similar approach is set forth in a proposal submitted to Citigroup's shareholders for a vote in late April 2015. The proposal would defer for ten years a substantial portion of top executives' pay, allowing the money to be used to cover fines if the bank violates the law, regardless of whether the executives were deemed responsible for the violations.

Policymakers and regulators in many different jurisdictions are grappling with the problems in banking revealed in the 2008 crisis. Beyond the substantive regulatory changes regarding what banks and bankers do, there is an increasing focus on the banking ethos, particularly as it affects banker behavior.[12] In Holland, the Advisory Committee on the Future of Banks in the Netherlands, in a report called Restoring Trust, recommended that bank executives sign an ethics and morality oath pledging to, among other things, adhere to the law and consider the interests of clients, shareholders, employees, and society as a whole in their work.[13] The oath was initially required only for top banking executives, but, starting in 2015, it will be required of all ninety thousand Dutch bankers.[14]

In a recent major speech, Mark Carney, the governor of the Bank of England, called for a new spirit of responsibility: "We can help to create an environment in which financial market participants are encouraged to think of their roles as part of a broader system. By building a sense of responsibility for the system, individuals will act in ways that reinforce the bonds of social capital and inclusive capitalism."[15] As we explain in the next chapter, a personal liability regime for bankers should not only change bankers' monetary incentives but should also foster an ethos of responsibility of the sort Governor Carney envisions.

6 RESPONSIBLE BANKING

I n chapter 5, we proposed covenant banking: that if a bank fails, is bailed out at a loss to a government, is assessed a fine, or is found liable for a civil judgment involving fraud, or enters into a settlement in lieu of a fine or a possible fraud-based judgment, its most highly compensated bankers would bear some personal liability. Here we discuss how and why covenant banking may encourage more responsibility in banker behavior—and a new banking ethos.

Under covenant banking, if a bank fails or is bailed out, its most highly paid bankers would bear true downside risk, from personal assets. Imposing losses should be more effective than simply limiting gains. Reactions to potential gains and losses are not symmetric. As discussed in chapter 3, bankers may experience some of their money, especially stock-based compensation they have received from their bank, as being "house money"—money that they view as "profits" that they can lose, rather than their "capital." They may be less concerned with not taking home their full possible allotment of house money than with losing money they think of as already theirs.[1]

Moreover, the marginal utility of money is different at different levels of wealth. The amounts for which a banker could be liable on account of his bank's insolvency might be significant, potentially affecting the banker's standard of living. The possibility of having a much diminished standard of living may be far more motivating than the prospect of a much smaller bonus or diminution in the value of stock options (or stock) awarded as part of compensation. Indeed, bankers might experience potential losses in a covenant banking regime as qualitatively different and more consequential, not just as an offset in their computations against possible upside gains. Finally, a loss might have symbolic force in a way a foregone gain would not.

Under covenant banking, bankers would also be personally liable to pay some portion of their banks' debts, fines, fraud-based judgments, and settlements. They should therefore be strongly motivated to avoid conduct that could lead to bank insolvency or liability. Because the bankers' liability would not just turn on their own actions, they would be strongly motivated to be aware of and to the extent possible address problematic behavior by their colleagues, subordinates, and superiors, and they would be reluctant to work at banks at which they thought their colleagues, subordinates, or superiors were behaving in a manner that could yield insolvency or liability. They would be reluctant to hire people who they thought were particularly apt to behave in ways that could make bank insolvency or liability significantly more likely. Potentially liable bankers would be particularly vigilant about financial or legal risk taking on behalf of the bank. Ultimately, bankers might demand higher upside rewards, but that should be a price worth paying.

The fear of downside exposure should encourage caution. In chapter 5, we responded to arguments that it might lead to too much caution. Indeed, the examples in chapter 1 clearly demonstrate that more caution is warranted: the fear that "good" risk taking or innovation will be reduced is overblown when the relative benefits and costs are considered.

Why not just try limiting upside compensation that encourages problematic behavior? Even putting aside the considerable difficulties of getting the compensation design right and identifying the problematic behavior it seeks to avoid, designing a plan of this sort would leave in place the underlying ethos that causes the problematic behavior, one notably revolving around narrow material gain. It would reinforce the view that bankers primarily "work to bonus." The expertise bankers use in financial maneuvering may very well permit them to do end runs around the "improved" and more sensitive compensation formulas. Changing the ethos is critical; changes to upside compensation alone, especially prospective upside compensation, will likely not accomplish that task.[2]

That imposing real downside risk on bankers could move them toward a more other-regarding ethos might seem paradoxical. Any change in banker behavior might seem to simply reflect a banker's self-interest in avoiding liability. But the concept of personal liability has its own power, expressing not just the instrumental fact that one's assets are at risk but also the reason for the liability, the ethos of responsibility. Old-style partnerships of bankers reflected such an ethos, the partners standing behind their businesses with all of their personal assets.

Restoring some measure of personal liability for bankers should motivate a change in culture toward increased professionalism. For senior bankers in a position to try to influence bank culture from the top, the change in culture would have the most profound effect. The changed culture should make banks far less attractive to people who are of a mind to make money through inappropriate risk taking, maneuvering, conflicted behavior, market manipulation, and law breaking. Moreover, in the common imagination, liability is usually related to responsibility; when we think of a situation where someone "ought to pay" for some damage, it is because we think they are in some sense responsible. Bankers' personal liability would send a powerful message. Bankers would get the burden of having to stand behind what they and their colleagues were doing, but they would also get the benefit of providing credible ways of demonstrating to their clients, customers, regulators, creditors, and shareholders their personal commitment to their bank.

Banking is, and should be conceived of as, a profession. Just as lawyers are officers of the broader justice system, bankers should be officers of the broader financial system. They should bear liability for harm their banks do—not just to motivate them to change their behavior but also because liability is part of a broader conception of what banking is: a profession whose members collectively bear personal and professional responsibility.

What would responsible banking entail? There are two guiding principles: honesty, and concern for others (including customers, clients, and the greater society). Concern for others particularly entails not attempting to profit by externalizing losses onto others and not substantially increasing the aggregate risk in society purely to allow or to make side bets. Honesty and concern for others are closely linked; dishonesty in banking is not infrequently linked to an attempt to fool others, who may then incur losses. Dishonesty is clearly implicated in many of the examples given in chapter 1, as is lack of concern for others. Risk taking may be irresponsible because the person or institution ultimately bearing the risk was not told the (whole) truth and would very likely not have taken on the risk if he had been told. In chapter 1, we provided examples in which this was apparently the case; sometimes, the risk taker was the bank's customer or client and at other times, it was the bank itself, and its shareholders and creditors. In some cases of irresponsible risk taking, the risk taker kept the risk but was not in a position to bear the losses that could have resulted: if the risk taker becomes insolvent, those risks would have to have been borne by others. Some risk taking is irresponsible because it is zero (or even negative)-sum, consisting of side bets with no other business purpose, such as a legitimate hedge. Side bets can add to overall risk in society without commensurate benefit; some side bets also contribute to a general misallocation of capital.[3] Financial maneuvering is another problem, being by definition either deceptive or intended to subvert rules, regulations, or contractual agreements. Dishonesty and lack of regard for others, or both, are involved. Enron's prepay transactions and Lehman's Repo 105, for example, were apparently designed to help depict the firms' financial conditions as far better than they were in an attempt to fool people; Greece's cross-currency swap was apparently intended to help subvert a regulatory regime and conceal the extent of Greece's debt to at least some market participants.

A responsible approach to banking would make honesty a central value for individuals and banks. Honest disclosure would tell a buyer what he should know, not what sellers are legally required to tell him, unless the buyer has no reasonable expectation that he is relying on the banker for advice and the banker is merely executing a transaction the buyer initiated. Complete honesty should extend, too, to shareholders, regulators, and others with whom bankers deal.

Beyond honesty, a responsible approach to banking would also involve concern for clients and customers as well as the greater society. The examples we discussed in chapter 1 suggest that for some bankers the most important unit of account is the self, with the banking firm perhaps being second and client/customer interests being third place. The well-being of the financial system and society as a whole is a distant and far less relevant fourth consideration.

Such an ordering of priorities does not reflect the expectations we have of people in other lines of work. One can imagine what the world would be like if we not only tolerated but actually expected doctors, journalists, teachers, military leaders, and clergy to act this way. Selfishness affects these professions also, but the consensus is that predominantly selfish behavior is outside the socially acceptable norm. The consensus about these and many other professions is that there is an obligation to serve the public good. A professional who openly states that his or her priorities are defined by self-interest and the limits of the law will most likely be ostracized and a professional organization that hires him might be ostracized as well.

Businesspeople may or may not think of themselves as professionals, depending on the type of business they conduct, but most businesspeople talk a great deal about the value of their business to others, principally customers but also employees and the community. Businesspeople who talked mostly about the importance of making money would in many instances be less successful because they would earn the distrust of customers, not to mention others affected by the way business is conducted. Companies without public shareholders thus often avoid discussion of profits and disclose their balance sheets and earnings on a need-to-know basis with shareholders and creditors while focusing public discourse on the value they provide for customers and the community.

Banks also talk about the value of what they do for their customers and communities. But there is a difference, certainly in rhetoric and, it seems, in values as well. Society has become used to the notion that bankers' principal, if not only, objective may be to make money for themselves and for their banks. As discussed in chapter 2, the shift away from service-oriented banking—underwriting and brokerage services—and toward proprietary banking—trading and sale of derivative products—has exacerbated this trend. The change from investment banking partnerships to public companies, also discussed in chapter 2, has meant that shareholders, analysts, and media outlets want bankers to talk more about how much money their banks make. The fact that many people no longer understand the complex products that bankers sell and the services bankers provide pushes the conversation further toward the one variable that most people do understand: money. The successful banker makes more money than the unsuccessful banker and for many observers this simplistic observation is apparently the end of the conversation.

In sum, society tolerates the notion that the acquisition of money can be the sole objective of bankers' work. Society does not try very hard to articulate other objectives of bankers' work, and few bankers are in any rush to suggest them.

A comparison with lawyers is illustrative. The legal profession at least purports to put the interests of clients and the legal system ahead of the interests of the individual lawyer and his firm. A lawyer who publicly embraced an ordering of priorities consisting of self first, firm second, clients third, and the public last would not be highly thought of by other lawyers, would be strongly criticized by legal ethics authorities, and might be considered unfit to practice law. The ethics rules of most jurisdictions, the American Bar Association Model Rules of Professional Conduct, bar opinions, and judicial opinions are full of references to lawyers' two principal obligations—to the client and to the judicial system—and difficulties that arise when these obligations conflict with each other. A lawyer's obligations to his law firm are supposed to be far down the list of priorities, and the lawyer's own personal interests are supposed to be subordinate as well. The American Bar Association and state bar associations have been steadfast in refusing to permit lawyers to work for firms that are owned by anyone but lawyers, in part to avoid lawyers incurring obligations to persons not bound by a code of ethics that subordinates self-interest.

Some lawyers may cheat clients, lie to third parties, and do other things that harm others. Much of bankers' gaming of the system is enabled by lawyers who put perceived obligations to fee-paying clients ahead of lawyers' obligation to the legal system and society as a whole. The standard these lawyers are judged against, however, at least says that the interests of clients and the justice system come first (which of the two comes first depends on the circumstances and is not always clear). At least the lawyer does not justify conduct by saying that he is permitted, within the bounds of the law, to act only in his own self-interest.

Unlike lawyers, bankers are not bound by a code of professional ethics that articulates specific ways in which they are expected to prioritize clients' interests or the interests of the broader system, in their case the financial system, over self-interest. Some bankers, such as brokers in a fiduciary relationship with clients, are subject to, and adhere to, fiduciary and other standards, but many other bankers do not. Federal and state regulation of bankers' activities is intense and complex, particularly after the Dodd-Frank Act, but this externally imposed regulation is about the government telling bankers what they can and cannot do—for example, when selfish behavior crosses the line and becomes illegal. No internally generated profession-wide code of ethics defines acceptable conduct. Perhaps because bankers have less opportunity to regulate their own conduct and that of competitors through professional associations, bankers are probably less likely than lawyers to engage in thoughtful discussion with each other about what they should and should not do as a profession.

After the financial crisis of 2008, some bankers forcefully described their work itself as a public service. Goldman Sachs CEO Lloyd Blankfein claimed to be doing the Lord's work, leading to jests about "divine compensation" levels, stock options, and why rabbis and ministers should not be similarly rewarded. Such claims about investment banking's public mission elicited considerable scorn, especially as further scandals unfolded.

Blankfein and others also argued that meritocratic banks such as Goldman Sachs contribute to society by giving talented persons of all backgrounds a chance to succeed (Blankfein grew up in a public housing project). Entirely apart from Goldman Sachs and the rest of Wall Street, however, the top 1 percent—or in this case the top 0.01 percent—in America has long been open to self-made men. This social mobility mantra is hardly a justification for what one does to get to the top and does not address at all the question of whether the bottom 99.99 percent is worse off as a result. (Irresponsible banking that throws the economy into a recession also probably decreases social mobility overall.) Lloyd Blankfein's own Horatio Alger story may appeal to people inside the industry who are frustrated with memories of the insularity and snobbishness of investment banks in an earlier era. His tale says nothing about whether a few people making themselves suddenly and fabulously rich makes the world a better place: the state lottery accomplishes this same objective at perhaps less social cost.

Ironically, much of bankers' conduct showing lack of regard for others occurred during a time—the 1990s and early years of the twenty-first century—of enormous philanthropic commitments by bankers. These donations help bankers boast of professional success—"keeping score"—among a competitive group of people who also have far more money than they can spend on themselves. Charity also may be a rationalization (i.e., an excuse) for running a business with relatively little regard for the impact of that business on others. In the worst cases, such as that of Bernard Madoff, charity is an instrument for building credibility with investors and achieving selfish ends. (How can a man who donates so much money to religious causes be a cheat?) Finally, some bankers make charitable contributions because they genuinely want to help other people even if they have not found a satisfying way of doing so at work. Compartmentalized ethical systems separate the ruthless self-seeking that sometimes characterizes the banking profession from the more beneficent goals these bankers have for their personal lives, and charity is an outlet for the latter.

A business, of course, is not a charity. Capitalism succeeds as an economic system because most businesses *both* make money *and* contribute to a greater social good. A successful business probably does not focus exclusively on helping others, but most successful businesses thrive because they do good things for other people and often for society as a whole. Businesses that do not further something other than their own self-interest in the long run don't survive.

Of course tension exists between self-interest and the interest of others. Few people devote their lives exclusively to the interests of others with no thought of what they want for themselves. Few people, however, only think of their own self-interest and not of others. Most people achieve some balance between the two. What is unacceptable — particularly for a profession such as banking that has an enormous impact on society as a whole — is for tension between these two competing concerns repeatedly to be resolved exclusively in the direction of self-interest.

A banker fulfills a social and economic purpose if he does something useful while he is making money, for example, if he facilitates access to capital for businesses, provides investors with sound investment opportunities, enhances the growth and stability of the financial system, and/or contributes to the well-being of the community in some other way. And the banker who cares about others will avoid conduct that is harmful, such as using excessive leverage in transactions and helping clients conceal their own financial weaknesses from regulators and investors.

In sum, the "greed is good" ethos may have a long history on Wall Street, but it has been an unhappy history. At times, such as in 1929 and again in 2008, this ethos has had a devastating impact on overall wealth. This ethos of self-interest needs to be counterbalanced by an ethos that emphasizes collective welfare and an understanding of the way in which self-interest and collective welfare often reinforce each other. Personally and professionally responsible investment bankers understand the impact of their work on others and make decisions with these interests in mind.

Responsible bankers would be forthright and truthful with their clients and customers, regulators, and the broader market. They would not engage in conflicted behavior, they would not manipulate markets, their disclosures would be true and complete, and they would not violate the law or help others to do so. Responsible bankers would also take care not to use financial engineering techniques to engage for themselves or for their clients in financial maneuvering—that is, to deceive or to subvert a regulatory scheme or private agreement. Responsible bankers are well situated to make the necessary assessments.

How should responsible bankers approach risk taking, either as to their own banks' risks or as to risks they help a client take?

Responsible risk taking has several characteristics. Most responsible risk taking has a socially beneficial objective, such as facilitating access to capital for a worthwhile enterprise. Responsible risk taking also is not excessive in proportion to the expected benefit. Responsible risk, furthermore, is not undertaken in an environment of "moral hazard" in which the person deciding to take the risk (which for this purpose includes the banker and typically the bank as well) makes the decision in part because he will not pay the cost of the risk if things don't work out. Responsible risk taking also involves informing others who should know about the risks before they consent and does not involve imposing unsuitable risks on persons unable to bear those risks. Finally, responsible financial risk is taken seriously, with due regard to its gravity; by contrast, in popular "real life" books about banking, risk sometimes is taken quite cavalierly, sometimes seemingly for the thrill of it.

These characteristics of responsible risk taking are best understood as part of a continuum, with obviously irresponsible risk at one end and risk taking that is obviously responsible at the other end. Different risks will involve different mixtures of these characteristics—or their opposites—but risks that fall short with respect to many of these characteristics, or that severely fail with respect to a few of them, are likely to be irresponsible.

The first characteristic of responsible risk taking, an expected social benefit from risk, is typified by the core mission that investment bankers traditionally had of raising capital for new business ventures. Bankers presented with many ventures seeking financing select those that deserve access to public and private capital because they are likely to be successful, rejecting those that are not. In many instances these bankers also put their banks' money at risk by conducting "firm commitment" underwritings, committing to buy for their own account an issuer's securities that cannot be sold to investors. Other risks taken by bankers help assure the pricing accuracy and liquidity of secondary markets. These risks include trading on a bank's own account, which serves a useful function when it does not create conflicts of interest or otherwise interfere with bankers' other more essential functions. All of these functions provide an identifiable social benefit.

Mortgage securitization transactions, as problematic as many of them were in the 2008 financial crisis, frequently have provided a social benefit. In the earlier securitization transactions, and also in some securitization transactions during the crisis, mortgages were made according to conventional (or if novel, still sound) lending criteria and then were pooled, and interests were sold to investors. More funds became available to make more mortgages, and loan rates were equalized and lowered throughout the country. Securitizations of cross-border cash flows also enabled sound businesses in countries with high political risk to get access to capital at low rates. The sound and familiar securitization transactions set the stage for the problematic transactions that led to the crisis. Bankers structured and sold to eager investors higher-yielding AAA subprime mortgage securities, causing demand for "product" in the form of subprime loans and, thus, higher demand and prices for housing, stoking more demand for the loans, and, critically, the erosion of credit standards to increase supply— leading to a collapse that in hindsight seems all too predictable. Whatever social benefit there may have been when subprime mortgages began to be securitized, costs began to appreciably exceed the benefits in increasing numbers of cases. Hopefully, in the future, a negative trajectory will be spotted and stopped before real damange is done.

The second characteristic of responsible risk taking is that the risk not be disproportionate to the expected social benefit. This balance needs to be assessed not only from the perspective of the risk taker but—because most risks have social externalities—also from the perspective of society. It is, for example, a good thing for working families to have access to mortgages they can afford, and some mortgage-backed securities further this goal, but society can be far worse off if mortgage-backed securities allow many loans likely to end up in foreclosure to be made. The social harm exceeds the social costs. Regardless of whether there is a willing borrower and a willing investor in such loans, it is personally and professionally irresponsible for bankers to facilitate these transactions.

Responsible bankers thus should inform themselves of the potential social costs of risk relative to the potential social benefits from risk and act based on this information. At a minimum, they should refrain from facilitating risks when the expected social costs are far higher than the expected social benefits.

The third characteristic of responsible risk taking is that the person or institution taking the risk shares in the risk—that is, will suffer a significant downside if the risk does not pay off. (Otherwise the moral hazard problem moves to the fore as risk takers avoid the consequences of their actions.)

Even the risks that banks themselves take can do poorly by this measure. While many bankers had significant stockholdings in their banks, and lost a great deal of money in the crisis, many did not.[4] More important, many of those responsible for risk taking were insulated from a significant downside because even their worst-case scenario, in which they lost a great deal of money, did not put at risk their personal assets outside the bank. As pointed out in chapter 3, considerable evidence suggests that people can view different portions of their assets differently and have different risk preferences over those different portions. As long as a banker will have enough money to maintain his high standard of living even in the worst-case scenario, he may be willing to risk a large amount of his net worth, particularly the portion acquired by taking similar risks. If bankers' worst-case scenarios potentially compromised their standards of living, as they would under the covenant banking regime suggested in this book, they would have thought much longer and harder before incurring the big risks that sank their firms and the economy—they might have come to very different conclusions and made different decisions.

A fourth characteristic of responsible risk taking is that the persons who ultimately bear a risk understand and consent to it. Appropriate disclosure is made. This is where honesty—another topic already discussed above—is important. But disclosure is not enough. A common problem is that investment managers with short-term time horizons may "consent" to taking a risk where the risk is not suitable for the people on whose behalf they are investing. Even some individual or institutional investors may themselves take on risks that they should not. Broker-dealer regulation recognizes this problem and addresses it with the concept of "suitability." The suitability rule governs broker-dealers' dealings with customers: a broker should not put an investor's money into an investment if the risk is not suitable for that particular investor. A concept like suitability should be more broadly applied to investment managers who manage other investors' money or the money of unions, foundations, charities, and municipalities. Good business practice would be that banks selling investments to such investors also consider suitability of the investment for the customer. Some of the risks foisted off on these investors in past transactions thus were not acceptable because they were not suitable for the persons who ultimately bore them.[5] Orange County, for example, incurred large losses on complex securities sold to them by Merrill Lynch, which ultimately had to pay the county for some of these losses. The county declared bankruptcy. Taxpayers paid a significant price; county services suffered as well. A similar story can be told about the far more recent purchase by Jefferson County of complex securities from JP Morgan, and the county's subsequent bankruptcy.

Some of the risks incurred in banking are borne by even more attenuated parties, such as neighbors of homeowners who default on risky loans, municipalities with vastly diminished property tax revenues when home values plummet, investors who lose money when markets as a whole collapse as they did in 2008, taxpayers who pay for bailouts, and people who lose their jobs in the recessions and depressions that almost invariably come on the heels of reckless conduct in the banking sector. Few of these people gave "informed consent" to what happened to them, and many were exposed to risks that in any event were not suitable under the circumstances. Bankers should not be expected to calculate all of these risks but they should be aware of and consider them.

Finally, risk taking should not be an end itself. Bankers who derive psychic satisfaction from taking big risks can be a threat to their banks as well as customers and creditors and the banking system as a whole. Banks need to send a sober message that people who value risk for its own sake should go elsewhere, as should people who are not open with others—their colleagues, shareholders, or regulators—about the risks they are taking or causing others to take.

In sum, responsible banking does not mean avoiding all or even most risk. A lot of risk taking is beneficial for investors, for the economy, and for society as a whole. Responsible risk taking, however, occurs when there is some social benefit from the risk, the social benefit is reasonable in relation to the potential downside from the risk, the risk taker assumes part of the risk, and other persons who bear risk give informed consent to risks that are suitable for them under the circumstances.

Responsible bankers will be responsible about financial and legal risk. They will be responsible in other respects as well, avoiding behavior that may help their banks' immediate bottom line but ultimately hurts the bank, the bank's customers or clients, or the greater society.

CONCLUSION

Not nearly enough has changed since the 2008 financial crisis. Many sensible (and some not so sensible) proposals have been made; some have been adopted. Some lessons may have been learned, and some excesses may have been restrained. But far more is needed—the next crisis has scarcely been averted.

It is time for a new approach. Much of what has been proposed, and much of what has been enacted, addresses the behavior of banks. More of a focus needs to be on individual bankers and the present-day culture of banks.

Until comparatively recently, many investment banks were organized as general partnerships, with each general partner unlimitedly liable from his personal assets for liabilities of the partnership. The present-day culture owes much to the fact that investment banks shifted from partnership to corporate form. Those who would have been partners in partnerships are now officers in corporations, able to enjoy a considerable upside without a commensurate, or even a significant, downside. This would not be a problem—as indeed it is not in many corporations—were there not particular ways in which banks, or more precisely, bankers, could cause significant problems for the greater society. This is not to say that all or even most bankers behave in problematic ways. But the continuing trajectory of scandals suggests that significant problematic banker behavior continues.

In this book, we have argued that the most highly compensated bankers—those that, had banks been organized as general partnerships, would probably have been general partners—should bear more personal liability for what happens at their banks. They should bear significant liability if their banks fail, and they should have to pay a portion of fines, civil judgments involving fraud, and settlements in lieu of such fines or judgments. Ideally, banks would adopt regimes providing for such liability voluntarily, perhaps in response to pressure by some of their stakeholders, such as shareholders, creditors, or customers and clients. To encourage banks to adopt such regimes, regulators might agree to waive certain aspects of the present rules and regulations otherwise applicable to banks. A virtuous circle might begin, in which banks could tout their bankers' willingness to stand behind their products and services, thereby gaining a competitive advantage. As adoption of personal liability regimes became more common, those banks not doing so might suffer a competitive disadvantage.

The solution we propose in this book, covenant banking, is in a sense about money, insofar as exposure to liability would change bankers' monetary incentives. But money is not nearly as important a part of the story as it has been thought to be. Behavior is far more complicated—in ways that matter to an understanding of the problem and to a formulation of effective solutions. Bankers, banks, and the broader society have gotten caught up in a race for more—more money, but also more symbols of accomplishment or "points." In the banking industry, points are awarded for some things that hurt society and run counter to what "professionals" should be doing. Ability to maneuver around rules, contractual agreements, and bonus formulas is rewarded, as is "salesmanship" that may sometimes consist of convincing buyers that low-quality investments are actually of high quality. The problem is thus about more than just money. It is also about the values of the industry and some of the people who work in it.

It could be otherwise. Viewing the problem from the vantage point of people rather than money, and the possibility of changing the people in banking rather than just their financial incentives, envisions a broader goal, one that warrants cautious optimism. What people value is determined by their peers as well as by society. Sometimes, banks have valued and thus encouraged behavior that has hurt many people in the broader society. In some cases, the hurt was not anticipated; in other cases it was. In some cases, the hurt may even have been a source of "points" to the bankers. This can and should change: bankers should not be heedless of the broader social consequences of their actions. Liability can be seen as society's way of making people take responsibility. Stressing banker responsibility—the core of covenant banking—could help banking reclaim the esteem warranted by a true profession.

Governor Mark Carney of the Bank of England vividly describes what banking has been and could become:

The answers start from recognising that financial capitalism is not an end in itself, but a means to promote investment, innovation, growth and prosperity. Banking is fundamentally about intermediation—connecting borrowers and savers in the real economy.

In the run-up to the crisis, banking became about banks not businesses; transactions not relations; counterparties not clients. New instruments originally designed to meet the credit and hedging needs of businesses quickly morphed into ways to amplify bets on financial outcomes.

When bankers become detached from end-users, their only reward becomes money. Purely financial compensation ignores the non-pecuniary rewards to employment, such as the satisfaction from helping a client or colleague succeed.

This reductionist view of the human condition is a poor foundation for ethical financial institutions needed to support long-term prosperity. To help rebuild that foundation, financiers, like all of us, need to avoid compartmentalisation—the division of our lives into different realms, each with its own set of rules. Home is distinct from work; ethics from law; the individual from the system.

This process begins with boards and senior management defining clearly the purpose of their organisations and promoting a culture of ethical business throughout them. Employees must be grounded in strong connections to their clients and their communities. To move to a world that once again values the future, bankers need to see themselves as custodians of their institutions, improving them before passing them along to their successors.[1]

ACKNOWLEDGMENTS

We thank the participants at the first symposium of the Adolf A. Berle Jr. Center on Corporations, Law and Society at Seattle University School of Law, organized by Professor Charles O'Kelley, where the ideas in this book were first presented and developed. Hill also thanks participants at the Canadian Law and Economics Association conference, the European Law and Economics Association conference, the Midwestern Law and Economics Association conference, the Gruter Institute conference, the Boston University Review of Banking and Financial Law symposium on shadow banking, Notre Dame's symposium on corporate governance and business ethics in a postcrisis world, *University of St. Thomas Law Journal*'s symposium, beyond crisis-driven regulation, and participants at seminars and presentations at the University of British Columbia Faculty of Laws, Florida State University College of Law, Fordham Law School's Corporate Law Center, the University of Illinois at Champaign-Urbana, the Interdisciplinary Center/Herzliya (Israel), the Université de Paris–Nanterre, the Faculty of Laws of Queen's University (Canada), and the Western Ontario Faculty of Laws. Painter thanks participants in faculty colloquia at the University of Minnesota, the University of St. Thomas, the University of Nebraska, Valparaiso University, and the University of Illinois at Champaign-Urbana for helpful suggestions, as well as participants in the Henry Kaufman symposium on religion and business at the University of Maryland. Painter thanks the Safra Center for Ethics at Harvard University, where he is a fellow for the 2014–15 academic year, for financial support during the latter stages of this project, as well as for very helpful suggestions from participants in weekly seminars at the Safra Center.

Hill and Painter also thank the following people for very useful conversations and reviews of the manuscript: Bill Black, Susanna Blumenthal, Gene Borgida, June Carbone, Mary Anne Case, Boudewijn de Bruin, Allan Erbsen, Michael Frankel, Tamar Frankel, Erik Gerding, Stuart Green, Sean Griffith, Jill Herbert, Martin Hellwig, Peter Huang, Wulf Kaal, Leo Katz, Jonathan Knee, Art Markman, Brett McDonnell, Bill McGeveran, Justin

O'Brien, Saule Omarova, Frank Partnoy, Sharon Reich Paulsen, Paul L. Rubin, Malcolm Salter, Janis Sarra, Dan Schwarcz, Susan Sered, Bobbie Spellman, Kathleen Vohs, Chuck Whitehead, and Jennifer Wilson. We have also discussed the book with many other people in a variety of settings, and we are grateful for the many helpful suggestions we have received.

Hill and Painter also thank David Pervin, our original editor at University of Chicago Press, who encouraged us in early stages and helped us get the project through the proposal stage, and Joe Jackson, who succeeded David Pervin, and who helped us in the later stages. Both David and Joe made the book much better than it would otherwise have been. In addition, Yvonne Zipter's assistance in manuscript preparation has been invaluable.

Rashida Adams, Dan Cohn, Kyle Kurowski, Stephanna Szotkowski, Andrew Thompson, John M. Schwietz, Anna Luczkow, and Michael Burke provided able research and editing assistance, as did the following librarians: Connie Lenz, Mary Rumsey, Suzanne Thorpe, and David Zopfi-Jordan. Julie Friesner provided excellent editorial assistance. Hill and Painter also thank the community at the University of Minnesota, mostly the law school, but also other parts of university, for providing an environment where people have a considerable stake in contributing to their colleagues' work.

Finally, Claire Hill thanks her partner Eric Hillemann, who did all the usual wonderful things partners do in these situations, and more.

Richard Painter is grateful to the two people to whom he has dedicated this book for insightful conversations over many years about the broker-dealer industry: his grandfather, the late Sidney Homer Jr., who spent his life working in the bond business, and his father William H. Painter, whose perspective on broker-dealer regulation informed Congress, regulators, lawyers, and several generations of law students.

NOTES

Introduction

1 Carney, "Inclusive Capitalism: Creating a Sense of the Systemic," May 27, 2014.
2 Dudley, "Ending Too Big to Fail," November 7, 2013. Dudley came to the Federal Reserve from Goldman Sachs, where he worked from 1986 to 2007.
3 The CFTC's fines totaled $1.475 billion and were assessed against Citibank, JPMorgan, RBS, UBS, and HSBC; the Office of the Controller of the Currency's fines totaled $950 million and were assessed against Bank of America, JPMorgan, and Citibank; the Financial Conduct Authority of Britain's fines totaled £1.1 billion ($1.768 billion), and were assessed against Citibank, HSBC, JPMorgan, RBS, and UBS; and the Swiss Financial Market Supervisory Authority FINMA's fines were assessed against UBS, for $138 million. U.S. Commodities Futures Trading Commission, "CFTC Orders Five Banks to Pay over $1.4 Billion in Penalties," November 12, 2014; Office of the Comptroller of the Currency, "OCC Fines Three Banks $950 Million," November 12, 2014; and Financial Conduct Authority, "FCA Fines Five Banks £1.1 Billion for FX Failings," November 12, 2014.
4 See, e.g., Bray, "Switzerland Opens Criminal Inquiry," November 13, 2014; Viswanatha and Freifeld, "Global Banks Entering Higher-Stake Phase," November 13, 2014; McLaughlin, "Banks Get December Deadline," November 14, 2014; and Farrell, "Lawsky Said to Probe," December 11, 2014.
5 U.S. Department of Justice, "BNP Paribas Agrees to Plead Guilty," June 30, 2014.
6 U.S. Department of Justice, "Credit Suisse Pleads Guilty to Conspiracy to Aid and Assist U.S. Taxpayers in Filing False Returns," May 19, 2014.
7 In September of 2013, JPMorgan agreed to pay $920 million to four regulators, three in the United States (the SEC, the Federal Reserve, and the Office of the Comptroller of the Currency) and the UK's Financial Conduct Authority. U.S. SEC, "JPMorgan Chase Agrees to Pay $200 Million," September 19, 2013. In October 2013, JPMorgan agreed to pay $100 million to the CFTC. Order, *In re* JPMorgan Chase Bank, N.A. CFTC Docket No. 14-01 (Commodity Futures Trading Commission, October 16, 2013).
8 Griffin and Campbell, "U.S. Bank Legal Bills Exceed $100 Billion," August 28, 2013. Some other articles discussing the large costs incurred by banks include Silver-Greenberg, "Hampered by Legal Costs, JPMorgan's Profit Falls 7.3%"; Alden, "Legal Costs Weighed on Wall Street's First-Half Profits," January 14, 2014; Bray, "Profit Falls 26% at Barclays, Weighed Down by Legal Costs," October 30, 2014, and "R.B.S. Profit Weighed Down by $1.25 Billion for Legal Costs," October 31, 2014; and Popper, "Under Investigation, JPMorgan Increases Its Potential Legal Costs," November 3, 2014.
9 Board of Governors of the Federal Reserve System, "Independent Foreclosure Review to Provide $3.3 Billion in Payments, $5.2 Billion in Mortgage Assistance," Janu-

ary 7, 2013; U.S. Department of Justice, "$25 Billion Mortgage Servicing Agreement Filed in Federal Court" March 12, 2012.

10 Schwartz, "James Gorman of Morgan Stanley, Going against Type," June 28, 2014; and Trefis Team, "A Look at Barclays' Revamped Strategy and Its Impact on the Bank's Shares," May 15, 2014. See also Solomon, "In Tough Market, Investment Banks Seek Shelter or Get Out," June 10, 2014.

11 See, e.g., Barclays response to a critique of its behavior in "Barclays Response to the *Salz Review*," April 2013; and Deutsche Bank's website page, "Responsibility: Cultural Change and Corporate Values," updated October 22, 2014.

12 The September 26, 2007, e-mail from Peter Kraus, co-head of Goldman's Investment Banking Division, to Blankfein is included in the Staff of Senate Permanent Subcommittee on Investigations, 112th Cong., *Wall Street and the Financial Crisis: Anatomy of a Financial Collapse*, April 13, 2011, 625 (hereafter cited as *Levin-Coburn Report*). Also see Greg Smith's interview with Anderson Cooper on *60 Minutes*— "Goldman Sachs VP Explains Why He Quit," October 21, 2012. The following interchange occurs between 8:42 and 9:30 in the interview:

Anderson Cooper: Smith says he grew even more disillusioned after the Senate hearings, when he and a Goldman Sachs partner met in Asia with a major client, the head of one of the biggest funds in the world.

Greg Smith: And he looks me and a partner in the eye and says, "Let me be honest with you guys. We don't trust you at all. But don't worry. There's nothing to worry about. We're gonna keep doing business with you because you're the biggest bank. You're the smartest. And actually we have to do business with you." Now my jaw almost dropped because hearing from one of your biggest clients that they don't trust you when your whole mantra and reputation is built on trust, to me, it was the worst possible thing you can hear. And then I leave the meeting and the partner from Goldman Sachs who I was with is jubilant. "This is great news. The client is gonna keep doing business with us because they have to."

13 Financial Crisis Inquiry Commission, *Financial Crisis Inquiry Commission Report* (hereafter cited as *FCIC Report*), January 2012, 236. The FCIC was bipartisan, but all four Republican members dissented from its report, although they agreed with parts of it.

14 Obama, "Remarks by the President at Presentation of Medal of Honor to Sergeant Kyle J. White, US Army," May 13, 2014.

15 UK House of Commons, Treasury Committee, *Financial Institutions—Too Important to Fail*, vol. 2, *Oral and Written Evidence*, March 29, 2010 (testimony of E. Gerald Corrigan, February 2010), Ev 52.

16 Lewis, *Liar's Poker*, 33 (quoting Salomon bond analyst Sidney Homer).

17 Michael Lewis may be going a bit further than is necessary when he says in the last sentence of his review of Greg Smith's book on Goldman Sachs: "The ultimate goal should be to create institutions so dull and easy to understand that, when a young man who works for one of them walks into a publisher's office and offers to write up his experiences, the publisher looks at him blankly and asks, 'Why would anyone want to read that?'" (Lewis, "The Trouble with Wall Street," February 4, 2013).

18 For a discussion of Catholic social thought and ethics in investment banking, see Painter, "The Moral Responsibility of Investment Bankers."

19 Deutsche Bank, "Responsibility: Cultural Change and Corporate Values."
20 Goldman Sachs, *Business Standards Committee Impact Report.*
21 Ibid., 3.
22 Ibid., 4.
23 Ibid.
24 Ibid., inside front cover (before p. 1).
25 Barclays PLC, "Barclays Response to the *Salz Review*," 2, and passim.
26 Dudley, "Enhancing Financial Stability by Improving Culture in the Financial Services Industry," October 20, 2014. Dudley suggested, among other reforms, that bankers be required to post "performance bonds" from compensation to cover the cost of regulatory fines. This concept is discussed further in chapter 5 of this book.

Chapter 1

1 Smith, "Goldman Sachs VP Explains." A former employee of Lehman provides a similar account on his blog, an extensive quote from which is reproduced in the text accompanying n. 30, chap. 3, of this book (Chirls, "My Time at Lehman," April 9, 2013).
2 This chapter describes many settlements, some quite large; in a fair number of cases, a bank settles allegations that are quite similar to previous allegations it has settled.
3 Wyatt, "Promises Made, and Remade, by Firms in S.E.C. Fraud Cases," November 7, 2011. One example is settlements by Goldman Sachs in both 2012 and 2003 concerning the potential misuse of nonpublic information. The 2012 settlement was for $22 million and the earlier settlement was for $9.3 million. The behavior at issue in the 2012 settlement occurred between 2006 and 2011. U.S. SEC, "SEC Charges Goldman, Sachs & Co. Lacked Adequate Policies and Procedures for Research 'Huddles,'" April 12, 2012. Goldman had also entered into a consent order in 2011 with the Massachusetts Securities Division relating to the same conduct at issue in the 2012 SEC settlement. *In re* Goldman Sachs, Co., Consent Order, No. 2009-079 (Commonwealth of Massachusetts, June 9, 2011).
4 U.S. SEC, "Ten of Nation's Top Investment Firms Settle Enforcement Actions Involving Conflicts of Interest between Research and Investment Banking," April 28, 2003. Deutsche Bank also settled similar allegations in 2004. U.S. SEC, "SEC, NY Attorney General, NASD, NASAA, NYSE and State Regulators Announce Historic Agreement to Reform Investment Practices; $1.4 Billion Global Settlement Includes Penalties and Funds for Investors," December 20, 2002.
5 See *The Impact of the Global Settlement: Hearing Before the U.S. Senate Committee on Banking, Housing, and Urban Affairs*, 108th Cong. 611, 2003. For other examples where analysts' glowing public assessments of investments contrasted with private assessments that were quite negative, see In the Matter of an Inquiry by Eliot Spitzer, Affidavit in Support of Application for an Order Pursuant to General Business Law Section 354 (N.Y. Sup. Ct. 2002).
6 In the Matter of an Inquiry by Eliot Spitzer, Affidavit, 13; see also Complaint, SEC v. Grubman, No. 03 CV 2938 (S.D.N.Y. Apr. 28, 2003).
7 See Powers. Troubh, and Winokur, *Report of Investigation of Special Investigative Committee of the Board of Directors of Enron Corp.* (hereafter cited as *Powers Report*), February 1, 2002. The Library of Congress has dedicated a webpage of Congressional reports on Enron's collapse (only some of which focus on investment

banker behavior). See "Enron Hearings." Contrary to many other commentators, Frank Partnoy claims that Enron actually was profitable. See Partnoy, *Infectious Greed*, 297.

8 The types of transactions Enron used to improve its financial appearance, including prepay transactions, are detailed at length in various reports, including the *Powers Report* and Hearings before the U.S. Senate Permanent Subcommittee on Investigations, *The Role of Financial Institutions in Enron's Collapse*, app. B.

9 "In a prepay transaction . . . the purchaser pays for a commodity upfront, in full, at the time the contract is made, and the seller agrees to deliver the subject commodity on future dates, often over the course of several years" (U.S. SEC, "SEC Charges J. P. Morgan Chase in Connection with Enron's Accounting Fraud," July 28, 2003).

10 U.S. SEC, "SEC Settles Enforcement Proceedings against J. P. Morgan Chase and Citigroup," July 28, 2003.

11 White, "Deploying the Full Enforcement Arsenal," September 26, 2013.

12 U.S. SEC, "SEC Settles Enforcement Proceedings," July 28, 2003.

13 Lehman, CIBC, and Bank of America also settled. After they settled, the Supreme Court ruled in *Stoneridge Inv. Partners, LLC v. Scientific-Atlanta, Inc.*, 552 U.S. 148 (2008), that private plaintiffs could not bring an action under Section 10b-5 against secondary actors, parties who had not made direct statements to investors for conspiring with primary violators; other banks had been sued as well but had not yet settled. *Regents of the Univ. of Calif. v. Credit Suisse First Boston* (USA), Inc. 482 F. 3d 327 (5th Cir. 2007), *cert. denied sub nom. Regents of University of California v. Merrill Lynch, Pierce, Fenner & Smith, Inc.*, 128 S. Ct. 1120 (2008). After the Supreme Court's ruling, the cases against those other banks were terminated without those banks having made any payment.

14 *Role of Financial Institutions in Enron's Collapse*, 1:232. The SEC's allegations included that "J. P. Morgan Chase and Citigroup engaged in, and indeed helped their clients [Enron and Dynegy] design, complex structured finance transactions. The structural complexity of these transactions had no business purpose aside from masking the fact that, in substance, they were loans" (U.S. SEC, "SEC Settles Enforcement Proceedings"). The transactions helped Enron appear to have less debt than it actually had; it also helped Enron appear to have "cash flow from operations" rather than "cash flow from financing"—that is, it helped Enron appear to have generated funds from its business when it was simply borrowing money. The SEC alleged that Chase and Citi both knew that Enron's aim was "specifically to allay investor, analyst, and rating agency concerns about its cash flow from operating activities and outstanding debt. Citigroup knew that Dynegy had similar motives for its structured finance transaction" (ibid.). A Senate subcommittee had this to say about Enron's prepays:

> The participants in Enron's "prepays" were not only aware that the transactions were driven by Enron's desire to manipulate its financial statements, the financial institutions actively aided Enron in designing and implementing financial structures that created and maintained the fiction that the transactions were trades rather than loans. (*Role of Financial Institutions*, 235)
> In addition to helping Enron design and execute multiple "prepay" transactions, the financial institutions complied with Enron requests to restrict

disclosure of the nature and extent of its prepay activities. By design and intent, the "prepays" structured by Enron and the financial institutions made it impossible for investors, analysts, and other financial institutions to uncover the true level of Enron's indebtedness. (Ibid., 237)

There are many possible explanations for why major financial institutions were willing to go along with and even expand upon Enron's "prepay" activities. One obvious incentive was the fees paid by Enron which provided lucrative business deals to a number of financial institutions on Wall Street and elsewhere. Citi earned approximately $167 million from 1997 through 2001. (Ibid., 240)

One banker, from JP Morgan, wrote in an e-mail: "Enron loves these deals as they are able to hide funded debt from their equity analysts because they (at the very least) book it as deferred rev[enue] or (better yet) bury it in their trading liabilities." (Ibid., 3)

Even beyond the prepay transactions, Enron's financial statements were marvels of deception, depicting a company quite different from the real Enron. Not only was "debt" understated using various techniques including prepays, income was overstated, including through sales by Enron to entities falsely purporting to be independent of assets at inflated prices, where the entities paid with promissory notes (secured by Enron stock); also, cash flow was overstated, as Enron and its bankers found creative ways to characterize amounts borrowed as cash flow.

15 *Levin-Coburn Report*, 11. The *Levin-Coburn Report* and the *FCIC Report* are among the most important government reports on the financial crisis.

16 See Hill, "Securitization: A Low-Cost Sweetener for Lemons." There is a very long and successful history of crafting securities from prime mortgages. Lenders, including some banks, make mortgages but would rather not hold onto them, preferring to have cash to make more mortgages. Investors would like to make investments, especially safe ones, in different asset classes—investing in the right to get mortgage payments nicely complements a portfolio of stocks and bonds and offers a bit more yield than do comparably rated securities. So, banks buy many mortgages and sell the right to receive payments from the mortgages. The pool will contain mortgages selected for their quality, and for their lack of "positive correlation"—that the mortgages are sufficiently dissimilar on relevant dimensions that what affects the value of one mortgage should not affect the value of the pool as a whole—which for purposes of mortgages means that the mortgaged properties are in different regions.

There is no reason why a subprime security could not be safe—the key is in how it's structured. Some subprime mortgages will pay off and others not. Again, the keys are that the mortgages' performances not be positively correlated—as with prime mortgages, this means that they not be located in the same geographic area— and that they be carefully selected. The higher priority securities issued by a pool can be safe and appropriately highly rated. Transaction structures may, however, be tempted to make the higher priority tranches too large, such that they are less safe and their high ratings are incorrect.

17 Evidence suggests that many mortgage originators knew what was going on. See generally *Levin-Coburn Report*. Evidence also suggests there was pressure on appraisers to give the desired appraisals. See in this regard the *FCIC Report*, which dis-

cusses the issue and notes that "from 2000 to 2007 a coalition of appraisal organizations circulated and ultimately delivered to Washington officials a public petition
signed by 11,000 appraisers . . . [I]t charged that lenders were pressuring appraisers
to place artificially high prices on properties. According to the petition, lenders were
'blacklisting honest appraisers' and instead assigning business only to appraisers
who would hit the desire price targets." Ibid. at 18. See also New York State Office
of the Attorney General, "A. G. Schneiderman Secures $7.8 Million Settlement with
First American Corporation and Eappraiseit for Role in Housing Market Meltdown," September 28, 2012.

18 The recruiting even went on in church basements. See Geller, "Neighborhood
Swayed by 'Liar's Loans,'" May 26, 2007.

19 See Sepe and Whitehead, "Paying for Risk."

20 U.S. Department of Justice, "Justice Department, Federal and State Partners Secure
Record $13 Billion Global Settlement with JPMorgan," November 16, 2013.

21 Ibid.

22 JPMorgan Settlement Agreement, Annex 1: Statement of Facts, [November 19,
2013], 3–5 (emphasis added).

23 U.S. Department of Justice, "Justice Department, Federal and State Partners Secure
Record $7 Billion Global Settlement with Citigroup," July 14, 2014.

24 Citigroup Settlement Agreement, Annex 1: Statement of Facts, July 14, 2014, 7–8
(emphasis added).

25 Federal Housing Finance Agency, "FHFA's Update on Private Label Securities Actions," September 12, 2014.

26 Federal Housing Finance Agency, "Releases." The complaints are at Federal Housing
Finance Agency, "Litigation." For various reasons, some of the releases for specific
settlements recite higher settlement amounts; the amounts listed in the text are
taken from the comprehensive chart dated September 12, 2014, "FHFA's Update on
Private Label Securities Actions." Other settlements include ones by the SEC with
Goldman Sachs, for $20 million and one with JPMorgan, for $296.9 million. See
U.S. SEC, "SEC Charges J. P. Morgan and Credit Suisse with Misleading Investors
in RMBS Offerings," November 16, 2012, which describes settlements with both for
a total of $400 million. J. P. Morgan was charged with, among other things, "mis-
stat[ing] information about the delinquency status of mortgage loans that provided
collateral for an RMBS offering in which it was the underwriter. J. P. Morgan received fees of more than $2.7 million, and investors sustained losses of at least $37
million on undisclosed delinquent loans." What Credit Suisse is alleged to have
done is a bit different, and it is something JPMorgan was also alleged to have done:
when a defective mortgage was repurchased by a mortgage originator, rather than
giving the money to the investors who bought the security that included the mortgage, they kept it. Morgan Stanley settled charges similar to those against JPMorgan,
for misrepresenting the "delinquency status of mortgage loans underlying two subprime RMBS securitizations," for $275 million. U.S. SEC, "Morgan Stanley to Pay
$275 Million for Misleading Investors in Subprime RMBS Offerings," July 24, 2014.
Many more suits have been brought: some have settled, some are making their way
through the pipeline, and some have been dismissed.

27 U.S. Department of Justice, "Bank of America to Pay $16.65 Billion in Historic Jus-

tice Department Settlement," August 21, 2014. Also, Bank of America, in its capacity as successor in interest to Countrywide Financial Corporation has been assessed a civil penalty of nearly $1.3 billion for Countrywide's "intentional scheme" to misrepresent the quality of some mortgage loans it processed. U.S. v. Countrywide Financial Corporation, Inc., 996 F. Supp. 2nd 247 (S.D. N.Y. 2014). Another example involving allegations of misrepresentations involves auction rate securities. In 2008 and 2009, Citi, UBS, JPMorgan, Morgan Stanley, Deutsche Bank, Credit Suisse, and other banks settled allegations that they sold investors risky auction-rate securities (ARS) as safe and highly liquid, comparing the securities' liquidity to that of money market investments. See U.S. SEC, "SEC Finalizes ARS Settlements with Citigroup and UBS," December 11, 2008 ($22.7 billion to UBS customers and $7 billion to Citi customers, for a total of $30 billion), "SEC Finalizes ARS Settlement[with] Wachovia," February 5, 2009 (more than $7 billion to Wachovia customers), "SEC Finalizes ARS Settlements with Bank of America, RBC, and Deutsche Bank," June 3, 2009 (approximately $4.5 billion to Bank of America customers, $800 million to RBC customers, and $1.3 billion to Deutsche Bank customers, for a total of nearly $6.7 billion), and "SEC Enforcement Division Announces Preliminary Settlement with Merrill Lynch to Help Auction Rate Securities Investors," August 22, 2008 (Merrill Lynch to restore $7 billion to investors). When investors tried to sell the securities after the financial markets collapsed, those banks allegedly had stopped supporting the ARS market, so that the securities were completely illiquid. The settlements, with the SEC and various state regulators, required the banks to pay penalties and repurchase more than $61 billion of the securities from investors. See U.S. SEC, "Citigroup Agrees in Principle to Auction Rate Securities Settlement," August 7, 2008 (Citi agrees to return $7.5 billion to investors, small businesses, and charities); New York State Office of the Attorney General, "Attorney General Cuomo Announces Settlement with UBS to Recover Billions for Investors in Auction Rate Securities," August 8, 2008; and Minnesota Department of Commerce, "Auction Rate Securities Settlements."

28 U.S. Department of Justice, "Bank of America to Pay $16.65 Billion." The settlement almost derailed as two SEC commissioners argued for additional sanctions, but it ultimately went through. Michaels, Schmidt, and Geiger, "BofA Mortgage Settlement Stalls over SEC Political Fight," October 27, 2014; In re Bank Of America, N.A. and Merrill Lynch, Pierce, Fenner & Smith, Inc., Waiver Order, Securities Act Release No. 9682, November 25, 2014.

29 For simplicity, we do not discuss "hybrid" CDOs that have both actual mortgage exposure and bets with others on such exposure. The Stack-1 transaction discussed in the text accompanying n. 53, chap. 1, of this book was a hybrid.

30 One reason why CDOs were created is that some of the more junior interests were far less popular than either the senior or most junior interests. With appropriate structuring, a pool of these less popular interests could be formed that would be able to sell interests in itself, also at different levels of seniority. But the problem remained: the new "structuring" that turned B (relatively junior) pieces into more senior pieces generated more B pieces, which had to be sold to still other CDOs, kicking the can farther down the road.

31 In a few instances, however, investors apparently received oral or even written rep-

resentations seemingly contradicting the boilerplate disclaimers. See Basis Yield Alpha Fund (Master) v. Goldman Sachs, 37 Misc.3d 1212(A) (N.Y. Sup. Ct. Oct. 18, 2012), aff'd as modified, Basis Yield Alpha Fund (Master) v. Goldman Sachs Group, Inc., 115 A.D.3d 128 (2014). We cannot know whether representations contradicting boilerplate disclaimers were given more often, but it does seem possible.

32 See U.S. SEC, "Goldman Sachs to Pay Record $550 Million," July 15, 2010.

33 Ibid.

34 Protess, "Ex-Goldman Trader Tourre Fights S.E.C. Penalties in Fraud Case," January 22, 2014. Tourre was fined $650,000 and was required to give up a $175,463 "bonus plus interest linked to the transaction" (Raymond and Stempel, "Big Fine Imposed on Ex-Goldman Trader Tourre in SEC Case," March 12, 2014). In May 2014, Tourre decided not to appeal his case (Protess, "Former Goldman Trader Tourre Says He Will Not Appeal," May 27, 2014). At this writing, Tourre is enrolled in an economics PhD program at the University of Chicago. He had been scheduled to teach a course at the school, but this arrangement was terminated before the course began (Abrams, "In Change, Tourre Won't Be Teaching University of Chicago Course," March 4, 2014).

35 SEC v. Citigroup Global Markets Inc., Complaint, No. 11-CV-7387 (S.D.N.Y. Oct. 19, 2011), at 10.

36 U.S. SEC, "Citigroup to Pay $285 Million," October 19, 2011; and In re Credit Suisse Alternative Capital, LLC. Order Instituting Administrative and Cease-and-Desist Proceedings, LLC, Securities Act Release No. 9268, Investment Advisers Act Release No. 3302, Administrative Proceeding File No. 3-14594 (Oct. 19, 2011).

37 In re Credit Suisse Alternative Capital, LLC., at 4.

38 U.S. SEC, "Citigroup to Pay $285 Million." The settlement with Credit Suisse (Credit Suisse Alternative Capital and its successor in interest, Credit Suisse Asset Management) is in In re Credit Suisse. The Citi employee who wrote the e-mail quoted in the text, Brian Stoker, was also sued by the SEC in connection with this transaction. Mr. Stoker was found not liable (U.S. SEC, "Brian Stoker Found Not Liable," November 21, 2012). See also Lattman, "S.E.C. Gets Encouragement from Jury That Ruled against It," August 3, 2012.

39 SEC v. Citigroup Global Markets Inc., 827 F.Supp.2d 328 (S.D.N.Y. 2011).

40 SEC v. Citigroup Global Markets Inc. 752 F.3d 285 (2nd Cir. 2014) (vacating and remanding the District Court's decision); SEC v. Citigroup Global Markets Inc. 34 F. Supp. 3d 397 (S.D.N.Y. 2014) (on remand, approving the settlement). See also U.S. SEC, "Statement on 2nd Circuit Decision," June 4, 2014.

41 Or more precisely, its commercial paper conduit. SEC v. J.P. Morgan Securities LLC, Complaint, No. 11-04206 (S.D.N.Y. June 21, 2011), at 2.

42 U.S. SEC, "J. P. Morgan to Pay $153.6 Million," June 21, 2011.

43 U.S. SEC, "SEC Charges Merrill Lynch with Misleading Investors in CDOs," December 12, 2013. See also Eisinger and Bernstein, "The Magnetar Trade," April 9, 2010; and New York Times Dealbook, "Magnetar's Big Subprime Trade," April 15, 2010.

44 Pursuit Partners, LLC v. UBS AG, 48 Conn. L. Rptr. 557, 565 (2009).

45 Ibid., 557. UBS dropped its appeal, "State of Connecticut Judicial Branch Supreme and Appellate Court Case Detail: SC 18533," February 15, 2011.

46 Pursuit Partners. UBS also settled with the SEC for $50 million for violating securi-

ties laws when structuring and marketing other CDO deals. According to the SEC, UBS received upfront payments while acquiring CDS for its ACA ABS 2007-2 CDO but failed to transfer the payments to the CDO and did not report to investors that it retained the upfront payments. U.S. SEC, "UBS to Pay $50 Million," August 6, 2013.

47 Childs, "Citigroup Lost $15 Million," February 13, 2013.

48 *Levin-Coburn Report*, 394–95. Timberwolf is one of the deals at issue in a private party suit against Goldman.

49 *FCIC Report*, 235–36.

50 *Levin-Coburn Report*, 394. The 36 percent number is from p. 10 of the report.

51 Ibid., 331–32. Deutsche Bank wasn't able to sell the whole deal, and lost a considerable amount from pieces it retained.

52 Deutsche Bank settled with Lehman over Gemstone CDO for $42 million. See Motion to Settle, *In re* Lehman Brothers Holding Inc., No. 08-13555 (Bankr. S.D.N.Y. Aug. 24, 2012). Deutsche Bank settled for $55 million with M&T Bank. See M&T Bank Corp. v. Gemstone CDO VII, LTD., 68 A.D.3d 1747 (N.Y. Sup. Ct., 4th Dep't 2009).

53 China Development Industrial Bank v. Morgan Stanley & Co. Inc., 86 A.D.3d 435, 436 (N.Y. A.D. 2011). Morgan Stanley was also sued by Basis Yield Alpha Fund in connection with Basis's purchase of Stack 2006-1 securities; the judge allowed some of Basis's claims to proceed. Basis Yield Alpha Fund Master v. Morgan Stanley & Co. LLC., 2013 WL 942539 (N.Y. Sup. Ct. 2013).

54 "China Development Industrial Bank v. Morgan Stanley, Affirmation of Jason C. Davis," March 16, 2007. Morgan Stanley reportedly made the following statement on the issue of these and the other like names discussed for the transaction: "While the e-mail in question contains inappropriate language and reflects a poor attempt at humor, the Morgan Stanley employee who wrote it was responsible for documenting transactions," the bank wrote in a statement to *ProPublica*. "It was not his job or within his skill set to assess the state of the market or the credit quality of the transaction being discussed." Eisinger, Financial Crisis Suit Suggests Bad Behavior at Morgan Stanley," January 23, 2013. See also, Chatterjee, "Morgan Stanley Knew about 'Nuclear Holocaust' Mortgage Loans," January 23, 2013; and Levine, "Morgan Stanley Finalizes Its Entry," January 23, 2013.

55 The full e-mail chain is available at China Development Industrial Bank v. Morgan Stanley & Co., Report of Mark N. Froeba, Exhibit A, No. 650957/2010 (N.Y. Sup. Ct., Aug. 13, 2012), at 2–6.

56 "SEC Settles with Former Officers of Subprime Lender," August 2, 2010; McLean and Nocera's *All the Devils Are Here*, describes New Century's slide into bankruptcy (251–52, and 256).

57 David Jacob, a former executive managing director of Global Structured Finance at Standard & Poor's (S&P), wrote in a letter to the SEC: "I was and remain a strong advocate for securitization. However, somewhere along the way, bad practices began to rot the foundation of this innovative market. One of these practices was how issuers and Wall Street pressured and manipulated the credit rating agencies (CRAs) to obtain higher ratings, and how the CRAs allowed this to happen to maintain or grow their market share. . . . The problems arising from this bad behavior were magnified and created great systemic risk. Rating shopping and criteria cater-

ing led to the downward spiral of credit risk miss-estimation by the CRAs" (Jacob, letter to SEC Secretary Elizabeth M. Murphy, June 3, 2013).

Securities issuers didn't used to have the power to play off agencies against each other. Moody's and Standard & Poor's had a "partner monopoly," in which both agencies' ratings were needed for market acceptance; issuers therefore had to go to both. Fitch's ascendance as a plausible third rater in the sphere of structured finance is an important part of the story by which ratings shopping became realistic (and common). Hill, "Why Did Rating Agencies Do Such a Bad Job?" and "Rating Agencies Behaving Badly."

58 The August 20, 2007, e-mail is in *Levin-Coburn Report Exhibits*, ex. 95b; see also Ovide, "Inside S&P," September 27, 2011. The bank involved was the U.S. investment banking subsidiary of Japanese bank Mizuho; Mizuho agreed to pay $127.5 million to settle SEC charges in connection with this deal. See U.S. SEC, "SEC Charges Mizuho Securities," July 18, 2012.

59 They would also press rating agencies for ratings so quickly that the agencies did not have time to do proper reviews. See various May 2007 e-mails from Eric Kolchinsky of Moody's to Yvonne Fu and Uri Yoshizawa, also of Moody's, in *Levin-Coburn Report Exhibits*.

60 Salmon, "Why Did All Those Super-Seniors Exist?" April 28, 2010.

61 See Fligstein and Goldstein, "The Transformation of Mortgage Finance and the Industrial Roots of the Mortgage Meltdown," June 2014, 28, and generally. For a discussion of Lehman and Bear Stearns' (and insurance giant AIG's) failures, see Madden, "A Weapon of Mass Destruction Strikes" (Fall, 2008). For more Merrill Lynch coverage, see Bernstein and Eisinger, "The 'Subsidy,'" December 22, 2010. For UBS coverage, see Salmon, "How UBS Lost Money on Super-Senior Bonds," April 23, 2008.

62 Citigroup agreed to pay $75 million to the SEC to settle claims that it lied to its investors about its subprime exposure, omitting from its disclosures two types of subprime assets, super-senior tranches of CDOs and "liquidity puts." See U.S. SEC, "SEC Charges Citigroup Inc. in Connection with Misleading Disclosures," July 29, 2010; *FCIC Report*, 137–39. See also Alloway, "Citi to Pay $730m in Subprime Settlement," March 18, 2013. The two settlements were approved by U.S. District Court Judge Sidney Stein. *In re* Citigroup Inc. Securities Litigation, 965 F.Supp.2d 369 (S.D.N.Y. 2013); *In re* Citigroup Inc. Bond Litigation, 296 F.R.D. 147 (S.D.N.Y. Aug. 20, 2013).

63 U.S. SEC, "SEC Charges Citigroup and Two Executives for Misleading Investors," 29, 2010; and *In re* Gary L. Crittenden and Arthur H. Tildesley, Jr., Securities Act Release No. 62593 Administrative Proceeding File No. 3-13985 (July 29, 2010).

64 *FCIC Report*, 261 (emphasis added). This exposure to super-senior losses was what caused AIG's meltdown. AIG and a few other entities, but mostly AIG, wrote— that is, sold—insurance against them, in the form of credit-default swaps. So, some banks' exposure was hedged, some banks' exposure was not. Goldman's largely was—the U.S. Treasury's "bailout" of AIG largely went to pay Goldman for the insurance AIG had written. Many banks, and AIG, wildly underestimated the actual risk involved. That mistake was a significant factor in the banks' and AIG's need for bailouts.

65 See generally, Acharya and Richardson, "Causes of the Financial Crisis."

66 According to Lucas, Goodman, and Fabozzi, there was $1.1 trillion dollars of issu-
ance as of 2005 (*Collateralized Debt Obligations*, 3).

67 The discussion here is partly adapted from Hill, "Bankers Behaving Badly?" 680–81.
"Repo" is short for "repurchase agreement." In a standard repurchase agreement,
one party sells securities to another, agreeing to repurchase the securities in the
(usually, very near) future at a price higher than the sales price.

68 In 2007, banks started to feel pressure to reduce their leverage, lest they be downgraded by the rating agencies. *In re* Lehman Brothers Holdings, Inc., Report of
Anton R. Valukas, Examiner, No. 08-13555 (Bankr. S.D.N.Y. Mar. 11, 2010), at 736–37.

69 Ibid., 6–8 (emphasis added). The discussion of Repo 105 takes up an entire volume
of the examiner's nine-volume report.

70 Ibid., 735.

71 Ibid., 739.

72 Various e-mails between Michael McGarvey and Jormen Vallecillo of Lehman
Brothers, dated July 2, 2008 (FOIA Confidential Treatment Requested by Lehman
Brothers Holding, Inc., LBEX-DOCID 3379145. See also *In re* Lehman Brothers
Holdings, at 739–40.

73 Ibid., 744.

74 Ibid., 742.

75 U.S. Department of the Treasury, "Remarks of Secretary Lew at Pew Charitable
Trusts," December 5, 2013.

76 Tewary, "Portfolio Hedging Is Alive and Well under Volcker," December 30, 2013.

77 Board of Governors of the Federal Reserve, press release, December 18, 2014.

78 *JPMorgan Chase Whale Trades*, 1; emphasis added (hereafter cited as *Levin-McCain
Report*).

79 *Merriam-Webster Dictionary*, online, s.v. "hedge."

80 *Levin-McCain Report*, 253.

81 Ibid., 4.

82 Ibid., 57.

83 Ibid., 4

84 Ibid., 240. "Notional," for this purpose, means "face value." An example is a transaction in which one party exchanges fixed interest payments on $10,000,000 for
floating interest payments on that amount. The "notional" amount is $10,000,000.

85 Ibid., i–iii.

86 *Levin-McCain Report Exhibits*, ex. 54 See also the e-mail quoted in n. 89, this
chapter.

87 *Levin-McCain Report*, 196 (emphasis added).

88 Ibid., 14.

89 See the following e-mail correspondence, included in the *Levin-McCain Exhibits*,
ex. 79d (e-mail addresses have been deleted):
    From: MRM Reporting
    Sent: Monday, January 23, 2012 3:31 PM
    To: Dimon, Jamie; Hogan, John J.
    CC: Drew, Ina; Staley, Jes; Weiland, Peter; Bacon, Ashley; Waring, Mick; Doyle,
        Robin A.; Bisignano, Frank J; Tocchio, Samantha X; Lochtefeld, Thomas A;

GREEN, IAN; Gondell, Sarah N; MRM Firmwide Reporting; Intraspect—
LIMITS

Subject: APPROVAL NEEDED: JPMC 95% 10Q VaR One-Off Limit Approval
Importance: High

This email is to request your approval to implement the temporary increase of the Firm's 95% 10Q VaR limit from $125mm to $140mm, expiring on January 31st, 2012. There is a pending approval for a new model for the CIO Intl Credit Tranche book. If the new model is approved and implemented prior to January 31st, the Firm's 95% 10Q VaR limit will revert back to the original $125mm level.

CIO 95% VaR has become elevated as CIO balances credit protection and management of its Basel III RWA. In so doing, CIO has increased its overall credit spread protection (the action taken thus far has further contributed to the positive stress benefit in the Credit Crisis (Large Flattening Sell-off) for this portfolio which has increased from +$1.4bn to +$1.6bn) while increasing VaR during the breach period.

Action has been taken to reduce the VaR and will continue. In addition, CIO has developed an improved VaR model for synthetic credit and has been working with MRG to gain approval, which is expected to be implemented by the end of January.

From: Hogan, John J.
To: MRM Reporting; Dimon, Jamie
CC: Drew, Ina; Staley, Jes; Weiland, Peter; Bacon, Ashley; Waring, Mick; Doyle, Robin A.; Bisignano, Frank J; Tocchio, Samantha X; Lochtefeld, Thomas A; GREEN, IAN; Gondell, Sarah N; MRM Firmwide Reporting; Intraspect—
LIMITS

Sent: Mon Jan 23 17:44:41 2012
Subject: Re: APPROVAL NEEDED: JPMC 95% 10Q VaR One-Off Limit Approval
I approve.

From: Dimon, Jamie
Sent: Mon, 23 Jan 2012 23:13:18 GMT
To: Hogan, John J.; MRM Reporting
CC: Drew, Ina; Staley, Jes; Weiland, Peter; Bacon, Ashley; Waring, Mick; Doyle, Robin A.; Bisignano, Frank J; Tocchio, Samantha X; Lochtefeld, Thomas A; GREEN, IAN; Gondell, Sarah N; MRM Firmwide reporting; Intraspect—
LIMITS

Subject: Re: APPROVAL NEEDED: JPMC 95% 10Q VaR One-Off Limit Approval
I approve.

90 Note that Ina Drew told the Office of the Comptroller of the Currency that "investment decisions are made with full understanding of executive management including Jamie Dimon" and that "everyone knows what is going on" (OCC, "OCC Assesses $300 Million Civil Money Penalty," September 19, 2013). See text accompanying n. 99 chap. 1, of this book, for more context.

91 *Levin-McCain Report*, 11, 156.

92 One exhibit in the report is a list of "inaccurate public statements" made on an April 13, 2012, earnings call:

Re Risk Managers: "All of those positions are put on pursuant to the risk management at the firm-wide level."

Re Regulators: "All those positions are fully transparent to the regulators."

Re Long-Term Decisions: "All of those decisions are made on a very long-term basis."

Re Hedging: "We also need to manage the stress loss associated with that portfolio . . . so we have put on positions to manage for a significant stress event in Credit. We have had that position on for many years. . . ."

Re Volcker Rule: "We believe all of this is consistent with what we believe the ultimate outcome will be related to Volcker."

Levin-McCain Report Exhibits, ex. 1 f.

93 Ibid., ex. 83.
94 *Levin-McCain Report*, 252.
95 Ibid.
96 *Levin-McCain Report Exhibits*, ex. 1i.
97 Ibid.
98 Ibid., ex. 96.
99 Ibid., ex. 71. The conversation took place in May 2012.
100 *Levin-McCain Report*, 3.
101 See Financial Conduct Authority, "JPMorgan Chase Bank N.A. Fined," September 19, 2013; U.S. SEC, "JPMorgan Chase Agrees to Pay $200 Million and Admits Wrongdoing to Settle SEC Charges," September 19, 2013; OCC, "OCC Assesses $300 Million Civil Money Penalty," September 19, 2013; U.S. CFTC, "CFTC Files and Settles Charges against JPMorgan Chase Bank," October 16, 2013; SEC v. Martin-Artajo, No. 13-05677 (S.D.N.Y. Aug. 14, 2013); United States v. Martin-Artajo, No. 13-MAG-1975, sealed complaint (S.D.N.Y. Aug. 9, 2013). The CFTC required JPMorgan to admit wrongdoing—that its traders acted recklessly. Protess, "A Regulator Cuts New Teeth," October 16, 2013. Grout and Martin-Artajo have both recently appealed UK civil findings against the bank that might adversely affect their cases. Binham, "Ex-JPMorgan Trader Challenges 'Whale' Findings," July 6, 2014; Brinded, "Ex-JPM 'London Whale Conspirator' Julien Grout Appeals Civil Case," July 7, 2014. For a full overview see Hurtado, "The London Whale," updated March 5, 2015.
102 Kopecki, "JPMorgan's Drew Forfeits 2 Years' Pay as Managers Ousted," July 13, 2012.
103 Eavis, "Big Raise for JPMorgan's Dimon Despite a Rough Year," January 24, 2014; and Yang, "Jamie Dimon Got a Huge Pay Cut. Or a Huge Raise. It's Hard to Tell," April 11, 2014. See also Kopecki, "JPMorgan Awards CEO Jamie Dimon $23 Million Pay Package"; and Fitzpatrick, "Dimon Takes a 'Whale' of a Pay Cut," April 4, 2012.
104 As explained in the Financial Services Authority settlement of June 27, 2012, with Barclays:

The London Interbank Offered Rate ("LIBOR") and the Euro Interbank Offered Rate ("EURIBOR") are benchmark reference rates fundamental to the operation of both UK and international financial markets, including markets in interest-rate derivatives contracts.

LIBOR and EURIBOR are by far the most prevalent benchmark reference rates used in euro, US dollar and sterling over the counter ("OTC") interest rate derivatives contracts and exchange-traded interest rate contracts. The notional amount outstanding of OTC interest rate derivatives contracts in the first half of 2011 has been estimated at 554 trillion US dollars. The total value of volume of short-term interest rate contracts traded on LIFFE [London International Financial Futures Exchange] in London in 2011 was 477 trillion euro including over 241 trillion euro relating to the three month EURIBOR futures contract (the fourth largest interest rate futures contract by volume in the world).

Financial Services Authority, "Final Notice to Barclays Bank plc," June 27, 2012, 1; see also *Salz Review*, 64–66.

105 The FSA report described Barclays's misconduct as including:

making submissions which formed part of the LIBOR and EURIBOR setting process that took into account requests from Barclays' interest rate derivatives traders. These traders were motivated by profit and sought to benefit Barclays' trading positions;

seeking to influence the EURIBOR submissions of other banks contributing to the rate setting process; and

reducing its LIBOR submissions during the financial crisis as a result of senior management's concerns over negative media comment.

Financial Services Authority, "Barclays Fined £59.5 Million," June 27, 2012.

As a result of the scandal, the procedure by which LIBOR is set has been changed. The administrator now charged with administering LIBOR aims "to re-turn credibility, trust and integrity to benchmarks" (ICE Services, "ICE Benchmark Administration: Overview").

106 According to some sources, it has been going on a lot longer, maybe even since 1991. See Keenan, "My Thwarted Attempt to Tell of Libor Shenanigans," July 26, 2012; see also Gongloff, "Libor Fraud Was Happening in 1991," July 27, 2012.

107 U.S. CFTC, "CFTC Orders Barclays to Pay $200 Million Penalty"; U.S. Department of Justice, "Barclays Bank PLC Admits Misconduct," June 27, 2012.

108 Muñoz and Colchester, "Top Officials at Barclays Resign over Rate Scandal," July 4, 2012.

109 See U.S. CFTC, "CFTC Orders UBS to Pay $700 Million Penalty," December 19, 2012 (in addition to the $700 million, UBS agreed to pay $259.2 million to FSA, $500 mil-lion to the Department of Justice, and $64.3 million to the Swiss Financial Market Authority, for a total of $1.52 billion), "CFTC Orders the Royal Bank of Scotland," February 6, 2013 (the Royal Bank of Scotland plc and RBS Securities Japan Limited were collectively fined $150 million by the U.S. Department of Justice, $325 million by the CFTC, and $137 million by the FSA, for a total of $612 million); "Deutsche Bank to Pay $800 Million Penalty to Settle CFTC Charges of Manipulation, At-tempted Manipulation, and False Reporting of LIBOR and Euribor," April 23, 2015 ($800 million by the CFTC; $775 million by the DOJ; £266.8 by the FCA, and $600 million by the New York State Department of Financial Services); and Finch, For-tado and Brush, "RBS Fined $612M by Regulators," February 6, 2013. See also En-rich, "Banks to Be Hit with Rate Fines." November 5, 2013.

110 See European Commission, "Antitrust: Commission Fines Banks € 1.71 Billion," December 4, 2013. Barclays and UBS assisted the European Commission with its investigation and avoided fines. Broker-dealer firm RP Martin was also fined (ibid.).

111 Financial Conduct Authority, "Lloyds Banking Group Fined £105m," July 7, 2014.

The Financial Conduct Authority is a successor to the Financial Services Authority. As of April 2013 the Financial Services Authority split into the Financial Conduct Authority and the Prudential Regulatory Authority. U.S. CFTC, "CFTC Charges Lloyds Banking Group," July 28, 2014. As of July 28, 2014, the CFTC's total penalties in connection with LIBOR and other benchmark interest rates have been $1.87 billion (ibid.). U.S. Department of Justice, "Lloyds Banking Group Admits Wrongdoing," July 28, 2014.

112 The CFTC fined Rabobank $475 million for its involvement in the LIBOR scandal. The Department of Justice also imposed a fine of $325 million, and the FCA fined Rabobank $170 million. U.S. CFTC, "Rabobank to Pay $475 Million Penalty," October 29, 2013; U.S. Department of Justice, "Rabobank Admits Wrongdoing," October 29, 2013; Financial Conduct Authority, "The FCA Fines Rabobank £105 Million," October 29, 2013.

113 Currier, "Beyond Barclays," July 6, 2012; New York Times Dealbook, "Understanding the Rate-Fixing Inquiry," updated July 28, 2014; Taibbi, "Everything Is Rigged," April 25, 2013; and Scannell, Hall, and Schäfer, "NY Regulator Opens Currency Probe," February 5, 2014. Indeed, both federal and state regulators, notably the New York and Connecticut attorneys general, are among those investigating (Albergotti and Eaglesham, "9 More Banks Subpoenaed over Libor," October 25, 2012). Other regulators, as well as private parties, are also investigating and, in some cases, bringing lawsuits. See In re Libor-Based Financial Instruments Antitrust Litigation, 935 F. Supp. 2d 666 (S.D.N.Y. 2013), reversed in part by Gelboim v. Bank of America Corp. 135 S. Ct. 897 (2015), which holds that plaintiffs who had their cases dismissed in the consolidated action had a right of immediate appeal. A recent suit against the banks that were charged by the Federal Deposit Insurance Corporation (FDIC) with setting LIBOR alleged that they "fraudulently and collusively suppressed USD LIBOR, and they did so to their advantage" (Federal Deposit Insurance Corporation v. Bank of America Corporation, Complaint, No. 14-01757 (S.D.N.Y. Mar. 14, 2014), at 1). See also Armour, "FDIC Sues Banks over Libor," March 14, 2014. Also, the EU recently charged HSBC, JPMorgan, and Crédit Agricole with participating in a cartel to manipulate interest rate derivatives deriving their value from EURIBOR. European Commission, "Antitrust: Commission Sends Statement of Objections to Crédit Agricole, HSBC and JPMorgan," May 20, 2014.

114 Financial Services Authority, "Final Notice to Barclays Bank plc.," 19.

115 Ibid., 40 (emphasis added).

116 U.S. CFTC, "CFTC Orders the Royal Bank of Scotland plc." Here are findings from Lloyd's settlement with the CFTC:

> Before the acquisition of HBOS [banking and insurance company] by Lloyds Banking Group in January 2009, the Sterling and US Dollar LIBOR submitters at each bank individually altered LIBOR submissions on occasion to benefit the submitters' and traders' cash and derivatives trading positions. Upon the consolidation of the two companies, the submitters, who were located in separate offices, coordinated with one another to adjust LIBOR submissions to benefit their respective trading positions.
>
> From at least mid-2006 to October 2008, the Lloyds TSB Yen LIBOR submitter colluded with the Yen LIBOR Submitter at Coöperatieve Centrale Raiffeisen-Boerenleenbank B.A. (Rabobank) to adjust their respective Yen

LIBOR submissions to benefit the trading positions of Lloyds TSB and Rabobank.

During the global financial crisis in the last quarter of 2008, HBOS, through the acts of its submitters and a manager, improperly altered and lowered HBOS's Sterling and U.S. Dollar LIBOR submissions to create a market perception that HBOS was relatively financially healthy and not a desperate borrower of cash. Specifically, the manager who supervised the HBOS Sterling and U.S. Dollar LIBOR submitters directed the submitters to make LIBOR submissions at the rate of the expected published LIBOR so that the bank did not stand out as a material outlier from the rest of the submitting banks. The submitters followed these instructions, making submissions through the end of the year that did not reflect their honest assessment of HBOS's cost of borrowing unsecured interbank funds, and, accordingly, were not consistent with the BBA LIBOR definition.

In 2006, Lloyds TSB and HBOS submitters on certain occasions increased their bids for Sterling in the cash market in an attempt to manipulate the published Sterling LIBOR fixing higher, thereby benefitting specific trading positions that were tied to Sterling LIBOR.

U.S. CFTC, "CFTC Charges Lloyds Banking Group," July 28, 2014.

117 U.S. CFTC, "CFTC Orders the Royal Bank of Scotland plc," February 6, 2013.

118 Recently, the UK brought criminal actions against a former trader at Citi and UBS. The trader was charged with "eight counts of conspiracy to defraud" for his involvement in the manipulation of LIBOR rates. See Croft and Schäfer, "First Banker to Be Charged," June 21, 2013. Other individuals are under investigation as well. In October, 2013 UK prosecutors notified twenty-two individuals that they are being investigated for involvement in LIBOR rigging, and thirteen have been charged as of April 2014. See Bray, "22 under Investigation in Libor Case in Britain," October 21, 2013; and UK Serious Fraud Office, "Further Charges in LIBOR Investigation," April 28, 2014.

119 Bray, "3 Who Worked at Barclays Face Charges in Libor Case," February 17, 2014.

120 U.S. Department of Justice, "Former Rabobank LIBOR Submitter Pleads Guilty," August 18, 2014. See also Hurtado and Schoenberg, "Rabobank Ex-Traders Charged with Yen Libor Rigging," January 14, 2014; and Protess, "Three Former Rabobank Traders Charged," January 13, 2014. Three former brokers of ICAP Plc also face criminal charges in the United States for manipulation of LIBOR. See Reuters, "Three Ex-Brokers Face Criminal Charges over Libor Scandal," September 25, 2013. An additional Rabobank trader pleaded guilty to conspiring with the original three. Stempel and Viswanatha, "UPDATE 2—U.S. Wins First Guilty Plea," June 10, 2014.

121 According to one news account, the foreign exchange rate–rigging scandal is anticipated to be just as bad as LIBOR. See Strauss and Schäfer, "Forex Claims 'as Bad as Libor.'" Various pension retirement funds have filed class action lawsuits against banks for manipulating the foreign currency exchange market from 2003 to 2013. See, e.g., Fresno County, Employees' Retirement Association v. Barclays Bank PLC, Class Action Complaint, No. 14-CV-00902 (S.D.N.Y. Feb. 11, 2014); City of Philadelphia, Board of Pensions and Retirement v. Barclays Bank PLC, Class Action Com-

plaint, No. 14-00876 (S.D.N.Y. Feb. 11, 2014); Value Recovery Fund LLC v. Barclays Bank PLC, Class Action Complaint, No. 14-CV-00867 (S.D.N.Y. Feb. 10, 2014).

122 See Leising, Fortado, and Brunsden, "Meet ISDAfix, the Libor Scandal's Sequel," April 18, 2013; Armitstead, "Terry Smith Warned Authorities ISDAfix Was Vulnerable to Manipulation," April 11, 2013; and Braithwaite, Mackenzie, and Scannell, "Brokers at ICAP in CFTC Rate Swaps Probe," April 9, 2013. Effective August 1, 2014, a new administrator has been selected to assume administration of ISDAfix, the Intercontinental Exchange Benchmark Administration, or IBA.

123 FERC, "FERC Approves Market Manipulation Settlement," January 22, 2013.

124 See Silver-Greenberg and Protess, "JPMorgan Caught in Swirl of Regulatory Woes," May 2, 2013. See also Federal Energy Regulatory Commission v. J. P. Morgan Ventures Energy Corp, No. 12-00352 (D.D.C. July 2, 2012).

125 FERC, "FERC, JP Morgan Unit Agree," July 30, 2013, and "FERC Orders $453 Million in Penalties," July 16, 2013. See also FERC, *FY 2014 Congressional Performance Budget Request*, April 2013, 30; and *Salz Review*, 204. Barclays is contesting the penalties (24/7 Wall St., "Barclays Refusing to Pay 470 Million US Penalty," July 17, 2013). See Federal Energy Regulatory Commission v. Barclays Bank PLC et al., No. 2:13-cv-02093 (E.D. Cal. Oct. 9, 2013).

126 Indeed, a Congressional investigation recently concluded that "Wall Street banks have become heavily involved with physical commodities markets, increasing risks to financial stability, industry, consumers and markets." See the press release from Senator Carl Levin's website, "Subcommittee Finds Wall Street Commodities Actions Add Risk to Economy, Businesses, Consumers," November 19, 2014.

127 European Commission, "Antitrust: Commission Sends Statement of Objections to 13 Investment Banks," July 1, 2013.

128 Dunbar, "Revealed: Goldman Sachs' Mega-Deal for Greece," July 1, 2003; and Croucher, "Eurozone Crisis," November 15, 2011. ("In a series of deals, Goldman Sachs bought Greek debt held in dollars or yen using euros, but for an off-market, made-up exchange rate. The inflated value given to the Greek debt resulted in an extra €1billion credit for Greece. This was to help Greece meet strict debt-to-GDP criteria to join the single currency laid out in the Maastricht treaty. This extra billion did not show up as Greek debt, though it would have to be paid back, in addition to the pay-out on maturity of the bonds, at a later date. The deal was originally reported by *Risk Magazine* back in 2003. Greece was allowed to continue borrowing as it hadn't disclosed the debt from its currency swap deals. It borrowed as much as €5.3billion more because of the off-market deals, according to a Eurostat report" [Croucher, "Eurozone Crisis," November 15, 2011].) See also Balzli, "Greek Debt Crisis," February 8, 2010; and Dunbar, "Goldman Swap Shows Greece Was Europe's Subprime Nation," January 24, 2012. One prominent blogger, Yves Smith of *Naked Capitalism*, said: "This is why I am dubious of customized OTC derivatives (as opposed to plain vanilla products, like most interest rate and currency swaps). Their main uses are regulatory arbitrage . . . (generally with very rich fees attached) or to shift risk onto chumps" ("Goldman Helped Greece Disguise Deficit," February 9, 2010).

129 Dunbar and Martinuzzi, "Goldman Secret Greece Loan," March 5, 2012; European Commission, Eurostat, *Report on the EDP Methodological Visits to Greece in 2010.*

130 Dunbar, "Revealed." A Federal Reserve investigation of the Goldman-Greece swaps was apparently abandoned without charges being brought. Robb, "Fed Ends Goldman, Greece Probe with No Action," April 14, 2010. See also Dunbar and Martinuzzi, "Goldman Secret Greece Loan," March 5, 2012.

131 Dunbar, "Goldman Swap Shows," January 14, 2014.

132 European Commission, Eurostat, *Report on the EDP,* 16–17, and "Information Note on Greece," February 24, 2010.

133 Ishmael, "Corrigan or Eurostat," February 23, 2010; and Dunbar and Martinuzzi, "Goldman Secret Greece Loan."

134 Dunbar, "Revealed." See also his report for BBC's *Newsnight,* "How Goldman Sachs Masked Greece's Debt," February 20, 2012.

135 Salmon, "How Greece Hid Its Borrowing," February 9, 2010." See also Piga, "Do Governments Use Financial Derivatives Appropriately?"; Chaffin and Hope, "EU Demands Details on Greek Swaps," February 15, 2010; and Story, Thomas, and Schwartz, "Wall St. Helped to Mask Debt Fueling Europe's Crisis," February 13, 2010.

136 UK House of Commons, Treasury Committee, *Financial Institutions,* Ev 54. For Goldman's response see Goldman Sachs, "Goldman Sachs Transactions with Greece," February 21, 2010.

137 Moore, "Goldman Would Refuse Another Greece Swap," November 21, 2013.

138 On the dispositions of various lawsuits, see n. 142 below. Holding against Deutsche Bank in a case involving a small-business customer who had incurred losses because of an interest-rate swap, a German court "concluded that Deutsche Bank had failed to adequately warn its customer, a supplier of paper products, about the risks of the transaction. . . . The bank 'deliberately designed the risk structure of the transaction to the disadvantage of the client, in order to immediately resell the risk at a profit.'" "The swaps had a negative market value of 80,000 euros on the day of the transaction, the court said, a fact that Deutsche Bank did not disclose to the customer" (Ewing and Nicholson, "German Court Rules against Deutsche Bank," March 22, 2011). At least twenty-five similar suits were brought. Another suit that raises some similar issues has been brought by the city of Pforzheim against JPMorgan (Matussek, "Pforzheim-JPMorgan Swaps").

139 Croft, "Deutsche Bank Accused of Mis-Selling Swap," October 15, 2013.

140 The case also contains allegations about Deutsche Bank's manipulation of LIBOR. Colchester, "Court Clears Way for Investor Suits over Libor," July 4, 2012; Beioley, "Freshfields and A&O's Client Deutsche Bank Loses Latest Unitech Court Outing," October 8, 2014.

141 Martinuzzi and Sirletti, "Deutsche Bank Forfeits 221 Million Euros," December 19, 2013; Bernabei and Jewkes, "Update 4-Former Monte Paschi Management Convicted as Crisis Mounts," October 31, 2014.

142 There had been criminal convictions of both banks and individuals, both of which were reversed (Legorano, "Milan Court Overturns Fraud Derivatives Case Verdict," March 7, 2014). The banks had agreed to unwind the swaps early. The case may still be appealed. See Sirletti and Martinuzzi, "JPMorgan, UBS Convictions Overturned," March 7, 2014. Milan was scarcely the only municipality entering into these sorts of deals (ibid.). Also see Elliott, "Public Health Warning," April 9, 2014. The

Italian region of Piedmont recently lost a case relating to its derivatives purchases against several European banks; it had previously settled with Merrill Lynch (Piovaccari and Landini, "Italy's Piedmont Loses Lawsuit over Derivative Contracts," July 17, 2013).

143 Walsh, "In Alabama, a County That Fell off the Financial Cliff," February 18, 2013. When Jefferson County filed for bankruptcy, it was $4.2 billion in debt. Detroit filed for bankruptcy on July 13, 2013, with approximately $19 billion in debt.

144 Most recently, the judge denied a motion by LeCroy and McFaddin for summary judgment. SEC v. LeCroy et al., No. 09-CV-02238. and partial summary judgment (N.D. Ala., S Div. September 5, 2014); Hammer, "SEC Has Jurisdiction over County's Swap Deals with JPMorgan, Judge Rules," September 10, 2014.

145 SEC v. LeCroy, Complaint, at 1–2. See also Taibbi, "Looting Main Street," March 31, 2010. Some of the payments at issue even came from the bank trying to preserve its business. ("JP Morgan at one point even paid Goldman Sachs $3 million just to back . . . off" [Taibbi, "Looting Main Street"].)

146 SEC v. LeCroy, Complaint; Whitmire and Walsh, "High Finance Backfires," March 12, 2008. See also Selway and Braun, "JPMorgan Swap Deals Spur Probe," August 11, 2011.

147 SEC v. LeCroy, Complaint at 24.

148 Ibid.

149 Ibid., 25.

150 Ibid., 30.

151 In re J. P. Morgan Securities Inc., Securities Act Release No. 9078 (Nov. 4, 2009), 4–6.

152 Ibid., 3.

153 Whitmire and Walsh, "High Finance Backfires."

154 Bond Girl, "The Incredible Story of the Jefferson County Bankruptcy," October 23, 2011. One estimate was that the swaps cost twice what they should have (Selway, "Jefferson County's Journey," September 16, 2011). Another estimate was that JPMorgan had overcharged the county by $100 million, charging $120 million for swaps that should have cost $20 million (Selway and Braun, "JPMorgan Swap Deals Spur Probe").

155 Selway and Braun, "JPMorgan Proves Bond Deal Death," August 11, 2011.

156 Walsh, "J.P. Morgan Settles Alabama Bribery Case," November 4, 2009.

157 Walsh, "In Alabama."

158 Church and McCarty, "Jefferson County Files to End Bankruptcy," July 1, 2013. With forgone fees, the "cost" to JPMorgan is about $1.5 billion (Corkery, "How Much Did Jefferson County Cost J. P. Morgan?" June 5, 2013). Per Newkirk and Edwards ("Jefferson County in New Creditors Deal with JPMorgan Concessions," November 1, 2013), "JPMorgan, the biggest U.S. bank by assets, took the lead in arranging risky securities deals that pushed the county into bankruptcy in 2011. The bank had already agreed to forgive $842 million of the $1.22 billion it was owed. Under the debt-reduction settlement, bond insurers agreed to $40 million in additional concessions; hedge funds, $17.5 million; and liquidity banks, $2.8 million. JPMorgan additionally pledged to provide a 40-year letter of credit up to $180 million, commissioners were told." See also Church, "Jefferson County JPMorgan Deal Called Safer

Than Suing," November 20, 2013. In "Bankruptcy Deal Poses New Risks for Jefferson County and Wall Street, Analysts Say," June 4, 2013, Whitmire reports: "Robert Brooks, a professor of finance at the University of Alabama, says that JPMorgan's willingness, or even eagerness, to get away from Jefferson County [agreeing to forgive $842 million of the $1.2 billion sewer debt it holds] sends a somewhat different message. 'Doesn't that strike you as extremely generous?' Brooks said. 'I wonder if perhaps there is a reason for their generosity other than they are really nice people. Obviously, you don't give up that kind of money unless you believe that your firm has inflicted harm on Jefferson County.'"

159 Wright, "Deal Puts Jefferson County on Path," June 5, 2013, "The other creditors agreeing are 'bond insurers Assured Guaranty, FGIC and Syncora and seven hedge funds' which, with JPMorgan, 'hold about $2.4 billion of the $3.078 billion sewer debt'" (Wright, "Deal Puts Jefferson County on Path"). See also Walsh, "A County in Alabama Strikes a Bankruptcy Deal." For a description of the judge's ruling in the sewer customers' appeal, see Faulk, "Federal Judge," October 1, 2014.

160 Selway and Braun, "JPMorgan Proves Jefferson County," August 11, 2011. LeCroy was sentenced to three months of incarceration followed by two years of supervised release; he paid a $15K fine, $200 special assessment, and $50K restitution prior to sentencing. Snell, the other banker charged in the matter, was sentenced to ninety days of house arrest and three years' probation and was ordered to pay the same fine and special assessment as LeCroy but did not need to pay restitution since LeCroy agreed to pay the full amount. *In re* Anthony C. Snell and Charles E. LeCroy, S.E.C. Admin. Proc. File No. 3-12359. Release No. 330 (May 3, 2007), at 19. J. P. Morgan Securities, Inc., terminated their employment. *In re* Anthony C. Snell and LeCroy, S.E.C. Admin. Proc. File No. 3-12359. Release No. 630 (October 18, 2006). Both LeCroy and Snell were charged with two counts of wire fraud; they both pleaded guilty (ibid., at 2). LeCroy was almost hired as a pension consultant by the Florida Senate, but an outcry caused his offer to be rescinded. See FBI, "White, Kemp, and 10 Others Charged in Philadelphia Corruption Case," June 29, 2004; Shiffman, "Former Executive Gets Jail, Probation Charles LeCroy Pleaded Guilty in January to Making an Illegal Payment to Ron White," June 9, 2005.

161 U.S. SEC, "Commission Declares Initial Decision Final as to Snell And LeCroy, June 4, 2007.

162 Ibid.

163 Walsh, "In Alabama." FBI, "Federal Judge Sentences Former Birmingham Mayor," December 2, 2008. One thing that emerges from the news accounts is a prominent role for Langford's great interest in clothes and shopping. Langford was beholden to Blount for paying his debts in connection with clothes acquisitions; there are mentions of Langford being taken by Blount on shopping expeditions, including to New York, courtesy of JPMorgan's largesse. Whitmire and Nossiter, "Birmingham Mayor Accused," December 2, 2008. Another commissioner, Mary Buckelew, also had a weakness for clothes and was also taken on shopping expeditions. She was "convicted in connection with accepting bribes from Blount." She pled guilty to obstruction of justice, cooperated with prosecutors, and was sentenced to three years of probation (FBI, "Federal Judge Sentences Former Birmingham Mayor," December 2, 2008).

164 Hume, "JPMorgan to Pay $228M for Municipal Bond Bid-Rigging," July 7, 2011. See also Selway and Braun, "FBI Probe of JPMorgan Fees Focuses on Swaps Roiling Muni Debt," October 27, 2008.

165 JPMorgan paid a $22 million penalty. *In re* JPMorgan Chase Bank, N.A., Consent Order, No. 2011-105, AA-EC-11-63 (Comptroller of the Currency, July 6, 2011), at 2–3. This settlement was part of a broader settlement discussed in the text accompanying n. 171, chap. 1. See also Hume, "JPMorgan to Pay," describing MacFaddin's alleged involvement in the conduct at issue. Wells Fargo entered into a similar consent agreement with the OCC, agreeing to pay a $20 million civil penalty (*in re* Wells Fargo Bank, N.A., Consent Order for a Civil Money Penalty AC-EC-11-97, December 8, 2011); Wells Fargo was also required to pay $14 million to various organizations. See also U.S. SEC, "SEC Charges Goldman Sachs," September 27, 2012, which describes a settlement on these charges with Goldman Sachs, and ongoing proceedings involving the former Goldman vice president, who eventually settled. Kantor, "SEC: Ex-Goldman Banker Fined," May 23, 2013.

166 See Maharaj and Grad, "Seducing Citron"; Martin, "Robert Citron, Culprit in California Fraud, Dies at 87," January 18, 2013: see also Greenwald and Baumohl, "The California Wipeout," December 19, 1994; and Wilmarth, "The Transformation of the U.S. Financial Services Industry," 1975, 365 ("[Orange County treasurer] Citron's highly leveraged investments [consisting of complex derivatives and other interest-sensitive securities] ultimately inflicted losses of more than $1.6 billion on Orange County"). See also Parsons, "Citron on the Witness Stand."

167 See, generally, Wayne and Pollack, "Merrill Makes Strategic Move in Ending Suit," June 4, 1998. The $430 million settlement(s) to Orange County related to the complex derivatives bought for the county by its treasurer, Robert Citron (Pollack and Wayne, "Ending Suit, Merrill Lynch to Pay California County $400 Million," June 3, 1998, settlement with county. The $2 million related to alleged misstatements in the county's notes offering underwritten by Merrill. *In re* Merrill Lynch, Pierce, Fenner & Smith Inc. Settlement. E.C. Release No. 7566 (August 24, 1998).

Another well-known example—not involving a municipality but following the same general pattern—of allegedly targeting an unsophisticated party to buy unsuitable complex derivatives, involves Bankers Trust. In the early 1990s, Bankers Trust sold Procter & Gamble and Gibson Greetings complex derivatives that caused them to lose significant amounts of money. Procter & Gamble's loss in 1994 was $157 million, "the largest derivatives loss by a nonfinancial firm" (*FCIC Report*, 47). Procter & Gamble sued Bankers Trust for fraud in connection with two transactions done in 1993; they settled, with Bankers Trust forgiving amounts they claimed were owed to them by P&G.

The sophistication of the buyers was hotly disputed, but in the course of litigation, tapes were uncovered in which Bankers Trust bankers made many compromising remarks as to their less than flattering views of their clients and how they intended to make money from their dealings with those clients. *Business Week* fought for, and won, the right to report on the material in the tapes. Procter & Gamble Co. v. Bankers Trust Co., 78 F.3d 219 (6th Cir. 1996). The *Business Week* story included the following:

It's Nov. 2, 1993, and two employees of Bankers Trust Co. are discussing a leveraged derivative deal the bank had recently sold to Procter & Gamble Co. ". . . They would never be able to know how much money was taken out of that," says one employee, referring to the huge profits the bank stood to make on the transaction. "Never, no way, no way," replies her colleague. "That's the beauty of Bankers Trust." . . .

[In] a videotaped training session for new employees . . . a bank employee tells his charges that, in a hypothetical derivative transaction among Sony, IBM, and Bankers Trust, "what Bankers Trust can do for Sony and IBM is get in the middle and rip them off—take a little money." The employee then adds: "Let me take that back. I just realized that I'm being filmed." A Bankers spokesman played six minutes of the videotape of the session for BW, which the bank says lends support to the bank's contention that the employee's comment was "a very poor attempt at humor, but nothing more," in an "otherwise dull presentation" and that the comment was taken out of context. [. . .]

An internal document about a proposed derivative for Federal Paper Board allegedly says that Bankers would make $1.6 million on the deal, including a "7 [basis point] rip-off factor." In a different instance, two Bankers employees are discussing a client's loss on a trade. One then tells the other: "Pad the number a little bit." P&G quotes another Bankers Trust employee saying to a colleague: "Funny business, you know? Lure people into that calm and then just totally f—— 'em."

In responding to conversations by Bankers Trust employees quoted in this story, a bank spokesman says that "the stupid and crude comments between Bankers Trust employees on these tapes were the basis for our disciplinary actions against these individuals last year." A number of the employees quoted in the documents have left Bankers, been disciplined, or been reassigned. (Holland, Himelstein, and Schiller, "Bankers Trust Tapes," October 16, 1995)

The *Business Week* story also reports on tapes of Bankers Trust employees talking about some deals with Procter & Gamble as "a massive huge future gravy train" and a "wet dream."

Bankers Trust also settled with Gibson Greetings, to which it had sold derivatives between 1991 and 1994. In 1994, Gibson had lost $20.7 million on the derivatives, an amount that exceeded its 1993 profits (Loomis, Barlyn, and Ballen, "Untangling the Derivatives Mess," March 20, 1995). Bankers agreed not to seek some of the payments it claimed Gibson owed to Bankers on account of the derivatives. It also paid the CFTC and the SEC a fine of $10 million to settle allegations that it had misled Gibson. A Bankers Trust employee was fined $100,000 in connection with the case. See *In re* Gary S. Missner, Securities Act Release No. 7304 (June 11, 1996). The *New York Times* reported that "the investigation relied on tapes of telephone conversations between the executive and a co-worker in which the executive worries about how to tell Gibson that it has lost money and decides to lie about the losses. 'We told him $8.1 million when the real number was $14' million, the document quotes the executive as saying. 'So now if the real number is $16, we'll tell him it is $11' million. The Government also said that Bankers Trust understated Gibson's losses on derivatives by more than 50 percent in information provided for the company's 1992 and 1993 financial statements" (Hansell, "Settlement by Bankers Trust Unit," December 23, 1994).

168 U.S. SEC, "SEC Settles with Ten Brokerage Firms," April 6, 2000.

169 When municipalities issue new debt to pay off old expensive debt, funds from new bonds are placed in escrow. The funds are then used to purchase securities to pay off debt on old bonds; typically, U.S. Treasury bills (T-bills) are purchased. However, to retain tax-exempt status, the securities purchased to pay off the old debt cannot earn a higher yield than the newly issued bonds. Bankers marketed and sold T-bills to municipalities above their fair market value and therefore lowered the yields to appear to be in compliance with the law, and banks made a profit from this financial maneuver (yield burning).

170 Typically in bid rigging, competitors (not necessarily all) agree in advance which competitor will win on a contract (in this instance, on federal, state, or local government contracts) and agree to refrain from bidding or withdraw a previously submitted bid, to submit bids that are too high or with terms that they know will not be accepted, or to rotate who will submit the lowest bid.

171 U.S. SEC, "SEC Charges Wachovia with Fraudulent Bid Rigging," December 8, 2011; see also, "SEC Charges J. P. Morgan Securities with Fraudulent Bidding," July 7, 2011; "SEC Charges UBS with Fraudulent Bidding," May 4, 2011; "SEC Charges Banc of America Securities with Fraud," February 9, 2005; and Hume, "JPMorgan to Pay."

172 See FINRA, "FINRA Fines J. P. Morgan Securities," December 13, 2007.

173 FINRA, "FINRA Sanctions Five Firms $4.4 Million," December 27, 2012.

174 The breakdown is as follows: JPMorgan— $465,700 fine and $166,676 in restitution; Citigroup— $888,000 fine and $391,106 in restitution; Merrill Lynch— $787,000 fine and $287,200 in restitution; Goldman Sachs— $568,000 fine and $115,997 in restitution; Morgan Stanley— $647,700 fine and $170,054 in restitution). Ibid.

175 U.S. Department of Justice, "BNP Paribas Agrees to Plead Guilty," June 30, 2014.

176 Ibid.

177 Ibid.

178 U.S. Department of Justice, "Exhibit A: Factual Statement," December 16, 2009, at 1.

179 Ibid. Credit Suisse's press release announcing the settlement is at Credit Suisse, "Credit Suisse Announces Settlement with US Authorities." Also see Credit Suisse's earlier press release announcing that the settlement was likely: "Credit Suisse Confirms Settlement Discussions with US Authorities," December 15, 2009.

180 U.S. Department of Justice, "Credit Suisse Agrees to Forfeit $536 Million," December 16, 2009.

181 U.S. Department of Justice, "Exhibit A: Factual Statement," at 3, agreed in connection with Deferred Prosecution Agreement; U.S. Department of Justice, "Credit Suisse Agrees to Forfeit $536 Million."

182 See U.S. Department of the Treasury, "JPMorgan Chase Bank N.A. Settles," August 25, 2011. (JPMorgan Chase sent $178.5 million transfers to Cuban persons in apparent violation of Cuban assets control regulations, made a $2.9 million loan to the bank issuer of a letter of credit involving a vessel blocked pursuant to Weapons of Mass Destruction Proliferations Sanctions Programs, and failed to respond promptly and completely to an Office of Foreign Assets Control subpoena.) JPMorgan has also been under investigation for hiring relatives of people from whom they hope to get

business in China in an alleged violation of U.S. bribery (Foreign Corrupt Practices Act) laws (Kopecki, "JPMorgan Bribe Probe Said to Expand," April 4, 2012).

183 U.S. Department of Justice, "HSBC Holdings Plc. and HSBC Bank USA N.A. Admit to Anti-Money Laundering and Sanctions Violations," December 11, 2012 (HSBC), and "Standard Chartered Bank Agrees to Forfeit $227 Million," December 10, 2012 (Standard Chartered); and New York State Department of Financial Services, "Statement From Benjamin M. Lawsky," December 11, 2012 (Standard Chartered); Board of Governors of the Federal Reserve System, "Press Release," December 10, 2012 (Standard Chartered).

184 *Salz Review*, 55. See also Protess and Silver-Greenberg, "HSBC to Pay $1.92 Billion," December 10, 2012.

185 U.S. Department of Justice, "Credit Suisse Pleads Guilty." See also Tucker and Gordon, "Credit Suisse Pleads Guilty." Credit Suisse, Switzerland's second-largest bank, had hoped to avoid the guilty plea with a deferred prosecution agreement as UBS, Switzerland's largest bank, had in 2009. See Silver-Greenberg and Protess, "In Tax Case, Credit Suisse Is Denied Milder Penalty," May 19, 2014.

186 U.S. Department of Justice, "Credit Suisse Pleads Guilty," April 12, 2013.

187 U.S. Department of Justice, "UBS Enters into Deferred Prosecution Agreement"; United States v. UBS Ag, No. 09-600033 (S.D. Fla 2009); Voreacos, "UBS Tax-Fraud Charge Is Dropped," October 22, 2010.

188 See, generally, Acharya and Richardson, "Causes of the Financial Crisis"; and UBS, "Shareholder Report on UBS's Write-Downs," April 18, 2008.

189 *FCIC Report*, 236.

190 Zibel and Johnson, "U.S. Reaches $968 Million Mortgage Settlement," June 17, 2014; Corkery and Silver-Greenberg, "SunTrust Settles with Justice Dept," June 17, 2014.

191 U.S. Department of Justice, "Federal Government and State Attorneys General Reach Nearly $1 Billion Agreement," June 17, 2014 ($968 million settlement).

192 U.S. Department of Justice, "Federal Government and State Attorneys General Reach $25 Billion Agreement," February 9, 2012.

193 U.S. Department of Justice, "Federal Government and State Attorneys General Reach Nearly $1 Billion Agreement with SunTrust," June 17, 2014.

194 Lauricella and Burne, "Chasing Yield, Investors Plow into Riskier Bonds," May 19, 2014. Some have shown willingness, at least for a time, to invest in repackaged versions of the securities of the sort whose value plummeted in the crisis (Scism and Smith, "Wall Street Wizardry Reworks Mortgages," October 1, 2009). See also Sinnock, "Market 'Overheated' for Nonperforming Mortgages," June 19, 2014.

195 Moore, "Goldman Would Refuse."

196 *In re* Del Monte Foods, 25 A.3d 813 (Del. Ch. 2011). See generally, Bratton and Wachter, "Bankers and Chancellors," which considers this and other chancery court decisions discussing bankers, including decisions critical of bankers.

197 FINRA, "FINRA Fines 10 Firms," December 11, 2014.

Chapter 2

1 *Securities Industry Study*, United States Senate, Committee on Banking, Housing, and Urban Affairs, S. Res. 109, 92nd Cong. (1972), at 7. The increase was so rapid in 1968, and old fashioned processing methods were so slow (these included use of physical stock certificates to settle trades), that a "back office" crisis crippled broker-

dealers when paperwork could not keep up with trades. Broker-dealers invested heavily in automation and other support operations only to see trading volume fall off sharply with the market decline of 1970. Brokerage profits fell precipitously, and many firms went out of business. As many as 110 broker-dealers were forced into liquidation in 1969 and 1970 (at 8).

2 See Popper and Eavis, "Errant Trades Reveal Risk," August 3, 2012.

3 U.S. v. Morgan, 118 F. Supp. 621 (S.D.N.Y. 1953).

4 Silver v. New York Stock Exchange, 373 U.S. 341 (1963).

5 For a description of Goldman Sachs' journey from partnership to LLC to public company, see Mandis, *What Happened to Goldman Sachs?* 101–7.

6 The rule was adopted on a temporary basis in 1982 and adopted permanently in 1983.

7 A court recently disallowed the use of a tax shelter marketed by Goldman Sachs, assessing penalties against the taxpayer, Dow Chemical (Chemtech Royalty Associates, L.P. v. United States, Memorandum Ruling, Nos. 05-944, 05-285, and 07-405, 2013 WL 704037 (M.D. La. 2013). The court said that "SLIPs was a marketed tax shelter presented to Dow by Goldman Sachs" (22). The court discussed Goldman's participation, noting that "Goldman and Dow worked together to ensure the banks' [other necessary participants in the deals] risk of loss would be de minimis" (26). The case refers to Goldman as having developed the transaction: "The constant refrain of business objectives [that it was necessary to say the deal had] is contrived, and wholly consistent with what Andrews & Kurth told Goldman Employees who developed SLIPs—that a business purpose was needed in order for the transaction to work" (28). The holding was affirmed on appeal, but the penalty award was vacated and remanded. Chemtech Royalty Associates, L. P., v. United States, 766 F. 3d. 453 (5th Cir. 2014). Other banks involved in tax shelter deals included Deutsche Bank, Merrill Lynch, and Bankers Trust. For further discussion on the rise of tax shelters, see Rostain and Regan, *Confidence Games*. See also *Tax Shelters: Who's Buying, Who's Selling, and What's the Government Doing about It?*

8 Copeland, "Income Evolution at BHCs," July 23, 2012.

9 *Salz Review*, 82.

10 Colchester and Enrich, "Barclays Dashes Its Global Dreams," May 9, 2014.

11 See Kaufman's foreword to Homer and Leibowitz, *Inside the Yield Book*, 1st ed., ix–xii.

12 See Painter, "Ethics and Corruption in Business and Government," July 28, 2006, 4.

13 *Broderick v. Rosner*, 294 U.S. 629 (1935).

14 Ibid., 643–44.

15 See, generally, Morrison and Willhelm, "Investment Banking: Past, Present, and Future."

16 For a brief history of Salomon Brothers, see Funding Universe, "Salomon Inc. History." For further discussion on the history of Salomon Brothers, see Ellis and Vertin, *Wall Street People*, 303–8.

17 In a recent article, "Regulatory Contrarians," Brett McDonnell and Daniel Schwarcz argue that regulatory agencies should have contrarians that help the agencies focus sufficiently on differing perspectives.

18 Kaufman, "Kaufman on Civility," June 20, 2011.

19 Ibid.

20 Sadly, as described on this book's dedication page, William Salomon passed away at the age of one hundred. See Arnold, "William Salomon Dies at 100; Wall Street Pillar Modernized Salomon Bros," December 9, 2014, for more on this exceptional man's achievements.

21 SEC v. Gutfreund et al., Administrative Proceeding No. 3-7930 (Dec. 3, 1992).

22 For discussion of Warren Buffett's role at Salomon, see Lowenstein, *Buffett: The Making of an American Capitalist*, 368–410.

23 Bennett, "City: King Salomon's Mine!" September 28, 1997.

24 Dash, "Citigroup Considers Changes at Phibro," August 7, 2009 ("Citigroup executives are considering what to do next. One option would be to transform Phibro into a partnership headed by Mr. Hall."). See also Enrich, Casselman, and Solomon, "How Occidental Scored Citi Unit Cheaply," October 12, 2009.

25 Kaufman, "Kaufman on Civility."

26 Smith, "Why I Am Leaving Goldman Sachs."

27 McLean and Nocera, *All the Devils Are Here*, 155.

28 See, e.g., Stout, *The Shareholder Value Myth*.

29 In one version of the story, academic economists are unwitting dupes, believing the incentive alignment story wholly and naively. See Dobbin and Zorn, "Corporate Malfeasance," 6–7.

30 Sociologist Dirk Zorn observes that "corporate finance had been a back-office function performed by treasurers or controllers, whose duties were confined to tasks like bookkeeping and preparing tax statements" ("Here a Chief, There a Chief," 345). Zorn argues that, "in response to an ambiguous regulatory change in accounting rules in 1979, which threatened to reduce reported earnings further at a time when corporate earnings already were under great strain, corporate leaders and finance professionals reconstructed the CFO as a solution. The CFO's popularity quickly surged as a result, and the role kept expanding in the following years to focus on managing shareholders and stock prices."

31 In the early 1960s, no firm in Zorn's sample (of four hundred industrial firms) had a CFO; by 2000, 80 percent did (ibid., 354–56). Zorn argues that "the CFO came to manage relations with shareholders, market expectations, and the firm's stock price" (352). Companies had had "bean counters"; now they had "spin doctors" (345).

32 The "stylized dance" analogy is developed more fully in Hill's 1997 article, "Why Financial Appearances Might Matter: An Explanation for 'Dirty Pooling' and Other Financial Cosmetics."

33 Dobbin and Jung, "The Misapplication of Mr. Michael Jensen," 39–40; Hill, "Why Financial Appearances Might Matter," 142.

Chapter 3

1 *Salz Review*, 177.

2 Abrams and Lattman, "Ex-Credit Suisse Executive Sentenced," November 22, 2013.

3 Tarullo, "Good Compliance, Not Mere Compliance," October 20, 2014.

4 A banker writing on the respected financial blog *Naked Capitalism* (one of the most visited such sites on the web, see Gongol, "EconDirectory.com: Traffic Rankings," as of May 15, 2013), Edward Harrison (who has his own blog, *Credit Writedowns*) writes: "You learn very quickly in investment banking that status is not all about the titles, it's more about the money. Read any account from investment banking

like *Predator's Ball* or *Liar's Poker* you will quickly notice that even the higher level guys are driven to earn a lot of money, not only for the money itself but for what that money says about their status and value relative to their peers" (Harrison, "A Banker's Perspective," February 24, 2010).

5 See, generally, Frank, *Luxury Fever*. Considerable evidence in the psychological literature bears this out. See Mandel, Petrova, and Cialdini, "Images of Success"; and Dubois and Duquesne, "The Market for Luxury Goods." A broader debate concerns whether preferences are fixed or constructed, with the authors cited here clearly on the "constructed" side. For a nuanced take on the question, see Hsee et al., "Wealth, Warmth, and Well-Being." The article argues that happiness from money and acquisition is relative (and hence could be constructed) but that happiness from consumption may sometimes be absolute, if the consumption is "inherently evaluable" (396).

6 Some recent research making this point is Salganik, Dodds, and Watts, "Experimental Study of Inequality and Unpredictability."

7 See Lea and Webley, "Money as Tool."

8 *Levin-Coburn Report*, 394.

9 *Salz Review*, 6. See also Advisory Committee on the Future of Banks in the Netherlands, *Restoring Trust*. The committee was set up in November 2008 by the board of the Netherlands Bankers' Association and the report was released April 7, 2009. The report states that "a situation in which profits accrue to the shareholders and bonus schemes while the losses are charged to taxpayers, clients and employees is no longer acceptable. A fundamental change of mentality and reorientation are therefore required in the banking sector" (7).

10 In this regard, some research suggests that disclosure of conflicts might make the discloser take more advantage than he otherwise might. See Loewenstein, Sah, and Cain, "The Unintended Consequences," February 15, 2012.

11 The *Star Trek* episode is "A Taste of Armageddon," 1967. People generally respond less strongly to difficulties faced by huge numbers of people who are mere statistics than to difficulties faced by one iconic victim. See Loewenstein and Small, "Statistical, Identifiable and Iconic Victims." Charity solicitations often prominently feature a very small number of such victims; outpourings of support are much greater than those for solicitations that feature statistics on hundreds of thousands of victims affected. See Slovic, "If I Look at the Mass."

12 Some banks are now urging bankers to not work one or more days during the weekend (Swarns, "Banks Urge Young Analysts," March 23, 2014). It will be interesting to see what effect, if any, this has.

13 In Waytz and Epley, "Social Connection Enables Dehumanization," the authors go further, arguing that just being "socially connected to close others . . . creates disconnection from more distant others." Ibid. at abstract.

14 Epley and Caruso, "Egocentric Ethics," 173.

15 Vohs, Mead, and Goode, "Merely Activating," 208, and "Psychological Consequences of Money," 1154. In one striking experiment, people were asked to draw either a dollar sign or an *S* on their foreheads. Those drawing the dollar sign were more likely to draw the sign facing themselves than were those drawing the *S*. This suggests that bankers, who are continually primed with the concept of money, might experience their own benefits as far more salient than the costs imposed on

others by their and their colleagues' behavior. Interestingly, in another experiment, when people were given financial rewards for seeing others' perspectives, they were better able to do so, making up for the detrimental effect of being primed to think about money in general. The experiment called for participants to help others navigate a maze. Participants "primed" with money, in the form of a screensaver depicting currency, did worse than those primed with a screensaver of fish: they "made more errors at adjusting their directions to their partner." But when participants "were given a cash incentive to give good directions," those primed with money did no worse than those primed with fish. For more details on both experiments see Mead et al., "There is No 'You' in Money." This suggests that monetary primes may be influencing bankers to keep their own perspectives and interests in the forefront, but that they could do otherwise and be more mindful of others if other incentives, including, somewhat paradoxically, monetary incentives, were used.

16 Reminders of money may trigger a "business decision frame," which "entails objectification of social relationships . . . in a cost-benefit calculus in which self-interest is pursued over others' interests," weakening "the pull of morality" (Kouchaki et al., "Seeing Green," 54). The article distinguishes between different "frames" that people can have, including in the context of being employees. Other possible frames include "market pricing orientation" and "economic decision." The authors find evidence that reminders of money may make a person characterize the situation he is in as a "business," a context in which what one does is "focus on one's gains and losses largely to the exclusion of benefits and costs to others." The market orientation frame takes into account proportionality of a bargain, and equity to participants in a bargain; the economic decision frame takes into account material gain. The "unethical behavior" at issue in the authors' experiment included stealing copy paper from a workplace, lying, and willingness to hire a job candidate who would provide confidential information that he was presumably not supported to provide. Nonetheless, it is interesting that the authors of an empirical paper on unethical banker behavior discussed in the text and cited in the note below found that it was banker identity, and not salience of money, that was associated with increases in banker unethical behavior.

17 Cohn, Fehr, and Maréchal, "A Culture of Cheating?" December 4, 2104, 86 and 87. The authors also found that neither the strength of a banker's desire to compete and win nor a banker's view that others were more apt to be cheating, explained why making banker identity more salient increased cheating.

18 See Schurter and Wilson, "Justice and Fairness"; and Smith, *Econned*.

19 Blankfein was speaking on gay rights at a financial industry forum. Moore and Harper, "Blankfein's Gay-Rights Stance Shows Wall Street's Dilemma," May 3, 2012.

20 Markman and Medin, "Similarity and Alignment in Choice," provides evidence that in some contexts decision makers prefer to choose among options based on alignable differences.

21 See Hsee et al., "Overearning."

22 A recent article by David Brooks depicts the ethos:

Let's say you are a student at a good high school. You may want to have a normal adolescence. But you are surrounded by all these junior workaholics who have been preparing for the college admissions racket since they were 6. You find you can't unilaterally withdraw from the rat race and still get into the college of your choice. So you also face enormous pressure to behave in a way you detest. You might call these situations brutality cascades. In certain sorts of competitions, the most brutal player gets to set the rules. Everybody else feels pressure to imitate, whether they want to or not. (Brooks, "The Brutality Cascade," March 4, 2013.)

23 See, generally, Stout, "Killing Conscience."

24 Serageldin, Higgs, and Salmaan Siddiqui all pled guilty to felonies; they, and Faisal Siddiqui, have all settled with the SEC. Serageldin was sentenced to two and a half years in jail, and the SEC fined him a little over $1 million dollars (the same amount he forfeited in the criminal case; he received dollar for dollar credit toward the civil penalty). U.S. Department of Justice, "Former Credit Suisse Managing Director Sentenced," November 22, 2013; Hurtado, "Ex-Credit Suisse CDO Chief Must Pay," January 21, 2014. The resolution of the US Attorney's cases was that Higgs had to pay nearly $1,000,000, and Siddiqui had to pay $150,000; both were sentenced to "time served" (U.S. Department of Justice, "Former Credit Suisse Managing Director Sentenced," and "Former Credit Suisse Vice President Sentenced," November 22, 2013). Higgs and Siddiqui were sued by the SEC as well as the Justice Department; Faisal Siddiqui was only sued by the SEC. For the SEC's complaint against all four, see SEC v. Serageldin, No. 12-00796 (S.D.N.Y. Feb. 1, 2012). The FBI press release describing the SEC's charges as well as those brought by the U.S. attorney is titled "Manhattan U.S. Attorney and FBI Assistant Director in Charge Announce Charges," April 12, 2013. Higgs and Siddiqui had pled guilty immediately on being charged and cooperated with authorities. An FBI press release describes the global structured credit head's guilty plea and the charges against him. See FBI, "Former Credit Suisse Managing Director Pleads Guilty." See also Lattman, "Former Credit Suisse Executive," April 12, 2013; and Vaughan, "Ex-Credit Suisse Trader Pleads Guilty," April 12, 2013. See also Eisinger, "Why Only One Top Banker," April 30, 2014.

25 This is discussed in Hill, "Tax Lawyers are People Too."

26 The concept was developed by E. Tory Higgins, a psychology professor at Columbia University. Higgins's regulatory focus theory "describes two fundamental self-regulatory systems, promotion focus and prevention focus, and the goal-pursuit strategic means preferred by each—eagerness and vigilance, respectively" (Cesario, Higgins, and Scholer, "Regulatory Fit and Persuasion," 445). See also Higgins, *Beyond Pleasure and Pain*.

27 HigginsLab, "Regulatory Focus."

28 See, e.g., Ariely, *The (Honest) Truth*.

29 See also sec. 6 of UBS, "Shareholder Report on UBS's Write-Downs," April 18, 2008, 28–42, which attributes part of UBS's difficulties to the silos in which bankers were operating.

An article of interest is Schurr et al., "Is That the Answer You Had in Mind?" The authors found that people taking a narrower perspective were less apt to see certain behavior as being unethical than were those taking a broader perspective, or to consider the consequences not just of the isolated action but of other choices and actions together.

The factors discussed in chapter 3 of this book work with more generic factors such as sunk costs, confirmation bias, motivated reasoning, and cognitive dissonance. These all lead people to be reluctant to revisit what they already think, do, and are.

30 Chirls, "My Time at Lehman."

31 Testosterone levels may be associated with risk preferences. See Apicella et al., "Testosterone and Financial Risk Preferences." The authors find that "risk-taking in an investment game with potential for real monetary payoffs correlates positively with salivary testosterone levels and facial masculinity, with the latter being a proxy of pubertal hormone exposure" (384).

32 See Zaleskiewicz, "Beyond Risk Seeking."

33 Ibid.

34 Thus, by "risk," we mean as it is colloquially understood, which maps somewhat, but not perfectly, onto the formal definition. How much risk one takes may be in part a function of one's views as to the costs one would have to bear if there were bad results. People who are more collectively oriented, or more aware of their interdependence with others, may be more inclined to take financial risks since their losses might be covered by people in their social groups but less inclined to take social risks since their embarrassment might be greater. See also Hsee and Weber, "Cross-National Differences," comparing attitudes toward financial and social risk in the United States and Asia. See also Mandel, "Shifting Selves," who finds that, when people's interdependent selves are "activated," they are more likely to take a financial risk and less likely to take a social risk than when their independent selves are activated.

35 See also Sjöberg and Engleberg, "Attitudes to Economics Risk-Taking." The authors find evidence of a "postulated cluster" of attitudes and values in students of finance. The students were "high in economic risk-taking and gambling, low in money importance and concern/worry, high in sensation seeking and success orientation, relatively low in emotional intelligence in comparison with other students, on the average, and low in altruistic values. It is reasonable to draw the conclusion that people with such characteristics also tend to invest their own and other people's money in risky projects with little regard for altruistic values."

36 Recent research supporting this proposition is found in Schurr and Ritov, "The Effect of Giving." Assigning a higher value to giving up a particular type of thing than acquiring that same type of thing may only happen if one is giving up one's last such thing.

37 See, e.g., Thaler, *Quasi-Rational Economics*. The term first appears in a paper by Thaler and Johnson, "Gambling with the House Money." A later exploration of the issue is in Ackert et al., "Examination of the House Money Effect."

38 The seminal article on this phenomenon is Kahneman and Tversky, "Prospect Theory."

39 BBC News, "How Leeson Broke the Bank," June 22, 1999. Leeson now has parlayed his notoriety into a second career as a corporate executive and dinner speaker. His website (www.nickleeson.com) welcomes visitors as follows: "Welcome to the official website of Nick Leeson—the original Rogue Trader whose unchecked risk-taking caused the biggest financial scandal of the 20th century."

40 Kahneman and Tversky also discuss "gain frames," but the "gain frames" tend to be between a sure thing and a less sure thing. With bankers, there may be no direct

analogue—there is no "sure (enough)" thing. Also, the less sure thing may contemplate a huge payoff, and there may be considerable social pressure to "shoot for the moon." Finally, the "sure thing" in the short term may not be "sure" in the moderate term—the "slow and steady" performer is scarcely assured of a job at the bank in the moderate term.

41 See, generally, Coates, *The Hour between Dog and Wolf.*

42 Ibid., 4–5. On market participant physiology causing problematic behavior, see Lo, "Fear, Greed, and Financial Crises."

43 Werdigier and Scott, "Ex-Trader Sentenced in Loss," November 20, 2012.

44 Shirbon, "Accused UBS Rogue Trader." Adoboli's attempt to get permission to appeal was denied. Croft, "Judges Refuse," June 4, 2014.

45 Dunbar, *The Devil's Derivatives*, xii. The former motivation can be characterized as avoidance and the latter can be characterized as approach. See, generally, the handbook edited by a leading researcher in this area, Andrew J. Elliot, ed., *Handbook of Approach and Avoidance Motivation.* Going further, the "true nature" of approach/avoidance has been characterized using regulatory focus theory, discussed in n. 26, chap. 3 of this book. Promotion focus causing "eagerness" is akin to what we mean here by liking to win; similarly, prevention focus causing vigilance is akin to hating to lose. While it is well beyond our scope, we consider it possible that some of the work done in these areas might suggest psychological techniques that, at least in the short term, might influence behavior in directions we would consider felicitous.

46 This suggests a nostalgia or at least aspiration for boring banking and bankers. See Elizabeth Warren, "Banking Should Be Boring," May 22, 2012; and Liaquat Ahamed, Pulitzer Prize–winning author of the 2009 book *Lords of Finance: The Bankers Who Broke the World* (see also Ahamed, "Bankers Should Be Boring," June 19, 2012, among others).

47 "Calling Clients 'Muppets.'"

Chapter 4

1 Some regulatory solutions directed at banking institutions in theory could work, such as significant increases in capital requirements. For instance, in *The Banker's New Clothes*, Admati and Hellwig have proposed a capital requirement of 20 percent, far above existing requirements. History suggests that banks will make adoption of any such requirements very difficult.

2 A Google search in mid-2014 for "EU bonus cap" yielded the following article titles and short descriptions on its first page of results:

> From BBC News, March 5, 2014: "Lloyds and Barclays Avoid EU Bonus Cap by Paying Shares": "Two UK banks are handing out massive share awards to senior executives amid EU limits on bonuses."
>
> From the *New York Times*, January 16, 2014: "For Goldman in Europe, a 3rd Way to Get Paid": "To navigate bonus caps in Europe, Goldman Sachs will offer a new kind of pay class for bankers in Britain and on the Continent" (Anderson, "For Goldman in Europe").
>
> From the *Wall Street Journal*, February 4, 2014: "A Q &A on the EU Bonus Cap and the Ways around It."

3 European Banking Authority, "EBA Discloses Probe into EU Bankers Allowances,"

October 15, 2014. And there are real questions as to whether the bonus cap is on balance a good idea; one criticism is that if more of a banker's pay is fixed, it will be harder for the bank to scale back that pay to reflect worse performance by the banker or the bank.

4 See U.S. SEC, "Chairman Cox Announces," September 26, 2008.

5 See Carton, "SEC to Receive 2% Budget Increase in FY 2014, Far Below 26% Requested Increase," January 14, 2014.

6 See Anderson, "British Bank Regulators Pine," June 4, 2014.

7 In the aftermath of a high-profile corporate bribery case brought by the Serious Fraud Office in 2013, SFO V. Victor Dahdelah, Painter provided expert testimony to the Crown Court Southwark on ethics and other problems created when the SFO outsourced its investigatory work for a criminal prosecution to a U.S. law firm that represented the alleged victim. The law firm at the last minute refused to produce witnesses for trial testimony, causing the SFO prosecution to collapse with an acquittal. See Dahdelah v. MacDougall and Akin Gump, Crown Court Southwark, Case No. T20117607 & T20117073, Judge Loraine-Smith (opinion dated Friday, 21 March 2014). The court blasted the SFO for its mishandling of the case. See Binham, "Dahdaleh Lawyers Argue over Nuances," March 12, 2014, discussing expert testimony on alleged conflicts between promises that law firm Akin Gump made to the SFO and its duty to its client under U.S. law. See also Dean, "Judge Lays Blame for Dahdaleh," March 22, 2014. This outsourcing arrangement and other ill-advised prosecution strategies are probably inevitable when the SFO's budget is so small compared with the resources available to defendants the SFO is up against.

8 The quote can be found in Popper and Protess, "To Regulate Rapid Traders," October 7, 2012.

9 A few recent papers have suggested precisely such a regime—an "FDA" (or like mechanism) for prior approval of new financial products. See Posner and Weyl, "An FDA For Financial Innovation"; and Omarova, "License to Deal."

10 For discussion of the role of lawyers in working around regulations, see Painter, "Transaction Cost Engineers."

11 For a discussion of the role of lawyers in representing S&Ls prior to the early 1990s S&L crisis and Salomon Brothers in the 1991 Treasury auction scandal, see Painter, "The Moral Interdependence of Corporate Lawyers and Their Clients."

12 See Levitt, *Take on the Street*, 303–24, reprinting letters to Levitt from Enron CEO Ken Lay and similar letters from members of Congress criticizing the SEC's efforts to regulate auditors; and Painter, "Standing Up to Wall Street," reviewing Levitt, *Take on the Street.*

13 Protess, "Wall Street Seeks to Tuck Dodd-Frank Changes in Budget Bill," December 9, 2014.

14 Eavis, "Wall St. Wins a Round in a Dodd-Frank Fight," December 12, 2014; and Cleary Gottlieb News, "Pres. Obama Signs Bill," December 17, 2014.

15 Morrison v. National Australia Bank, 561 U.S. 247 (2010).

16 See Painter, "The Dodd-Frank Extraterritorial Jurisdiction Provision," 1.

17 Securities Litigation Uniform Standards Act of 1998, Pub. L. No. 105-353, 112 Stat. 3227. For a critique of the rationale given for the preemption of state law, see Painter, "Responding to a False Alarm: Federal Preemption of State Securities Fraud Causes of Action."

18 *In re* Citigroup Inc. Shareholder Derivative Litigation, 964 A.2d 106, 131 (Del. Ch., 2009).

19 The business judgment rule is a "presumption that in making a business decision the directors of a corporation acted on an informed basis, in good faith and in the honest belief that the action taken was in the best interests of the company" Aronson v. Lewis, 473 A. 2d. 805, 812 (Del. 1984)

20 See Benedetti-Valentini and Deen, "BNP Fine Stirs French Anger," June 2, 2014: "*Le Figaro* newspaper said the U.S. was making an example of BNP to deflect criticism it had been "lenient with the American banks responsible for the financial crisis." Also: "The right-wing National Front, which beat France's two mainstream political parties in the May 25 [2014] European parliamentary elections . . . called on the government to 'defend the national interest' in the case."

Chapter 5

1 There are, of course, people who are risk loving. Particularly if higher rewards are offered in exchange for potential exposure to downside risk, risk-loving people might continue to be attracted to banking. But the situation would still be better than the present situation, where even non-risk-loving bankers are rewarded for taking risks, since the risks are to their customers or employers or the society at large, not themselves.

2 Some of this section and the succeeding sections are adapted from Hill and Painter, "Berle's Vision beyond Shareholder Interests." Our proposal that some bankers be personally responsible for (a portion of) regulatory fines is based on our 2012 op-ed, "Why SEC Settlements Should Hold Senior Executives Liable," May 29, 2012.

3 Although few if any corporations now use assessable stock, experts studying financial institutions still examine its use as a tool for banking regulation. See Macey and Miller, "Double Liability of Bank Shareholders."

4 See, e.g., Langevoort, "On Leaving Corporate Executives."

5 These commentators argue that the business judgment rule is only appropriate in fault-based suits brought against outside directors. See, e.g., Johnson, "Corporate Officers and the Business Judgment Rule," 439.

6 Recall, however, that as explained in the introduction, only those involved in banking would be covered.

7 A higher par value for stock issued to managers could result in additional franchise taxes for the corporation. This would impose a small additional tax on compensation over $1 million, an amount that could be offset by a federal tax credit if the franchise tax were deemed a disincentive for using high par value assessable stock. Alternatively, as discussed in the text, an assessment could be imposed without relating the amount of the assessment to the stock's "par value" but instead to the trading price of the stock at the time of issuance. This would allow the assessable stock to have a low par value as does most common stock in recent times.

8 Oral testimony and written statement of Richard W. Painter in *Hearing before the Committee on Financial Services*, May 17, 2012.

9 Professor Wulf Kaal's recent study examining 257 such agreements between 1993 and 2013 found that most of these agreements were entered into after 2003 and required significant changes in the composition of the board of directors and/or the duties and activities of the board, changes in top management, increased moni-

toring and reporting, use of independent monitoring firms, and implementation of compliance programs. See Kaal and Lacine, "The Effect of Deferred and Non-Prosecution Agreements."

10 Judges may have less discretion, or believe they have less discretion, to reject regulatory agency settlements after the Second Circuit's June 2014 decision, discussed in chapter 1 and this chapter, that U.S. District Judge Jed Rakoff exceeded his authority in rejecting the SEC's 2011 settlement of a major case against Citigroup.

11 Volcker, "Think More Boldly," December 14, 2009. For a measured defense of innovation, see Litan, "In Defense of Much," February 17, 2010. Litan concludes that "there has been more socially useful financial innovation over the past several decades" (47). He talks about how such innovations could be encouraged. But his is not a blanket endorsement of innovation. He concludes that "we should stand readier to correct abuses when they appear and not let destructive financial innovations wreak the kind of economic havoc we have unfortunately just witnessed" (47).

12 Some legal initiatives that will soon come into force seem especially focused on individual banker conduct. In particular, the UK's new Banking Reform Act includes a provision by which senior managers are identified to regulators and the regulators obtain heightened regulatory powers over such managers' conduct of their duties (Financial Services Act, c.33, 2013, pt. 4). The law also will impose criminal liability for senior bankers for "reckless conduct leading to the insolvency of a bank," but the showings required make the imposition of liability under this provision exceedingly unlikely (Financial ServicesAct, pt. 4, sec. 36).

13 One bank's translation of the pledge reads as follows:
I swear/promise that I will exercise my function properly and carefully.
I swear/promise that I will duly weigh all the interests involved in the enterprise, i.e. those of the clients, the shareholders, the employees and the society in which the enterprise is active.
I swear/promise that in this weighing I will focus on the client's interest and that I will inform the client to the best of my ability.
I swear/promise that I will act in accordance with the laws, regulations and codes of conduct which apply to me.
I swear/promise that I will observe secrecy about anything to which I have been entrusted.
I swear/promise that I will not abuse my knowledge.
I swear/promise that I will maintain an open and verifiable attitude and I know my responsibility towards society.
I swear/promise that I will perform to the best of my abilities to maintain and promote confidence in the financial services sector.
So help me God!/This I declare and promise! (NIBC, "Banker's Oath/Solemn Affirmation of Policymaker")

14 Alderman, "With 'So Help Me God.'" For the full text of the new charter, rules, and code of conduct, see Dutch Banking Association. *Future-Oriented Banking: Social Charter, Banking Code, Rules of Conduct*, October, 14, 2014.

15 Carney, "Inclusive Capitalism," 4.

Chapter 6

1 More evidence that people view amounts they don't regard as (already) theirs differently than amounts they do regard as (already) theirs is provided by the "Save More Tomorrow" plan promoted by the scholar most associated with research on house money, Thaler, "Save More Tomorrow"; see also the discussion on house money in the text accompanying n. 37, chap. 3 of this book.

In the Save More Tomorrow plan, employees who had not agreed that some portion of their present paychecks should go into a savings vehicle were apparently willing to agree to put into such a vehicle a portion of their future raises. A future raise is regarded differently—the amount does not go into a person's baseline. The employee would get less in the future rather than giving something up. Bankers might also regard giving up future compensation as relatively easy, too, and might take legal or inappropriate financial risks even if these risks threaten future compensation. They would be motivated by the prospective loss of future compensation, but less so than they would be by potentially giving up something they think of as theirs now.

2 There are many proposals to change upside compensation. One is by Bhagat, Bolton, and Romano, in "Getting Incentives Right." They argue that "bank executives, significant employees, and directors' incentive compensation should consist only of restricted stock and restricted stock options—restricted in the sense that the executive cannot sell the shares or exercise the options for two to four years after his or her last day in office" (61). They also note that because bankers at banks approaching insolvency may no longer be motivated to take a long-term perspective even if they have restricted equity, banks should have more equity, either as a function of assets or in the form of contingent debt that converts to equity (61). Another proposal to change upside compensation is that of Lucian Bebchuk and Holger Spamann. They suggest that bankers' compensation be tied to the performance of the bank's debt securities, not just its stock ("Regulating Bankers' Pay"). These proposals are clearly a great deal better than linking compensation principally to reported earnings and stock performance, which have proven too easy to game. But they still involve no risk of loss for bankers—only forgone gains—if creditors are not paid. As discussed in chapter 3, the baseline counts: forgoing "gains" may be far easier than incurring actual losses. None of this is to say we are opposed to these types of proposals, just that we think they do not suffice.

3 Harvard political economy professor Benjamin Friedman notes that:

As of 2009, the value of credit swaps outstanding in US markets was $36 trillion—three times the entire amount of bonds issued by all US corporations combined and a far larger multiple of the indebtedness of the specific companies against which the swap contracts were written. The vast majority of these swaps, therefore, had nothing to do with how participants in the financial markets spread the risk of genuine losses of wealth. Instead, their purpose was simply to create gains for the firms that bet correctly on how the contracts' prices would move, exactly matched by losses for whoever bet incorrectly on the other side. (Friedman, "Is Our Financial System Serving Us Well?" 20–21)

Not surprisingly, banks have a different view:

Goldman executives agreed that synthetic CDOs were "bets" that magnified overall risk, they also maintained that their creation had "social utility" because it added liquidity to the market and enabled investors to customize the exposures they wanted in their portfolios. In testimony before the Commission, Goldman's President and Chief Operating Officer Gary Cohn argued: "This is no different than the tens of thousands of swaps written every day on the U.S. dollar versus another currency. Or, more importantly, on U.S. Treasuries . . . This is the way that the financial markets work." (*FCIC Report*, 146)

4 How much they "lost" depends, of course, on how we compute what they "had"— do we compute at the peak of the market or at some lower valuation? There can be many defensible ways to approach this computation, some of which would suggest that even bankers who "lost" a great deal still came out better off than they had been when they started working at their banks.

5 Congress, in 2010, asked the SEC to study whether broader fiduciary obligations should be imposed, but for many broker-customer relationships, the suitability standard remains the norm. As discussed in the text, banker behavior in the crisis would not be consistent even with the existing, more relaxed suitability standard.

Conclusion

1 Carney, "Inclusive Capitalism," 8–9.

REFERENCES

The following references include scholarly publications, general interest books, newspaper articles, internal reports and press releases of financial institutions, and other descriptive material. We also include press releases of government agencies, congressional committees, and members of Congress. While some of these press releases describe official actions such as an investigation or settlement of a case, they are descriptive in nature and, like press releases from financial institutions, often present a particular point of view. At the end of this bibliography is a list of statutes, regulations, legal briefs, opinions (of courts or administrative agencies), filings, and administrative documents of an official nature that either do something such as resolve a case or contain testimony and/or official findings of fact (such as a congressional committee hearing or report). These documents also sometimes contain particular points of view, but generally they have been created through an official process in which other viewpoints were considered as well.

Abrams, Rachel. "In Change, Tourre Won't Be Teaching University of Chicago Course." *New York Times DealBook*, March 4, 2014. http://dealbook.nytimes.com/2014/03/04 /in-change-tourre-wont-be-teaching-university-of-chicago-course/?_php=true& _type=blogs&_r=0.

Abrams, Rachel, and Peter Lattman. "Ex-Credit Suisse Executive Sentenced in Mortgage Bond Case." *New York Times DealBook*, November 22, 2013. http:// dealbook.nytimes.com/2013/11/22/ex-credit-suisse-executive-sentenced-in -mortgage-case/.

Acharya, Viral V., and Matthew P. Richardson. "Causes of the Financial Crisis." *Critical Review* 21, nos. 2–3 (2009): 195–210.

Acharya, Viral V., Philipp Schnabl, and Gustavo Suarez. "Securitization without Risk Transfer." *Journal of Financial Economics* 107, no. 3 (2013): 515–36.

Ackert, Lucy F., Narat Charupat, Bryan K. Church, and Richard Deaves. "An Experimental Examination of the House Money Effect in a Multi-Period Setting." Federal Reserve Bank of Atlanta Working Paper No. 2003-13, September 2003. http://www.frbatlanta.org/filelegacydocs/wp0313.pdf.

Admati, Anat, and Martin Hellwig. *The Bankers' New Clothes: What's Wrong with Banking and What to Do about It*. Princeton, NJ: Princeton University Press, 2013.

Advisory Committee on the Future of Banks in the Netherlands (Maas Committee). *Restoring Trust*, April 7, 2009. http://www.nvb.nl/en/media/document/001225 _090407-rapport-adviescommissie-toekomst-banken-uk.pdf.

Ahamed, Liaquat. "Bankers Should Be Boring." *Atlantic*, June 19, 2012. http://www .theatlantic.com/magazine/archive/2012/07/bankers-should-be-boring/309043/.

———. *Lords of Finance: The Bankers Who Broke the World*. New York: Penguin Press, 2009.

Albergotti, Reed, and Jean Eaglesham. "9 More Banks Subpoenaed over

Libor." *Wall Street Journal*, October 25, 2012. http://online.wsj.com/article
/SB10001424052970203897404578079413742864842.html.

Alden, William. "Legal Costs Weighed on Wall Street's First-Half Profits." *New York Times DealBook*, October 7, 2014. http://dealbook.nytimes.com/2014/10/07/legal
-costs-weighed-on-wall-streets-first-half-profits/.

Alderman, Liz. "With 'So Help Me God' Ethics Oath, Dutch Banks Seek Redemption." *New York Times DealBook*, December 12, 2014. http://dealbook.nytimes.com/2014
/12/12/netherlands-asks-bankers-to-swear-to-god/?hpw&rref=business&action=
click&pgtype=Homepage&module=well-region&region=bottom-well&WT.nav=
bottom-well.

Alloway, Tracy. "Citi to Pay $730m in Subprime Settlement." *Financial Times*, March 18, 2013. http://www.ft.com/intl/cms/s/0/6cbdcc82-901c-11e2-9239-00144feabdc0.html
#axzz2Rnx2dWCL.

Anderson, Jenny. "British Bank Regulators Pine to Win a Big Case." *New York Times DealBook*, June 4, 2014. http://dealbook.nytimes.com/2014/06/04/british-bank
-regulators-pine-to-win-a-big-case/?_php=true&_type=blogs&_r=0.

———. "For Goldman in Europe, a 3rdWay to Get Paid." *New York Times DealBook*, January 16, 2014. http://dealbook.nytimes.com/2014/01/16/at-goldman-in-europe
-theres-salary-bonus-and-a-new-option/.

Apicella, Coren L., Anna Dreber, Benjamin Campbell, Peter B. Gray, Moshe Hoffman, and Anthony C. Little. "Testosterone and Financial Risk Preferences." *Evolution and Human Behavior* 29, no. 6 (2008): 384–90. doi:10.1016/j.evolhumbehav.2008
.07.001.

Ariely, Dan. *The (Honest) Truth about Dishonesty: How We Lie to Everyone—Especially Ourselves*. New York: Harper Perennial, 2013.

Armitstead, Louise. "Terry Smith Warned Authorities ISDAfix Was Vulnerable to Manipulation." *Telegraph*, April 11, 2013. http://www.telegraph.co.uk/finance
/newsbysector/banksandfinance/9985601/Terry-Smith-warned-authorities-ISDAfix
-was-vulnerable-to-manipulation.html.

Armour, Stephanie. "FDIC Sues Banks over Libor." *Wall Street Journal*, March 14, 2014. http://online.wsj.com/news/articles/SB10001424052702303730804579439442827174438.

Arnold, Laurence. "William Salomon Dies at 100; Wall Street Pillar Modernized Salomon Bros." *Los Angeles Times*, December 9, 2014. http://www.latimes.com
/local/obituaries/la-me-william-salomon-20141210-story.html.

Balzli, Beat. "Greek Debt Crisis: How Goldman Sachs Helped Greece to Mask Its True Debt." *Spiegel Online International*, February 8, 2010. http://www.spiegel.de
/international/europe/greek-debt-crisis-how-goldman-sachs-helped-greece-to
-mask-its-true-debt-a-676634.html.

Barclays PLC. "Barclays Response to the *Salz Review*." April 2013. http://www.barclays
.com/content/dam/barclayspublic/documents/news/471-392-250413-salz-response
.pdf.

Barrett, Devlin, Dan Fitzpatrick, and Nick Timiraos. "J. P. Morgan Settles with FHFA." *Wall Street Journal*, October 25, 2013. http://online.wsj.com/news/articles
/SB10001424052702303615304579157931846055864.

BBC News. "Foreign Exchange Allegations 'As Bad as Libor,' Says Regulator." BBC, February 4, 2014. http://www.bbc.co.uk/news/business-26041039.

———. "How Leeson Broke the Bank." *Business: The Economy*, June 22, 1999. http://news.bbc.co.uk/2/hi/business/375259.stm

———. "Lloyds and Barclays Avoid EU Bonus Cap by Paying Shares." March 5, 2014. http://www.bbc.com/news/business-26453390.

———. "Morgan Stanley to Pay out $1.25bn to Settle Lawsuit." February 4, 2014. http://www.bbc.co.uk/news/business-26043498.

———. "Osborne Abandons Challenge to EU Cap on Bankers' Bonuses." November 20, 2014. http://www.bbc.com/news/business-30125780.

———. "Timeline: Libor-Fixing Scandal." February 6, 2013. http://www.bbc.co.uk/news/business-18671255.

Bebchuk, Lucian A., and Holger Spamann. "Regulating Bankers' Pay." *Georgetown Law Journal* 98 (2010): 247–87.

Beioley, Kate. "Freshfields and A&O's Client Deutsche Bank Loses Latest Unitech Court Outing." *The Lawyer*, October 8, 2014. http://www.thelawyer.com/news/practice-areas/litigation-news/freshfields-and-aos-client-deutsche-bank-loses-latest-unitech-court-outing/3026846.article.

Benedetti-Valentini, Fabio, and Mark Deen. "BNP Fine Stirs French Anger, Pressuring Hollande to Act." *Bloomberg*, June 2, 2014. http://www.bloomberg.com/news/2014-06-01/bnp-fine-stirs-french-anger-putting-pressure-on-hollande-to-act.html.

Bennett, Neil. "City: King Salomon's Mine! Sandy Weill, Head of Travelers, Has Snapped up Wall Street's Most Famous Brokerage House for $9bn. Neil Bennett Reveals How the Deal Was Done and Why Weill Moved in Where Others Have Walked Away." *Sunday Telegraph London*, September 28, 1997.

Benson, Clea, and Elena Logutenkova. "UBS to Pay $885 Million to Settle U.S. Mortgage Suit." *Bloomberg*, July 26, 2013. http://www.bloomberg.com/news/2013-07-25/ubs-agrees-to-pay-885-million-to-settle-u-s-securities-suit.html.

Bernabei, Stefano, and Stephen Jewkes. "Update 4-Former Monte Paschi Management Convicted as Crisis Mounts." Reuters, October 31, 2014. http://www.reuters.com/article/2014/10/31/italy-banks-montepaschi-idUSL5N0SQ1TX20141031.

Bernstein, Jake, and Jesse Eisinger. "The 'Subsidy': How a Handful of Merrill Lynch Bankers Helped Blow up Their Own Firm." *ProPublica*, December 22, 2010. http://www.propublica.org/article/the-subsidy-how-merrill-lynch-traders-helped-blow-up-their-own-firm.

Bhagat, Sanjai, Brian Bolton, and Roberta Romano. "Getting Incentives Right: Is Deferred Bank Executive Compensation Sufficient?" *Yale Journal on Regulation* 31 (2014): 523–64.

Binham, Caroline. "Dahdaleh Lawyers Argue over Nuances of US Law in London." *Financial Times*, March 12, 2014. http://www.ft.com/intl/cms/s/0/7a2ca72c-aa14-11e3-8bd6-00144feab7de.html#axzz34S629ftx.

———. "Ex-JPMorgan Trader Challenges 'Whale' Findings." *Financial Times*, July 6, 2014. http://www.ft.com/intl/cms/s/0/32daf9ee-038a-11e4-817f-00144feab7de.html?siteedition=uk#axzz3MeYKF0AR.

Board of Governors of the Federal Reserve System. "Independent Foreclosure Review to Provide $3.3 Billion in Payments, $5.2 Billion in Mortgage Assistance." January 7, 2013. http://www.federalreserve.gov/newsevents/press/bcreg/20130107a.htm.

———. "Press Release." December 10, 2012. http://www.federalreserve.gov/newsevents/press/enforcement/20121210a.htm.

———. "Press Release." December 18, 2014. http://www.federalreserve.gov /newsevents/press/bcreg/20141218a.htm.

Bond Girl. "The Incredible Story of the Jefferson County Bankruptcy—One of the Greatest Financial Ripoffs of All Time." *Business Insider*, October 23, 2011. http:// www.businessinsider.com/the-incredible-story-of-the-jefferson-county-bankruptcy -one-of-the-greatest-financial-ripoffs-of-all-time-2011-10.

Braithwaite, Tom, Michael Mackenzie, and Kara Scannell. "Brokers at ICAP in CFTC Rate Swaps Probe." *Financial Times*, April 9, 2013. http://www.ft.com/intl/cms/s/0 /c19afd04-a08b-11e2-88b6-00144feabdc0.html#axzz2SFrelegK.

Bratton, William W., and Michael L. Wachter, "Bankers and Chancellors." *Texas Law Review* 93, no. 1 (2014): 1–84.

Bray, Chad. "BNP Paribas Says U.S. Penalties May Top the $1.1 Billion It Set Aside." *New York Times DealBook*, April 30, 2014. http://dealbook.nytimes.com/2014/04/30 /bnp-paribas-warns-1-1-billion-might-not-be-enough-to-cover-u-s-fines/.

———. "Profit Falls 26% at Barclays, Weighed Down by Legal Costs." *New York Times DealBook*, October 30, 2014. http://dealbook.nytimes.com/2014/10/30/barclays -profit-falls-on-weaker-investment-banking-and-legal-costs/.

———. "R.B.S. Profit Weighed Down by $1.25 Billion for Legal Costs." *New York Times DealBook*, October 31, 2014. http://dealbook.nytimes.com/2014/10/31/r-b-s-posts -profit-as-it-sets-aside-1-25-billion-for-legal-costs/.

———. "Swiss Regulator Opens Currency Inquiry." *New York Times DealBook*, March 31, 2014. http://dealbook.nytimes.com/2014/03/31/swiss-competition-commission -opens-currency-inquiry/.

———. "Switzerland Opens Criminal Inquiry of Currency Traders." *New York Times DealBook*, November 13, 2014. http://dealbook.nytimes.com/2014/11/13/switzerland -opens-criminal-inquiry-into-forex-traders/?_r=0.

———. "3 Who Worked at Barclays Face Charges in Libor Case." *New York Times DealBook*, February 17, 2014. http://dealbook.nytimes.com/2014/02/17/3-former -barclays-employees-accused-in-libor-scandal/?_php=true&_type=blogs&_r=0.

———. "22 under Investigation in Libor Case in Britain." *New York Times DealBook*, October 21, 2013. http://dealbook.nytimes.com/2013/10/21/22-named-as-co -conspirators-in-libor-case-in-britain/?pagewanted=print&_r=1.

Brinded, Lianna. "Ex-JPM 'London Whale Conspirator' Julien Grout Appeals Civil Case." *International Business Times*, July 7, 2014. http://www.ibtimes.co.uk/ex-jpms -london-whale-conspirator-julien-grout-appeals-against-civil-case-1455560.

Brooks, David. "The Brutality Cascade." Op-Ed., *New York Times*, March 4, 2013. http://www.nytimes.com/2013/03/05/opinion/brooks-the-brutality-cascade.html ?ref=opinion&_r=1&.

Brunsden, Jim, and Ben Moshinsky, "Millionaire Bankers Win Chance of EU Bonus-Caps Reprieve." *Bloomberg News*, March 4, 2014. http://www.bloomberg.com/news /2014-03-04/bankers-may-win-bonus-rule-exemptions-in-eu-commission-plan .html.

"Calling Clients 'Muppets' and Worse." *60 Minutes*, CBS News, October 21, 2012. http:// www.cbsnews.com/videos/calling-clients-muppets-and-worse/.

Carney, Mark. "Inclusive Capitalism: Creating a Sense of the Systemic." Speech presented at the Conference on Inclusive Capitalism, London, May 27, 2014. http:// www.bankofengland.co.uk/publications/Documents/speeches/2014/speech731.pdf.

Carton, Bruce. "SEC to Receive 2% Budget Increase in FY 2014, Far Below 25% Requested Increase." *Compliance Week*, January 14, 2014. http://www .complianceweek.com/blogs/enforcement-action/sec-to-receive-2-budget-increase -in-fy-2014-far-below-26-requested-increase#.VBhruVf8-vk.

Cesario, Joseph, E. Tory Higgins, and Abigail A. Scholer. "Regulatory Fit and Persuasion: Basic Principles and Remaining Questions." *Social and Personality Psychology Compass* 2, no. 1 (2008): 444–63.

Chaffin, Joshua, and Kerin Hope. "EU Demands Details on Greek Swaps." *Financial Times*, February 15, 2010. http://www.ft.com/intl/cms/s/0/cc82f954-1a3f-11df-b4ee -00144feab49a.html#axzz2tdOTHRRO.

Chatterjee, Pratap. "Morgan Stanley Knew about 'Nuclear Holocaust' Mortgage Loans, Taiwanese Lawsuit Reveals." *CorpWatch* (blog), January 23, 2013. http://www .corpwatch.org/article.php?id=15810.

Childs, Mary. "Citigroup Lost $15 Million with UBS's 'Crap' CDO Blessed by S&P." *Bloomberg*, February 13, 2013. http://www.bloomberg.com/news/2013-02-14 /citigroup-lost-15-million-with-ubs-s-crap-cdo-blessed-by-s-p.html.

Chirls, Nick. "My Time at Lehman." *Thoughts from Brooklyn, NY* (blog), April 9, 2013. http://nickchirls.com/my-time-at-lehman.

Church, Steven. "Jefferson County JPMorgan Deal Called Safer Than Suing." *Bloomberg*, November 20, 2013. http://www.bloomberg.com/news/2013-11-20 /jefferson-county-seeks-approval-to-end-2-year-bankruptcy.html.

Church, Steven, and Dawn McCarty. "Jefferson County Files to End Bankruptcy, Adjust Debt." *Bloomberg*, July 1, 2013. http://www.bloomberg.com/news/2013-06-30 /jefferson-county-files-to-end-bankruptcy-adjust-debt.html.

Citigroup Class V Funding III, Ltd, and Class V Funding III, Corp. *Offering Circular*. March 29, 2007. http://s3.documentcloud.org/documents/12769/class-v-iii -prospectus.pdf.

Cleary Gottlieb News. "Pres. Obama Signs Bill Enacting Significant Amendments to Swaps Push-Out Requirements." December 17, 2014. http://www.cgsh.com /pres-obama-signs-bill-enacting-significant-amendments-to-swaps-push-out -requirements/.

Coates, John. *The Hour between Dog and Wolf: Risk Taking, Gut Feelings and the Biology of Boom and Bust*. New York: Penguin Press, 2012.

Cohn, Alain, Ernst Fehr, and Michel André Maréchal. "A Culture of Cheating? Dishonesty and Business Culture in the Banking Industry." *Nature* 516 (December 4, 2014): 86–89. doi:10.1038/nature13977.

Colchester, Max. "Court Clears Way for Investor Suits over Libor: Barclays, Deutsche Bank Lose Bid to Block Link between Rate-Manipulation Charges and Derivatives Sales." *Wall Street Journal*, November, 8, 2013. http://online.wsj.com/news/articles /SB10001424052702303309504579185891601440598.

Colchester, Max, and David Enrich. "Barclays Dashes Its Global Dreams: U.K. Lender to Cut Investment Bank Nearly in Half, Retrench in Western Europe." *Wall Street Journal*, May 9, 2014. http://www.wsj.com/articles/SB10001424052702304431104579549002925322362.

Consumer Financial Protection Bureau (CFPB). "CFPB Orders Bank of America to Pay $727 Million in Consumer Relief for Illegal Credit Card Practices." Press release, April 9, 2014. http://www.consumerfinance.gov/newsroom/cfpb-orders

-bank-of-america-to-pay-727-million-in-consumer-relief-for-illegal-credit-card
-practices.

Copeland, Adam. "Income Evolution at BHCs: How Big BHCs Differ." *Liberty Street Economics* (blog). Federal Reserve Bank of New York. July 23, 2012. http://libertystreeteconomics.newyorkfed.org/2012/07/income-evolution-at-bhcs-how-big-bhcs-differ.html.

Copley, Caroline, and Albert Schmieder. "Switzerland Probes Banks over Possible Forex Rigging." Reuters, October 4, 2013. http://www.reuters.com/article/2013/10/04/us-swiss-probe-forex-idUSBRE9930B420131004.

Corkery, Michael. "How Much Did Jefferson County Cost J. P. Morgan?" *MoneyBeat* (blog), *Wall Street Journal*, June 5, 2013. http://blogs.wsj.com/moneybeat/2013/06/05/how-much-did-jefferson-county-cost-j-p-morgan/.

Corkery, Michael, and Jessica Silver-Greenberg. "$772 Million Penalty for Bank of America Credit Card Practices." *New York Times DealBook*, April 9, 2014. http://dealbook.nytimes.com/2014/04/09/800-million-penalty-for-bank-of-america-credit-card-practices/.

———. "SunTrust Settles with Justice Dept. over Mortgages; Talks Continue for Citigroup and Bank of America." *New York Times DealBook*, June 17, 2014. http://dealbook.nytimes.com/2014/06/17/suntrust-settles-with-justice-dept-over-mortgages-talks-continue-for-citigroup-and-bank-of-america/?_php=true&_type=blogs&_r=0.

Credit Suisse. "Credit Suisse Announces Settlement with US Authorities Related to US Dollar Payments Involving Parties Subject to US Sanctions." Press release, December 16, 2009. https://www.credit-suisse.com/us/en/about-us/media/latest-news/media-release.html?ns=41372&p=x.html.

———. "Credit Suisse Confirms Settlement Discussions with US Authorities Related to US Dollar Payments Involving Parties Subject to US Sanctions." Press release, December 15, 2009. https://www.credit-suisse.com/us/en/about-us/media/latest-news/media-release.html?ns=41371&p=x.html.

Croft, Jane. "Deutsche Bank Accused of Mis-Selling Swap." *Financial Times*, October 15, 2013. http://www.ft.com/intl/cms/s/0/5acefd90-358d-11e3-952b-00144feab7de.html#axzz3589xZieB.

———. "Judges Refuse ex-UBS Trader Kweku Adoboli's Appeal Request." *Financial Times*, June 4, 2014. http://www.ft.com/intl/cms/s/0/b568b0f2-ebfe-11e3-ab1b-0014feabdc0.html#axzz3bq1RKSo8.

Croft, Jane, and Daniel Schäfer. "First Banker to Be Charged over Libor Faces Court in UK." *Financial Times*, June 21, 2013. http://www.ft.com/intl/cms/s/0/0496d07a-d998-11e2-bab1-00144feab7de.html.

Croucher, Shane. "Eurozone Crisis: Greece-Goldman Deal That Sparked Debt Mayhem Not Repeated." *International Business Times*, November 15, 2011. http://www.ibtimes.co.uk/articles/249767/20111115/eurozone-crisis-greece-goldman-deal-sparked-debt.htm#ixzz1mDYc7ZEO.

Currier, Cora. "Beyond Barclays, Laying out the Libor Investigation." *ProPublica*, July 6, 2012. http://www.propublica.org/article/beyond-barclays-laying-out-the-libor-investigations.

Dash, Eric. "Citigroup Considers Changes at Phibro." *New York Times*, August 7, 2009. http://www.nytimes.com/2009/08/07/business/07phibro.html?_r=0.

Davidoff [Solomon], Steven M., and Claire A. Hill. "Limits of Disclosure." *Seattle University Law Review* 36 (2013): 599–637.

Dean, James. "Judge Lays Blame for Dahdaleh Collapse on SFO, *Times* (London), March 22, 2014. http://www.thetimes.co.uk/tto/law/article4040769.ece.

Deutsche Bank. "Deutsche Asset Management Finalizes Market Timing Settlement with Securities and Exchange Commission and New York Attorney General." News release, December 21, 2006. https://www.db.com/medien/en/content/press _releases_2006_3277.htm.

Disavino, Scott, and David Sheppard. "Deutsche Bank Settles U.S. Power Market Manipulation Case." Reuters, January 22, 2013. http://www.reuters.com/article/2013 /01/22/us-ferc-deutschebank-idUSBRE90L0SW20130122.

Dobbin, Frank, and Jiwook Jung. "The Misapplication of Mr. Michael Jensen: How Agency Theory Brought Down the Economy and Why It Might Again." In *Markets on Trial: The Economic Sociology of the US Financial Crisis, pt. B*, edited by Michael Lounsbury and Paul M. Hirsch, 29–64. Research in the Sociology of Organizations, vol. 30. Bingley, UK: Emerald Group Publishing Limited, 2010.

Dobbin, Frank, and Dirk Zorn. "Corporate Malfeasance and the Myth of Shareholder Value." *Political Power and Social Theory* 17 (2005): 179–98.

Dubois, Bernard, and Patrick Duquesne. "The Market for Luxury Goods: Income versus Culture." *European Journal of Marketing* 27, no. 1 (1993): 35–44.

Dudley, William, "Ending Too Big to Fail." Speech, Remarks presented at the Global Economic Policy Forum, New York City, November 7, 2013. http://www.newyorkfed .org/newsevents/speeches/2013/dud131107.html.

———. "Enhancing Financial Stability by Improving Culture in the Financial Services Industry." Remarks at the Workshop on Reforming Culture and Behavior in the Financial Services Industry, Federal Reserve Bank of New York, New York, October 20, 2014. http://www.newyorkfed.org/newsevents/speeches/2014/dud141020a .html.'

Dunbar, Nicholas. *The Devil's Derivatives: The Untold Story of the Slick Traders and Hapless Regulators Who Almost Blew Up Wall Street . . . and Are Ready to Do It Again*. Boston: Harvard Business Review Press, 2011.

———. "Goldman, Greece and a Troubling Tango." *Nick Dunbar* (blog), February 18, 2010. http://nickdunbar.net/2010/03/01/goldman-greece-and-a-troubling-tango/.

———. "Goldman Swap Shows Greece Was Europe's Subprime Nation." *Nick Dunbar* (blog), January 24, 2012. http://www.nickdunbar.net/articles/goldman-swap-shows -greece-was-europes-subprime-nation/.

———. "How Goldman Sachs Masked Greece's Debt." BBC *Newsnight* report. February 20, 2012. http://www.bbc.co.uk/news/world-europe-17108367.

———. "Revealed: Goldman Sachs' Mega-Deal for Greece." *Risk Magazine*, July 1, 2003. http://www.risk.net/risk-magazine/feature/1498135/revealed-goldman-sachs -mega-deal-greece.

Dunbar, Nicholas, and Elisa Martinuzzi. "Goldman Secret Greece Loan Shows Two Sinners as Client Unravels." Bloomberg, March 5, 2012. http://www.bloomberg .com/news/2012-03-06/goldman-secret-greece-loan-shows-two-sinners-as-client -unravels.html.

Dutch Banking Association. *Future-Oriented Banking: Social Charter, Banking Code, Rules of Conduct*. October, 14, 2014. http://www.nvb.nl/nieuws/2014/3392/nvb

-presenteert-definitief-pakket-toekomstgericht-bankieren-na-brede-consultatie-in
-de-samenleving.html.

Eavis, Peter. "Big Raise for JPMorgan's Dimon Despite a Rough Year." *New York Times
DealBook*, January 24, 2014. http://dealbook.nytimes.com/2014/01/24/dimons-pay
-jumps-to-20-million-in-a-year-of-legal-woes-for-jpmorgan-chase/.

———. "Wall St. Wins a Round in a Dodd-Frank Fight." *New York Times DealBook*,
December 12, 2014. http://dealbook.nytimes.com/2014/12/12/wall-st-wins-a-round
-in-a-dodd-frank-fight/.

Economist. "The Rotten Heart of Finance." July 7, 2012. http://www.economist.com
/node/21558281.

Eisinger, Jesse. Financial Crisis Suit Suggests Bad Behavior at Morgan Stanley." *New
York Times DealBook*, January 23, 2013. http://dealbook.nytimes.com/2013/01/23
/financial-crisis-lawsuit-suggests-bad-behavior-at-morgan-stanley/?_php=true&
_type=blogs&_r=0.

———. "Why Only One Top Banker Went to Jail for the Financial Crisis." *New York
Times Magazine*, April 30, 2014. http://www.nytimes.com/2014/05/04/magazine
/only-one-top-banker-jail-financial-crisis.html?_r=0.

Eisinger, Jesse, and Jake Bernstein. "The Magnetar Trade: How One Hedge Fund
Helped Keep the Bubble Going." *ProPublica*, April 9, 2010. http://www.propublica
.org/article/all-the-magnetar-trade-how-one-hedge-fund-helped-keep-the-housing
-bubble.

Elliot, Andrew J., ed. *Handbook of Approach and Avoidance Motivation.* New York:
Psychology Press, 2008.

Elliott, Dominic. "Public Health Warning." *Breakingviews*, April 9, 2014. http://www
.breakingviews.com/banks-swap-rewards-for-risk-on-public-deals/21140429.article

Ellis, Charles D., and James R. Vertin. *Wall Street People: True Stories of Today's Masters
and Moguls.* New York: J. Wiley, 2001.

Enrich, David. "Banks to Be Hit with Rate Fines." *Wall Street Journal*, November 5,
2013. http://www.wsj.com/news/articles/SB10001424052702303936904579179583
913317604?KEYWORDS=libor+fines.

Enrich, David, Ben Casselman, and Deborah Solomon. "How Occidental Scored Citi
Unit Cheaply: Bailout, Andrew Hall Factor Hurt Bank's Bargaining Position; 'Why
Should I Pay a Premium?'" *Wall Street Journal*, October 12, 2009. http://online.wsj
.com/articles/SB125509326073375979.

Epley, Nicholas, and Eugene Caruso. "Egocentric Ethics." *Social Justice Research* 17, no.
2 (2004): 171–87.

European Banking Authority (EBA). "EBA Agrees on Definition of Identified Staff
for Remuneration Purposes." December 13, 2013. http://www.eba.europa.eu/-/eba
-agrees-on-definition-of-identified-staff-for-remuneration-purposes.

———. "EBA Discloses Probe into EU Bankers Allowances." Press release, October
15, 2014. https://www.eba.europa.eu/-/eba-discloses-probe-into-eu-bankers
-allowances.

European Commission. "Antitrust: Commission Fines Banks € 1.71 Billion for
Participating in Cartels in the Interest Rate Derivatives Industry." Press release,
December 4, 2013. http://europa.eu/rapid/press-release_IP-13-1208_en.htm.

———. "Antitrust: Commission Sends Statement of Objections to 13 Investment

Banks, ISDA and Market in Credit Default Swaps Investigation." Press release, July 1, 2013. http://europa.eu/rapid/press-release_IP-13-630_en.htm.

———. "Antitrust: Commission Sends Statement of Objections to Crédit Agricole, HSBC and JPMorgan for suspected participation in euro interest rate derivatives cartel," Press release, May 20, 2014. http://europa.eu/rapid/press-release_IP-14-572 _en.htm.

Ewing, Jack, and Chris V. Nicholson. "German Court Rules against Deutsche Bank in Swaps Case." *New York Times DealBook*, March 22, 2011. http://dealbook.nytimes .com/2011/03/22/german-court-rules-against-deutsche-bank-in-swaps-case/.

Farrell, Greg. "Lawsky Said to Probe Barclays, Deutsche Bank FX Algorithm." *BloombergBusinessweek*, December 11, 2014. http://www.businessweek.com/news /2014-12-10/ny-regulator-said-to-probe-deutsche-bank-barclays-fx-algorithms.

Farrell, Sean. "Financial Watchdog Publishes Libor Warnings to Two Bankers." *Guardian* (London), February 3, 2014. http://www.theguardian.com/business/2014 /feb/03/fca-libor-warnings-bankers.

Faulk, Kent. "Federal Judge: Jefferson County Sewer Rate Hike Schedule Could Be Scrapped under Bankruptcy Plan Appeal." AL.com, October 1, 2014. http://www .al.com/news/birmingham/index.ssf/2014/10/federal_judge_jefferson_county.html.

Federal Bureau of Investigation (FBI), "Federal Judge Sentences Former Birmingham Mayor and Former Jefferson County Commission President to 15 Years for Bribery Scheme." Press release, March 5, 2010. http://www.fbi.gov/birmingham/press -releases/2010/bh030510.htm.

———. "Former Credit Suisse Managing Director Pleads Guilty in Connection with Scheme to Hide Losses in Mortgage-Backed Securities Trading Book." Press release, April 12, 2013. http://www.fbi.gov/newyork/press-releases/2013/former-credit -suisse-managing-director-pleads-guilty-in-connection-with-scheme-to-hide -losses-in-mortgage-backed-securities-trading-book.

———. "Manhattan U.S. Attorney and FBI Assistant Director in Charge Announce Charges against Two Former Credit Suisse Managing Directors and Vice President for Fraudulently Inflating Subprime Mortgage-Related Bond Prices in Trading Book." Press release, February 1, 2012. http://www.fbi.gov/newyork/press-releases /2012/manhattan-u.s.-attorney-and-fbi-assistant-director-in-charge-announce -charges-against-two-former-credit-suisse-managing-directors-and-vice-president -for-fraudulently-inflating-subprime-mortgage-related-bond-prices-in-trading -book.

Federal Energy Regulatory Commission (FERC). "FERC Approves Market Manipulation Settlement with Deutsche Bank." Press release, January 22, 2013. http://www.ferc.gov/media/news-releases/2013/2013-1/01-22-13.asp.

———. "FERC, JP Morgan Unit Agree to $410 Million in Penalties, Disgorgement to Ratepayers." Press release, July 30, 2013. http://www.ferc.gov/media/news-releases /2013/2013-3/07-30-13.asp#.UuodjZNev48.

———. "FERC Orders $453 Million in Penalties for Western Power Market Manipulation." Press release, July 16, 2013. https://www.ferc.gov/media/news -releases/2013/2013-3/07-16-13.asp#.UvKnSZNesQ5.

———. *FY 2014 Congressional Performance Budget Request.* April 2013. http://www .ferc.gov/about/strat-docs/fy14-budg.pdf.

Federal Housing Finance Agency (FHFA). "FHFA Announces Settlement with Goldman Sachs." News release, August 22, 2014. http://www.fhfa.gov/Media/PublicAffairs/Pages/FHFA-Announces-Settlement-with-Goldman-Sachs.aspx.

———. "FHFA's Update on Private Label Securities Actions." September 12, 2014. http://www.fhfa.gov/Media/PublicAffairs/Pages/FHFAs-Update-on-Private-Label-Securities-Actions.aspx.

———. "Releases." Available at http://www.fhfa.gov/Media/Pages/News-Releases.aspx.

Feely, Jef. "JPMorgan Settles Military Mortgage Suits for $56 Million." *Bloomberg*, April 21, 2011. http://www.bloomberg.com/news/2011-04-21/jpmorgan-chase-settles-military-mortgage-overcharging-suit-for-56-million.html.

Financial Conduct Authority [United Kingdom]. "FCA Fines Five Banks £1.1 Billion for FX Failings and Announces Industry-Wide Remediation Programme." Press release, November 12, 2014 (last modified November 13, 2014). http://www.fca.org.uk/news/fca-fines-five-banks-for-fx-failings.

———. "JPMorgan Chase Bank N.A. Fined £137,610,000 for Serious Failings Relating to Its Chief Investment Office's 'London Whale' Trades." Press release, September 19, 2013. http://www.fca.org.uk/news/jpmorgan-chase-bank-na-fined.

———. "Lloyds Banking Group Fined £105m for Serious LIBOR and Other Benchmark Failings." Press release, July 7, 2014. http://www.fca.org.uk/news/press-releases/lloyds-banking-group-fined-105m-libor-benchmark-failings.

———. "The FCA Fines Rabobank £105 Million for Serious LIBOR-Related Misconduct." Press release, London, October 29, 2013. http://www.fca.org.uk/news/the-fca-fines-rabobank-105-million-for-serious-libor-related-misconduct.

Financial Industry Regulatory Authority (FINRA). "FINRA Fines J. P. Morgan Securities $500,000 for Failing to Disclose Use of Payments to Consultants to Obtain Numerous Municipal Securities Offerings." News release, December 13, 2007. http://www.finra.org/Newsroom/NewsReleases/2007/P037611.

———. "FINRA Fines Merrill Lynch $1 Million for Failure to Arbitrate Disputes with Employees." News release, January 25, 2012. http://www.finra.org/Newsroom/NewsReleases/2012/P125455.

———. "FINRA Fines 10 Firms a Total of $43.5 Million for Allowing Equity Research Analysts to Solicit Investment Banking Business and for Offering Favorable Research Coverage in Connection With Toys"R"Us IPO." News release, December 11, 2014. http://www.finra.org/Newsroom/NewsReleases/2014/P602059.

———. "FINRA Sanctions Five Firms $4.4 Million for Using Municipal and State Bond Funds to Pay Lobbyists." Press release, December 27, 2012. http://www.finra.org/Newsroom/NewsReleases/2012/P197554.

Financial Services Authority [United Kingdom]. "Barclays Fined £59.5 Million for Significant Failings in Relation to LIBOR and EURIBOR." Press release, June 27, 2012. http://www.fsa.gov.uk/library/communication/pr/2012/070.shtml.

———. "Final Notice to Barclays Bank Plc." June 27, 2012. http://www.fsa.gov.uk/static/pubs/final/barclays-jun12.pdf.

Finch, Gavin, Lindsay Fortado, and Silla Brush. "RBS Fined $612M by Regulators for Manipulating Libor Rate." *Bloomberg*, February 6, 2013. http://www.bloomberg.com/news/2013-02-05/rbs-said-to-face-up-to-783-million-fine-for-manipulating-libor.html.

Fitzpatrick, Dan. "Dimon Takes a 'Whale' of a Pay Cut: J. P. Morgan Chief's Compensation Halved after Trading Debacle; Bank Posts Record Net Income in 2012." *Wall Street Journal*, January 16, 2013. http://online.wsj.com/news/articles/SB10001424127887323968304578245352454016848.

Fligstein, Neil, and Goldstein, Adam. "The Transformation of Mortgage Finance and the Industrial Roots of the Mortgage Meltdown." Working paper, June 2014. Available at http://sociology.berkeley.edu/sites/default/files/faculty/fligstein/Rise%20and%20Fall%20Revised%20June%202014%20Final%20Version.pdf.

Fortado, Lindsay. "Former Barclays Employees Charged over Libor Rigging." *BloombergBusinessweek*, February 18, 2014. http://www.businessweek.com/news/2014-02-17/three-ex-barclays-employees-charged-over-libor-rigging-in-london.

Fortado, Lindsay, and Silla Brush. "Barclays Fined by U.K., U.S. for Falsifying Libor Rates." *Bloomberg*, June 27, 2012. http://www.bloomberg.com/news/2012-06-27/barclays-said-to-be-nearing-libor-settlement-with-fsa-cftc.html.

Frank, Robert. *Luxury Fever: Why Money Fails to Satisfy in an Era of Excess*. New York: Free Press, 1999.

Friedman, Benjamin. "Is Our Financial System Serving Us Well?" *Daedalus* 139, no. 4 (2010): 9–21.

Funding Universe. "Salomon Inc. History." http://www.fundinguniverse.com/company-histories/Salomon-Inc-Company-History.html.

Gandel, Stephen. "Barclays Settles Allegations That It Manipulated Key Lending Rates." *CNN Money*, June 27, 2012. http://finance.fortune.cnn.com/2012/06/27/barclays-libor/.

Geller, Adam. "Neighborhood Swayed by 'Liar's Loans.'" *Washington Post*, May 26, 2007. http://www.washingtonpost.com/wp-dyn/content/article/2007/05/26/AR2007052600545_pf.html.

Gerding, Erik. *Law, Bubbles, and Financial Regulation*. London: Routledge, Taylor and Francis Group, 2014.

Goldman Sachs. *Business Standards Committee Impact Report*. May 2013. http://www.goldmansachs.com/a/pgs/bsc/files/GS-BSC-Impact-Report-May-2013-II.pdf.

Goldman Sachs. "Goldman Sachs Transactions with Greece." News release, February 21, 2010. http://www.goldmansachs.com/media-relations/comments-and-responses/archive/greece.html.

Gongloff, Mark. "Libor Fraud Was Happening in 1991, Trader Says, 17 Years Before Timothy Geithner Claims He Knew." *Huffington Post*, July 27, 2012. http://www.huffingtonpost.com/mark-gongloff/libor-fraud-timothy-geithner_b_1710225.html.

Gongol, Brian. "EconDirectory.com: Traffic Rankings for Business and Economics Websites." May 15, 2013. http://www.gongol.com/lists/bizeconsites/2013/05/.

Goodley, Simon. "Foreign Exchange Trading Faces SFO Criminal Investigation." *Guardian* (London). July 21, 2014. http://www.theguardian.com/business/2014/jul/21/foreign-exchange-trading-criminal-investigation-serious-fraud-office.

Greenwald, John, and Bernard Baumohl. "The California Wipeout." *Time*, December 19, 1994. http://www.time.com/time/magazine/article/0,9171,982029,00.html.

Griffin, Donal, and Dakin Campbell. "U.S. Bank Legal Bills Exceed $100 Billion." *Bloomberg News*, August 28, 2013. http://www.bloomberg.com/news/2013-08-28/u-s-bank-legal-bills-exceed-100-billion.html.

Gumbel, Peter. "In the Netherlands, Bankers Turn to God-by Law." *Analysis and*

Opinion: The Great Debate (blog), Reuters, February 12, 2014. http://blogs.reuters
.com/great-debate/2014/02/12/in-the-netherlands-bankers-turn-to-god-by-law/.

Hamermesh, Lawrence A., and A. Gilchrist Sparks III. "Corporate Officers and the
Business Judgment Rule: A Reply to Professor Johnson." *Business Lawyer* 60 (2005):
865–76.

Hammer, Peter. "SEC Has Jurisdiction over County's Swap Deals with JPMorgan,
Judge Rules." *The Knowledge Effect* (blog), Reuters, September 10, 2014. http://blog
.thomsonreuters.com/index.php/sec-has-jurisdiction-over-countys-swap-deals
-with-jpmorgan-judge-rules/.

Hansell, Saul. "Settlement by Bankers Trust Unit." *New York Times*, December 23, 1994.
http://www.nytimes.com/1994/12/23/business/settlement-by-bankers-trust-unit
.html.

Harris, Lasana T., and Susan Fiske. "Dehumanized Perception: A Psychological Means
to Facilitate Atrocities, Torture, and Genocide?" *Zeitschrift für Psychologie* 219, no. 3
(2011): 175–81.

———. "Dehumanizing the Lowest of the Low: Neuroimaging Responses to Extreme
Out-Groups." *Psychological Science* 17 (October 2006): 847–53.

Harrison, Edward. "A Banker's Perspective of the Greece Derivatives Debt Dodge."
Naked Capitalism (blog), February 24, 2010. http://www.nakedcapitalism.com/2010
/02/a-bankers-perspective-of-the-greece-derivatives-debt-dodge.html.

Higgins, E. Tory. *Beyond Pleasure and Pain: How Motivation Works*. Oxford: Oxford
University Press, 2011.

HigginsLab. "Regulatory Focus." 2013. http://www.columbia.edu/cu/psychology
/higgins/research.html.

Hill, Claire A. "Bankers Behaving Badly? The Limits of Regulatory Reform." *Review of
Banking and Financial Law* 31 (2012): 675–93.

———. "Rating Agencies Behaving Badly: The Case of Enron." *Connecticut Law
Review* 35, no. 3 (Spring 2003): 1145–56.

———. "Securitization: A Low-Cost Sweetener for Lemons." *Washington University
Law Quarterly* 74 (1996): 1061–1126.

———. "Tax Lawyers Are People Too: Commentary on Victor Fleischer's Options
Backdating, Tax Shelters and Corporate Culture." *Virginia Tax Review* 26
(2007):1065–68.

———. "Why Did Anyone Listen to the Rating Agencies after Enron?" *Journal of
Business and Technology Law* 4 (2009): 283–94.

———. "Why Did the Rating Agencies Do Such a Bad Job Rating Subprime
Securities?" *University of Pittsburgh Law Review* 71, no. 3 (2009): 585–608.

———. "Why Financial Appearances Might Matter: An Explanation for 'Dirty
Pooling' and Some Other Types of Financial Cosmetics." *Delaware Journal of
Corporate Law* 22 (1997): 141–96.

Hill, Claire, and Richard Painter. "Berle's Vision beyond Shareholder Interests: Why
Investment Bankers Should Have Some Personal Liability." *Seattle University Law
Review* 33, no. 4 (2010): 1173–99.

———. "A Simpler Rein Than the Volcker Rule." *New York Times DealBook*, October
28, 2011. http://dealbook.nytimes.com/2011/10/28/another-view-a-simpler-rein
-than-the-volcker-rule/.'

———. "Why S.E.C. Settlements Should Hold Senior Executives Liable." *New York

Times DealBook, May 29, 2012. http://dealbook.nytimes.com/2012/05/29/why-s-e-c
-settlements-should-hold-senior-executives-liable/.

Holland, Kelley, Linda Himelstein, and Zachary Schiller. "The Bankers Trust
Tapes." *Business Week*, October 16, 1995. Last updated June 13, 1997. http://www
.businessweek.com/1995/42/b34461.htm.

Homer, Sidney, and Martin Leibowitz. *Inside the Yield Book.* 2nd ed. Bloomberg
Financial Series. Hoboken, NJ: John Wiley and Sons, 2004.

Hsee, Christopher K., and Elke U. Weber. "Cross-National Differences in Risk
Preference and Lay Predictions." *Journal of Behavioral Decision Making* 12, no. 2
(1999): 165–79.

Hsee, Christopher K., Yang Yang, Naihe Li, and Luxi Shen. "Wealth, Warmth, and Well-
Being: Whether Happiness Is Relative or Absolute Depends on Whether It Is about
Money, Acquisition, or Consumption." *Journal of Marketing Research* 46, no. 3
(June 2009): 396–409.

Hsee, Christopher K., Jiao Zhang, Cindy F. Cai, and Shirley Zhang. "Overearning."
Psychological Science 24, no. 6 (2013): 852–59.

Hume, Lynne "JPMorgan Chase to Pay $228M for Municipal Bond Bid-Rigging,"
American Banker, July 7, 2011. http://www.americanbanker.com/issues/176_130
/jpmorgan-pay-investment-bid-rigging-charges-1039806-1.html?zkPrintable=1&
nopagination=1.

Hume, Neil. "How to Borrow €1bn without Adding to Your Public Debt Figures." *FT
Alphaville* (blog), February 15, 2010. http://ftalphaville.ft.com//2010/02/15/149351
/how-to-borrow-e1bn-without-adding-your-public-debt-figures.

Hurtado, Patricia. "Ex-Credit Suisse CDO Chief Must Pay More Than $1 Million."
Bloomberg, January 21, 2014. http://www.bloomberg.com/news/2014-01-21/ex
-credit-suisse-cdo-chief-must-pay-more-than-1-million.html.

———. "The London Whale." *Bloomberg QuickTake*, updated March 5, 2015. http://
www.bloombergview.com/quicktake/the-london-whale.

Hurtado, Patricia, and Tom Schoenberg. "Rabobank Ex-Traders Charged with Yen
Libor Rigging." *Bloomberg*, January 14, 2014. http://www.bloomberg.com/news
/2014-01-13/rabobank-ex-traders-charged-with-yen-libor-rigging-u-s-says.html.

Intercontinental Exchange, Inc.(ICE) Services. "ICE Benchmark Administration:
Overview." https://www.theice.com/iba.

Ishmael, Stacie-Marie. "Corrigan or Eurostat: Whom Would You Believe?" *FT
Alphaville* (blog), February 23, 2010. http://ftalphaville.ft.com/2010/02/23/156591
/corrigan-or-eurostat-whom-would-you-believe/.

Isidore, Chris. "JPMorgan's Dimon Gets 74% Pay Hike Despite Legal Woes." *CNN
Money*, January 24, 2014. http://money.cnn.com/2014/01/24/news/companies
/dimon-pay/.

Jacob, David P. Letter to SEC Secretary Elizabeth M. Murphy. June 3, 2013. Comment
Letters, US Securities and Exchange Commission. http://www.sec.gov/comments
/4-661/4661-25.pdf.

Johnson, Lyman P. Q. "Corporate Officers and the Business Judgment Rule" *Business
Lawyer* 60 (February 2005): 439–69.

"JPMorgan, Morgan Stanley Fined $1.8 billion for Concealing Pre-Crisis Mortgage
Risk." RT.com, February 5, 2014. http://rt.com/business/morgan-stanley-mortgage
-penalty-673/.

Kaal, Wulf A., and Timothy Lacine, "The Effect of Deferred and Non-Prosecution Agreements on Corporate Governance: Evidence from 1993–2013." *Business Lawyer* 70 (Winter 2014–15): 61–119.

Kahneman, Daniel, and Amos Tversky. "Prospect Theory: An Analysis of Decision under Risk." *Econometrica* 47 (1979): 263–91.

Kantor, Ira. "SEC: Ex-Goldman Banker Fined, Barred in Cahill Pay-to-Play Case." *Boston Herald Biz Smart*, May 23, 2013. http://bostonherald.com/business/business _markets/2013/05/sec_ex_goldman_banker_fined_barred_in_cahill_pay_to_play _case.

Kaufman, Henry. Foreword to *Inside the Yield Book*, by Sidney Homer and Martin Leibowitz. Englewood Cliffs, NJ: Prentice-Hall, 1972.

———. "Kaufman on Civility in the Financial Sector." *Carnegie Council*, June 20, 2011. http://www.carnegiecouncil.org/studio/multimedia/20110620/index.html.

Keenan, Douglas. "My Thwarted Attempts to Tell of Libor Shenanigans." *Financial Times*, July 26, 2012. http://www.ft.com/intl/cms/s/0/dc5f49c2-d67b-11e1-ba60 -00144feabdc0.html#axzz2XgH5S9Wl.

Kolhatkar, Sheelah. "Mary Jo White Is the Woman Who Makes Wall Street Admit Guilt." *BloombergBusinessweek*, October 16, 2013. http://www.businessweek.com /articles/2013-10-16/mary-jo-white-is-the-woman-who-makes-wall-street-admit -guilt.

Kopecki, Dawn. "JPMorgan Awards CEO Jamie Dimon $23 Million Pay Package." *Bloomberg*, April 4, 2012. http://www.bloomberg.com/news/2012-04-04/jpmorgan -awards-ceo-jamie-dimon-23-million-pay-package.html.

———. "JPMorgan Bribe Probe Said to Expand in Asia as Spreadsheet Is Found." *Bloomberg*, August 28, 2013. http://www.bloomberg.com/news/2013-08-29 /jpmorgan-bribe-probe-said-to-expand-in-asia-as-spreadsheet-found.html.

———. "JPMorgan's Drew Forfeits 2 Years' Pay as Managers Ousted." *BloombergBusinessweek*, July 13, 2012. http://www.businessweek.com/news/2012-07 -13/dimon-says-ina-drew-offered-to-return-2-years-of-compensation.

Kouchaki, Maryam, Kristin Smith-Crowe, Arthur P. Brief, and Carlos Sousa. "Seeing Green: Mere Exposure to Money Triggers a Business Decision Frame and Unethical Outcomes." *Organizational Behavior and Human Decision Processes* 121, no. 1 (2013): 53–61. http://dx.doi.org/10.1016/j.obhdp.2012.12.002.

Lacapra, Lauren Tara. "Morgan Stanley Settles with MBIA, Sets $1.8 Billion Charge." Reuters, December 13, 2011. http://www.reuters.com/article/2011/12/13/us -morganstanley-mbia-idUSTRE7BC1AH20111213.

Langevoort, Donald. "On Leaving Corporate Executives Naked, Homeless and without Wheels: Corporate Fraud, Equitable Remedies and the Debate over Entity versus Individual Liability." *Wake Forest Law Review* 42 (2007): 627–61.

Lattman, Peter. "Former Credit Suisse Executive Pleads Guilty to Inflating the Value of Mortgage Bonds." *New York Times DealBook*, April 12, 2013. http://dealbook .nytimes.com/2013/04/12/ex-credit-suisse-executive-pleads-guilty-to-inflating -value-of-mortgage-bonds/?src=recg.

———. "S.E.C. Gets Encouragement from Jury That Ruled against It." *New York Times DealBook*, August 3, 2012. http://dealbook.nytimes.com/2012/08/03/s-e-c-gets -encouragement-from-jury-that-ruled-against-it./.

Lauricella, Tom, and Katy Burne. "Chasing Yield, Investors Plow into Riskier

Bonds." *Wall Street Journal*, May 19, 2014. http://online.wsj.com/news/articles
/SB10001424052702304422704579572390216147878.

Lea, Stephen E. G., and Paul Webley. "Money as Tool, Money as Drug: The Biological
Psychology of a Strong Incentive." *Behavioral and Brain Sciences* 29, no. 2 (2006):
161–209.

Leeson, Nick. "Welcome." http://www.nickleeson.com.

Legorano, Giovanni. "Milan Court Overturns Fraud Derivatives Case Verdict."
Wall Street Journal, March 7, 2014. http://online.wsj.com/news/articles
/SB10001424052702304554004579424712672889106.

Leising, Matthew, Lindsay Fortado, and Jim Brunsden. "Meet ISDAfix, the Libor
Scandal's Sequel." *BloombergBusinessweek*, April 18, 2013. http://www.businessweek
.com/articles/2013-04-18/meet-isdafix-the-libor-scandals-sequel.

Levin, Carl, U.S. Senator, Michigan. "Subcommittee Finds Wall Street Commodities
Actions Add Risk to Economy, Businesses, Consumers." Press release, November
19, 2014. http://www.levin.senate.gov/newsroom/press/release/subcommittee-finds
-wall-street-commodities-actions-add-risk-to-economy-businesses-consumers.

Levine, Matt. "The Goldman Sachs Aluminum Conspiracy Lawsuit Is Over."
Bloomberg View, September 3, 2014. http://www.bloombergview.com/articles/2014
-09-03/the-goldman-sachs-aluminum-conspiracy-lawsuit-is-over.

———. "Morgan Stanley Finalizes Its Entry in the 'Who Said the Worst Things about
Its Own Products?' Competition." *Dealbreaker*, January 23, 2013. http://dealbreaker
.com/2013/01/morgan-stanley-finalizes-its-entry-in-the-who-said-the-worst-things
-about-its-own-products-competition/#fn02.

Levitt, Arthur. *Take on the Street: What Wall Street and Corporate America Don't Want
You to Know*. New York: Pantheon, 2002.

Lewis, Michael. *Flash Boys*. New York: W. W. Norton, 2014.

———. *Liar's Poker*. New York: W. W. Norton, 1989.

———. *Panic: The Story of Modern Financial Insanity*. New York: W.W. Norton, 2009.

———. "The Trouble with Wall Street: The Shocking News That Goldman Sachs Is
Greedy." *New Republic*, February 4, 2013. http://www.newrepublic.com/article
/112209/michael-lewis-goldman-sachs.

Litan, Robert. "In Defense of Much, But Not All, Financial Innovation." *Brookings
Institution*, February 17, 2010. http://www.brookings.edu/research/papers/2010/02
/17-financial-innovation-litan.

Lo, Andrew. "Fear, Greed, and Financial Crises: A Cognitive Neurosciences
Perspective." In *Handbook on Systemic Risk*, edited by Jean-Pierre Fouque and
Joseph A. Langsam, 622–62. Cambridge: Cambridge University Press, 2013. http://
ssrn.com/abstract=1943325.

Loewenstein, George, Sunita Sah, and Daylian M. Cain. "The Unintended
Consequences of Conflict of Interest Disclosure." *Journal of the American Medical
Association* 307, no. 7 (February 15, 2012): 669–70.

Loewenstein, George, and Deborah A. Small. "Statistical, Identifiable and Iconic
Victims." In *Behavioral Public Finance*, edited by Edward J. McCaffery and Joel
Slemrod, 32–46. New York: Russell Sage Foundation, 2006.

Logutenkova, Elena, and Lindsay Fortado. "UBS Fined $1.5 Billion by Regulators for
Rigging Libor." *Bloomberg*, December 19, 2012. http://www.bloomberg.com/news
/2012-12-19/ubs-fined-1-4-billion-swiss-francs-for-manipulating-libor-rate.html.

Loomis, Carol J., Suzanne Barlyn, and Kate Ballen. "Untangling the Derivatives Mess They Didn't Melt Down the Financial System. But These Red-Hot Instruments Proved Too Tempting for Both Buyers and Sellers. This Is the Story of How Lies, Leverage, Ignorance—and Lots of Arrogance—Burned Some Big Players." *Fortune*, March 20, 1995. http://archive.fortune.com/magazines/fortune/fortune_archive /1995/03/20/201945/index.htm.

Lowenstein, Roger. *Buffett: The Making of an American Capitalist.* New York: Main Street Books, 1995.

Lucas, Douglas J., Laurie S. Goodman, and Frank J. Fabozzi. *Collateralized Debt Obligations: Structures and Analysis.* 2nd ed. Hoboken, NJ: Wiley, 2006.

Macey, Jonathan R., and Geoffrey P. Miller. "Double Liability of Bank Shareholders: History and Implications." *Wake Forest Law Review* 27 (1992): 31–62.

Madden, Jerome A. "A Weapon of Mass Destruction Strikes: Credit Default Swaps Bring Down AIG and Lehman Brothers." *Business Law Brief* 5, no.1 (Fall 2008): 15–22.

Maharaj, Davan, and Shelby Grad. "Seducing Citron: How Merrill Influenced Fund and Won Profits." *Los Angeles Times*, July 26, 1998. http://articles.latimes.com/1998 /jul/26/news/mn-7391.

Mandel, Naomi. "Shifting Selves and Decision Making: The Effects of Self-Construal Priming on Consumer Risk-Taking." *Journal of Consumer Research* 30, no. 1 (2003): 30–40.

Mandel, Naomi, Petia K. Petrova, and Robert B. Cialdini. "Images of Success and the Preference for Luxury Brands." *Journal of Consumer Psychology* 16, no. 1 (2006): 57–69.

Mandis, Steven. *What Happened to Goldman Sachs?* Boston: Harvard Business Review Press, 2013.

Markman, Arthur B., and Dedre Gentner. "Thinking." *Annual Review of Psychology* 52 (2001): 223–47.

Markman, Arthur B., and Douglas L. Medin. "Similarity and Alignment In Choice." *Organizational Behavior and Human Decision Processes* 63, no. 2 (August 1995): 117–30.

Martin, Douglas. "Robert Citron, Culprit in California Fraud, Dies at 87." *New York Times*, January 18, 2013. http://www.nytimes.com/2013/01/18/business/robert-citron -culprit-in-california-fraud-dies-at-87.html.

Martinuzzi, Elisa, and Sonia Sirletti. "Deutsche Bank Forfeits 221 Million Euros from Monte Paschi Deal." *Bloomberg*, December 19, 2013. http://www.bloomberg.com /news/2013-12-19/monte-paschi-reaches-accord-with-deutsche-bank-on-santorini -deal.html.

Matussek, Karin. "Pforzheim-JPMorgan Swaps Prompt Charges against Officials." *BloombergBusinessweek*, February 20, 2013. http://www.businessweek.com/news /2013-02-20/pforzheim-jpmorgan-swaps-prompt-charges-against-officials.

McCoy, Kevin. "Banks Caught in Widening Foreign Exchange Probes." *USA Today*, April 7, 2014. http://www.usatoday.com/story/money/business/2014/04/05/foreign -exchange-investigations-expand/7252681/.

McDonnell, Brett and Daniel Schwarcz. "Regulatory Contrarians." *North Carolina Law Review* 89 (2010): 1629–82.

McLaughlin, David. "Banks Get December Deadline to Come Clean on FX Rigging."

New York Times DealBook, November 14, 2014. http://dealbook.nytimes.com/2014 /11/03/jpmorgan-raises-estimate-for-legal-costs/.

McLean, Bethany, and Joe Nocera. *All the Devils Are Here: The Hidden History of the Financial Crisis*. New York: Portfolio/Penguin, 2010.

Mead, Nicole L., Eugene M. Caruso, Kathleen D. Vohs, and Roy F. Baumeister. "There Is No 'You' in Money: Reminders of Money Reduce the Motivation to Be Liked and Accepted." *Journal of Personality and Social Psychology* (forthcoming).

Michaels, Dave, Robert Schmidt, and Keri Geiger "BofA Mortgage Settlement Stalls over SEC Political Fight." *Bloomberg*, October 27, 2014. http://www.bloomberg.com /news/2014-10-27/bofa-mortgage-settlement-stalls-over-sec-political-fight.html.

Minnesota Department of Commerce. "Auction Rate Securities Settlements." //mn.gov /commerce/topics/enforcement/auction-rate-securities-settlements.jsp.

Mollenkamp, Carrick. "Deutsche Bank Agrees $55 Mln Settlement with M&T." Reuters, January 17, 2012. http://in.reuters.com/article/2012/01/18/idINL1E8CI03020120118.

Moore, Michael J. "Goldman Would Refuse Another Greece Swap, Sherwood Says." *Bloomberg*, November 21, 2013. http://www.bloomberg.com/news/2013-11-22 /goldman-would-refuse-another-greece-swap-sherwood-says.html.

Moore, Michael J., and Christine Harper. "Blankfein's Gay-Rights Stance Shows Wall Street's Dilemma." *Bloomberg*, May 3, 2012. http://www.bloomberg.com/news/2012 -05-02/blankfein-s-gay-rights-support-shows-wall-street-s-obama-dilemma.html

Morrison, Alan D., and William J. Willhelm. "Investment Banking: Past, Present, and Future." *Journal of Applied Corporate Finance* 19, no. 1 (Winter 2007): 8–20.

Muñoz, Sara Schaefer, and Max Colchester. "Top Officials at Barclays Resign over Rate Scandal." *Wall Street Journal*, July 4, 2012. http://online.wsj.com/news/articles /SB10001424052702304299704577503974000425002.

Muolo, Paul. "JPMorgan Admits Guilt in Massive FHA Fraud Case, Will Pay $614 Million in Damages." *Inside Mortgage Finance*, February 5, 2014. http://www .insidemortgagefinance.com/imfnews/1_283/daily/jpmorgan-chase-admits-guilt -in-fha-case-1000026047-1.html?ET=imfpubs:e4254:56441a:&st=email&s =imfnews.

Newkirk, Margaret, and Kathleen Edwards. "Jefferson County in New Creditors Deal with JPMorgan Concessions." *BloombergBusinessweek*, November 1, 2013. http:// www.businessweek.com/news/2013-10-31/jefferson-county-commission-reaches -new-creditors-deal-correct.

New York State Department of Financial Services. "Statement from Benjamin M. Lawsky, Superintendent of Financial Services, Regarding Standard Chartered Bank." Press release, August 14, 2012. http://www.dfs.ny.gov/about/press/pr1208141 .htm.

New York State Office of the Attorney General. "A. G. Schneiderman Secures $7.8 Million Settlement with First American Corporation and Eappraiseit for Role in Housing Market Meltdown." Press release, September 28, 2012. http://www.ag.ny .gov/press-release/ag-schneiderman-secures-78-million-settlement-first-american -corporation-and.

———. "Attorney General Cuomo Announces Settlement with UBS to Recover Billions for Investors in Auction Rate Securities." Press release, August 8, 2008. http://www.ag.ny.gov/press-release/attorney-general-cuomo-announces-settlement -ubs-recover-billions-investors-auction.

———. "New York State Mortgage Settlement." February 2012. http://www
.nysmortgagesettlement.com/.

———. "NY Attorney General Sues First American and Its Subsidiary for Conspiring
with Washington Mutual to Inflate Real Estate Appraisals." Press release,
November 1, 2007. http://www.ag.ny.gov/press-release/ny-attorney-general-sues
-first-american-and-its-subsidiary-conspiring-washington.

New York Times DealBook. "Barclays to Pay $298 Million for Violating Trade Law."
August 16, 2010. http://dealbook.nytimes.com/2010/08/16/barclays-to-pay-298
-million-for-violating-trade-law/.

———"Magnetar's Big Subprime Trade." April 15, 2010. http://dealbook.nytimes.com
/2010/04/15/magnetar-death-star-of-subprime/.

———. "Understanding the Rate-Fixing Inquiry." Updated July 28, 2014. http://www
.nytimes.com/interactive/2012/07/16/business/dealbook/20120716-libor-interactive
.html#/#banks.

NIBC Bank, N.V. "Banker's Oath/Solemn Affirmation of Policymaker." http://www
.nibc.com/investor-relations/dutch-banking-code/bankers-oath.html.

Obama, Barack. "Remarks by the President at Presentation of Medal of Honor to
Sergeant Kyle J. White, US Army." Speech given on May 13, 2014. http://www
.whitehouse.gov/the-press-office/2014/05/13/remarks-president-presentation
-medal-honor-sergeant-kyle-j-white-us-army.

Office of the Comptroller of the Currency (OCC). "OCC Assesses $300 Million Civil
Money Penalty against JPMorgan Chase, N.A., Related to Derivatives Trading
Activity." Press release, September 19, 2013. http://www.occ.gov/news-issuances
/news-releases/2013/nr-occ-2013-140.html.

———. "OCC Fines Three Banks $950 Million for FX Trading Improprieties." News
Release, November 12, 2014. http://www.occ.gov/news-issuances/news-releases
/2014/nr-occ-2014-157.html.

Omarova, Saule T. "License to Deal: Mandatory Approval of Complex Financial
Products." *Washington University Law Review* 90, no. 1 (2012): 63–140.

Ovaska, Michael, and Margot Patrick. "The Libor Settlements." *Wall Street Journal*,
March 5, 2014. http://online.wsj.com/news/interactive/LIBOR0213?ref=
SB10001424127887324178904578342012085837302.

Ovide, Shira. "Inside S&P: Fears over an Ill-Fated CDO Deal." *Wall Street Journal*,
September 27, 2011. http://blogs.wsj.com/deals/2011/09/27/inside-sp-fears-over-an
-ill-fated-cdo-deal/.

Painter, Richard W. "The Dodd-Frank Extraterritorial Jurisdiction Provision: Was It
Effective, Needed or Sufficient?" *Harvard Business Law Review* 1 (2011): 195–229.

———. *Ethics and Corruption in Business and Government: Lessons from the South
Sea Bubble and the Bank of the United States.* Chicago: Law School, University of
Chicago, 2006.

———. "The Moral Interdependence of Corporate Lawyers and Their Clients."
Southern California Law Review 67 (1994): 507–84.

———. "The Moral Responsibility of Investment Bankers." *St. Thomas University Law
Review* 8 (2011): 5–28.

———. "Responding to a False Alarm: Federal Preemption of State Securities Fraud
Causes of Action." *Cornell Law Review* 84 (1998): 1–108.

————. "Standing Up to Wall Street (and Congress)." *Michigan Law Review* 101 (2003): 1512–31.

————. "Transaction Cost Engineers, Loophole Engineers or Gatekeepers: The Role of Business Lawyers after the Financial Meltdown." In *Research Handbook on the Economics of Corporate Law*, edited by Claire Hill and Brett McDonnell, 255–72. Northampton, MA: Edward Elgar, 2012.

Parsons, Dana. "Citron on the Witness Stand Was One Way to Court Disaster." *Los Angeles Times*, June 5, 1998. http://articles.latimes.com/1998/jun/05/local/me -56764.

Partnoy, Frank. *Infectious Greed: How Deceit and Risk Corrupted the Financial Markets.* New York: Times Books, 2003.

Piga, Gustavo. "Do Governments Use Financial Derivatives Appropriately?" *International Finance* 4 (Summer 2001): 189–219.

Piovaccari, Giulio, and Francesca Landini. "Italy's Piedmont Loses Lawsuit over Derivative Contracts." Reuters, July 17, 2013. http://uk.mobile.reuters.com/article /article/idUKL6N0FN1K320130717.

Pollack, Andrew, and Leslie Wayne. "Ending Suit, Merrill Lynch to Pay California County $400 Million." *New York Times*, June 3. 1998. http://www.nytimes.com/1998 /06/03/business/ending-suit-merrill-lynch-to-pay-california-county-400-million .html?pagewanted=all&src=pm.

Popper, Nathaniel. "Under Investigation, JPMorgan Increases Its Potential Legal Costs." *New York Times DealBook*, November 3, 2014. http://dealbook.nytimes.com /2014/11/03/jpmorgan-raises-estimate-for-legal-costs/?_r=0.

Popper, Nathaniel, and Peter Eavis. "Errant Trades Reveal a Risk Few Expected." *New York Times DealBook*, August 3, 2012. http://dealbook.nytimes.com/2012/08/02 /errant-trades-reveal-a-risk-few-expected/.

Popper, Nathaniel, and Ben Protess. "To Regulate Rapid Traders, SEC Turns to One of Them." *New York Times*, October 7, 2012. http://www.nytimes.com/2012/10/08 /business/sec-regulators-turn-to-high-speed-trading-firm.html?pagewanted=all.

Posner, Eric A., and E. Glen Weyl. "An FDA for Financial Innovation: Applying the Insurable Interest Doctrine to Twenty-First-Century Financial Markets." *Northwestern University Law Review* 107, no. 3 (2013): 1307–58.

Powers, William C., Jr., Raymond S. Troubh, and Herbert S. Winokur Jr. *Report of Investigation of Special Investigative Committee of the Board of Directors of Enron Corp. (Powers Report.)* February 1, 2002. http://i.cnn.net/cnn/2002/LAW/02/02 /enron.report/powers.report.pdf.

Protess, Ben. "Bank of America Pays $137 Million in Bid-Rigging Case." *New York Times DealBook*, December 7, 2010. http://dealbook.nytimes.com/2010/12/07/bofa -pays-137-million-to-settle-bid-rigging-charges/.

————. "Ex-Goldman Trader Tourre Fights S.E.C Penalties in Fraud Case." *New York Times DealBook*, January 22, 2014. http://dealbook.nytimes.com/2014/01/22/tourre -seeks-leniency-in-s-e-c-case/.

————. "Former Goldman Trader Tourre Says He Will Not Appeal." *New York Times DealBook*, May 27, 2014. http://dealbook.nytimes.com/2014/05/27/former-goldman -trader-tourre-says-he-will-not-appeal/.

————. "A Regulator Cuts New Teeth for JPMorgan in London Whale Case." *New*

York Times DealBook, October 16, 2013. http://dealbook.nytimes.com/2013/10/16
/jpmorgan-to-pay-100-million-and-make-admission-of-wrongdoing-in-london
-whale-pact/.

———. "Three Former Rabobank Traders Charged in Libor Case." *New York Times
DealBook*, January 13, 2014. http://dealbook.nytimes.com/2014/01/13/three-former
-rabobank-traders-charged-in-libor-case/.

———. "Wall Street Seeks to Tuck Dodd-Frank Changes in Budget Bill." *New York
Times DealBook*, December 9, 2014. http://dealbook.nytimes.com/2014/12/09/wall
-street-seeks-to-tuck-dodd-frank-changes-in-budget-bill/.

Protess, Ben, and Jessica Silver-Greenberg. "HSBC to Pay $1.92 Billion to Settle
Charges of Money Laundering." *New York Times DealBook*, December 10, 2012.
http://dealbook.nytimes.com/2012/12/10/hsbc-said-to-near-1-9-billion-settlement
-over-money-laundering/

———. "JPMorgan Is Penalized $2 Billion over Madoff." *New York Times DealBook*,
January 7, 2014. http://dealbook.nytimes.com/2014/01/07/jpmorgan-settles-with
-federal-authorities-in-madoff-case/.

Raymond, Nate, and Jonathan Stempel. "Big Fine Imposed on Ex-Goldman Trader
Tourre in SEC Case." Reuters, March 12, 2014. http://www.reuters.com/article/2014
/03/12/us-goldmansachs-sec-tourre-idUSBREA2B11220140312.

Reckard, E. Scott, and Michael Wagner. "Broker to Settle with O.C. for $437 Million."
Los Angeles Times, June 3, 1998. http://articles.latimes.com/1998/jun/03/news/mn
-56057/2.

Reuters. "Former JPMorgan Executive Challenges U.K.'s London Whale Report."
October 21, 2013. http://www.reuters.com/article/2013/10/21/us-jpmorgan-whale
-idUSBRE99K16A20131021.

———. "Here Are the 16 Banks under Investigation over the Libor Scandal." July 11,
2012. http://www.huffingtonpost.com/2012/07/11/libor-rate-scandal_n_1664737
.html.

———. "Judge OKs JPMorgan Overdraft Fee Settlement." May 25, 2012. http://www
.reuters.com/article/2012/05/25/jpmorgan-overdraft-settlement-idUSL1E8GP3
ZY20120525.

———. "Three Ex-Brokers Face Criminal Charges over Libor Scandal." *Huffington
Post*, September 25, 2013. http://www.huffingtonpost.com/2013/09/25/criminal
-charges-libor_n_3987890.html.

Robb, Greg. "Fed Ends Goldman, Greece Probe with No Action." *Market Watch*, April
14, 2010. http://www.marketwatch.com/story/fed-ends-goldman-greece-probe
-with-no-action-2010-04-14.

Rostain, Tanina, and Milton C. Regan Jr. *Confidence Games: Lawyers, Accountants, and
the Tax Shelter Industry.* Cambridge, MA: MIT Press, 2014.

Salganik, Matthew J., Peter Sheridan Dodds, and Duncan J. Watts. "Experimental Study
of Inequality and Unpredictability in an Artificial Cultural Market." *Science* 311
(February 10, 2006): 854–56. Available at http://qssi.psu.edu/files/salganik_dodds
_watts06_full.pdf.

Salmon, Felix. "The Greek Derivatives Aren't Goldman's Fault." *Analysis and Opinion:
Felix Salmon* (blog), Reuters, February 16, 2010. http://blogs.reuters.com/felix
-salmon/2010/02/16/the-greek-derivatives-arent-goldmans-fault/.

———. "How Greece Hid Its Borrowing in the Swaps Market." *Analysis and Opinion: Felix Salmon* (blog), Reuters, February 9, 2010. http://blogs.reuters.com/felix -salmon/2010/02/09/how-greece-hid-its-borrowing-in-the-swaps-market/.

———. "How UBS Lost Money on Super-Senior Bonds." *Seeking Alpha* (blog), April 23, 2008. http://seekingalpha.com/article/73558-how-ubs-lost-money-on-super -senior-bonds."

———. "Why Did All Those Super-Seniors Exist?" *Analysis and Opinion: Felix Salmon* (blog), Reuters, April 28, 2010. http://blogs.reuters.com/felix-salmon/2010/04/28 /why-did-all-those-super-seniors-exist/.

Salz, Anthony. *Salz Review: An Independent Review of Barclays Best Practices.* London: Barclays, 2013.

Scannell, Kara, Camilla Hall, and Daniel Schäfer. "NY Regulator Opens Currency Probe." *Financial Times*, February 5, 2014. http://www.ft.com/intl/cms/s/0/3911ef32 -8e7f-11e3-98c6-00144feab7de.html#axzz3CCtBrGNa.

Schurr, Amos, and Ilana Ritov. "The Effect of Giving It All Up on Valuation: A New Look at the Endowment Effect." *Management Science* 60, no. 3 (2013): 628–37.

Schurr, Amos, Ilana Ritov, Yaakov Kareev, and Judith Avrahami. "Is That the Answer You Had in Mind? The Effect of Perspective on Unethical Behavior." *Judgment and Decision Making* 7, no. 6 (2012): 679–88.

Schurter, Karl, and Bart J. Wilson. "Justice and Fairness in the Dictator Game." *Southern Economic Journal* 76, no. 1 (2009): 130–45.

Schwarcz, Steven L. "Excessive Corporate Risk-Taking and the Decline of Personal Blame." *Emory Law Journal* 65, no. 2 (2015). http://ssrn.com/abstract=2553511.

Schwartz, Nelson D. "James Gorman of Morgan Stanley, Going against Type." *New York Times*, June 28, 2014. http://www.nytimes.com/2014/06/29/business/james -gorman-of-morgan-stanley-going-against-type.html.

Schwartz, Nelson D., and Eric Dash. "Banks Bet Greece Defaults on Debt They Helped Hide." *New York Times*, February 24, 2010. http://www.nytimes.com/2010/02/25 /business/global/25swaps.html?dbk.

Scism, Leslie, and Randall Smith. "Wall Street Wizardry Reworks Mortgages." *Wall Street Journal*, October 1, 2009. http://online.wsj.com/news/articles /SB125434502953253695.

Sebag, Gaspard. "JPMorgan to HSBC Accused by EU over Rate-Rigging Cartel." *Bloomberg*, May 20, 2014. http://www.bloomberg.com/news/2014-05-20/jpmorgan -to-hsbc-accused-by-eu-over-rate-rigging-cartel.html.

Selway, William. "Jefferson County's Journey from Sewer-Bond Scandal to Settlement: Timeline." *Bloomberg*, September 16, 2011. http://www.bloomberg.com/news/2011 -09-16/jefferson-county-alabama-s-path-from-scandal-to-debt-settlement-timeline .html.

Selway, William, and Martin Z. Braun. "FBI Probe of JPMorgan Fees Focuses on Swaps Roiling Muni Debt." *Bloomberg*, October 27, 2008. http://www.bloomberg.com /apps/news?sid=alL9gsK5wG40&pid=newsarchive.

———. "JPMorgan Proves Bond Deal Death in Jefferson County No Bar to New Business." *Bloomberg*, August 11, 2011. http://www.bloomberg.com/news/2011-08-12 /jpmorgan-proves-bond-deal-death-in-jefferson-county-no-bar-to-new-business .html.

————. "JPMorgan Swap Deals Spur Probe as Default Stalks Alabama County." *Bloomberg*, May 22, 2008. http://www.bloomberg.com/apps/news?sid=aF _f8gLLNvn0&pid=newsarchive.

Sepe, Simone M., and Charles K. Whitehead. "Paying for Risk." *Cornell Law Review* 100 (2015): 655–702.

Shah, Aman, and Nate Raymond "Morgan Stanley to Pay $1.25 Billion to Resolve Mortgage Lawsuit." Reuters, February 4, 2014. http://www.reuters.com/article/2014 /02/05/us-morganstanley-fhfa-idUSBREA131PX20140205.

Shiffman, John. "Former Executive Gets Jail, Probation[,] Charles LeCroy Pleaded Guilty in January to Making an Illegal Payment to Ron White." philly.com (blog), June 9, 2005. http://articles.philly.com/2005-06-09/news/25438780_1_probation -illegal-payment-fbi-agents.

Shirbon, Estelle. "Accused UBS Rogue Trader: 'I Lost Control.' " Reuters, October 30, 2012. http://uk.reuters.com/article/2012/10/30/ubs-trial -idUKL5E8LUEUO20121030.

Shotter, James, and Caroline Binham. "Swiss Investigate Individuals in Forex Case." *Financial Times*, November 13, 2014. http://www.ft.com/intl/cms/s/0/4aa4557a -6b40-11e4-be68-00144feabdc0.html?siteedition=uk#axzz3LzByZdZq.

Silver-Greenberg, Jessica. "Hampered by Legal Costs, JPMorgan's Profit Falls 7.3%." *New York Times DealBook*, January 14, 2014. http://dealbook.nytimes.com/2014/01 /14/hurt-by-legal-costs-jpmorgan-earnings-fall-7-3-for-quarter/.

Silver-Greenberg, Jessica, and Ben Protess. "In Tax Case, Credit Suisse Is Denied Milder Penalty." *New York Times DealBook*, May 19, 2014. http://dealbook.nytimes .com/2014/05/19/feeling-the-force-of-the-law/.

————. "JP Morgan Caught in Swirl of Regulatory Woes." *New York Times DealBook*, May 2, 2013. http://dealbook.nytimes.com/2013/05/02/jpmorgan-caught-in-swirl-of -regulatory-woes/.

Sinnock, Bonnie. "Market 'Overheated' for Nonperforming Mortgages, Advisors Say." *Mortgage Servicing News*, June 19, 2014. http://www.nationalmortgagenews .com/news/servicing/market-overheated-for-nonperforming-mortgages-advisors -1042001-1.html?utm_medium=email&ET=nationalmortgage%3Ae4010451%3Aa %3A&utm_campaign=-jun%2019%202014&utm_source=newsletter&st=email.

Sirletti, Sonia, and Elisa Martinuzzi. "JPMorgan, UBS Convictions Overturned in Milan Swaps Case." *Bloomberg*, March 7, 2014. http://www.bloomberg.com/news /2014-03-07/jpmorgan-ubs-convictions-overturned-in-milan-swaps-case.html.

Sjöberg, Lennart, and Elisabeth Engleberg. "Attitudes to Economic Risk-Taking, Sensation Seeking and Values of Business Students Specializing in Finance." *Journal of Behavioral Finance* 10, no. 1 (2009): 33–43. http://dx.doi.org/10.1080/154275609 02728712.

Slovic, Paul. " 'If I Look at the Mass I Will Never Act': Psychic Numbing and Genocide." *Judgment and Decision Making* 2, no. 2 (2007): 79–95.

Smith, Greg. "Goldman Sachs VP Explains Why He Quit." Interview by Anderson Cooper, *60 Minutes*, CBS, October 21, 2012. http://dx.doi.org/10.1080/15427560 902728712.

————. "Why I Am Leaving Goldman Sachs." Op-ed, *New York Times*, March 14, 2012. http://www.nytimes.com/2012/03/14/opinion/why-i-am-leaving-goldman-sachs .html?pagewanted=all&module=Search&mabReward=relbias%3Ar.

Smith, Yves. ECONned: How Unenlightened Self Interest Undermined Democracy and Corrupted Capitalism. New York: Palgrave Macmillan, 2011.

———. "Goldman Helped Greece Disguise Deficit." Naked Capitalism (blog), February 9, 2010. http://www.nakedcapitalism.com/2010/02/goldman-helped -greece-disguise-deficit.html#TLeOJXWLvyKfvJdR.99.

———. "Libor Manipulation Well Known in London by 1991." Naked Capitalism (blog), July 27, 2012. http://www.nakedcapitalism.com/2012/07/libor-manipulation -well-known-in-london-by-1991.html#D4e3c6TwmCFcWdBg.99.

Solomon, Steven Davidoff. "In Tough Market, Investment Banks Seek Shelter or Get Out." New York Times DealBook, June 10, 2014. http://dealbook.nytimes.com/2014 /06/10/in-tough-market-investment-banks-seek-shelter-or-get-out/.

State of Connecticut Judicial Branch. "Supreme and Appellate Court Case Detail: SC 18533." February 15, 2011. http://appellateinquiry.jud.ct.gov/CaseDetail.aspx?CRN= 13888&Type=CaseName.

Stempel, Jonathan. "JPMorgan to Pay $150 Million over Failed Sigma SIV." Reuters, March 20, 2012. http://www.reuters.com/article/2012/03/20/us-jpmorgan-sigma -settlement-idUSBRE82J0S820120320.

Stempel, Jonathan, and Aruna Viswanatha. "UPDATE 2—U.S. wins first guilty plea from individual in Libor probe." Reuters, June 10, 2014. http://uk.reuters.com /article/2014/06/10/rabobank-libor-idUKL2N0OR1TF20140610.

Story, Louise, Landon Thomas Jr., and Nelson D. Schwartz. "Wall St. Helped to Mask Debt Fueling Europe's Crisis." New York Times, February 13, 2010. http://www .nytimes.com/2010/02/14/business/global/14debt.html?scp=4&sq=goldman&st= cse.

Stout, Lynn A. "Killing Conscience: The Unintended Behavioral Consequences of 'Pay for Performance.'" Journal of Corporation Law 39 (2014): 525–61.

———. The Shareholder Value Myth: How Putting Shareholders First Harms Investors, Corporations, and the Public. San Francisco: Berrett-Koehler, 2012.

Strauss, Delphine, and Daniel Schäfer. "Forex Claims 'as Bad as Libor,' Says FCA." Financial Times, February 4, 2014. http://www.ft.com/intl/cms/s/0/6d2f697a-8da8 -11e3-bbe7-00144feab7de.html#axzz2sTxN7hUI.

Swarns, Rachel L. "Banks Urge Young Analysts to Do the Unthinkable: Take Weekends Off," New York Times, March 23, 2014. http://www.nytimes.com/2014/03/24 /nyregion/banks-urge-young-analysts-to-do-the-unthinkable-take-the-weekends -off.html.

Taibbi, Matt. "Everything Is Rigged: The Biggest Price-Fixing Scandal Ever." Rolling Stone, April 25, 2013. http://www.rollingstone.com/politics/news/everything-is -rigged-the-biggest-financial-scandal-yet-20130425.

———. "Looting Main Street." Rolling Stone, March 31, 2010. http://www.rollingstone .com/politics/news/looting-main-street-20100331.

Tarullo, Daniel K. "Good Compliance, Not Mere Compliance." Speech at the Federal Reserve Bank of New York Conference, "Reforming Culture and Behavior in the Financial Services Industry," New York, October 20, 2014. www.federalreserve.gov /newsevents/speech/tarullo20141020a.htm.

Tewary, Akshat. "Portfolio Hedging Is Alive and Well under Volcker." American Banker, December 30, 2013. http://www.americanbanker.com/bankthink/portfolio -hedging-is-alive-and-well-under-volcker-1064564-1.html.

Thaler, Richard H. *Quasi-Rational Economics*. New York: Russell Sage Foundation, 1994.

———. "Save More Tomorrow." Capital Ideas: Selected Papers from the Center for Decision Research, The University of Chicago Graduate School of Business. http://www.chicagobooth.edu/capideas/sept04/savemoretomorrow.html

Thaler, Richard H., and Eric J. Johnson. "Gambling with the House Money and Trying to Break Even: The Effects of Prior Outcomes on Risky Choice." *Management Science* 36, no. 6 (1990): 643–60.

Treanor, Jill. "Barclays Fined £290m as Bid to Manipulate Interest Rates Is Exposed." *Guardian* (London), June 27, 2012. http://www.theguardian.com/business/2012/jun/27/barclays-chief-bob-diamond-bonus-fine.

———. "Europe's Banking Regulator to Relax Cap on Bonuses for Highest-Paid Staff Plans to Lift Pay Restrictions from 12,000 Bankers Have Angered Campaigners but Are Welcomed by Industry Figures." *Guardian* (London), December 13, 2013. http://www.theguardian.com/business/2013/dec/13/europe-banking-regulator-relaxes-bonus-cap.

Trefis Team, "A Look at Barclays' Revamped Strategy and Its Impact on the Bank's Shares." *Forbes*, May 15, 2014. http://www.forbes.com/sites/greatspeculations/2014/05/15/a-look-at-barclays-revamped-strategy-and-its-impact-on-the-banks-shares/.

Tucker, Eric, and Marcy Gordon. "Credit Suisse Pleads Guilty in U.S. Tax Evasion Case." *Associated Press*, May 19, 2014. http://bigstory.ap.org/article/credit-suisse-charged-tax-evasion-case.

24/7 Wall St. "Barclays Refusing to Pay 470 Million US Penalty." *Wall Street Journal Marketwatch*, July 17, 2013. http://www.marketwatch.com/story/barclays-refusing-to-pay-470-million-us-penalty-2013-07-17.

UBS. "Shareholder Report on UBS's Write-Downs." April 18, 2008. http://www.ubs.com/1/ShowMedia/investors/agm?contentId=140333&name=080418ShareholderReport.pdf.

UK Serious Fraud Office. "Further Charges in LIBOR Investigation." Press release, April 28, 2014. http://www.sfo.gov.uk/press-room/latest-press-releases/press-releases-2014/further-charges-in-libor-investigation.aspx.

U.S. Commodity Futures Trading Commission (U.S. CFTC). "CFTC Charges Lloyds Banking Group and Lloyds Bank with Manipulation, Attempted Manipulation, and False Reporting of LIBOR." Press release, July 28, 2014. http://www.cftc.gov/PressRoom/PressReleases/pr6966-14.

———. "CFTC Files and Settles Charges against JPMorgan Chase Bank, N.A., for Violating Prohibition on Manipulative Conduct in Connection with 'London Whale' Swaps Trades." Press release, October 16, 2013. http://www.cftc.gov/PressRoom/PressReleases/pr6737-13.

———. "CFTC Orders Barclays to Pay $200 Million Penalty for Attempted Manipulation of and False Reporting concerning LIBOR and Euribor Benchmark Interest Rates." Press release 6289-12, June 27, 2012. http://www.cftc.gov/PressRoom/PressReleases/pr6289-12.

———. "CFTC Orders Five Banks to Pay over $1.4 Billion in Penalties for Attempted Manipulation of Foreign Exchange Benchmark Rates." Press release PR7056-14, November 12, 2014. http://www.cftc.gov/PressRoom/PressReleases/pr7056-14.

———. "CFTC Orders the Royal Bank of Scotland plc and RBS Securities Japan Limited to Pay $325 Million Penalty to Settle Charges of Manipulation, Attempted Manipulation, and False Reporting of Yen and Swiss Franc Libor." Press release 6510-13, February 6, 2013. http://www.cftc.gov/PressRoom/PressReleases/pr6510-13.

———. "CFTC Orders UBS to Pay $700 Million Penalty to Settle Charges of Manipulation, Attempted Manipulation and False Reporting of LIBOR and Other Benchmark Interest Rates." Press release 6472-12, December 19, 2012. http://www.cftc.gov/PressRoom/PressReleases/pr6472-12.

———. "Deutsche Bank to Pay $800 Million Penalty to Settle CFTC Charges of Manipulation, Attempted Manipulation, and False Reporting of LIBOR and Euribor." Press release 7159-15, April 23, 2015. http://www.cftc.gov/PressRoom/PressReleases/pr7159-15.

———. "Rabobank to Pay $475 Million Penalty to Settle Manipulation and False Reporting Charges Related to LIBOR and Euribor." Press release 6752-12, October 29, 2013. http://www.cftc.gov/PressRoom/PressReleases/pr6752-13.

U.S. Department of Justice. "Attorney General Holder Delivers Remarks at Press Conference Announcing Significant Law Enforcement Action." Press conference, June 30, 2014. http://www.justice.gov/iso/opa/ag/speeches/2014/ag-speech-1406301.html.

———. "Bank of America to Pay $16.65 Billion in Historic Justice Department Settlement for Financial Fraud Leading up to and during the Financial Crisis." Press release, August 21, 2014. http://www.justice.gov/opa/pr/bank-america-pay-1665-billion-historic-justice-department-settlement-financial-fraud-leading.

———. "Barclays Bank PLC Admits Misconduct Related to Submissions for the London Interbank Offered Rate and the Euro Interbank Offered Rate and Agrees to Pay $160 Million Penalty." Press release, June 27, 2012. http://www.justice.gov/opa/pr/2012/June/12-crm-815.html.

———. "Barclays Bank PLC Agrees to Forfeit $298 Million in Connection with Violations of the International Emergency Economic Powers Act and the Trading with the Enemy Act." Press release, August 18, 2010. http://www.justice.gov/opa/pr/2010/August/10-crm-933.html.

———. "BNP Paribas Agrees to Plead Guilty and to Pay $8.9 Billion for Illegally Processing Financial Transactions for Countries Subject to U.S. Economic Sanctions." Press release, June 30, 2014. http://www.justice.gov/opa/pr/2014/June/14-ag-686.html.

———. "Credit Suisse Agrees to Forfeit $536 Million in Connection with Violations of the International Emergency Economic Powers Act and New York State Law." Press release, December 16, 2009. http://www.justice.gov/opa/pr/2009/December/09-ag-1358.html.

———. "Credit Suisse Pleads Guilty to Conspiracy to Aid and Assist U.S. Taxpayers in Filing False Returns." Press release, May 19, 2014. http://www.justice.gov/opa/pr/2014/May/14-ag-531.html.

———. "Federal Government and State Attorneys General Reach Nearly $1 Billion Agreement with SunTrust to Address Mortgage Loan Origination as Well as Servicing and Foreclosure Abuses." Press release, June 17, 2014, http://www.justice.gov/opa/pr/2014/June/14-civ-638.html.

———. "Federal Government and State Attorneys General Reach $25 Billion

Agreement with Five Largest Mortgage Servicers to Address Mortgage Loan Servicing and Foreclosure Abuses." Press release, February 9, 2012. http://www .justice.gov/opa/pr/federal-government-and-state-attorneys-general-reach-25 -billion-agreement-five-largest.

———. "Former Credit Suisse Managing Director Sentenced in Manhattan Federal Court in Connection with Scheme to Hide Losses in Mortgage-Backed Securities Trading Book." Press release, June 24, 2014. http://www.justice.gov/usao/nys /pressreleases/June14/davidhiggssentencing.php.

———. "Former Credit Suisse Managing Director Sentenced in Manhattan Federal Court to 30 Months in Prison in Connection with Scheme to Hide Losses in Mortgage-Backed Securities Trading Book." Press release, November 22, 2013. http://www.justice.gov/usao/nys/pressreleases/November13 /KareemSerageldinSentenc.php.

———. "Former Credit Suisse Vice President Sentenced in Manhattan Federal Court in Connection with Scheme to Hide Losses in Mortgage-Backed Securities Trading Book." Press release, July 31, 2014. http://www.justice.gov/usao/nys/pressreleases /July14/SalmaanSiddiquiSentencing.php.

———. "Former Rabobank LIBOR Submitter Pleads Guilty for Scheme to Manipulate Yen LIBOR." Press release, August 18, 2014. http://www.justice.gov/opa/pr/2014 /August/14-crm-872.html.

———. "HSBC Holdings Plc. and HSBC Bank USA N.A. Admit to Anti-Money Laundering and Sanctions Violations, Forfeit $1.256 Billion in Deferred Prosecution Agreement." Press release, December 11, 2012. http://www.justice.gov/opa/pr/2012 /December/12-crm-1478.html.

———. "Justice Department, Federal and State Partners Secure Record $7 Billion Global Settlement with Citigroup for Misleading Investors about Securities Containing Toxic Mortgages." Press release, July 14, 2014. http://www.justice.gov /opa/pr/2014/July/14-ag-733.html.

———. "Justice Department, Federal and State Partners Secure Record $13 Billion Global Settlement with JPMorgan for Misleading Investors about Securities Containing Toxic Mortgages." Press release, updated November 20, 2013. http:// www.justice.gov/opa/pr/justice-department-federal-and-state-partners-secure -record-13-billion-global-settlement.

———. "Lloyds Banking Group Admits Wrongdoing in LIBOR Investigation, Agrees to Pay $86 Million Criminal Penalty." Press release, July 28, 2014. http://www.justice .gov/opa/pr/lloyds-banking-group-admits-wrongdoing-libor-investigation-agrees -pay-86-million-criminal.

———. "Rabobank Admits Wrongdoing in Libor Investigation, Agrees to Pay $325 Million Criminal Penalty." Press release, October 29, 2013. http://www.justice.gov /opa/pr/2013/October/13-crm-1147.html.

———. "Standard Chartered Bank Agrees to Forfeit $227 Million for Illegal Transactions with Iran, Sudan, Libya, and Burma." Press release, December 10, 2012. http://www.justice.gov/opa/pr/2012/December/12-crm-1467.html.

———. "$25 Billion Mortgage Servicing Agreement Filed in Federal Court." Press release, March 12, 2012. http://www.justice.gov/opa/pr/25-billion-mortgage -servicing-agreement-filed-federal-court.

———. "UBS Enters into Deferred Prosecution Agreement." Press release, February 18, 2009. http://www.justice.gov/tax/txdv09136.htm.

U.S. Department of the Treasury. "JPMorgan Chase Bank N.A. Settles Apparent Violations of Multiple Sanctions Programs." August 25, 2011. http://www.treasury .gov/resource-center/sanctions/OFAC-Enforcement/Pages/20110825.aspx.

———. "Remarks of Secretary Lew at Pew Charitable Trusts." Press release, December 5, 2013. http://www.treasury.gov/press-center/press-releases/Pages /jl2232.aspx.

U.S. Securities and Exchange Commission (SEC). "AIG to Pay $800 Million to Settle Securities Fraud Charges by SEC." Press release 2006-19, February 9, 2006. http:// www.sec.gov/news/press/2006-19.htm.

———. "American International Group, Inc. Agrees to Pay $126 Million to Settle Fraud Charges Arising out of Its Offer and Sale of an Earnings Management Product." Press release 2004-163, November 30, 2004. http://www.sec.gov/news /press/2004-163.htm.

———. "Banc of America Capital Management, BACAP Distributors and Banc of America Securities to Pay $375 Million, Exit Mutual Fund Clearing Business, and Make Other Remedial Reforms to Settle SEC Market Timing and Late Trading Charges." Press release 2005-16, February 9, 2005. http://www.sec.gov/news/press /2005-16.htm.

———. "Bank of America Agrees in Principle to ARS Settlement." Press release 2008-247, October 8, 2008. http://www.sec.gov/news/press/2008/2008-247.htm.

———. "Bank of America Agrees to Pay $150 Million to Settle SEC Charges." Litigation release 21407, February 4, 2010. http://www.sec.gov/litigation/litreleases /2010/lr21407.htm.

———. "Brian Stoker Found Not Liable." Litigation release 22541, November 21, 2012. http://www.sec.gov/litigation/litreleases/2012/lr22541.htm.

———. "Chairman Cox Announces End of Consolidated Supervised Entities Program." Press release 2008-230, September 26, 2008. http://www.sec.gov/news /press/2008/2008-230.htm.

———. "CIO Task Force Update: JPMorgan Chase & Co." July 13, 2012. http://www .sec.gov/Archives/edgar/data/19617/000001961712000248/jpmc2q12exhibit993.htm.

———. "Citigroup Agrees in Principle to Auction Rate Securities Settlement: Firm will Provide Liquidity and Remediate Losses." Press release 2008-168, August 7, 2008. http://www.sec.gov/news/press/2008/2008-168.htm.

———. "Citigroup to Pay $208 Million to Settle Charges Arising from Creation of Affiliated Transfer Agent to Serve Its Proprietary Mutual Funds." Press release 2005-80, May 31, 2005. http://www.sec.gov/news/press/2005-80.htm.

———. "Citigroup to Pay $285 Million to Settle SEC Charges for Misleading Investors about CDO Company Profited from Proprietary Short Position Former Citigroup Employee Sued for His Role in Transaction." Litigation Release No. 22134, October 19, 2011. http://www.sec.gov/litigation/litreleases/2011/lr22134.htm.

———. "Citigroup to Pay $285 Million to Settle SEC Charges for Misleading Investors about CDO Tied to Housing Market." Press release 2011-214, October 19, 2011. http://www.sec.gov/news/press/2011/2011-214.htm.

———. "Court Approves SEC Settlements with Two Former Bear Stearns Hedge Fund

Portfolio Managers; SEC Bars Managers from Regulated Industries." Litigation release 22398, June 25, 2012. http://www.sec.gov/litigation/litreleases/2012/lr22398 .htm.

———. "Deutsche Bank Securities to Pay $87.5 Million, Including Penalty of $7.5 Million for Failing to Timely Produce All E-mail; Thomas Weisel Partners to Pay $12.5 Million." Press release 2004-120, August 26, 2004. http://www.sec.gov/news /press/2004-120.htm.

———. "Enforcement Proceedings: Commission Declares Initial Decision Final as to Snell and LeCroy." SEC News Digest, no. 2007-106 (June 4, 2007). http://www.sec .gov/news/digest/2007/dig060407.txt.

———. "Enforcement Proceedings: SEC Settles with Former Officers of Subprime Lender New Century." SEC News Digest, no. 2010-143 (August 2, 2010). http://www .sec.gov/news/digest/2010/dig080210.htm.

———. "Goldman Sachs to Pay Record $550 Million to Settle SEC Charges Related to Subprime Mortgage CDO." Press release 2010-123, July 15, 2010. http://www.sec.gov /news/press/2010/2010-123.htm.

———. "JPMorgan Chase Agrees to Pay $200 Million and Admits Wrongdoing to Settle SEC Charges." Press release 2013-187, September 19, 2013. http://www.sec.gov /News/PressRelease/Detail/PressRelease/1370539819965#.UvPypGJdXHU.

———. "J. P. Morgan Settles SEC Charges in Jefferson County, Ala. Illegal Payments Scheme." Press release 2009-232, November 4, 2011. http://www.sec.gov/news/press /2009/2009-232.htm.

———. "J. P. Morgan to Pay $153.6 Million to Settle SEC Charges of Misleading Investors in CDO Tied to U.S. Housing Market." Press release 2011-131, June 21, 2011. http://www.sec.gov/news/press/2011/2011-131.htm.

———"Morgan Stanley to Pay $275 Million for Misleading Investors in Subprime RMBS Offerings." Press release 2014-144, July 24, 2014. http://www.sec.gov/News /PressRelease/Detail/PressRelease/1370542355594#.U9IDYONdVHU.

———. "Morgan Stanley to Pay $7.9 Million to Settle Best Execution Case with SEC." Press release 2007-91, May 9, 2007. http://www.sec.gov/news/press/2007/2007-91 .htm.

———. "SEC and NYSE Settle Enforcement Actions against Goldman Sachs Unit for Role in Customers' Illegal Trading Scheme." Press release 2007-41, March 14, 2007. http://www.sec.gov/news/press/2007/2007-41.htm.

———. "SEC Announces Securities Laws Violations by Wachovia Involving Mortgage-Backed Securities." Press release 2011-83, April 5, 2011. http://www.sec .gov/news/press/2011/2011-83.htm.

———. "SEC Charges Banc of America Securities with Fraud in Connection with Improper Bidding Practices Involving Investment of Proceeds of Municipal Securities." Press release 2010-239, December 7, 2010. http://www.sec.gov/news /press/2010/2010-239.htm.

———. "SEC Charges Citigroup and Two Executives for Misleading Investors about Exposure to Subprime Mortgage Assets: Citigroup Agrees to Pay $75 Million Penalty." Press release 2010-136, July 29, 2010. http://www.sec.gov/news/press/2010 /2010-136.htm.

———. "SEC Charges Citigroup Inc. in Connection with Misleading Disclosures

Regarding Its Exposure to Sub-Prime Assets." Litigation Release 21605, July 29, 2010. http://www.sec.gov/litigation/litreleases/2010/lr21605.htm.

———. "SEC Charges Goldman, Sachs & Co. Lacked Adequate Policies and Procedures for Research 'Huddles.'" Press release 2012-61, April 12, 2012, http://www.sec.gov/news/press/2012/2012-61.htm.

———. "SEC Charges Goldman Sachs and Former Vice President in Pay-to-Play Probe Involving Contributions to Former Massachusetts State Treasurer." Press release 2012-199, September 27, 2012. http://www.sec.gov/news/press/2012/2012-199.htm.

———. "SEC Charges J. P. Morgan and Credit Suisse with Misleading Investors in RMBS Offerings." Press release 2012-233, November 16, 2012. http://www.sec.gov/news/press/2012/2012-233.htm.

———. "SEC Charges J. P. Morgan Chase in Connection with Enron's Accounting Fraud." Litigation release 18252, July 28, 2003. http://www.sec.gov/litigation/litreleases/lr18252.htm.

———. "SEC Charges J. P. Morgan Securities with Fraudulent Bidding Practices Involving Investment of Municipal Bond Proceeds." Press release 2011-143, July 7, 2011. http://www.sec.gov/news/press/2011/2011-143.htm.

———. "SEC Charges Merrill Lynch with Misleading Investors in CDOs." Press release, 2013-261, December 12, 2013. http://www.sec.gov/News/PressRelease/Detail/PressRelease/1370540492377#.U91fteNdVHU.

———. "SEC Charges Mizuho Securities USA with Misleading Investors by Obtaining False Credit Ratings for CDO: Firm to Pay $127.5 Million to Settle Charges." Press release 2012-139, July 18, 2012. http://www.sec.gov/news/press/2012/2012-139.htm.

———. "SEC Charges Morgan Stanley with Inadequate Disclosure in Mutual Fund Sales; Morgan Stanley Pays $50 Million to Settle SEC Action." Press release 2003-159, November 17, 2003. http://www.sec.gov/news/press/2003-159.htm.

———. "SEC Charges UBS with Fraudulent Bidding Practices Involving Investment of Municipal Bond Proceeds." Press release 2011-105, May 4, 2011. http://www.sec.gov/news/press/2011/2011-105.htm.

———. "SEC Charges Wachovia with Fraudulent Bid Rigging in Municipal Bond Proceeds." Press release 2011-257, December 8, 2011. http://www.sec.gov/news/press/2011/2011-257.htm.

———. "SEC Enforcement Division Announces Preliminary Settlement with Merrill Lynch to Help Auction Rate Securities Investors." Press release 2008-181, August 22, 2008. http://www.sec.gov/news/press/2008/2008-181.htm.

———. "SEC Finalizes ARS Settlement to Provide $7 Billion in Liquidity to Wachovia Investors." Press release 2009-17, February 5, 2009. http://www.sec.gov/news/press/2009/2009-17.htm.

———. "SEC Finalizes ARS Settlements with Bank of America, RBC, and Deutsche Bank." Press release 2009-127, June 3, 2009. http://www.sec.gov/news/press/2009/2009-127.htm.

———. "SEC Finalizes ARS Settlements with Citigroup and UBS, Providing Nearly $30 Billion in Liquidity to Investors." Press release 2008-290, December 11, 2008. http://www.sec.gov/news/press/2008/2008-290.htm.

———. "SEC, NY Attorney General, NASD, NASAA, NYSE and State Regulators

Announce Historic Agreement to Reform Investment Practices; $1.4 Billion Global Settlement Includes Penalties and Funds for Investors; $1.4 Billion Global Settlement Includes Penalties and Funds for Investors." Press release 2002-179, December 20, 2002. http://www.sec.gov/news/press/2002-179.htm.

———. "SEC Reaches Agreement in Principle to Settle Charges against Bank of America for Market Timing and Late Trading." Press release 2004-33, March 15, 2004. http://www.sec.gov/news/press/2004-33.htm.

———. "SEC Settles Action Charging Wachovia Corporation with Proxy Disclosure and Other Reporting Violations Involving the 2001 Merger between First Union Corporation and Old Wachovia Corporation." Press release 2004-152, November 4, 2004. http://www.sec.gov/news/press/2004-152.htm.

———. "SEC Settles Enforcement Proceedings against J. P. Morgan Chase and Citigroup." Press release 2003-87, July 28, 2003. http://www.sec.gov/news/press/2003-87.htm.

———. "SEC Settles Fraud Charges with Bear Stearns for Late Trading and Market Timing Violations." Press release 2006-38, March 16, 2006. http://www.sec.gov/news/press/2006-38.htm.

———. "SEC Settles with Ten Brokerage Firms as Part of Global Resolution of Yield Burning Claims." Press release 2000-45, April 6, 2000. http://www.sec.gov/news/press/2000-45.txt.

———. "SEC Sues J. P. Morgan Securities Inc. for Unlawful IPO Allocation Practices J. P. Morgan Agrees to Settlement Calling for Injunction and Payment of $25 Million Penalty." Press release 2003-129, October 1, 2003. http://www.sec.gov/news/press/2003-129.htm.

———. "SG Cowen and Lehman Brothers Settle Enforcement Actions with SEC and NYSE for Supervisory Failures in Frank Gruttadauria Case." Press release 2003-96, August 14, 2003. http://www.sec.gov/news/press/2003-96.htm.

———. "Statement on 2nd Circuit Decision." Public statement, June 4, 2014. http://www.sec.gov/News/PublicStmt/Detail/PublicStmt/1370541993346#.U9FiFPldWGo.

———. "Ten of Nation's Top Investment Firms Settle Enforcement Actions Involving Conflicts of Interest between Research and Investment Banking." Press release 2003-54, April 28, 2003. http://www.sec.gov/news/press/2003-54.htm.

———. "UBS Agrees to Pay $200 Million to Settle SEC Charges for Violating Registration Requirements." Press release 2009-29, February 18, 2009. http://www.sec.gov/news/press/2009/2009-29.htm.

———. "UBS to Pay $50 Million to Settle SEC Charges of Misleading CDO Investors." Press release 2013-146, August 6, 2013. http://www.sec.gov/News/PressRelease/Detail/PressRelease/1370539751175.

Vaughan, Bernard. "Ex-Credit Suisse Trader Pleads Guilty in U.S. Mortgage Case." Reuters, April 12, 2013. http://www.reuters.com/article/2013/04/12/us-creditsuisse-serageldin-plea-idUSBRE93B0SI20130412.

Viswanatha, Aruna, and Karen Freifeld. "Global Banks Entering Higher-Stake Phase of Forex Probes." Reuters, November 13, 2014. http://www.reuters.com/article/2014/11/13/us-banks-forex-settlement-criminal-idUSKCN0IX01H20141113.

Vohs, Kathleen D., Nicole L. Mead, and Miranda R. Goode. "Merely Activating the Concept of Money Changes Personal and Interpersonal Behavior." Current Directions in Psychological Science 17, no. 3 (2008): 208–12.

———. "The Psychological Consequences of Money." *Science* 314 (November 2006): 1154–56. http://www.sciencemag.org/content/314/5802/1154.full.pdf?sid=1c879857 -ec62-47b7-842a-4e0631dafa26 DOI: 10.1126/science.1132491.

Volcker, Paul. "Think More Boldly." *Wall Street Journal*, December 14, 2009. http:// online.wsj.com/article/SB10001424052748704825504574586330960597134.html.

Voreacos, David. "UBS Tax-Fraud Charge Is Dropped by U.S. Prosecutors." *Bloomberg*, Oct. 22, 2010. http://www.bloomberg.com/news/2010-10-22/u-s-ends-ubs-deferred -prosecution-accord-in-conspiracy-case.html.

Walsh, Mary Williams. "A County in Alabama Strikes a Bankruptcy Deal." *New York Times DealBook*, June 4, 2013. http://dealbook.nytimes.com/2013/06/04/a-county -in-alabama-strikes-a-bankruptcy-deal/.

———. "In Alabama, a County That Fell off the Financial Cliff." *New York Times*, February 18, 2013. http://www.nytimes.com/2012/02/19/business/jefferson-county -ala-falls-off-the-bankruptcy-cliff.html.

———. "J.P. Morgan Settles Alabama Bribery Case." *New York Times*, November 4, 2009. http://www.nytimes.com/2009/11/05/business/05derivatives.html.

Warren, Elizabeth. "Banking Should Be Boring." *Elizabeth Warren for Senate* (blog). May 22, 2012. http://elizabethwarren.com/blog/banking-should-be-boring.

Wayne, Leslie, with Andrew Pollack. "Merrill Makes Strategic Move in Ending Suit." *New York Times*, June 4, 1998. http://www.nytimes.com/1998/06/04/business /merrill-makes-strategic-move-in-ending-suit.html.

Waytz, Adam, and Nicholas Epley. "Social Connection Enables Dehumanization." *Journal of Experimental Social Psychology* 48, no. 1 (2012): 70–76.

Werdigier, Julia. "Britain Sues to Stop Cap on Bonuses for Bankers." *New York Times DealBook*, September 25, 2013. http://dealbook.nytimes.com/2013/09/25/britain -sues-over-caps-on-bankers-bonuses/.

———. "Former UBS Trader Seeks to Appeal Fraud Conviction." *New York Times DealBook*, March 1, 2013. http://dealbook.nytimes.com/2013/03/01/former-ubs -trader-requests-to-appeal-fraud-conviction/.

———. "JPMorgan Penalized by Regulator in Britain." June 3, 2010. http://www .nytimes.com/2010/06/04/business/global/04fine.html.

Werdigier, Julia, and Mark Scott. "Ex-Trader Sentenced in Loss at UBS." *New York Times DealBook*, November 20, 2012. http://dealbook.nytimes.com/2012/11/20/jury -finds-former-ubs-trader-guilty-of-fraud/?ref=business.

White, Mary Jo "Deploying the Full Enforcement Arsenal." Speech to Council of Institutional Investors conference, Chicago, September 26, 2013. http://www.sec.gov /News/Speech/Detail/Speech/1370539841202#.VI9HuHuRb09.

Whitmire, Kyle. "Bankruptcy Deal Poses New Risks for Jefferson County and Wall Street, Analysts Say." *Al.com* (blog), June 4, 2013. http://blog.al.com/spotnews/2013 /06/bankruptcy_deal_poses_new_risk.html.

Whitmire, Kyle, and Adam Nossiter, "Birmingham Mayor Accused of Trading County Deals for Cash and Clothes." *New York Times*, December 2, 2008. http://www .nytimes.com/2008/12/02/us/02birmingham.html?pagewanted=print.

Whitmire, Kyle, and Mary Williams Walsh. "High Finance Backfires on Alabama County." *New York Times*, March 12, 2008. http://www.nytimes.com/2008/03/12 /business/12bama.html.

Wilmarth, Arthur E., Jr. "The Transformation of the U.S. Financial Services Industry,

1975–2000: Competition, Consolidation, and Increased Risks." *University of Illinois Law Review* 2 (2002): 215.

Wright, Barnett. "Deal Puts Jefferson County on Path to Exit Record-Setting Bankruptcy." *Al.com* (blog), June 5, 2013. http://blog.al.com/spotnews/2013/06/deal_puts_jefferson_county_on.html.

Wright, Ben. "A Q&A on the EU Bonus Cap (and the Ways around It)." *Wall Street Journal*, February 4, 2014. http://blogs.wsj.com/moneybeat/2014/02/04/on-the-eu-bonus-cap-and-ways-around-it/.

Wyatt, Edward. "Promises Made, and Remade, by Firms in S.E.C. Fraud Cases." *New York Times*, November 7, 2011. http://www.nytimes.com/2011/11/08/business/in-sec-fraud-cases-banks-make-and-break-promises.html.

Yang, Jia Lynn. "Jamie Dimon Got a Huge Pay Cut. Or a Huge Raise. It's Hard to Tell." *Wonkblog* (blog), *Washington Post*, April 11, 2014. http://www.washingtonpost.com/blogs/wonkblog/wp/2014/04/11/jamie-dimon-got-a-huge-pay-cut-or-a-huge-raise-its-hard-to-tell/.

Zaleskiewicz, Tomasz. "Beyond Risk Seeking and Risk Aversion: Personality and the Dual Nature of Economic Risk Taking." In "Personality and Economic Behaviour," special issue of *European Journal of Personality* 15, no. S1 (2001): S105–S122. doi:10.1002/per.426.

Zibel, Alan, and Andrew R. Johnson. "U.S. Reaches $968 Million Mortgage Settlement with SunTrust." *Wall Street Journal*, June 17, 2014. http://online.wsj.com/articles/u-s-reaches-968m-settlement-with-suntrust-banks-over-mortgage-issues-1403033015.

Zorn, Dirk. "Here a Chief, There a Chief: The Rise of the CFO in the American Firm." *American Sociological Review* 69, no. 3 (June 2004): 345–64.

Statutes, Regulations, Legal Briefs, Opinions, Filings, and Administrative Documents

Aronson v. Lewis, 473 A. 2d. 805 (Del. 1984).

Basis Yield Alpha Fund (Master) v. Goldman Sachs, 37 Misc.3d 1212(A) (N.Y. Sup. Ct. 2012), *aff'd. as modified*, Basis Yield Alpha Fund (Master) v. Goldman Sachs Group, Inc., 115 A.D. 3rd 128 (1st Dept. 2014).

Basis Yield Alpha Fund Master v. Morgan Stanley & Co. LLC., 2013 WL 942359 (N.Y. Sup. Ct. 2013).

Broderick v. Rosner, 294 U.S. 629 (1935).

Central Bank of Denver v. First Interstate Bank of Denver, 511 U.S. 164 (1994).

Chemtech Royalty Associates, L.P. v. United States, Memorandum Ruling, Nos. 05-944, 05-285, and 07-405, 2013 WL 704037 (M.D. La. 2013), *affirmed in part and vacated in part and remanded*, 766 F. 3d 453 (5th Cir. 2014).

China Development Industrial Bank v. Morgan Stanley & Co. Inc., 86 A.D.3d 435, 436, 927 N.Y.S.2d 52 (1st Dept. 2011).

China Development Industrial Bank v. Morgan Stanley, Affirmation of Jason C. Davis. ProPublica, March 16, 2007. http://www.propublica.org/documents/item/560332-cdibvms-affirmation-jcdavis#document/p9.

China Development Industrial Bank v. Morgan Stanley & Co., Expert Report of Mark N. Froeba, Exhibit A, No. 650957/2010 (N.Y. Sup. Ct., Aug. 13, 2012). Available at http://s3.documentcloud.org/documents/560571/china-development-industrial-bank-v-morgan.pdf.

Citigroup Settlement Agreement, Annex 1: Statement of Facts. July 14, 2014. http://
www.justice.gov/iso/opa/resources/558201471413645397758.pdf.

City of Philadelphia, Board of Pensions and Retirement v. Barclays Bank PLC, Class
Action Complaint, No. 14-00876 (S.D.N.Y. Feb. 11, 2014).

Credit Suisse Deferred Prosecution Agreement. "Exhibit A: Factual Statement."
[December 16, 2009.] http://www.justice.gov/criminal/pr/documents/12-16-09
-CreditSuisse-factualstatement.pdf.

Dahdelah v. MacDougall and Akin Gump, Judgment, Case No. T20117607 &
T20117073, (Southwark Ct., Mar. 21, 2014). Available at http://res.cloudinary.com
/lbresearch/image/upload/v1395768096/r_v_dahdaleh210314approvedjudgment
_252114_1721.pdf.

Department of Enforcement v. Grubman, Offer of Settlement (NASD Office of
Hearing Officers, Apr. 21, 2003). http://www.finra.org/web/groups/industry/@ip
/@enf/@da/documents/industry/p007678.pdf.

European Commission, Eurostat, *Report on the EDP Methodological Visits to Greece in
2010*. http://dfn.gr/files/pdf/eurostat.12.5.11.pdf.

———. "Information Note on Greece." 24.02.2010.ec.europa.eu/eurostat/documents
/4187653/5779465/INFO-GREECE-EN.pdf.

*Examining the Settlement Practices of U.S. Financial Regulators: Hearing Before the
Committee on Financial Services, U.S. House of Representatives, One Hundred
Twelfth Congress, second session, May 17, 2012*. Washington, D.C.: Government
Printing Office. http://www.gpo.gov/fdsys/pkg/CHRG-112hhrg75734/pdf/CHRG
-112hhrg75734.pdf.

———. (oral testimony and written statement of Richard W. Painter, Professor of Law,
University of Minnesota Law School).

Federal Deposit Insurance Corporation v. Bank of America Corporation, Complaint,
No. 14-01757 (S.D.N.Y. Mar. 14, 2014).

Federal Energy Regulatory Commission v. Barclays Bank PLC et al., No. 2:13-cv-02093
(E.D. Cal. Oct. 9, 2013).

Federal Energy Regulatory Commission v. J. P. Morgan Ventures Energy Corp, No. 12-
00352 (D.D.C. July 2, 2012).

Federal Housing Finance Agency. "Litigation." http://www.fhfa.gov/Supervision
Regulation/LegalDocuments/Pages/Litigation.aspx.

Financial Crisis Inquiry Commission (FCIC). *The Financial Crisis Inquiry Report: Final
Report of the National Commission on the Causes of the Financial and Economic
Crisis in the United States*. Pub. L. No. 111-21. Washington, DC: Government
Printing Office, January 2011. Available at http://fcic-static.law.stanford.edu/cdn
_media/fcic-reports/fcic_final_report_full.pdf.

Financial Services (Banking Reform) Act (U.K.), c33 2013. http://www.legislation.gov
.uk/ukpga/2013/33/contents/enacted.

Fresno County Employees' Retirement Association v. Barclays Bank PLC, Class Action
Complaint, No. 14-CV-00902 (S.D.N.Y. Feb. 11, 2014).

*The Impact of the Global Settlement: Hearing Before the U.S. Senate Committee
on Banking, Housing, and Urban Affairs*, 108th Cong. 611 (2003). Washington,
DC: Government Printing Office, 2004. http://www.gpo.gov/fdsys/pkg/CHRG
-108shrg95946/html/CHRG-108shrg95946.htm.

In re Anthony C. Snell and Charles E. LeCroy, Administrative Proceeding File No.

3-12359, Release No. 630 (October 18, 2006). http://www.sec.gov/litigation/aljdec /2006/ap630jtk.pdf.

In re Anthony C. Snell and Charles E. LeCroy, Administrative Proceeding File No. 3-12359, Release No. 330 (May 3, 2007). https://www.sec.gov/litigation/aljdec/2007 /id330jtk.pdf.

In re Anthony C. Snell and Charles E. LeCroy, Administrative Proceeding File No. 3-12359, SEC Release No. 55850 (June 1, 2007). https://www.sec.gov/litigation/aljdec /2007/34-55850.pdf.

In re Banc of America Securities LLC, Securities Act Release No. 63451, Admin. Proc. File No. 3-14153 (Dec. 7, 2010). http://www.sec.gov/litigation/admin/2010/34-63451 .pdf.

In re Bank of America, N.A., and Merrill Lynch, Pierce, Fenner & Smith, Inc., Waiver Order, Securities Act Release No. 9682, November 25, 2014.

In re Citigroup Inc. Bond Litigation, 296 F.R.D. 147 (S.D.N.Y. 2013).

In re Citigroup Inc. Securities Litigation, 965 F.Supp.2d 369 (S.D.N.Y. 2013).

In re Citigroup Inc. Shareholder Derivative Litigation, 964 A.2d 106 (Del. Ch., 2009).

In re Credit Suisse Alternative Capital, Order Instituting Administrative and Cease-and-Desist Proceedings, LLC, Securities Act Release No. 9268, Investment Advisers Act Release No. 3302, Administrative Proceeding File No. 3-14594 (Oct. 19, 2011). http://www.sec.gov/litigation/admin/2011/33-9268.pdf.

In re Del Monte Foods, 25 A. 3d 813 (Del. Ch. 2011).

In the Matter of an Inquiry by Eliot Spitzer, Affidavit in Support of Application for an Order Pursuant to General Business Law Section 354 (N.Y. Sup. Ct. 2002), http:// www.ag.ny.gov/sites/default/files/press-releases/archived/MerrillL.pdf.

In re Gary L. Crittenden and Arthur H. Tildesley, Securities Act Release No. 62593, Administrative Proceeding File No. 3-13985 (July 29, 2010). https://www.sec.gov /litigation/admin/2010/34-62593.pdf.

In re Gary S. Missner, Securities Act Release No. 7304, Exchange Act Release No. 37301, Accounting and Auditing Enforcement No. 791, Admin. Proc. File No. 3-9025 (June 11, 1996). http://www.sec.gov/litigation/admin/337304.txt.

In re Goldman Sachs & Co., Consent Order, No. 2009-079 (Commonwealth of Massachusetts, June 9, 2011).

In re Goldman Sachs & Co., SEC Release No. 66791, Cease and Desist Order (April 12, 2012). http://www.sec.gov/litigation/admin/2012/34-66791.pdf.

In re JPMorgan Chase Bank, N.A., Consent Order, Office of the Comptroller of the Currency, Agreement with JPMorgan. No. 2011-105, AA-EC-11-63 (Comptroller of the Currency, July 6, 2011). http://www.occ.gov/static/enforcement-actions/ea2011 -105.pdf.

In re JPMorgan Chase Bank, N.A., Order, CFTC Docket No. 14-01 (Commodity Futures Trading Commission, Oct. 16, 2013).

In re J. P. Morgan Securities Inc., Securities Act Release No. 9078, Exchange Act Release No. 60928, Admin. Proc. File No. 3-13673 (Nov. 4, 2009). https://www.sec .gov/litigation/admin/2009/33-9078.pdf.

In re Lehman Brothers Holding Inc., Motion & Order No. 08-13555 (Bankr. S.D.N.Y. Aug. 24, 2012).

In re Lehman Brothers Holdings, Inc., Report of Anton R. Valukas, Examiner, No. 08-13555 (Bankr. S.D.N.Y. Mar. 11, 2010).

In re Libor-Based Financial Instruments Antitrust Litigation, 935 F. Supp. 2d 666 (S.D.N.Y. 2013); *reversed in part by* Gelboim v. Bank of America Corp. 135 S. Ct. 897 (2015).

In re Merrill Lynch, Pierce, Fenner & Smith Inc., Settlement, S.E.C. Release No. 7566 (August 24, 1998).

In re Wells Fargo Bank, N.A., Consent Order for a Civil Money Penalty, No. AA-EC-11-97 (Comptroller of the Currency, Dec. 8, 2011). http://occ.gov/static/enforcement actions/ea2011-175.pdf.

Janus Capital Group, Inc. v. First Derivative Traders, 131 S.Ct. 2296 (2011).

JPMorgan Chase Bank, N.A., Order, No. 14-01 (Commodity Future Trading Commission Oct. 16, 2013). http://www.cftc.gov/ucm/groups/public/ @lrenforcementactions/documents/legalpleading/enfjpmorganorder101613.pdf.

JPMorgan Chase Whale Trades: A Case History of Derivatives Risks and Abuses. (*Levin-McCain Report*). United States Senate, Permanent Subcommittee on Investigations, Committee on Homeland Security and Governmental Affairs. March 15, 2013. http://www.hsgac.senate.gov/download/report-jpmorgan-chase-whale-trades-a -case-history-of-derivatives-risks-and-abuses-march-15-2013.

———. *Exhibits.* Committee on Homeland Security and Governmental Affairs. March 15, 2013. http://www.hsgac.senate.gov/download/?id=6BB34BFA-658F-4874-A6CD -5740264BC957.

JPMorgan Settlement Agreement, Annex 1: Statement of Facts, Department of Justice, November 19, 2013. http://www.justice.gov/iso/opa/resources/9432013111915103199 0622.pdf.

M&T Bank Corp. v. Gemstone CDO VII, LTD., 68 A.D.3d 1747 (N.Y. 4th Dep't 2009).

Morrison v. National Australia Bank, Ltd. 561 U.S. 247 (2010).

NASD Department of Enforcement v. Grubman, Offer of Settlement (NASD Office of Hearing Officers, Apr. 21, 2003). http://www.finra.org/web/groups/industry/@ip /@enf/@da/documents/industry/p007678.pdf.

New York v. First American Corp., No. 406796-2007 (N.Y. Sup. Ct. Nov. 1, 2007) (removed to Federal District Court, New York v. First American Corp., 07-CV-10397 (S.D.N.Y.)).

Procter & Gamble Co. v. Bankers Trust Co., 78 F.3d 219 (6th Cir. 1996).

Pursuit Partners, LLC v. UBS AG, 48 Conn. L. Rptr. 557 (2009).

Regents of the University of California v. Credit Suisse First Boston (USA), Inc., 482 F.3d 372 (5th Cir. 2007), *cert. denied sub nom.* Regents of the University of California v. Merrill Lynch, Pierce, Fenner & Smith, Inc., 552 U.S. 1170 (2008).

The Role of Credit Rating Agencies: Hearing on Wall Street and the Financial Crisis, United States Senate, Permanent Subcommittee on Investigations Exhibits (2010). http://www.hsgac.senate.gov//imo/media/doc/Financial_Crisis/042310Exhibits.pdf.

The Role of Financial Institutions in Enron's Collapse, vol. 1, *Hearings before the Permanent Subcommittee of Investigations of the Committee on Governmental Affairs US Senate,* 107th Congress, (2002). http://www.gpo.gov/fdsys/pkg/CHRG -107shrg81313/html/CHRG-107shrg81313.htm. This and the other "Enron Hearings" are available at http://www.loc.gov/law/help/guide/federal/enronhrgs.php.

———. *Appendices.* Available at http://www.hsgac.senate.gov/subcommittes /investigations/hearings/the-role-of-the-financial-institutions-in-enrons-collapse -day-one.

SEC v. Citigroup, Inc., Complaint (D.D.C. July 29, 2010) (No. 10-01277). http://www.sec
.gov/litigation/complaints/2010/comp21605.pdf.

SEC v. Citigroup Global Markets Inc., Complaint (S.D.N.Y. Oct. 19, 2011) (No. 11-CV-
7387). http://www.sec.gov/litigation/complaints/2011/comp-pr2011-214.pdf.

SEC v. Citigroup Global Markets Inc., 827 F. Supp.2d 328, 332 (S.D.N.Y. 2011) vacated
and remanded in 752 F.3d 285 (2d Cir. 2014), and approved, 34 F. Supp. 3d. 379
(S.D.N.Y. 2014).

SEC v. Citigroup Global Markets Inc. 2014 WL 3827497 (S.D.N.Y. Aug. 5, 2014)

SEC v. Grubman, Complaint, No. 03 CV 2938 (S.D.N.Y. Apr. 28, 2003).

SEC v. Gutfreund et al., Admin. Proc. File No. 3-7930 (Dec. 3, 1992).

SEC v. J. P. Morgan Securities LLC, Complaint, No. 11-04206 (S.D.N.Y. June 21, 2011).
http://www.sec.gov/litigation/complaints/2011/comp-pr2011-131-jpmorgan.pdf.

SEC v. LeCroy, Complaint, No. 09-02238, 2014 WL 4403147 (N.D. Ala. Nov. 4, 2009).

SEC v. LeCroy et al., No. 09-CV-02238 (N.D. Ala. Sept. 5, 2014).

SEC v. Martin-Artajo, No. 13-05677 (S.D.N.Y. Aug. 14, 2013).

SEC v. Serageldin, No. 12-00796 (S.D.N.Y. Feb. 1, 2012). https://www.sec.gov/litigation
/complaints/2012/comp-pr2012-23.pdf.

Securities Industry Study. U.S. Senate, Committee on Banking, Housing, and Urban
Affairs, S. Res. 109, 92nd Cong. (1972).

Securities Litigation Uniform Standards Act of 1998, Pub. L. No. 105-33, 105th Cong.
(1998).

Silver v. New York Stock Exchange, 373 U.S. 341 (1963).

Stoneridge Inv. Partners, LLC v. Scientific-Atlanta, Inc., 552 U.S. 148 (2008).

Tax Shelters: Who's Buying, Who's Selling, and What's the Government Doing about It?
Hearing before the Committee on Finance, Senate, 108th Congress, October 21,
2003. Washington, DC: US Government Printing Office, 2004. http://www.finance
.senate.gov/hearings/hearing/?id=48f12fa4-a393-ad37-ce49-43df4eb3806c.

UK House of Commons, Treasury Committee. *Financial Institutions—Too Important
to Fail, Too Important to Ignore.* Vol. 2, *Oral and Written Evidence.* Ninth Report
of the Session 2009–2010. London: Stationery Office, March 29, 2010. http://www
.publications.parliament.uk/pa/cm200910/cmselect/cmtreasy/261/261ii.pdf.

U.S. v. American Home Mortgage, Consolidated Third Amended Complaint, 10-
CV-01465 (D. S.C. Feb. 3, 2014). http://www.nationalmortgagenews.com/pdfs
/szymoniaklawsuit.pdf.

U.S v. Countrywide Financial Corporation, Inc., 996 F. Supp. 2nd 247 (S.D.N.Y. 2014).

U.S v. Martin-Artajo, No. 13-MAG-1975, sealed complaint (S.D.N.Y. Aug. 9, 2013).

U.S. v. Morgan, 118 F. Supp. 621 (S.D.N.Y. 1953).

U.S. v. UBS Ag, No. 09-600033 (S.D. Fla), Deferred Prosecution Agreement, entered
into February 18, 2009, available at http://www.justice.gov/tax/UBS_Signed
_Deferred_Prosecution_Agreement.pdf.

Value Recovery Fund LLC v. Barclays Bank PLC, Class Action Complaint, No. 14-CV-
00867 (S.D.N.Y. Feb. 10, 2014).

Wall Street and the Financial Crisis: Anatomy of a Financial Collapse. (*Levin-Coburn
Report*). United States Senate, Permanent Subcommittee on Investigations,
Committee on Homeland Security and Governmental Affairs. Washington, DC:
Government Printing Office, April 13, 2011. http://www.levin.senate.gov/imo/media
/doc/supporting/2011/PSI_WallStreetCrisis_041311.pdf.

INDEX

In this index, names of specific banks are followed by subentries that sometimes refer to specific types of misconduct that have been alleged by regulators or private parties against the bank listed in the entry. In many instances the misconduct has not been admitted or proven even if the allegation resulted in a substantial financial settlement by the bank.

84; infringement of antitrust rules, 53; settlement with FHFA, 64
Hudson transaction, 33

incentive alignment, 220n29. *See also* banker behavior
ING, dealings with and in sanctioned countries, 64
inside directors, 72, 165
inside information. *See* nonpublic information, misuse of
insider trading. *See* nonpublic information, misuse of
insolvency. *See* bankruptcy; banks: insolvency
institutional investors, 68, 74, 75, 78, 79, 80, 83, 101, 105, 165, 166, 188
insurance companies, 13, 73, 78, 84, 86, 87, 155, 209n116
Intercontinental Exchange (ICE), 71, 72, 208n105
Internal Revenue Service (IRS), 1, 65, 128
International Swaps and Derivatives Association, 53, 137
investment adviser, 13, 14, 171
investment bankers, 14, 61, 73, 82, 84, 87, 89, 95, 96, 97, 99, 100, 149, 152, 184, 185, 196n18
investment banking, 2, 13, 21, 42, 68, 70, 73, 76, 81, 82, 83, 84, 85, 86, 87, 89, 92, 95, 96, 98, 99, 100, 101, 103, 104, 133, 146, 154, 181
investment banks, 5, 13, 22, 42, 66, 72, 73, 74, 75, 76, 78, 79, 80, 81, 83, 84, 86, 87, 88, 89, 90, 91, 92, 93, 95, 97, 99, 100, 101, 104, 105, 130, 132, 143, 144, 149, 183, 190, 196n10, 211n127
investment funds, 13; suitability of covenant banking regime for controlling behavior of, 171. *See also* hedge funds; private equity funds
Iran, 1, 62, 63, 64
ISDAfix, 52, 211n122
Italy, 55, 86, 212n142

Japan, 76, 105, 208n109, 255
J. Aron, 104

Jefferson County, Alabama, 58, 59, 60, 61, 68, 114, 188, 213n143, 213n154, 213n158, 214nn159–60
Jenkins, Anthony, 86
Joint Venture/Partnership Agreement (JVPA), 149, 152, 153, 154, 155, 156, 157, 158, 159
JP Morgan, 25, 32, 60, 188, 199n14, 211n125, 213n145; acquisition of Bear-Stearns, 100; bid-rigging, 86; currency market manipulation, 53; energy market manipulation, 53; FINRA fines, 70; Global Settlement, 20; infringement of antitrust rules, 53; Jefferson County bond and swaps deal, 59; LIBOR manipulation, 52; London Whale, 42, 43, 47, 65, 66, 120; manipulation of municipal bond markets, 61, 62, 215nn164–65; mortgage backed securities (RMBS), 25; mortgage loan servicing and foreclosure abuse charges, 69; sale of derivatives to city of Milan, 57; sanctioned by FINRA, 62; Squared CDO, 32
J.P. Morgan & Co. *See* JP Morgan

Kaufman, Henry, 97, 101, 105, 193, 219n11, 219n18, 220n25
King, Mervyn, 86
Knight Capital, 75

Langford, Larry, 59, 60, 214n163
Laster, J. Travis, 69
law and lawmaking, 127; banks' use of advisors to get around laws, 134; banks' willingness to flout, 3; "crowding out morality," 116; difficulty of regulators in keeping up with financial innovations, 131; influence of bankers over rules governing new lines of business, 74, 83; limitations of financial penalties on bank behavior, 141; limitations of reining in bank behavior, 2, 19; limitations of state and corporate regulations, 127, 128; obstacles to legal action for fraud, 142; regulatory capture, 144; role of Congress in, 137;

Milan, sale of derivatives deal to, 58, 212n142

Mizuho, 204n58

money: happiness from, versus happiness from consumption, 221n5; house money, 120, 177, 224n37, 229n1; marginal utility of, 177; mindless accumulation of, 83, 116; pursuit of, 6, 8, 33, 110, 111; reminders of, 114, 115, 222n16

Montag, Thomas, 33, 67

Moody's, 37, 203n57, 203n59. *See also* rating agencies

moral hazard, 97, 100, 185, 187

Morgan Stanley, 2, 20, 27, 33, 36, 53, 61, 62, 70, 81, 82, 85, 90, 196n10, 200nn26–27, 203n54, 217n174; Global Settlement, 20; infringement of antitrust rules, 53; sanctioned by FINRA, 62; suit by China Development Industrial Bank, 36; toxic securities, 65; yield burning, 61

Morrison v. National Australia Bank, 139, 226n15

mortgage appraisers, pressure on appraisers, 199n17

mortgage-backed securities, 2, 23, 24, 25, 27, 28, 34, 36, 39, 68, 104, 116, 186. *See also* collateralized mortgage obligations (CMOs); residential mortgage-backed securities (RMBS)

mortgage loan pools, 26; dark, 75; importance of lack of positive correlation in choosing, 199n16

mortage originators, 23, 68, 199n17, 200n26

mortgage securitization transactions, history of, 23, 186, 199n16

mortgage servicing, 2, 69, 195n9

Municipal Bond Insurance Association (MBIA), 87

municipal bonds, 61, 62, 215n164

Myanmar. *See* Burma (Myanmar)

National Association of Securities Dealers (NASD), 20, 197n4

negotiated commissions, 80, 82, 100

Netherlands, required ethics and morality oath, 176, 221n9

neuroscience, 121

New Century, 35, 37, 203n56. *See also* mortgage originators

New York Attorney General, 21, 197n4, 199n17, 200n27

New York State Department of Financial Services, 64, 208n109, 218n183

New York Stock Exchange (NYSE), 21, 71, 72, 73, 74, 75, 77, 78, 79, 80, 92, 95, 96, 97, 166, 169, 197n4, 219n4

nonpublic information, misuse of, 197n3

North American Securities Administrators Association (NASAA), 21, 197n4

notional value, 45, 58, 59, 207n104; definition of, 205n84

Nuclear Holocaust 2007–1, 36, 203n54

Obama, Barack, 4, 138, 196n14, 226n14

Occidental Petroleum, 99, 220n24

off-exchange trading, of derivatives of stocks and other securities, 74

Office of Comptroller of the Currency (OCC), 48, 49, 61, 62, 195n3, 195n7, 206n90, 207n101, 215n165

Office of Foreign Assets Control (OFAC), 64, 217n182

options. *See* stock options

Orange County, California, 60, 61, 188, 215nn166–67. *See also* bankruptcy: Orange County

over the counter (OTC) interest rate derivatives, 74, 207n104, 211n128

Painter, Richard, 4, 9, 83, 129, 163, 193, 194, 196n18, 219n12, 226n7, 226nn10–12, 226nn16–17, 227n2, 227n8

partnerships, 5, 13, 72, 79, 92, 93, 95, 100, 103, 104, 144, 146, 149, 169, 178, 181, 190. *See also* general partnerships

Partnoy, Frank, 124, 194, 198n7

Paulson & Co., 30, 31

pay, 1, 2, 20, 21, 28, 30, 32, 33, 37, 38, 44, 50, 53, 58, 59, 60, 61, 62, 64, 65, 66, 72, 80, 82, 87, 93, 99, 105, 116, 127, 129, 130, 141, 143, 144, 145, 146, 149, 152, 153, 155, 156, 157, 159, 160, 161, 162, 163, 167, 176, 177, 179, 185, 187, 188, 190, 195n3, 195n7,